States of Terror

States of Terror
History, Theory, Literature

David Simpson

The University of Chicago Press :: Chicago and London

The University of Chicago Press, Chicago 60637
The University of Chicago Press, Ltd., London
© 2019 by The University of Chicago
Published 2019

28 27 26 25 24 23 22 21 20 19   1 2 3 4 5

ISBN-13: 978-0-226-60019-2 (cloth)
ISBN-13: 978-0-226-60022-2 (paper)
ISBN-13: 978-0-226-60036-9 (e-book)
DOI: https://doi.org/10.7208/chicago/9780226600369.001.0001

Library of Congress Cataloging-in-Publication Data

Names: Simpson, David, 1951– author.
Title: States of terror : history, theory, literature / David Simpson.
Description: Chicago ; London : The University of Chicago Press, 2019. |
    Includes bibliographical references and index.
Identifiers: LCCN 2018026815 | ISBN 9780226600192 (cloth :
    alk. paper) | ISBN 9780226600222 (pbk. : alk. paper) |
    ISBN 9780226600369 (e-book)
Subjects: LCSH: Language and languages–Etymology. | Language and
    languages–Semantics. | Terror (The English Word) | Terror–Social
    aspects. | Terror–Religious aspects. | Terror in literature. | Terror–
    History. | Political violence. | Terror–Philosophy.
Classification: LCC P324.5 .S56 2019 | DDC 412–dc23
LC record available at https://lccn.loc.gov/2018026815

♾ This paper meets the requirements of ANSI/NISO Z39.48-1992
(Permanence of Paper).

In the first place, what is terror?

JACQUES DERRIDA

What does it mean to live in and according to terror? What sort of concept is terror? In what way can it provide a social frame, rules to live by, an aporetic, an ethos? For whom?

JACQUES LEZRA

The declaration of war on terror is at once the most obvious, overdetermined, and obscure speech act of our era.

MARC REDFIELD

Quick, quick, a new word, a new label. . . . Anything that will stop the process of thought for a time, anything to . . . partition off, to compartmentalize.

DORIS LESSING

Contents

Preface

Those of us who are English speakers, and many others
who are not, live in a world where the invocation of terror
has become commonplace without ever being carefully
analyzed or historically contextualized. There has been
significant investment, financial and intellectual, in the
study of terrorism, which is well supported by journals,
institutes, academic programs, and research funds. Terrorism is comfortably established in the common idiom
as a designated evil that must be aggressively countered.
In contrast, there is no such clear assumption about the
nature of terror, and no institutional effort to understand
it, except as a simple index of what terrorists do. Terror
talk is an attention-getting language invoking some sort
of threat that requires urgent response; it substitutes coercion for critique, and its current semantic hegemony
displaces a range of related terms, near synonyms, and
cognates (fear, dread, horror, and so on) that might, if attended to, afford us a more measured understanding of
what it is that terror is conjured up to perform. To suppose that vulnerability to terror describes the situation of,
for example, the civilian populations of major European
cities, leaves no space for adequately describing what a
Yemeni or Afghan villager might be feeling while living
under drone surveillance. The word is the same, but the
experiences are very different in intensity and temporality.

It remains (so far) the case that comprehensively militarized states possess much greater powers of violence than even the best-organized and resourced nonstate agents (although the potential for access to nuclear or biological weapons could change this balance). Terror could, and perhaps should, also be used as the word describing what many women and children feel in the face of male violence, including sexual violence. When this becomes a weapon of war, it ceases to be a merely domestic phenomenon and becomes a form of state terror. State terror could, and perhaps should, also be used to publicize what many black Americans (especially young men) feel at the sight of a police officer heading their way. These are both directly and indirectly forms of state terror. But we mostly do not use the word in these cases, because we have been encouraged to sequester it outside the homeland and to identify it with the enemy other. Terror has become what is directed at the state, not what is performed or encouraged by it. But it has not always been this way.

For much of the twentieth century terror was understood in the West as the property of states, but they were *other* states, designated as enemies, not us. Pol Pot, Mao, Lenin, Stalin, and Hitler have all been ranged in a roster of competitive villainy as dispensers of terrors. These widely recognized atrocities served to displace any easy recognition of terrors deployed by, for example, Allied airplanes over Germany, British counterinsurgency operations against the dissolving empire, or US-sponsored interventions in Central and South America and Vietnam. With the turn to violence among national liberation movements (Kenya, Malaya, Palestine, Algeria, and Ireland, among others), it became opportune to designate terrorism as their defining practice, and terror as its object. But such terrorism has always been punctilious and spasmodic. Even when it is the product of a long-term cause that persists through time, acts of violence have to be very regular indeed to create a pervasive sense of terror. FLN (Algeria), ETA (Basque Country), and IRA (Ireland) bombings arguably came closest to this but never succeeded in pressuring large populations into the sort of radical insecurity that is best described as a state of terror. Conversely, populations under occupation or surveillance by overwhelming military force are more susceptible to terror. Such force has always been the property of nation-states.

After 9/11, terror talk was everywhere, as it had been in the summer of 1794 in Europe. *Terror* has colonized a part of the lexicon that has, over the years, been occupied by a range of other words—*horror, dread, fear, panic*—and it has displaced them all. Imagine, for example, that the media-political consensus had, after 9/11, declared a war on horror.

Yes, this has the unfortunate hint of a campaign against bad fiction or scary movies. But for much of its history, *horror* has been interchangeable or synonymous with *terror*, each evoking the other. Gothic novelists in the 1790s use *horror* and *terror* in this way, although there are efforts at a distinction, such as the one proposed by Ann Radcliffe in the early nineteenth century. In current popular speech, having a horrible time means much the same as having a terrible time. The history of these words reveals a sequence of identifications and distinctions, as will become apparent at various points in what follows. I would suggest that in current speech a normative distinction can be traced between horror, as the emotion one feels at a distance from a violent event, and terror, which suggests that one is intimately threatened within and without, with no safe space at hand. If this is so, then *horror* is a better descriptor of what all of those who witnessed the events of 9/11, whether from across the Hudson River or on TV in Tokyo, actually felt. Terror, reciprocally, describes what was felt by those about to die, or close enough to think that they might. To collapse the distinction—to make everything an experience of terror—eliminates the particular emotion felt by those facing death and arguably perpetrates an ethical failure. It also allows for the dissemination of a unitary terror as a binding rhetoric wrapping the entire nation (and even the world) into a state of extreme vulnerability. A war on terror admirably suits the grandiloquent propaganda of a militant state apparatus by interpellating a collective weakness in need of overarching protection. There was a purpose to keeping horror off the register of appropriate responses to 9/11. It was possible to do so, I think, because few people are motivated to suggest any difference between horror and terror, and this is an ellipsis supported by a slippery semantic history. Edmund Burke, for example, argued that terror does indeed presume safe distance.

US president Barack Obama made an attempt, in 2009, after a period of relative calm in the homeland, to lower the rhetorical temperature by opining that the then-current threat was that of terrorism, not terror. But the Benghazi attack and the growth of the Islamic State as both a land-based and a global threat restored terror to its position at the pinnacle of popular consciousness, where it still remains. A string of bombings, shootings, and vehicle and knife attacks continues to provide evidence for declaring a state of terror all over the Western world, although there are local deviations and distinctions: for example, in Britain in July 2005, a war on terror was deliberately not declared, even as *terrorism* was admitted to be a descriptive term. This might be explained as admirable restraint or as recognition (one anticipated by Burke in the 1790s) that it is dangerous to acknowledge one's enemy as possessing the power of terror. Terrorism, conversely, merely expresses an aspiration to that power, as a momentary recourse to a violence that can be sustained only unevenly or not at all.

Unlike *terrorism*, terror's neologist offspring that came into the world in 1794, *terror* has for centuries been an attribute of various threatening or avenging men and gods. In the eighteenth century, it became the centerpiece of an aesthetic experience and highly esteemed as the essence of the sublime. After 1794, it took on a dominantly political identity, and it was tossed around as at first a key component of the power of the state, and then something that nonstate agents directed at the state itself. It has been the leitmotif of national liberation movements and the bugaboo of state interests seeking to denigrate those same movements. At all points, it has been both something that comes at us from outside and at the same time the inner feeling or emotion that such outside forces arouse in us. We have been told both that it is good to feel terror—for example, at the face of God—and that terror is something we should absolutely not give way to. One person's terror is another's civic discipline.

Terror wanders in and out of English and into other languages, whether as a foreign loanword, as a neologism made necessary by its distinctly nonnative origin, or as attached to an already-existing native word. Its conceptual profile accordingly differs, but it always reveals the power of naming. It occurs in English as a translation, for example, of Homer and Aristotle, and it goes from English all around the world, as it did after the events of 9/11. It keeps company with, but is not the same as, *terrorism*, whose history, while not uncomplicated, can be and has been tracked with some diligence. It can still be said of terror—and Jacques Derrida said so after 9/11—that we do not know what we are talking about. More recently, *terror* continues to be debated as proper or not proper to the description of such acts of violence as have occurred in Benghazi, Boston, Paris, London, and Las Vegas (to name but five), with no end in sight. If I cannot bid you, as William Blake did, to mark well these words because they are of your eternal salvation, I will claim that they might be important to our collective clear thinking and ideally to our capacity to defend ourselves from those for whom words are circulated as the money of fools and the currency of scoundrels.

This is an exemplary rather than a comprehensive analysis. I do not, for instance, offer an extended discussion of the Nazi or the Soviet terrors, the two most widely acknowledged state terrors of modern times. Decolonization movements generated terror-terrorism dynamics of their

own, in which antistate terrorism was mostly countered by even more
systematic violence on behalf of the imperialist powers: Algeria, Vietnam, Malaya, Kenya, Israel and Palestine, Ireland, and many others all
call for a detailed historical understanding in which the relation between
terror and terrorism should be investigated rather than assumed. The
neoliberal policy of global policing that has replaced old-style imperial-
ism involves its own versions of terror-terrorism, whether in the form of
military occupation, weaponized drone systems, or slower-acting, life-
threatening coercive agencies like sanctions and blockades. All of these
require a careful reckoning, which is beyond my ambition here. What
they have in common, though, is recourse to a rhetoric, a way of legitimating and explaining to their various publics what they are doing and
why. This is what I will often refer to as "terror talk," which assumes
an agreement about what it is proper to call terror while displacing any
commitment to critical understanding and to alternative terminologies.
It is my hope that a critical-historical philology of the sort here attempted
might have a function both analytical and medicinal; that a deeper knowledge of what terror has been taken to be at various times and places
might make us less susceptible to being deceived by those whose vested
interests require a noncritical acquiescence in their own uses of words.
It should also make us more aware that our own governments often
disavow their own deployments of terror by focusing only on what is
done by their enemies.

The following chapters offer some formative case histories of both
the deployment and the avoidance of terror talk, which is often absent
from the places where I had expected to find it and apparent elsewhere in
ways I had not predicted. The preponderance of such talk in the United
States in the post-9/11 period is in many ways exceptional. Spokespersons for the state have often refrained from according their enemies
the power of terror. Both sides in World War Two accused the other
of deploying terror, and in the Cold War "balance" of terror, each of
the superpowers acknowledged its availability to the other. But in non-
catastrophic conditions the rhetoric of terror can be double-edged. To
allow the enemy the power of terror can be to disadvantage oneself. Doing so renders the enemy morally culpable, to be sure, but it also implies
one's own relative weakness and vulnerability, and it may thus threaten
the integrity of resistance. The self-respectability of the state often comes
to be measured by its having the power of terror but not using it, or using it only in exceptional conditions, or (more often) using it and calling
it something else. One way to read the efflorescence of terror talk after
9/11 is to see it as an overemphasis on the power of the enemy in order

to justify a massively violent response. Another would be to regard it as a way of intimidating the homeland into grateful passivity at the hands of its rulers. The two are not incompatible.

: : :

Chapter 1, "Weighing Our Words," introduces the potential of critical philology for the understanding of how we describe extreme emotions. Is terror a concept, and how does it figure in concept history as currently conceived in the work of Koselleck and others? Can one disambiguate terror from other words in the fear-terror cluster, and which purposes are served by doing so? I discuss the management of terror's ambiguities in recent political-military strategy literature and outline the usefulness of a historical critique, along the lines that others have applied to *security*, for bringing some clarity to the discussion of terror.

Chapter 2, "What Do We Talk about When We Talk about Terror?" begins the historical sequence with a discussion of a passage in Plato's *Protagoras* where Socrates takes issue with Prodicus's fussiness about the differences between two fear-terror words, *deos* and *phobos*. Does this matter, and if so why and to whom? Such decisions have affected the long tradition of translations of Homer and Aristotle (especially) and have influenced the currency of fear and terror and their surrogates in other languages. In the eighteenth century, *terror* and *fear* switch places as translations of *phobos*, with terror eventually winning out as constitutive of the sublime. Long before the present day, terror was aestheticized as a pleasurable experience. Here I develop further the model of a fear-terror cluster (by way of Charles Darwin and Jerome Kagan) as the most adequate way of expressing (in English or in translation) the relations of emotion terms to what they might signify.

Chapter 3, "Putting Terror into the Fear of God," explores the other major avenue (after the classics and aesthetic theory) through which terror becomes familiarized in English: the King James Bible, which departs from its precursors in so often choosing *terror* as the term for describing what God instills in his subjects. Conversely, and perhaps surprisingly, Bunyan's widely read *Pilgrim's Progress* does not make comparably heavy use of *terror*, while in the emerging novel tradition *Robinson Crusoe* has a highly diversified use of fear and terror words. The second part of the chapter focuses on two episodes from Judges that have received much attention both in themselves and as reworked by others: the Samson story (with Milton's dramatization) and the story of the Levite of Ephraim (rewritten by Rousseau). These stories have been important touchstones for the working through of terror in relation to divine and secular violence. In the third section of this chapter, I take up Walter Benjamin's much-discussed essay "Critique of Violence" in relation to the fantasy of radical change without terror.

Chapter 4, "From Terror to The Terror," begins with a rehearsal of the ongoing debates about the nature of the Jacobin Terror of 1793–1794 and whether it was or was not the essence of the Revolution itself. Here I present the state of the discussion among the historians and set it beside Burke's writings in the 1790s, which for interesting reasons seek to displace terror as the imagined core of the Revolution. I survey the career of the fear-terror cluster in the gothic novels of the 1790s and in various fictional representations of the Revolution during the following century, including those by Balzac, Hugo, Dumas, and Dickens. Almost all of these authors are, for various reasons, very reluctant to resort to the rhetoric of terror and assiduous in searching out more complex interpretations of revolutionary violence.

Chapter 5, "Terror against the State," traces the gradual emergence of terror as something directed against the state rather than (or as well as) deployed by it. The prototype is Dostoevsky's *The Devils* (also translated as *Possessed*). The "dynamite" movement of the 1880s also produces its fictional representations (works by Conrad and James among them), as does the Baader-Meinhof phenomenon in Germany in the 1970s. Once again, these sources reveal a skeptical and parsimonious response to the rhetoric of terror, and a sense that terror cannot simply be dismissed as the attribute of the other who is the enemy. That remains the case in post-9/11 fiction (as exemplified here by the case of Don DeLillo), and especially in that written by authors who are not simply to be identified with "the West" (Rushdie, Hamid, or Shamsie, for example).

Chapter 6, "Being in Terror, Being as Terror," offers an account of the place of extreme emotions (the fear-terror cluster) in describing subjectivity itself, what it is to be human. Central here are the writings of Sartre, Hegel, Heidegger, Freud, and Kojève, along with various exponents of modern affect theory. It is significant that the complex discussion of the fear-terror syndrome in Continental philosophy's theories of subjectivity has not been replicated in the anglophone world, where it is mostly psychology (and often popular psychology) that takes up the topic. This surely helps explain the critical vacuum into which the politicians and the media were able to market their own personifications of terror after 9/11. I discuss the recourse to *anxiety* as a key word in the 1950s, along with Cold War civil defense manuals, as examples of the effort to disseminate terms for the management of fear as alternatives to those apparent in today's terror talk.

My title is of course deliberately open to a flexible application. In speaking of states of terror, I mean to register the strong historical correlation (and the often unacknowledged persistence) of terror with the behavior of political states, as well as its rather weaker association with nonstate agents. Terror is also a state of mind or feeling, with a relation to external forces that is always to be specified and a pointer to internal emotions that are always open to alternative namings. All terror is some or other state of terror, in place and time. This being so, there is no such "thing" as terror.

Acknowledgments

Along with audiences at the various lectures and seminars I have given over the past six years, I owe special thanks to the following for ideas, hints, corrections, and advice: David Atwell, John Barrell, Paul Bové, Tim Brelinski, David Clark, Joshua Clover, Rebecca Comay, Jacob Dlamini, Omnia el-Shakri, Susanna Ferguson, Mehmet Şükrü Hanioğlu, Michael Holquist, Brian Leach, Jacques Lezra, David Lloyd, Sheldon Lu, Colin MacCabe, Sara Melzer, Flagg Miller, Liz Miller, David Palumbo-Liu, Padma Rangaran, Juliana Schiesari, Amy Smith, Rebecca Spang, Baki Teczan, Gordon Turnbull, George Vela, David Wagner, and Claire Waters. I am very grateful to Randy Petilos for last-minute technical help.

I am also deeply indebted to fellowships at the Stellenbosch Institute for Advanced Study (and Director Hendrik Geyer), which afforded me a remarkable learning experience late in the development of my argument; and at the Humanities Research Center at the Australian National University in Canberra (and Director Will Christie), where the final revisions were completed. These two successive residencies radically sharpened my awareness of the history of state terror directed at indigenous peoples. Black and Native Americans, among others, well know that history.

I have been fortunate to receive two reports on the manuscript that were both incisive and generous, and full of good advice. My warmest thanks to their authors. As always Margaret Ferguson has pondered and responded to everything here, from the smallest item of punctuation to the most ambitious idea.

: : :

I am grateful for permission to reprint or refigure material that has previously appeared, as follows: "'Sleep No More!': Romanticism, Terror and The Terror," in *The Wordsworth Circle* 46, no. 1 (2015): 12–20, appears in reworked form as part of chapter 4; "Toward a Theory of Terror," in *boundary 2* 41, no. 3 (2014): 1–25, offers an overview of the project as a whole, with some historical examples, and appears scattered throughout the book; "Putting Terror into the Fear of God: The King James Bible," in *Critical Quarterly* 59, no. 1 (2017): 123–36, embodies the first part of chapter 3; and "Terror-Talk and Political Management," in *boundary 2* 44, no. 4 (2017): 155–78, anticipates part of chapter 6.

1

Weighing Our Words

Throughout the Nazi years and during World War Two, while his life was routinely in exceptional danger because he was a Jew living with an Aryan wife, the literary scholar and Dresden resident Victor Klemperer kept a diary in which he recorded and discussed the changes visited upon his native German language by the political and media culture of the *Hitlerzeit*. He ends his account by recording a conversation in which a woman describes herself as having spent a year in prison "'cos of certain expressions."[1] She had dared to criticize the party and its leader, or had failed to reproduce its preferred words and phrases. This, for Klemperer, was the moment when he realized why he had been taking all those notes: because of certain expressions. It can be the "single word," he opined, "which reveals the way a particular epoch thinks" (148). Even after the end of Hitler, in the early years of postwar Germany, relics of Nazi speech habits could be heard in the language of ordinary people: "The remnants of linguistic usage from the preceding epoch confuse and seduce them" (2). These words operate "like arsenic," inducing a delayed toxic

---

1. Victor Klemperer, *The Language of the Third Reich, LTI—Lingua Tertii Imperii: A Philologist's Notebook*, trans. Martin Brady (London: Athlone Press, 2000), 286. Hereafter cited with page numbers in the text.

reaction (15), and when they are used, they change the value of other words around them, monopolizing meaning and colonizing what had once been common property.

Those of us who do not live in totalitarian states, despite the occasionally strenuous limits on our freedom of speech (for instance, on "hate speech"), are only rarely fined or sent to prison for using the wrong words. But that does not make us free. True freedom of choice about how to speak and what to say are inhibited not only by formal and informal speech codes but also by habit and familiarity. The speed and thoroughness with which speech cultures reproduce themselves is breathtaking, their exact origins seemingly impossible to track. Does anyone know for sure how and why and exactly when our fellow citizens began to use *like* as a filler in almost every sentence, often more than once? What explains the strange dissemination of creaky-voice speech (glottalization) among the under-thirties (and now often their elders) or, before it, of uptalk? What brings words into being and explains why they become widely current? We have no agreed origin for the familiar word *Yankee*, which in the nineteenth-century designated a New Englander and by 1945 described (in British English) all Americans. In today's common parlance, it is impossible to use the freestanding word *terrorism* for describing the behavior of a nation-state, even though that was its original sense and its most common use before about 1970, and even as the ability to deploy terror arguably remains dominantly the property of nation-states. Terrorism is understood to be what antistate groups perform. To resurrect the earlier sense, we need an adjective: *state terrorism*, which is enough of a term of art that many will wonder what it can possibly mean. The simplification of terrorism as meaning always and only the indiscriminate violence of counterstate agents has not gone uncontested: Noam Chomsky and others have for decades insisted on the terrorist activities of the United States.[2] Oppressed minorities have always known the nature and reality of state terror: recall the circulation of shirts bearing an image of Geronimo's band and the inscription: "The Original Homeland Security: Fighting Terrorism since 1492." But a few cogent books and articles, even when backed up by witty and astute T-shirts, do not a language revolution make. The national and global interests that stand to gain from a negation of terrorism as only ever the

2. See, for example, Edward Herman and Gerry O'Sullivan, eds., *The "Terrorism" Industry: The Experts and Institutions That Shape Our View of Terror* (New York: Pantheon, 1989); and Alexander George, ed., *Western State Terrorism* (Cambridge, UK: Polity, 1991).

strategy of the enemy other have proved far too powerful and pervasive to be diverted by an oppressed minority or by a few independent intellectuals, even those with the charismatic force of Chomsky or Edward Said. These interests operate not so much by fiat but by command of a working consensus among newspapers, television networks, and politicians in a world where victory goes to the mass-circulation media that can seemingly override occasional strong dissent (e.g., from the *London Review of Books* or the *New York Review of Books*) as long as the dissenters are kept well away from television talk shows and from "expert" consultation with governments and political parties. Words matter most when their usages remain uncontested.

What follows does address the question of terrorism but only indirectly: it is much more concerned with the career of *terror*, which has a longer and more intricate history, one which of course interacts with *terrorism* since (and for once we can be precise about this) 1794. Marc Redfield persuasively suggests that the invocation of terror is "*the* exemplary speech act of sovereignty for our era."[3] Redfield's commitment to understanding terror as part of a rhetoric is exemplary: rhetoric is what persuades or coerces, inclining the hearer or reader to agree with the person employing it. Nazi speech patterns as described by Klemperer were a rhetoric in exactly this sense. Words also carry with them a history, one that can be displaced or even inverted, one that can enforce, authenticate, contest, or qualify what particular writers and speakers are intending at their particular moment in time. As such they call for a philology, a history of their inventions and reinventions, one that contextualizes their transformations through social and linguistic time. Such history (and rhetoric) cannot alone change the direction of the governing consensus, as history itself has so often proved. Philology will not start a revolution; it may not even cause the governing powers more than a moment of anxiety, if that. But it does make clear that word choices are not self-evident, that they involve exclusions and silent contestations with alternative rhetorical possibilities, roadblocks, or roads not taken. These unmentioned or displaced histories carry with them information that unsettles the univocity so often assumed or imposed by the prevailing consensus. The history of *terror* reveals several twists and turns that can sometimes appear as complete inversions. In the sphere of aesthetic experience, in tragedy, for example, or in the gothic novel, a measure of terror has been proposed as the sine qua non of a positive experience:

---

3. Marc Redfield, *The Rhetoric of Terror: Reflections on 9/11 and the War on Terror* (New York: Fordham University Press, 2009), 51.

not just a good thing but also an essential contributor to appropriate reading or beholding. Terror is the kingpin of Edmund Burke's theory of the sublime. It has also been put to use by theologians as an important educative power in the hand of God. But for the current generation, terror has mostly become at once an entirely negative and a morally illicit practice carried out only and always by the enemy other. Trotsky noticed this ruling elite habit back in 1911: "They would like to label all the activities of the proletariat directed against the class enemy's interests as terrorism [*Terrorismus*]."[4] Anyone opposed to the Washington Consensus invites nomination as a terrorist; those on our side are exempt from such descriptors even when, as in the case of Jewish state formation in 1948, terrorism is the major component of political action.

The recent career of terror is one among many cases of a process eloquently described by Philip Fisher whereby "along the path of [an] almost three-thousand-year history the language that we now use, or find ourselves lacking, has been frozen into place at surprising moments." This is often the result of a "single salient case that steers response from behind the curtains of time."[5] In the case of modern ideas of terror, that salient example comes from the French Revolution, and specifically from its Jacobin phase from 1793 to 1794. If William Reddy is correct that emotions (and terror is one among them) "operate like overlearned cognitive habits," then one component of that learning is the historical accretion of a dominant meaning or meanings.[6] Such dominance affords opportunities for abuse, especially when the emotions are—like terror—highly charged. Many years ago, William Empson found in emotive uses of language "a protean confusion, harmful in a variety of fields and particularly rampant in literary criticism."[7] His privileged attention to literary criticism looks more than a little dated now, but the warning about harm remains timely, and especially so given the career of terror talk in the popular media and among our politicians. Empson, with appropriate modesty, does not think that he can solve the problem of protean confusion, but he urges critics to at least "try to clear an area" where

---

4. Leon Trotsky, "Why Marxists Oppose Individual Terrorism," *Der Kampf* (November 1911), https://www.marxists.org/archive/trotsky/1911/11/tia09.htm.

5. Philip Fisher, *The Vehement Passions* (Princeton, NJ: Princeton University Press, 2002), 4.

6. William M. Reddy, *The Navigation of Feeling: A Framework for the History of Emotions* (Cambridge: Cambridge University Press, 2001), 54.

7. William Empson, *The Structure of Complex Words* (Totowa, NJ: Rowman and Littlefield, 1979), 1. The book was first published in 1951.

they "will not do harm." This deserves to be the most minimal aspiration of any of us doing similar work. Whether we can indeed claim anything more is doubtful, but that should not in itself serve to dispel hopes and good intentions and perhaps intimations of better times to come. It might seem delusional to think that, for example, an appropriate understanding of the philology of terror could have prevented the American invasion of Iraq in 2003. But can we be sure that a populace more familiar with that philology would have permitted so many to be so easily fooled? The damage to which terror talk contributed is still being done, and there is continuing need for an adequate historical record that could contribute to preventing similar sleights of hand from working again and again. Furthermore, not doing harm, if conceived on the grand scale of a national politics, turns out to be a rather stringent criterion and one all too rarely observed.

Again, this inquiry concerns itself principally with terror, and only more tangentially with terrorism, but the operations of the one inevitably refigure those of the other. And the history of terrorism-talk offers some useful lessons, as well as some salient contrasts. It is relatively easy to map the major transitions in the common consensus about the meaning of terrorism. An exemplary instance of the coercive semantics gathering around this term is the 1986 book *Terrorism: How the West Can Win*, edited by Benjamin Netanyahu, who is also the major contributor. The book assembles short essays (based on conference proceedings) by high-profile politicians, journalists, and academics, mostly Americans and Israelis, and many with right-of-center affiliations. Its premise is that there is something called "the West," of which Israel is a leading representative, that is under sustained attack from international terrorism sponsored by the then Soviet Union and by a number of Arab states. The Palestinian Liberation Organization (PLO) is the chief offender in a global terrorist network described as or compared to a malignancy, organized crime, gangsterism, and cancer.[8] This network is a throwback to a "savage era" (11) and the marker of a radical distinction between barbarism and freedom (226). A Marxist-Muslim conglomerate, it is suggested, plays on the disunity and dismay of the West, and exploits the "sloppiness" of its thinking about the use of force (204). Given this declared crisis, there is no place for the "middle ground of neutrality," for mere economic self-interest or for "cowardice" (219, 223). Above all,

8. Benjamin Netanyahu, ed., *Terrorism: How the West Can Win* (New York: Farrar, Straus, and Giroux, 1986), 4, 31. Hereafter cited with page numbers in the text.

we are bidden to dispense with the fantasy that the relevant issues can be resolved by "politics" (224), that is, by anything short of punitive violence. The response to terrorism is terror.

What is notable is what the book does *not* mention. It gives no sense, for example, that there were two sides in the Cold War, each operating in similar ways in their various spheres of competition. It avoids any mention of the association of terrorism with national liberation movements, except (once and briefly) as a thing of the past. It mostly defines the new terrorism as a post-1968 phenomenon, but without any mention of the 1967 war in Israel-Palestine; and when it does indirectly signal that event, it is to accuse the PLO of being founded three years before the breaching of the Green Line, as if there had been no motive for Palestinian resistance before 1967 (i.e., no 1948). Significantly, it fails to mention the French Revolution and the Jacobin Terror, and thus effaces a long historical association of terrorism with the "Western" nation-state itself, whether in its internal disciplinary aspirations or in its behavior toward foreign or colonized populations. Terrorism, above all, now belongs wholly to the non-West, whereas the West itself is directed to destroy it and to follow the example of the West's exemplary representative in the Middle East, Israel.

Not every address to the topic of terrorism is as ideologically transparent as this one, although large numbers of specialist journals and government-sponsored reports still do not offer any alternatives to its presuppositions, and this despite a rich counterinsurgency literature that understands questions of terminology to be of crucial importance. One example: Frank Kitson began his career on active service in Kenya, where he devised ways of infiltrating the Mau Mau movement, whose members he referred to variously as gangs, gangsters, and terrorists.[9] Some years later, Kitson dropped the gangs and gangsters (which will be resurrected by Netanyahu) from his comprehensive list of terms from which to choose:

> In writing on this subject one of the most difficult problems concerns the matter of terminology. The British Army gives separate definitions of Civil Disturbance, Insurgency, Guerrilla Warfare, Subversion, Terrorism, Civil Disobedience, Communist Revolutionary Warfare, and Insurrection on the one hand and of Counter Insurgency, Internal Security, and Counter Revolutionary Operations on the other. Elsewhere conflicts are variously described as Partisan, Irregular or Unconventional Wars,

9. See Frank Kitson, *Gangs and Counter-Gangs* (London: Barrie and Rockliff, 1960).

and the people taking part in them have an even wider selection of labels attached to them. Furthermore, although a particular author will use one of these terms to cover one aspect of the business and another to cover another, a different author will use the same two terms in a totally different way.[10]

Kitson opts for subversion as the best term to describe everything that falls short of violence, and uses insurgency for the rest (3), but even these call for careful contextualization. Terror, notably, is not on Kitson's list, unless we assume that it is implicitly subsumed under terrorism as what terror performs. The 2001 war on terror is surely also a back-formation from terrorism, a seemingly natural association that sees terror as simply what terrorists do. In 1794, it was the other way around: the successors and enemies of the Jacobins first designated the "reign of terror" and then invented the word *terrorist* to describe those who carried it out.

For terror itself, the thing from which terrorism is derived and of which it is the executive arm, there is hardly any analytical tradition.[11] Until 9/11, *terror* occupied a somewhat quieter rhetorical register; and even after 9/11, it is still *terrorism* that attracts more attention and interest. The history of terror, though, is much longer, and the range of its associations and implications is larger. As an emotion (or affect or feeling), it subsists (in English) with a range of cognates or near synonyms that it can either displace or combine with; as an agent-object in the world (*a terror*), it can be described and redescribed in a seemingly limitless number of ways. And when one looks into the ways in which non-English terms are or are not translated as terror, the possibilities expand even further. Fundamental questions about what is and is not common between different persons in different times and places come to the surface when we ask, for example, whether the Greek *phobos* is best rendered in English as *fear* or *terror*. Terrorism, coined (in French) only in 1794, often passed into other languages in near-identical form (*terrorisme, terrorism, Terrorismus*). *Terror*, or what we have been *calling* terror, has wandered much more widely and in more mysterious ways.

10. Frank Kitson, *Low Intensity Operations: Subversion, Insurgency, Peace-Keeping* (London: Faber and Faber, 1971), 2.

11. Claire Sterling's *The Terror Network: The Secret War of International Terrorism* (New York: Holt, Rinehart and Winston, 1981) was briefly a media sensation, but it is little more than a lurid biography of various terrorists, and thus addresses terrorism without developing any concept of terror. Sterling's case for Soviet Russia as the sponsor of worldwide terrorism has since been widely discredited. Redfield's *The Rhetoric of Terror* and a few other studies are, in the wake of 9/11, beginning to fill in the gaps.

For example, terror has been argued by Wolfgang Sofsky, with un-impeachable moral seriousness, to be both the organizing principle (as a practice) and the object (as an effect) of the concentration-extermination camp system developed in Hitler's Europe.[12] The arbitrary power over life and death exercised by camp administrations did indeed create what many would agree to call a pervasive culture of terror. Closer to the other, trivial end of the spectrum, as NASA's Mars explorer was approaching its destination in the summer of 2012, the agency was sensing a lack of public interest in its big adventure. Accordingly, it released a video dramatizing the upcoming landing under the title *Seven Minutes of Terror*.[13] The reference was to the final stages of the landing sequence in which especially critical conditions would decide the fate of the mission. Why terror? The Mars lander itself has no emotions, so the terror instead describes what those watching it are going to feel. But their personal safety is not threatened, nor is the machine open to personification as something that itself either generates or feels terror. What is at stake here is at most anxiety, concern about what happens to another or, in this case, to one's long-cherished scientific hopes as embodied in a machine. This use of *terror* ought to make us think. And yet, at the same time, no one would have been perplexed had the machine failed and given rise to a comment that this was a terrible outcome. Since at least the eighteenth century, English speakers have used the word *terrible* as a simple emphatic, one that can describe both a terrible murder and a terrible meal. *Terror*, too, has been used in this way; I remember hearing any badly behaved boy described as "a little terror." But this use now seems outdated; *terror* has now been delegated to more serious tasks.

Anyone immersed in the popular language of the anglophone world after 9/11 is used to hearing about the more portentous use of terror on an almost daily basis. The so-called war on terror (sometimes global war on terror, hence GWOT in the relevant literature) was everywhere in the media at the end of 2001, and it still has a lively career. Its devilish charisma has been well described by Njabulo Ndebele, who finds in it a "terse encapsulation that ironically strains towards the economy of poetry but, unlike poetry, yields not insight but cleverness of the kind that

12. Wolfgang Sofsky, *Die Ordnung des Terrors* (1997), trans. William Templer as *The Order of Terror: The Concentration Camp* (Princeton, NJ: Princeton University Press, 1999). Hannah Arendt's *The Origins of Totalitarianism* (Orlando, FL: Harcourt, 1976) also asserts that terror is the property of an organized, administered state.

13. Kenneth Chang, "Simulated Space 'Terror' Offers NASA an Online Following," *New York Times*, July 10, 2012, http://www.nytimes.com/2012/07/11/science/space/seven -minutes-of-terror-video-grabs-online-audience-for-nasa.html.

supremely admires itself." It participates in the language of "a manipula-
tive state in which the desire for violence overwhelms the public capacity
to discern falsehood in argument."[14] Perhaps this is obvious to an alert
black South African writer: it has been less so in the United States, where
there was little negative criticism of this coinage, and rarely among the
kinds of people who were exploiting it. One notable dissenter was Zbigniew Brzezinski, who wrote in 2007 that "the damage these three words
have done—a classic self-inflicted wound—is infinitely greater than any
wild dreams entertained by the fanatical perpetrators of the 9/11 attacks
when they were plotting against us in distant Afghan caves."[15] The damage, he goes on to explain, was the creation of a culture of fear, one making it "easier for demagogic politicians to mobilize the public on behalf
of the policies they want to pursue." After "five years of almost continuous national brainwashing," he finds that America has indeed become
more paranoid. In 2003, Congress had identified 160 sites as potentially
important domestic targets for terrorist attack; by 2007, that number
had risen to about 300,000.

Brzezinski, as parts of this study will make clear, is applying good
Cold War (and Burkean) theory to the rhetoric of terror: inspiring panic
in a population is both empirically dangerous (people cannot be relied
on to behave calmly in a real crisis) and politically disabling (they risk
becoming the prey of all sorts of opportunists). President George W.
Bush got the point when he declared, in an address to a joint session of
Congress on September 20, 2001, that "as long as the United States of
America is determined and strong, this will not be an age of terror."[16]
This was solid, received doctrine, although it was overshadowed at the
time by Bush's famous imperative to carry on shopping. Bush further in-
sisted that "this country will define our times, not be defined by them."[17]

14. Njabulo S. Ndabele, *Fine Lines from the Box: Further Thoughts about Our
Country*, comp. Sam Thlalo Radithlalo (Cape Town: Umuzi, 2007), 202–3. Redfield
(*Rhetoric of Terror*, 66) argues that war is the inevitable "enactment of the sovereign exception," albeit that no other nation "could have attempted such a literary and violently
consequential speech act without falling into mere comic posturing."

15. Zbigniew Brzezinski, "Terrorized by 'War on Terror,'" *Washington Post*, March 25,
2007. The cultivation of fear as a means of disciplining a domestic population, especially
in the workplace, is explored in Corey Robin, *Fear: The History of a Political Idea* (Oxford: Oxford University Press, 2004). See also Caleb Carr, *The Lessons of Terror: A History of Warfare against Civilians* (New York: Random House, 2003).

16. *Selected Speeches of President George W. Bush, 2001–2008*, https://georgewbush
-whitehouse.archives.gov/infocus/bushrecord/documents/Selected_Speeches_George_W
_Bush.pdf.

17. This sentiment was given starkly specific form in the television series *House of
Cards* (episode 51), where the demonically charismatic President Frank Underwood

But in the same address, he spoke of "our war on terror," confirming the imprint of a phrase that had already, as they say, gone viral. The tide of terror in the affairs of language would prove hard to stem, and as soon as the rhetorical genie came out of the semantic bottle, it began to cause problems. The effort to limit the meaning of *terror* as designating the enemy other by way of simple personification—who the other is and what it does—would always be troubled and eroded by the tendency of *terror* to describe a subjective state, an emotion, or affect: terror as what we feel. Bush's address is thus compelled to assert that we will *not* feel terror at the terror with which we are at war, while inadvertently suggesting that the terror with which we are at war is already within us—in the manner of the "fear itself" that Franklin Roosevelt famously said we should not fear. In this way, the war against the other posits itself as also a war against what makes the self vulnerable: its own emotions. The one claim is credible, if grandiose; the other, beyond imagining.

Back in 1986, before Brzezinski, Christopher Hitchens wrote a scathing essay on the abuse of the word *terrorism*, showing how a word with "no meaning and no definition" had become the "buzzword of the eighties." He found it "the perfect instrument for the cheapening of public opinion and the intimidation of dissent," little more than a "junk word, designed to obliterate distinctions."[18] His point still stands, although thirty years on he seems to have lost his audience: terrorism is now almost completely uncontested in popular use as defining a violently bad thing done to us by others. Terror has come into the spotlight more recently and has not yet settled into complete referential complacency. And beyond the long-standing ambiguity of the word as designating both inner feeling and external agent, there is an aesthetic tradition identifying terror as able to inspire if not sheer pleasure then something very close to it. We are now more familiar with horror stories and horror movies, but around 1800 it was terror novels and tales of terror that loomed large in the literary marketplace. Edmund Burke made terror the essential and primary ingredient of his theory of the sublime long before the term was used to denigrate the Jacobins. Some legacies of this tradition surfaced in the aftermath of 9/11, when inevitable comparisons were made between the footage of the falling towers and similar images

---

(played by Kevin Spacey) pronounced that "we don't submit to terror . . . we make the terror." Episode 54 has the president announce that "terror is unacceptable" and that "fear is un-American."

18. Christopher Hitchens, "Wanton Acts of Usage—Terrorism: A Cliché in Search of a Meaning," *Harper's Magazine*, September 1, 1986, 66–70.

in the movies, so that the "real" event looked either eerily simulacral or subversively exciting, or both. Any inclination to associate the 9/11 event with the world of art was speedily condemned as tasteless or immoral (Karlheinz Stockhausen was the scapegoat here), but the association never quite went away. Thus there remained a mostly unspoken and indeed unnoticed but unmistakable connection between the falling towers and the Burkean sublime. This is not unimportant, because it helped to condition the words one could and could not use; most notably, it served, as we will see, to exclude any recourse to *horror* (rather than *terror*) as part of the permitted vocabulary for describing the events and the responses of various persons to them.

After 9/11, terror was not the order not just of the day but also of the decade; the strategic emptiness (or impossible fullness) of the term, signifying either or both a subjective response or a threatening object whose exact identity could never be specified, proved invaluable to the far-too-willing coalition of politicians and media pundits aiming to create and maintain a confused but warmongering patriotic consensus, a task in which they undoubtedly succeeded. While statistics cannot be exact, one scholar reports that George Bush's approval ratings hit 90 percent, while only some 20 percent thought that America's own policies had anything to do with the attacks on Washington and New York.[19] Notwithstanding the millions all over the world who marched against the war on Iraq, and the many who spoke out against it, the evidence is that terror talk was a highly effective tool for the manufacture of consent. Even the universities, where critical thought is supposed to flourish, mostly failed to provide a robust opposition, and indeed many salaried intellectuals fell enthusiastically into line with the government and media consensus.[20] Meanwhile, the phrase "war on terror" served as the enabling rhetoric for a war on whomever and whatever, wherever. The outcomes of that war have been and continue to be catastrophic. The creation of failed states and of more thoroughly failing states, and the massive loss of (mostly noncombatant) life, are the critical events of our generation, and

19. For these and other such indicators, see Richard Jackson, *Writing the War on Terrorism: Language, Politics and Counter-Terrorism* (Manchester: Manchester University Press, 2005), 162–63.

20. There was, of course, a good deal of formal and informal intimidation by media and government, exemplified by the black list published by the American Council of Trustees and Alumni; see Sandra Silberstein, *War of Words: Language, Politics and 9/11* (London: Routledge, 2002), 127–47. But many willingly offered up their endorsement, with attendant philosophical justifications, of the "homeland security" and foreign war-making initiatives.

they are overwhelmingly the responsibility of the "West," those who consistently assert themselves to be on the right side of everything and who largely dominate global politics.

It actually took a few days for the "war on terror" to be announced. It began as a "war on terrorism," a more familiar placeholder. By the evening of September 11, 2001, President Bush was already voicing the presence of "evil" and of "acts of terror," but what he first envisaged was a "war against terrorism." By September 20, this had become a "war on terror," which would eventually evolve into the "global war on terror."[21] *Terror* became the go-to word of the decade, until President Barack Obama's May 2013 speech to the National Defense University publicized a shift of rhetoric, in place for some time but not until then formally announced, by declaring that the bar had been set too high, that no one can promise "the total defeat of terror, and that the world we have now resembles the world before 9/11 where the threat comes not from terror but from terrorism." He holds on to the phrase *acts of terror*, but insists that "we must discipline our thinking, our definitions, our actions."[22] The war on terror, by this reckoning, appeared to be over, and we were back to responding to terrorism or to the weaker form, acts of terror. Obama's rhetorical climb-down, however, held good only until the rise of the Islamic State (IS) brought terror back into the limelight. And so we remain very much where Jacques Derrida thought we were in the days immediately after 9/11. In the heat of everyone else's moment, and apropos of the already-dominant telegraphic signature of the event *called* 9/11, he bluntly proposed that "we do not know what we are talking about."[23]

Obama's offering of "acts of terror" as the new term of art did not, moreover, diminish any of the polemical energy that made the interpellation of terror a critical measure of political propriety. In the debates leading up to the 2012 presidential election, challenger Mitt Romney took the president to task for waiting almost two weeks to declare the September 11, 2012 attack on the American consulate in Benghazi

---

21. The relevant speeches are transcribed in Jackson, *Writing the War on Terrorism,* 190–97.

22. White House, "Remarks by the President at the National Defense University." Notably, the British response to July 7, 2005, was rather sparing in its references to terror, as was the American reporting of the bombing of the Boston Marathon in April 2013, just a month or so before Obama's speech. W. J. T. Mitchell, in *Cloning Terror: The War of Images, 9/11 to the Present* (Chicago: University of Chicago Press, 2011), 23, dates the change to April 2009.

23. Giovanna Borradori, ed., *Philosophy in a Time of Terror: Dialogues with Jürgen Habermas and Jacques Derrida* (Chicago: University of Chicago Press, 2003), 86.

as an "act of terror." This was produced as evidence of the president's unfitness to manage foreign policy and defend the nation. But according to TV host Candy Crowley, who intervened in live time to set the record straight, Obama had indeed referred to terror in a Rose Garden speech one day after the event. So indeed he had, but not unambiguously. He had said that acts of terror would never deter America from pursuing its chosen policies, but he had (luckily or cleverly) left open a question about the exact fit between such acts of terror and the Benghazi attack, which his administration was attributing to the spontaneous violence aroused by the circulation of an American-made video insulting the prophet Muhammad. After the election, the same issues came back during the confirmation process of Susan Rice as the potential new secretary of state. Again, it was all about terror; specifically, had Rice deliberately misled the people by withholding evidence of the involvement of al-Qaeda affiliates in Benghazi? If so, then she would have been seeking to persuade us that the event was less serious than it really was. Terror involves coolheaded planning and premeditation, whereas mere violence is unpredictable and unconnected with larger plots. (The law, in similar fashion, distinguishes between premeditated crimes and crimes of passion.) Failure to predict and anticipate violence is excusable: it can happen anywhere at any time, rather like acts of God. But failure to anticipate a terror attack is a failure of diligence. Violence is a fact of life, but terror is Public Enemy No. 1. It now seems that the White House account of events was closer to the truth: there are apparently no records of organized involvement by al-Qaeda or anyone else.[24] But even if it had been a deliberate plot, its being the result of violence staged by organizations called terrorist would not of itself make it by all definitions an act of terror. It was not, for example, visibly designed to intimidate a passive civilian population by the threat of the unpredictable repetition of irresistible violence. It could have inspired terror in its immediate victims, but it did not have the sustained, wider power of terror, fully conceived (and neither did 9/11). That power, most of the time, resides with states, which possess armaments and delivery mechanisms well beyond those in the hands of most, if not all, nonstate agents. To imagine Benghazi as an act of terror rather than of mere terrorism is to participate once again in the hyperbolic rhetoric of the post-9/11 consensus. It interpellates the agents of violence into a global-international network that can

24. See David D. Kirkpatrick, "Deadly Mix in Benghazi: False Allies, Crude Video," *New York Times*, December 29, 2013.

be made credible as a long-term threat. Since Benghazi, all rhetorical bets are once again off. The appearance of ISIS as a partly land-based and partly global agent of both terrorism and terror has rendered, at least for the time being, Obama's effort to narrow down and rationalize the terminology more or less redundant. President Donald Trump continues to find terror talk indispensable. We are back with omnipresent terror.

And yet evidence of who really does hold the most pervasive power of terror is readily available, not just in the events unfolding daily in the real world but also in the documents governing US foreign policy. In 1996, well before Operation Shock and Awe (also known as Operation Iraqi Freedom) in 2003, the National Defense University Press published a book called *Shock and Awe*, in which the coauthors set out the conditions to be satisfied for US dominance of the battlefields of the future. They describe a comprehensive possession and application of the powers of terror through "(near) total control and signature management of the entire operational environment."[25] The aim is to "neuter the will of an adversary to resist," to "paralyze, shock, unnerve, deny, destroy," and to provide a "non-nuclear equivalent" of the Hiroshima and Nagasaki bombs, the results of which—the "ultimate military application of Shock and Awe"—are frequently invoked as a measure of political and military success.[26] Three conditions for rapid domination are especially notable. First, the US must be able to strike anywhere and anytime with the "element of impunity" (111); second, it must have "staying power" (14), that is, be able to prolong the threat through extended time; and third, there must be whole-field control of the entire environment, not only of the enemy's territory but also of the homeland as well (2). Clearly, these are conditions that can be met only by a nation-state—indeed, by a superpower. And clearly they are the conditions for the dissemination of terror. No nonstate agent could possibly command the resources required for such a program. The coauthors admit that it will be very hard to "sustain the current defense program over the long term without a real threat materializing to rally and coalesce public support" (5). Five years later, along came 9/11.

Ullman and Wade do use the phrase "reign of terror" (46), but only to describe Iraqi long-range rocket attacks on Tehran, never their own protocols. But the aspiration to control an entire lifeworld by violence

25. Harlan K. Ullman and James P. Wade, *Shock and Awe: Achieving Rapid Dominance* (Washington, DC: National Defense University Press, 1996), xi.
26. Ullman and Wade, *Shock and Awe*, xxv, xxix, xxvi, 110. Hereafter cited with page numbers in the text.

or the threat of violence is a classic instance of terror and of terrorizing (quite different from the more local, small-scale performances of terrorism). What is envisaged here is the total destruction of the personality and environment of the enemy, and the carefully restricted management of information at home. This is nothing less than a legitimation of the totalitarian state. Nothing is said about refashioning the law to control domestic opposition, but neither is such an option explicitly denied. We have come a long way from the declared need to create an informed and self-reliant citizenship of the sort that featured (however cynically) in Cold War policy. Naomi Klein has argued that we have seen the imposition of a long-term economic equivalent to shock and awe not only in the well-known US support for right-wing coups, and thus for torture and the repression of dissent by foreign governments (Chile, Nicaragua, Argentina, and so on), but also, more insidiously and less publicly, in the enforcement of neoliberal economic doctrines resulting in the massive redistribution of wealth across the globe.[27] The short-term terror of personal and collective violence and death is accompanied by a longer-term attrition of the conditions for flourishing. The creation of failed states creates further incentives for violent intervention, and the whole cycle begins again.[28]

So radical and comprehensive are these policies that, as Ullman and Wade fully realize, aggressive management of the domestic consensus is required to maintain support for state policy and state behavior. Not uncommonly (e.g., in Nicaragua and Iraq) this has involved lying and deception, and at the very least the tight control of information and of the ways in which it can be processed. For example, Richard Jackson has found that, of 414 stories airing on the major television networks between September 2002 and February 2003 (the months covering the run-up to the invasion of Iraq), "all but thirty four originated from three government agencies." Even the press, supposedly the guardian of our liberties, relied heavily (up to 75 percent) on government sources without

27. Naomi Klein, *The Shock Doctrine: The Rise of Disaster Capitalism* (New York: Picador, 2007).

28. US Army, *Field Manual* (sec. 3-24), published in 2006, offers a very different program for the control of occupied territories, placing political above military action as necessary for success. This attempt at creating a legitimacy-based counterinsurgent policy has, however, been criticized for imagining an impossible task for troops in the field; they must in theory master the local languages and cultures as well as provide, in the words of one commentator, everything "from security to sewage." See Beatrice Heuser, "The Cultural Revolution in Counter-Insurgency," *Journal of Strategic Studies* 30, no. 1 (2007): 153–71, esp. 168. The US Army's field manuals are also available online.

giving them serious scrutiny.[29] These kinds of direct and indirect manipulations of public opinion should have been common knowledge, since they had been an object of critique for some time. Chomsky and Said are only the best known among a number of writers and scholars who have explained the operations of the manufacture of consent in the context of previous crises.[30] But for all their eminence, they have been remarkably rare participants in television talk-show culture; it seems clear that their views are not welcome by those in charge of the major media. The rest of us plodding along with the job of critique are even more comprehensively ignored.

And yet the issue of consent remains crucial, and there is no more elementary consent than that governing the understandings of words: what they are taken to signify and who is doing the signifying. Terror and consent are in fact the two headline terms in Philip Bobbitt's bestselling book on the global situation after 9/11. Bobbitt proposes that terror does have a substantive meaning in the discussion of current world politics, despite his urgent sense that the US government has "no consensus" about what it is.[31] Terror is the capacity to disrupt and disable the healthy functions of consent states—those functions that require citizen approval of their governing classes. Such approval is based not only on the state's need to project legitimacy but also increasingly on its credibility as the protector of its citizens, to ensure security (202). Protecting civilians is more important than just killing terrorists (561). If terror succeeds in destroying our trust in basic security, then it has done its work; the state will destroy itself, either by implosion or by starting to govern by repression and intimidation: martial law (404). In the second case, it becomes itself a terror state and consent disappears. Effective terror in this respect can come either from human enemies or from natural disasters (215). The chaos of the federal responses to Hurricane Katrina (which was a significantly human-made catastrophe, but we may leave

29. Jackson, *Writing the War on Terrorism*, 167.

30. See, again, Herman and O'Sullivan, *The "Terrorism" Industry*; George, *Western State Terrorism*; Joseba Zulaika and William A. Douglass, *Terror and Taboo: The Follies, Fables and Faces of Terrorism* (London: Routledge, 1996); and Eqbal Ahmad, "The Lexicon of Terrorism," in *Confronting Empire: Interviews with David Barsamian* (Cambridge, MA: South End Press, 2000), 94–100. And for an influential instance of the formatting of the national imaginary with near-complete disregard for the truth, see Susan Faludi's account of the Jessica Lynch story in *The Terror Dream: Fear and Fantasy in Post-9/11 America* (New York: Henry Holt, 2007), 165–95.

31. Philip Bobbitt, *Terror and Consent: The Wars for the Twenty-First Century* (New York: Random House, 2009), 442, also 181–238. Hereafter cited with page numbers in the text.

that aside here) is as dangerous to democracy as is al-Qaeda, because it so emphatically spreads distrust of government and dismay at its failure to protect us.

Things are getting worse, Bobbitt argues, because we are in the middle of a major transition from nation-states to market states. Democratic nation-states are in theory somewhat coherent; they act as efficient collectives in which citizens agree to be represented by elected officials. Market states are more individually oriented, promising to maximize opportunities for each of us, often against the grain of any collective identity. Market states thus work to weaken representative democracy, even as they seem to fulfill one of its basic promises. Terrorist agencies also participate in market-state culture, one of whose attributes is the free (transnational) circulation of commodities available to individuals. Weapons are among those commodities. The market state thus erodes its own security by failing to restrain (and indeed encouraging) individual access to everything by all who can afford it. Terrorism becomes entrepreneurial and, subject to the sort of idiosyncratic financing typified by Osama bin Laden, relatively independent of any collective participation. Responding to such unpredictable threats, consent states become more prone to behave like terror states. The only thing that can inhibit this tendency is a clear and consistent commitment to the rule of law, including "civilian judicial review" of military tribunals (269) and the "decent treatment" of prisoners (285). Embodying democratic-consent culture and being seen to do so is critical to the survival of the state, both in itself and as a model for other states.

Not all consent states need be Western-style democracies (523), but the largest one in today's world happens to be so. Arguing that "elementary data mining" (308) would likely have resulted in the preemptive arrests of all of the 9/11 terrorists, and noting the subsequent revelations of torture at Abu Ghraib as well as the disgraceful federal response to Hurricane Katrina (217), Bobbitt finds (and finds reasonable) in America today a radical deficiency in the trust factor required for the proper functioning of a consent state. The prospect or promise of security sets a very high barrier for state competence, especially when that security is conceived as an individual demand in a society made up of very different individuals. This may be a relatively recent obsession: states have not always cast themselves as security states, and certain kinds of security have even been deemed inadvisable, unattainable, or impious, an almost blasphemous misunderstanding of our fragile lives as sinners or vulnerable beings. Noting the "severely overworked" status of the term in today's political and cultural lexicon as a "formidable instrument of life-management" whose credibility is based on a presumed universality, John T. Hamilton offers a powerful philological history, bringing out the deep ambivalence of the idea of security, which has been conceived of as everything from a natural right to a mortal sin. He finds that "security's semantic field begins to resemble . . . a rhizomatic network producing nearly infinite opportunities for interpretation and instrumentalization": exactly the situation I am claiming for the word *terror*.[32] The aspirational identification of security with the homeland or the *patrie* can subsist, as it has done in the work of Hobbes and Schmitt, only with the cultivation of the very fear it is supposed to preempt: citizens must be made fearful enough that they are willing to forgo liberties in order to feel themselves secure. The desire to be *sine cura*, without care (52), is simultaneously a form of negligence (carelessness) and an oxymoron, a "concern to be without concern" (27). It is itself a disruption of the very community it purports to protect, promising an *immunitas* that threatens to unbind the obligation to collective life (39). The urge for security—that is, the acceptance of a manufactured consensus as the highest good—requires acquiescence in the culture of fear. The operative syndrome is that which Derrida (and Esposito) call autoimmunity, where the state is "both self-protecting and self-destroying" and where it is in its own interest "to expose its vulnerability."[33] Adapting this model to the phenomenon of terror talk, we may suppose that in deploying a rhetoric that seeks to ensure its own incremental militarization, the homeland is at the same time inscribing its own inevitable weakness.

Mark Neocleous has proposed that security may be "little more than a semantic and semiotic black hole allowing authority to inscribe itself more deeply into human experience," a placeholder that works toward a "rejection of politics in any meaningful form."[34] Neocleous demonstrates (77–105) that the rhetoric of security, in the form of social security, first functions in the 1930s to describe the state's effort to ensure its citizens some protection against the worst excesses of a runaway liberal capitalism. The rhetoric of the New Deal understood this effort to be a form of "national" security well before that phrase came into common use, referring to foreign and domestic policing. Indeed, Neocleous ar-

---

32. John T. Hamilton, *Security: Politics, Humanity, and the Philology of Care* (Princeton, NJ: Princeton University Press, 2013), 7–8, 12. Hereafter cited with page numbers in the text.

33. Borradori, *Philosophy in a Time of Terror*, 108, 124.

34. Mark Neocleous, *Critique of Security* (Montreal: McGill-Queen's University Press, 2008), 4, 185.

gues, the support for a social safety net was always mediated through a desire to discourage popular interest in a (foreign-identified) socialist-communist alternative whose potential domestic availability was always more threatening than any military threat from the Soviet Union. The transposition of the security "problem" to the enemy other has been so successful that we refer routinely to social security benefits without ever making the connection, even as we are repeatedly being told that both kinds of security are under threat. It is worth noting that the expenditure on the one, the military and homeland security industries, directly threatens the flourishing of the other, the domestic health and safety complex. The one is marketed as necessary spending, the other as dispensable or discretionary. Although the declared demise of the Soviet alternative may for a time have allowed for the erosion of "social" security as a cherished political priority, and facilitated the elephantine expansion of the quite different operation called "homeland" security now directed at a very different enemy, there were signs from the 2016 election campaign responses (from both left and right) that the neoliberal strategy of relative pauperization is beginning to be recognized for what it is.

Like terror, security has an inner-outer flexibility in its rhetorical range: I can feel secure (or not) at the spectacle of security. And terror, like security, allows for the operation of a shell game in designating its possible origins and affiliates. So an interior terror, that which we feel, can be attributed to a chosen external agency (like the enemy other) to discourage us from understanding it in relation to quite other conditioning forces, such as economic vulnerability or social instability. In declaring the years of the middle twentieth century an "age of anxiety," as did Rollo May, among many others, there was a notable displacement or diminishing of references to terror, because anxiety cannot exist (verbally) as an external agent. I cannot be anxious at an anxiety outside myself; anxiety is within. This meant that the default cross-referencing was to psychoanalytic and philosophical conditions, states of mind or feeling. It was not so much the awareness of nuclear weapons (which were sometimes not even mentioned) as the modern mind that was up for discussion. While larger historical conditions were invoked, the primary site of adjudication mostly remained in the individual mind amenable to some form of therapy. If terror is now displacing, or at least disputing, the cultural territory with anxiety, then its semantic fungibility should alert us to a wider set of agencies influencing the current lexicon than those simply attributable to some or other ontological syndrome.

Here I fully endorse Marc Redfield's argument that, whatever else it is, terror is a "phantasmatic speech-act" designed to haunt us, and that "sovereign is he who decides on terror—who can call the other a terror-ist and make it stick."[35] The history and theory of terror must then come together: terror has no useful significance outside its history, and what that history records is, among other things, a constant pressure toward the production of theory or, more exactly, pseudotheory. While terror (and the fear-terror word cluster) have been discussed by philosophers, there cannot be a philosophy of terror, if one takes (following Derrida) conventional philosophy to require that there be no fudging of basic dis-tinctions in its operative vocabulary.[36] So *Verstand* must never be *Ver-nunft*, base must be kept apart from superstructure, and reason from imagination. What matters most, what is foundational, must mean one thing and one thing only; it must never have come into being by way of any kind of translation that is other than an absolute equivalence. Ac-cording to this criterion, terror must be distinguished from dread, or fear, or horror, or panic. But it is always, in its uses, slipping back and forth be-tween and among such associated terms, either failing to separate itself out or doing so in such obviously reductive ways that ulterior, polemical motives can be suspected.

If there cannot be a philosophy of terror, can there be a theory of terror? Yes, if theory be conceived as something necessarily inabsolute, a practice of thought that harks back to its Greek sense of looking into or seeking clues (although not any longer, in these our times, from the oracle). Such theory must not only cope with but also fully embrace the always-partial resolutions of words into meanings, and their functional displacement of other meanings. It must seek for a historical specificity, as far as it can, while accepting that any knowledge thus produced can-not be scientifically exact. There is a body of important work that has set about the task of refining our vocabulary in this domain: concept history or, in German, *Begriffsgeschichte*. This work amounts to something of a theory in the sense I have just suggested. It seeks to make general or collective statements about verbal-conceptual networks for which a set of common methods appears to produce conclusions that are enough alike to make us think that a theory is possible but also different enough that we cannot predict outcomes or preassign local deviations. Raymond Williams's *Keywords*, first published in 1976, is a foundational example

35. Redfield, *Rhetoric of Terror*, 4, 56. While recognizing the war on terror as a "deeply crazed" formulation (2), Redfield offers a powerful case for its inevitability within the phantasmagoric world of modern American sovereignty.

36. See, for one exemplary discussion, Derrida's *Dissemination*, trans. Barbara John-son (Chicago: University of Chicago Press, 1981), 61–171. Socrates's contribution to this orthodoxy is discussed in the next chapter.

and one that is always open to multiple fine-tunings in the face of prolif-
erating differences that Williams seems almost to delight in registering
as a protest against any idea of "proper" meaning: "We find a history
and complexity of meanings; conscious changes, or consciously different uses; innovation, obsolescence, specialization, extension, overlap,
transfer; or changes which are masked by a nominal continuity so that
words that seem to have been there for centuries, with continuous general meanings, have come in fact to express radically different or radically variable, yet sometimes hardly noticed, meanings and implications
of meaning."[37] Taking up for each of his entries "what can be called
a cluster" of "interrelated words and references," Williams finds connections that are "in some new ways systematic" (22), but he is wary
of suggesting any methodological closure, any comprehensive limits to
what might be expected.[38] Somewhat more demanding in this respect is
Quentin Skinner, who believes that "to apply any word to the world, we
need to have a clear grasp of both its sense and its reference" and, in the
case of "appraisive terms," we also need to know the "exact range of attitudes the term can standardly be used to express."[39] Skinner finds Williams
vague on the relation between word and concept: they are not the same
but nevertheless can be seen to have a "systematic relationship" (564).

   I do not share Skinner's sense of clarity and exactness in language use
as a decisive goal for concept analysis, whose complexities more often
rely on obfuscation. Clear distinctions are inevitably appealing in promising to clean up our thinking: Hannah Arendt, for example, laments
in her essay "On Violence" that political science does not "distinguish
among such key words as 'power,' 'strength,' 'force,' 'authority,' and,
finally, 'violence'—all of which refer to distinct, different phenomena
and would hardly exist unless they did. . . . To use them as synonyms not
only indicates a certain deafness to linguistic meanings, which would be
serious enough, but it has also resulted in a kind of blindness to the realities they correspond to."[40] This perfectly expresses philosophy's desire:
one word for one thing and thus a prospect of rational management. But

---

37. Raymond Williams, *Keywords: A Vocabulary of Culture and Society*, rev. ed.
(New York: Oxford University Press, 1983), 17.
   38. When I first came up with the phrase "fear-terror cluster," I did not know I was
reinventing one of Williams's terms, which I use rather more aggressively than he does.
   39. Quentin Skinner, "Language and Social Change," in *The State of the Language*,
ed. Leonard Michaels and Christopher Ricks (Berkeley: University of California Press,
1980), 562–78, esp. 566.
   40. Hannah Arendt, *Crises of the Republic* (Orlando, FL: Harcourt Brace and Co.,
1972), 142.

just a few pages later Arendt finds herself admitting that "these distinctions, though by no means arbitrary, hardly ever correspond to watertight compartments in the real world" (145). That real world notably includes both academic and popular writing, which often come together even as we might wish to keep them apart: the German *Gewalt*, as we shall see, can denote both actual violence and the power of violence. Like Arendt, Freud makes a pitch for clear distinctions in *Beyond the Pleasure Principle*, where he proposes to distinguish *Schreck*, *Furcht*, and *Angst* as different responses to danger. But as Jacques Lezra has pointed out, Freud himself is inconsistent, and elsewhere uses *Schreck* to denote what he here calls *Angst*.[41] As Lezra observes, *Schreck* is "nicely ambiguous, covering a range of senses, which run from horror to pleasant surprise" (25). Or, indeed, to terror.

More convincingly, Skinner does explain that there can be perspicacity in silence, in saying nothing. Silence, for example, is a telling form of reference when John Locke does not mention the ancient constitution, as almost everyone else did, in his work on government.[42] In this way, a normative vocabulary can be conceptually active by way of its absence, as it was (I would argue) when the word *horror* did not appear in any authorized accounts of the 9/11 events. *Begriffsgeschichte*, or concept history, as exemplified in the work of Reinhart Koselleck, is perhaps the closest critical model for what I am attempting to do with terror, and here too there seems to be a tentative or open relation between archive and theory. A primary question raised by Koselleck concerns the relation between concept history and social (or general) history: stated briefly (and somewhat obscurely), "language and history depend on each other but never coincide."[43] History is recorded in language but some things go undescribed. Concepts are necessary if there is to be any society or any political action, but concepts emerge from or subsist in systems that are far more complex than what can be registered in the language of concepts themselves (76). Similarly, concepts are associated with words, but not every word is a concept (84). And most importantly, while words can be rendered unambiguous in use, "a concept *must* remain ambiguous in order to be a concept" (85, my emphasis). Because a concept (e.g.,

41. Jacques Lezra, *Wild Materialism: The Ethic of Terror and the Modern Republic* (New York: Fordham University Press, 2010), 24–25.

42. Skinner, *The Foundations of Modern Political Thought*, vol. 1, *The Renaissance* (Cambridge: Cambridge University Press, 1978), xiv.

43. Reinhart Koselleck, *Futures Past: On the Semantics of Historical Time*, trans. Keith Tribe (New York: Columbia University Press, 2004), 222. Hereafter cited with page numbers in the text.

the state) is a "concentrate of several substantial meanings" and unites a "plenitude of meaning," it must be ambiguous even when it is clear. It "bundles up" a variety of things (85) and may at best "set a limit" to what can be made of it, so that its language is "a medium in which experiential capacity and theoretical stability can be evaluated" (86). Word-concept-history relations can seem to be resolved or transcended only to break out again into something "seemingly insoluble" (86).

These insights are very important. Koselleck does not suggest that concepts cannot have a history, as Marx and Althusser famously said about ideas (which, they claim, should always be referred back to the material transformations in modes of production which are responsible for their shifts and transformations), but that the history they do have is not the whole of history, nor can it be tracked back to that other history or histories in predictable and repeatable ways. At the same time, those histories cannot be described without the language of concepts themselves. How is this not an insoluble hermeneutic conundrum? There can be no absolute science of concepts, but there can be and are significant findings that are system forming. The information generated by a simultaneously synchronic and diachronic inquiry into concepts, their current and historical ranges, produces unpredictable findings that may be only "indices" for a social history (84), but social history cannot do without them. We will be looking for and finding in each case what Koselleck calls "the contemporaneity of the noncontemporaneous" (*Gleichzeitigkeit des Ungleichzeitigen*). Word meanings always reach beyond the "singularity" claimed by historical events (90), and some of these will almost always be excluded as any one concept is deployed in particular explanations. The exclusions will not however always (or perhaps ever) be the same. A process occurs that is comparable within limits but never fully repeatable, or never to be assumed fully repeatable. As Koselleck explains elsewhere, language is always self-reflexive, but in opening up inquiry into concepts, we have a way to gain insight into "what in past history was necessitated by language and what was not."[44] Each has "different speeds of transformation" and "distinguishable structures of repetition" (37). These differences interrupt any potential for a seamless identification of either with the other; that is, they inhibit the perfect closure of any hermeneutic circle.

---

44. Koselleck, *The Practice of Conceptual History: Timing History, Spacing Concepts*, trans. Todd Samuel Presner et al. (Stanford, CA: Stanford University Press, 2002), 27. Hereafter cited with page numbers in the text.

Koselleck's comments on *Bildung* (culture) are especially useful to my inquiry, because *Bildung*, like *terror*, is one of those words (and concepts) that designates both something interior, so, in English, one possesses culture, is cultured; and exterior, as in the fate of culture or culture studies (170–207). *Bildung*, like *terror*, is "both the process of producing and the result of having been produced" (176); and, like *terror*, it comes into its fully modern German meaning (along with *Geschichte*, history itself) in the eighteenth century. There is a comprehensive *Begriffsgeschichte* of terror-terrorism in the great multivolume dictionary-encyclopedia, of which Koselleck is one of the main editors, although in this case the entry is the work of Rudolf Walther.[45] This catalog of sources and analogues for terror and terrorism has been of inestimable use for my own project, not least because it routinely traverses four languages: German, English, French, and Latin (with an occasional foray into Greek). Significantly, the German noun *der Terror* emerges only in the 1790s as an import. It made some inroads previously in its French form, *terreur*, but even during and after the revolutionary period there remained a visible preference for translating it into German as *der Schreck or der Schrecken*. The two run together, and they still do. Meanwhile, *Schrecken* itself had already been put into service (along with *Furcht*) as Luther's translation of a range of Latin terms from the Vulgate: *metus, stupor, formido*, and, indeed, *terror*. Also needing to be made over into German were *timor* and *pavor*, which themselves were to be correlated with Greek precursors like *phobos* and *tromos*. Then there is the matter of the relation between biblical Greek and the significantly larger classical vocabulary of fear-terror words (*aidos, kedos, deos*, and so on) that figure in manuscripts from Homer to Aristotle and beyond. And then there is a further question of how all of these interact or not with the Hebrew, Aramaic, and other sources that we conveniently refer to as the (*the*) Bible. Every time a word crosses languages, the matter of what Saussure called its value becomes crucial. To translate French *mouton* into English, for example, one must take account of the fact that French uses the same word for what is in English both mutton and sheep. We can translate a word but not its value, which is a function of the signifying economy of its own language.

Terror, like *Bildung* and unlike many or most other concepts included in the *Geschichtliche Grundbegriffe*—tyranny, sovereignty, utopia, and

---

45. Rudolf Walther, "Terror-Terrorismus," in *Geschichtliche Grundbegriffe: Historisches Lexikon zur politisch-sozialen Sprache in Deutschland*, ed. Otto Bruner, Werner Conze, and Reinhart Koselleck (Stuttgart: Klett-Cotta, 1990), 6:323–444.

so on—is a doggedly reflexive word, and thus a particularly volatile concept. As I have noted, it denotes either or both a subjective emotion and an objective agency. The sight of terror afflicts me with terror: terror terrifies. Lezra describes this function as the "double genitive" in, for example, "fear of the masses," which can describe what the masses feel about something they encounter, or what the ruling elites feel about the masses.[46] (Horror works in the same way.) For Lezra, this reflexivity is critical to the function of terror in the modern republic and embodies a positive vulnerability of each to all that opens a space for ethical identification. But it also (unlike the residually objective terrorism) can be used to produce a less admirable undecidability, a false equivalence. He who deploys terror may indeed be himself in terror, but the terror of the powerless is very different in degree and perhaps in kind. What I feel when I see an armored drone overhead is not the same as what is felt by its operator. There may be a certain continuum of feeling, but there is a world of difference. Nibbling away at all serious reflection on terror is the tendency of this powerful concept-word to trivialize associations: the common use of *terrible* in modern English makes it near impossible to apply the word in its original sense as relating to terror.

Where does one stop? Should one stop? Can the evolution of a concept be circumscribed by describing its operations in a single language, or in one or two, or three, languages? Williams was clear that in some important cases his keywords can be adequately understood only "when other languages are brought consistently into comparison."[47] *Terror* in its current use is interesting here, because although the modern emphasis was refigured in French in the 1790s, the word (along with *terrorism*) now circulates globally in its dominant anglophone paradigms and, since 9/11, has been given a very particular spin.[48] Bakhtin's formulation of the social life of language is emphatic in claiming that no utterance

46. Lezra, *Wild Materialism*, 38–39.

47. Williams, *Keywords*, 20. Notably, the 1983 revised edition had no place for terror or terrorism, although this omission is supplied in the updated, online third edition, *Keywords Project*. See the website keywords.pitt.edu/williams_keywords.html.

48. The spin differs when languages incorporate the foreign word and its ready-made imprimatur, as German and English did with *terrorisme* in 1794, and as Italian and Spanish did soon after, and when they adopt an existing "native" term to describe a phenomenon, as Chinese and Arabic have done with *terror* and *terrorism*. Nineteenth-century Turkish prefers to transliterate *anarchist* to describe its own radicals, although from 1907 onward it also adopts *terrorism* from French. Paradoxically, resistance to foreign loanwords might seem to undermine the integrity of the native culture, which protects its language only to suggest that the (negative) concept is already at home. It can also, of course, disarm the concept by assimilating it to the already familiar.

takes place in isolation and that no speaker commands or is able to put beyond limits the entire "elastic environment of other, alien words about the same object" in a "dialogically agitated and tension-filled environment" that conditions the forming of concepts (*koncipirovanie*) and includes both demotic and foreign words. It is this plurality that impedes the rhetoric of restriction: expropriating language, "forcing it to submit to one's own intentions and accents, is a difficult and complicated process."[49] Or so one might hope. The view from the other side of *The Dialectic of Enlightenment* is less positive: it can be all too easy to make language submit to certain accents and intentions.

But I have not answered the question, Where does one stop? I think one does not stop, not because so doing will ever produce a complete or scientific model of a concept like terror (or any other), but because there is no predicting what will and will not be found significant for interpretation and understanding. I have, of course, been obliged to stop at places where my reading runs out or my language skills fall short, places where all of us have to stop. But in principle I am in favor of never stopping and of proposing our findings, however decisive they may seem, as always provisional. It is a long stretch of time and place from Lutheran *Schreck* to the war on terror, and an even longer one from Homeric *deos* to the so-called reign of terror in the French Revolution. Peter de Bolla, whose recent work on concepts is as close to state of the art as anything I know, finds it necessary to limit himself to an English database, aware as he is of the problem of values, whereby French *droits* is not identical to English *rights*. His work is premised on the debatable assumption that "different languages necessarily work with different concepts."[50]

I agree that a mixed-language informational set will not readily produce a coherent concept architecture open to computational text analysis, the core of de Bolla's method. But even a single-language set will not

49. M. M. Bakhtin, *The Dialogic Imagination: Four Essays*, trans. Caryl Emerson and Michael Holquist (Austin: University of Texas Press, 1981), 276, 279, 294.

50. Peter de Bolla, *The Architecture of Concepts: The Historical Formation of Human Rights* (New York: Fordham University Press, 2013), 3, 42. Hereafter cited with page numbers in the text. Significant here is the *Dictionary of Untranslatables: A Philosophical Lexicon*, ed. Barbara Cassin, trans. Emily Apter, Jacques Lezra, and Michael Wood (Princeton, NJ: Princeton University Press, 2013). This important project is a model for future work in its insistence on the congruence and incongruence of translational acts, even as it is motivated (in its original French edition) by a conscious resistance to the dominant anglophone global consensus. Only two of the terms with which I am principally concerned appear here: *anxiety* and *Sorge*. But there is a useful glossing of *concept* and *Begriff*. See also Ashfield and de Bolla, eds., *The Sublime* (Cambridge: Cambridge University Press, 1996).

produce that complete coherence, and within that single-language set there is always, as Williams confirms, a possible or demonstrable connection with other languages. This may be less the case in our relatively impoverished modern anglophone cultures than it was in earlier elite-print societies wherein writers routinely had fluency in more than one language, classical or modern. But if one's purpose is the analysis of a rhetoric intended to deflect or persuade, to limit or to supplement certain instances of language in use, then even when there is no avowed connection outside a single language, knowing something about the analogues and alternatives can be important. What did the phrase "war on terror" sound like to English-speaking German readers, of whom there are a good many? Echoes of both Baader-Meinhof and of the *Hitlerzeit* would be paramount for them, but largely nonexistent for most readers of the *Sacramento Bee*. They might also have recalled the terror of the concentration camps and the terror bombing of German cities. And would not many French readers and speakers have heard echoes of *la Terreur* of 1793–1794? Anglophone readers of the 1790s and beyond almost certainly recognized *terreur* in *terror*.

Peter de Bolla is understandably concerned that a translingual perspective will lead him to an unmanageable set of data, and in this he is probably right. What is exciting about his project is its use of digital databanks, large groups of texts open to sophisticated word searches for which various proximities are as significant as immediate contiguity; a word habitually found, for example, within a few phrases or sentences of another word can give evidence of an expanded conceptual architecture that would be missed by more localized attention. This, together with the sheer volume of texts now accessible, can promise insight into "patterns of linguistic behavior that can be said to be supra-agential: cultural all the way down" (31). Given that concepts range across numbers of words, this seems like a good way to capture them. Within the chosen language (here English), de Bolla confirms that concepts indeed "cannot be expressed in words without remainder"; there is always something left hanging, something supplementary. And "you always get the full panoply of terms even if you are attempting to direct attention to only one of them" (29). Along with the word, you always get what I am calling the cluster. Concepts are networks, and within them certain words attract other words; and each conceptual network interacts with others in a process de Bolla calls "orbital drag" (44). This assemblage is what he means by the "architecture" of concepts.

The orbital drag of contemporary terror talk is, I believe, predictable. Terrorism is already in place as that which "we" do not perpetrate, and terrorism is the enacting of terror. One would expect to see, within significant proximity, such terms as *barbarism, civilization, the West, homeland, fundamentalist, jihad, security, atrocity,* and so forth.[51] I shall not in what follows be attempting anything like the sophisticated digital databased taxonomy that de Bolla devotes to the eighteenth-century vocabulary of rights, but it is worth bearing in mind his method and his findings as heuristic for possible futures. My procedures have been more old fashioned and more haphazard: a lot of reading, following connections that are partly evidentiary and partly intuitive, supplemented with a bit of electronic text analysis where it is available.[52] I am interested in the diachronic as well as in the synchronic axis, in how emphasis within the fear-terror cluster (which at any given time may or may not amount to a concept) has shifted through time; but I have also given a lot of attention to shorter time spans when critical transformations seem to me to have been occurring, for example in the 1790s or in the production of the King James Bible. Much of the time my archive is multilingual, or as much so as I can make it. I am less concerned with pinning down the would-be-complete territory of terror (as a more or less tidy and delimited concept) than with tracking its continuities and transformations under certain pressures and incentives that are, broadly and narrowly, historical-political. Recall that Empson found "protean confusion" to be harmful in itself; it certainly has the potential to be turned to harm in the hands of the unscrupulous or the unaware. Raymond Williams did not endorse what he saw as the inflated ambitions of "that popular kind of inter-war and surviving semantics which supposed that clarification of difficult words would help in the resolution of disputes conducted in their terms and often evidently confused by them." There was to be no linguistic League of Nations. For him, what could be achieved by his sort of historical-philological work is "not resolution but perhaps, at times, just that extra edge of consciousness."[53] This is no small thing in a

---

51. *Western* was one of the words that Williams added to his revised *Keywords* in 1983.

52. For an example of the potential of a sophisticated large-corpus text analysis, see Ryan Heuser, Franco Moretti, and Erik Steiner, "The Emotions of London," *Pamphlet 13* (Stanford Literary Lab), October 2016, https://litlab.stanford.edu/LiteraryLab Pamphlet13.pdf. The findings are responsibly skeptical. Seeking to track fear-happiness extremes, and relying on consensus among the trackers about which (and how) words count, the coauthors find a high degree of emotional neutrality: cases in which it is hard to tell which emotions are being signaled. Fear terms are often linked to "geographical reticence" (8), that is, when places are described but not given exact locations. In general, they find more fear in the old city and more happiness in the West End.

53. Williams, *Keywords,* 24.

world where certain classes or interests have monopolized the production of consensus, and where whole categories of other persons have been taught to accept their findings. Peter de Bolla, too, is prompted by his sense that we inhabit "commonly held conceptual networks that in effect think *for* us, or at least provide the enclosures within which thinking takes place." He hopes that his work may make us "less likely to be trapped into situations in which concepts do our thinking for us in ways we might find surprising or even counter to our intentions."[54] These are goals I am more than willing to endorse and, I hope, contribute to furthering.

There is one pertinent, large-scale historical paradigm to be mentioned at this point and by way of further introduction. Koselleck's model of the modern age, wherein the *neueste Zeit* takes over from the *Neuzeit* that roughly corresponds to what others call the Renaissance, takes as its primary diagnostic the idea of the Enlightenment invention of an autonomous history that is revolutionary-progressive rather than cyclic-restorative and is driven by forces greater than contingent human intentions. This hypothesis involves the perceived onset of "acceleration," of things taken to be happening faster and faster.[55] It accords with the insights of *The Communist Manifesto* and of *Capital* about the speeding up of production, circulation, and accumulation that comes with the machine economy and the harnessing of steam power. If this or something like it is a true or convincing finding (and a commonplace sense of the increasing speed of change remains characteristic of the language that describes the contemporary virtual economy), then our experience of history itself is actually or potentially catastrophic, involving radical and unpredictable shifts that render the lifeworld more unstable than ever before. This registers in language and is recirculated and inflected by language. Koselleck notes that "for German-speaking areas from 1770 onward . . . both new meanings for old words and neologisms proliferate . . . establishing new horizons of expectation." Beginning around 1800, he finds "excessive use of the term *Zeit*," both standing alone and as a prefix (e.g., *Zeitgeist*), an increasing invocation of time itself.[56] We then inhabit a world premised on continual surprise, on variable temporality, and on the rapid displacement of habits that are never in place long enough to form traditions. Terror, as an emotion or affect, closely correlates with surprise, and as such it is an apt and ready term

54. de Bolla, *Architecture of Concepts*, 5, 44.
55. See, for example, Koselleck, *Futures Past*, 50, 269.
56. Koselleck, *Futures Past*, 79, 247.

(or concept) for describing such experience, especially if the changes that occur embody some element of threat, as indeed they now do for many who have to live outside the upper echelons of the Washington Consensus. *Terror*, and words like it, may then be likely to linger awhile, available for both use and exploitation. Surprise can all too readily be repackaged as terror.

It may, then, be useful to know that terror has a rich and controversial history beyond its recent appeal among politicians and the media. It (or its affiliates) can be tracked through literature from the Greeks to those contemporary writers seeking to represent the world during and after 9/11; it has a place in philosophy, especially that of the past hundred years or so; and it figures in what we have come to call theory, that which explores the interactive preoccupations of sociology, psychology, philosophy, anthropology, literature, and political science. The *history* in this book's title is the history of these things, of the most important things that have happened or been said in or under the name of terror. Or at least of some of them, enough, I hope, to amount to a significant account. It is easy to invoke the Jacobin Terror of 1793–1794, because the Jacobins used the term themselves, although much more sparingly than their opponents and successors. It is easy, too, to invoke the Nazi terror, because no one much disagrees about the excess of violence and its effects on Europe during World War Two. But the Stalinist Great Terror was a phrase coined by a Western historian, and only recently has it become acceptable, either in English or in German, to specify the bombing of German or Japanese cities in World War Two as terror bombing. Even in the case of the Jacobins, the established usage of the term *terror* has by no means resolved important questions about what was intended by it and how representative it was of either Jacobin policy or of the French Revolution itself. Above all—and this bears repeating—in recent times terror has been successfully identified with nonstate agencies who are enemies of the West rather than with the Western states themselves as they deploy their massive powers of destruction and intimidation on passive and often civilian populations. Those in Gaza whose rockets have caused at most one or two Israeli civilian deaths are publicized as terrorists, while those who have killed more than two thousand Palestinians, including many women and children, and reduced Gaza itself to a concentration camp, are allowed to pose merely as defenders of their national security.[57] Terror and terrorism are visibly manipulable

57. For a comprehensively documented case that Zionism was from the start (and well before the start) committed to terrorism in both establishing and maintaining

categories. They are not the only ones: *evil* also emerged very early in the descriptions of 9/11 as a theologically tinged attribute with metaphysical pretensions needing no further explanation.[58] And *civility*, though briefly out of fashion in the paranoid rhetorical climate immediately after 9/11, continues to do yeoman's work in political and academic circles as a purposively imprecise but increasingly legalistic absolute good, now mostly invoked as an inhibitor of free speech whenever the consensus is embarrassed by uncomfortable information.

But it is terror that arguably matters most, in the light of those urgent and destructive situations, which show no signs of ending, where terror and/or terrorism are invoked as the justification for further devastation and destruction of whoever is on the wrong side of the propaganda fence. Given this urgency, does it make sense to worry about what Homer might have meant by *deos* or *tromos*, of how and why *Furcht* and *Angst* function for Heidegger, of what is at stake when eighteenth-century translators transcribe Aristotle's *phobos* as either *fear* or *terror*, or of how various novelists employ vocabularies of violent emotions and affects? Is it not merely a melodramatic scholarly self-esteem that thinks that it can weigh in on these matters in ways that matter? Perhaps so. But one thing that the popular response to 9/11 revealed very clearly was the near-complete absence of any skepticism about the words being used to describe and make sense of events. Terror was again the order of the day, as it had been in 1794, and it was as such not subject to much critical scrutiny. One could simply berate the media and the politicians for their lamentable ignorance of the resources of the language, or (worse) for their cynical exploitation of the fudge factor inherent in that language; both of these are well worth doing. One can also use the occasion to explore some longer-term attributes of the vocabulary of violence, on the assumption that much still remains to be thought through and that terror is not yet a thing of the past, either as a term or as a state of affairs. This is my aim here. To echo and repurpose Donald Rumsfeld—who was himself citing a military intelligence protocol—we have not yet reached the point where we can stop thinking about what we think we know already.

Israel's statehood, see Thomas Suárez, *State of Terror: How Terrorism Created Modern Israel* (Northampton, MA: Olive Branch Press, 2017).

58. On the use of *evil* in post-9/11 rhetoric, see Laura Rediehs, "Evil," in *Collateral Language: A User's Guide to America's New War*, ed. John Collins and Ross Glover (New York: New York University Press, 2002), 65–78. In the same volume, John Collins (166), echoing Christopher Hitchens, notes that the optimum functioning of *terrorism* in the rhetoric of consensus requires that it not be defined at all.

One must also be aware of when we do not mention what we do know. Skinner argued for the purposive nature of Locke's silence about the ancient constitution, which anyone reading within the genre would have expected to see invoked. If we are working with positive evidence of what texts and speakers say, evidence we can see and enumerate, then we will miss (as Pierre Macherey argued in *A Theory of Literary Production*) the importance of silence, of things that do not appear as text and thus do not show up as countable or computable. But they are clearly part of what de Bolla calls the orbital drag, in any comprehensive sense of that term. Horror, as I have said, was almost never invoked in popular descriptions of the events of 9/11, with definite implications for what we were supposed to see and feel. Not mentioning horror made terror into a different thing, altering its rhetorical value. In the United States, for example, the most important silent partner of terror talk is arguably the word (or concept of) *race*. After the rumor of Arab or foreign responsibility for the Oklahoma City bombing was dispelled (as it soon was), there was comparatively little long-durational use of the words *terror* and *terrorism* in reference to the event. There was certainly no invocation of a war against either. Indeed, Timothy McVeigh's affiliations with white militia groups were played down rather than played up, as if no one had a motive for assigning terror and terrorism to white people. In November 2017, the mass shooting carried out by Devin Patrick Kelley in a Texas church was attributed by President Trump to a "very deranged individual" and called an "act of hatred," not terror. Kelley, of course, was white. The association of terror and terrorism with a racialized enemy was correspondingly emphatic after 9/11, and it belongs in a long but largely unspoken domestic tradition linking Black Americans with the threat of terror. The long and still-unresolved history of slavery in the homeland cannot be held apart from the responses to 9/11, which would have been different in places like Britain and Germany, where slavery was a more distant attribute of colonial domination and immigration has been mostly more recent.[59] The Haitian Revolution brought numbers of exiled plantation owners to the United States, where they contributed to an already-existing fear of slave revolt. Although many eyewitness accounts of the events of 1791–1804 were complicated by personal loyalties and local circumstances, with complex interactions between black and white (and indeed equally complex denotations of what was meant by black and white), there are certainly clear instances

59. Although the Irish have long been the go-to figure of terrorism in Britain, it is some time since they were fully racialized as black in the popular imagination.

of the ascription of terror to such happenings as the destruction of Cap-Français in June 1793.[60] Perhaps more significant, invocations of terror figure prominently in the accounts of both Caribbean and mainland slave revolts written by American authors like the abolitionist Thomas Wentworth Higginson for the domestic market.[61] Reputed events like the Gabriel conspiracy that caused "unutterable terror" to the Virginia planters three times in thirty years (50), as well as the documented revolts by the likes of Denmark Vesey and Nat Turner, are produced in an attempt to persuade readers that the culture of slavery must generate terror in the masters (as well as in the slaves who suffer within it). Adding special emphasis to this conviction is the New England tradition of legal terror associated with Jonathan Edwards, for whom an angry god (as God) is quite rightly prone to impose terror on sinful persons. John Brown, though himself a white abolitionist, is black by proxy in his designation as a homegrown American terrorist, and he has been theorized as such by a number of commentators.[62] Violence in a just cause remains an unresolved imperative in the lexicon of justice-seeking minorities, as it likely will do until the evidence of oppression is once and for all addressed. Its prospect, and indeed its history, still tends to remain in occlusion, unless, for example, one were living in South Africa after 1960. In an otherwise compelling recent study of "American terror," for example, Paul Hurh attributes Melville's strong sense of the "power of blackness" to Edwards's affective religious turn, as if the depravity of the species could displace or make light of the accumulating sins of the (white) race.[63] Melville's own *Benito Cereno* is read (226–28) as an allegory of the dread of the temporality of being-toward-death, but not at all as the imagining of a ticking clock within a national culture whose involvement in plantation slavery is as obvious to the alert reader as it is obscure to the naively well-disposed American ship's captain. The story's opening

60. See, for example, Jeremy D. Popkin, ed., *Facing Racial Revolution: Eyewitness Accounts of the Haitian Insurrection* (Chicago: University of Chicago Press, 2007), 229–32, 258–59. But horror remains notably more common than terror in the vocabulary of these apparent witnessings.

61. See Sujan Dass, ed., *Black Rebellion: Eyewitness Accounts of Major Slave Revolts* (Atlanta: Two Horizons Press, 2010), which reprints Higginson and other American authors. Higginson goes so far as to describe Nat Turner as generating a "Reign of Terror" (112).

62. See, for example, Ted A. Smith, *Weird John Brown: Divine Violence and the Limits of Ethics* (Stanford, CA: Stanford University Press, 2015).

63. Paul Hurh, *American Terror: The Feeling of Thinking in Edwards, Poe, and Melville* (Stanford, CA: Stanford University Press, 2015), 3. Edwards also had access to local memories and experiences of the destruction of Native American cultures.

atmosphere of pervasive grayness mixes the black and white of its pro-
tagonists into a wishful but unsustainable uniformity that Captain De-
lano cannot unperplex until it is almost too late.

Few writers have been as adept as Melville in communicating an unspoken terror implicit in racial oppression. Few political commentators
to this day are as able to articulate the surplus energy emanating from
the invocation of terror in America as one symptom of an unresolved
domestic history. After 1945, the racializing of the terror threat was re-
inforced by the spectacle of struggles for decolonization. All over the
world, black and brown people took up arms against their occupiers,
and they were bombed, tortured, and executed for their efforts. These
are the persons that none other than Winston Churchill, the poster boy
of Anglo-American militant heroism, referred to when he said, in 1919,
that he was "strongly in favour of using poisoned gas against the uncivi-
lized tribes . . . it would spread a lively terror."[64] On these matters, as on
many others implicated in the culture of terror talk, silence is not golden.
It represses not just the extra edge of consciousness but also consciousness itself; and of this we surely need all we can get.

64. This is a much-debated quote, and in an effort to take the most "conservative"
version, I cite from the website WinstonChurchill.org. To be sure, Churchill does claim
that he intends no lethal harm, that there would be no "serious permanent effects" on
"most" of those targeted. But to imagine this so soon after the gas warfare of World War
One seems at the very least disingenuous.

2

What Do We Talk about When We Talk about Terror?

Prodicus Laughs

With something that has become as platitudinously familiar as the word *terror*, it is bracing to begin far away and at another time, with words that have been rendered into English as *terror* but inhabit their own conceptual field, albeit one that cannot be definitively recovered. The fecundity of Homer's vocabulary for experiences of fear and terror is, by modern English standards, breathtaking. One could say that we now live with a much-diminished language, or that this particular word cluster is one we are thankful to see diminished. But this shrinking of our verbal options cannot simply be taken as evidence that we live in a less violent world. Life-threatening, in-your-face confrontations of Homeric intensity may be no less familiar now than then to many sectors of the population who live outside the elite enclaves of the developed world; even those who are lucky enough to live within such enclaves spend much of their time worrying about the incursion of violence from outside. Furthermore, we all live with an awareness of large-scale, fear-inducing agencies that were, with a few exceptions (like famine) quite unthinkable in ancient Greece: nuclear devastation, global environmental catastrophe, and omnipresent surveillance technology (itself death dealing for those who inhabit areas patrolled by weaponized drones).

We who speak English or other European languages may indeed have a smaller vocabulary than the poeticized Greeks and Trojans for specifying fear emotions, and this makes for fewer choices in describing them. But it does not tell us whether or to which degree we are having the same emotions, or that our feelings are more or less emphatic than theirs, nor does it instruct us in how to distinguish or conflate different words that seem to mean almost the same things.

Toward the end of the *Protagoras*, Socrates is quizzing Prodicus about whether there is an experience that involves the expectation of bad things (*ta kaka*) that he might call fear or dread. Prodicus says yes, but he thinks that the word should be dread (*deos*), not fear (*phobos*).[1] Never mind the name, says Socrates, would any man pursue such an experience if he could avoid it? No, admits Prodicus. Socrates seems to be telling him not to get tangled up with words, suggesting that what matters is whether such a thing could ever be a desired event. A few lines later, however, Socrates, as if to make his point, continues the discussion of dreadful things by using Prodicus's preferred word (*ta deina*). But this does not last. After a few more exchanges, we are back with compound forms of *phobos* to describe the same emotion (360B). Then, later still, *deos* returns once more.

Socrates would seem to be performing his point that it does not matter to this discussion which word we use. The exchange is a rerun of a similar interaction at 358A, where Socrates asks Prodicus not to sidetrack the debate by insisting on distinctions of terms (*diairesin ton onomaton*), in this case pleasure words, at the expense of attending to the sense of the question. Socrates is convincing in saying that both *deos* and *phobos* describe something that generates an aversive reaction, but this does not make them into exactly the same emotion. Much of this dialogue is indeed about the question that Socrates seems here to want to suppress: it is about whether there can be a sense of any question that is not also or even primarily a question about distinctions of terms. Protagoras, who gives this dialogue its name, is (like Prodicus) a famous sophist—a stranger, and one who takes money for his teaching—with whom the younger Socrates engages in debate.[2] Large parts of the dialogue are taken up with what we now call literary criticism, as the discussants set out to analyze an apparent contradiction in a poem by Simonides. An-

1. Plato, *Protagoras*, trans. W. R. M. Lamb (Cambridge, MA: Harvard University Press, 1924), 358D–E.

2. Socrates makes gentle fun of Prodicus's own "fifty drachma course of lectures" in *Cratylus*, 384D.

other long segment is given over to Protagoras's example of argument by fable or story (*muthos*) rather than by reason or demonstration (*logos*). There is a discussion of whether virtue (*arete*) can be taught or not, and of whether it is a single thing or an assemblage of various qualities. The official Socrates who figures in the tradition of what has come to be called Platonism would be expected to say that it is one thing that cannot be taught, but that is not quite where the dialogue ends up.

The incursion of etymological puzzles is too common in this text to be an accident. Setting up as a wordsmith does not seem to be the same as setting up as a carpenter or a saddle maker; it is not easily contained within a well-policed model of divided labor or by a conviction that each thing has only one opposite or outcome. Socrates takes issue with Protagoras's inclination for long, expository speeches (*makrologia*): he prefers the economy of cut and thrust that we have come to identify ever since with the Socratic method. But brevity, we are told, is what we owe to the Spartans (foreigners) rather than to the Athenians, and neither alternative is simply vindicated: Socrates himself indulges in a lengthy exposition during the discussion of Simonides. Word choices are not self-evident, but they can be inflected by regional dialects. Was Simonides making fun of Pittacus for speaking the dialect of Lesbos (341C)? Why does he use a Mytilenean word (346D)? At what point does a word come to designate one thing and not another? Should we agree to dismiss Prodicus's effort to choose between *deos* and *phobos* as a red herring that distracts us from the proper business of philosophy, or is there something to ponder here?

The *Protagoras* provides ample evidence that Jacques Derrida's curiosity about whether and to which degree Socrates and/or Plato might have been a closet or not-so-closet sophist is not misplaced. Socrates says that the adjective *deinos* (awful, terrible, dreadful) can simply be an emphatic applied to bad things, just as we might say "awful poverty" or "awful war" (341A–B). He cites Prodicus's claim that no one should apply the word *awful* to good things: we should not say that Protagoras is "an awfully wise man" (*sophos kai deinos*, wise and awful). In modern English we can do this, at least adverbially: we speak of a terrible war but might also declare ourselves terribly pleased to see you, or even dreadfully happy. How about in classical Greek? One commentator says that *sophos kai deinos* is "tolerably frequent in ironical characterization."[3] That would make Protagoras wise but a bit tricky, a bit too clever, but

---

3. *Platonis Protagoras*, ed. J. Adam and A. M. Adam (Cambridge: Cambridge University Press, 1962), 154. But such a man is "more clever than good" (155).

we can say it, and we do. And indeed the same word, *deinos*, has come up much earlier when the task of the sophist is being discussed (312D–E). Is it the sophist's job to create a "clever speaker" (*deinon legein*, used twice)? The sense of *deinos* as clever derives, according to the lexicon, from its association with power and wonder, which in turn looks back to the sense of dangerous or awful (i.e., awe inspiring). It is the "same" word but with a quite different "meaning." It is a word with more than one opposite (clever-stupid, tricky-trustworthy, frightening-innocuous). Another commentator notes of 341B that *deinos* can be used with a "favourable nuance," but that "terribly wise (*sophos kai deinos*) . . . does not have as much intensive force as the English."[4] So, perhaps Protagoras is wiser than usual but not excessively so? At least here, *deinos* does not stimulate an aversive reaction. And in the eighteenth century, in English, terror will come to be identified as a positive pleasure as it is made constitutive of the aesthetic sublime.

Greek seems to share with English confusion about how to use the word *terrible* (*deinos*). Protagoras and Prodicus are certainly wise enough to trouble Socrates's effort at controlling the debate. These are the sorts of questions that he is anxious not to take up when he bids Prodicus to follow only the sense of the question (at 358B) rather than worry over the aptness of words. Prodicus agrees, and then he laughs. Plato is not so full of laughs that one fails to notice when they occur, and laughter in general is elsewhere open to Socrates's disapproval (*Republic* 388E) as an index of a lapse in self-discipline. Yet I have found no comment on this moment. Could Prodicus be laughing ("as did the others") at the bluntness with which Socrates reveals that the best way to reach agreement is for everyone to agree with him? So "the sense of my question" that Prodicus is asked to respect (*pros ho boulomai apokrinai*) could be read as "let me have it my way" or "accede to my conditions." If we do, then of course Socrates will win the argument, and it is natural to laugh when we get such a message. Commentators do indeed find jokes and ironies at work in this dialogue. Although the authenticity of the dialogue has never been doubted, Adam and Adam note that no other work is "so full of fallacious reasoning"; thus, the nods to Crete and Sparta as sources of philosophy are deemed "of course ironical."[5] Is it ironic or not when Socrates implies that Prodicus is "inspired by the gods [*theois aner*]" as

4. Plato, *"Protagoras,"* trans. C. C. W. Taylor, rev. ed. (Oxford, UK: Clarendon Press, 1991), 142. The same phrase famously occurs in *Antigone* (332–33) in a passage that will be of central interest to Heidegger.

5. *Platonis Protagoras*, ix; *"Protagoras"* (Taylor), 144.

poets are?[6] And when we decide this, what are we to make of Socrates's identifying himself as a pupil or disciple of Prodicus (341A), the very person with whom he disputes about the choice of words? This same Socrates preaches the official line against the poets but has a soft spot for them notwithstanding. Does the apparent stalemate that ends the dialogue shows us a Socrates who spares Protagoras's feelings by not pushing home his advantage, or is it a decisive aporia?

Returning to our beginning, does it matter to us or to the Greeks whether it is *deos* or *phobos* that best describes their (our) anticipation of bad things? Is the feeling the same whatever we call it, as Socrates claims? Does it matter which English words we use to render the Greek? Does it matter when a different translator of the famous passage in *Republic* renders *deima* and *deina*, one letter and two lines apart, as *dread* and *terrors*? Why do these words differ so little as they differ?[7] According to received Platonism, the point here is to banish this whole vocabulary of terror and fear (*deina, phobera*) from anything that will be read by impressionable youth, anything of which the mere words can make them shudder (*phrittein*). If the physical effect is the same, who cares which particular word is used to stimulate it? Both should be discouraged. But scholars and translators are far from unanimous over how to render this pairing and how to make sense of their conjunction. In the nine English translations I have consulted, *deos* and *phobos* appear as *dread* and *fear* (three times), *fear* and *terror* (three times), *apprehension* and *fear*, *fright* and *fear*, and *fear* and *dread*. One of these has Prodicus declaring that *terror* and not *fear* is the correct word; another has him deciding for *fear* and against *terror*. Three commentators engage the question in some detail. One finds that "Prodicus's distinction is just, though often dropped in practice": *deos* is indeed anticipatory, whereas *phobos* is immediate and physical. A second disagrees, suggesting that "Greek usage supports Socrates; the two terms are frequently used without any indication of distinction." The third agrees with the first but

---

6. Adam and Adam, *Platonis Protagoras*, 188. Recent work on *Protagoras*, in the spirit of Derrida (whose name is, however, never mentioned), is willing to take seriously the substantive role of "literary" questions in suggesting that irony, skepticism, Sophism, and aporia may be constitutive rather than merely decorative components of the dialogue. See the essays in Olof Pettersson and Vigdis Songe-Møller, eds., *Plato's Protagoras: Essays on the Confrontation of Philosophy and Sophistry* (Cham, Switzerland: Springer International, 2017).

7. Plato, *Republic*, trans. Paul Shorey (Cambridge, MA: Harvard University Press, 1937), 386B. *Deima* is a Homeric word, and this seems to be its only occurrence in Plato, and Homer is of course the poet most under inspection at this point in the discussion.

attributes Prodicus's distinction to Homer in particular.[8] These different readings make clear that we are discussing a language that is not
one thing. What we are calling Greek includes a Homeric poem written
down perhaps in the eighth century BCE, telling of events in probably
the twelfth century BCE, and existing for us first in a manuscript from
the tenth century CE. It includes a fourth century BCE Platonic dialogue
(also surviving from later manuscripts) and a fifth century CE commentary by Ammonius, which is the source for Adam and Adam's judgment.
It would not be surprising if the kind of *deos* or *phobos* that someone
might have felt or described in ancient Troy were somewhat different
from what was being discussed more than a thousand years later. How
could we ever know?

Socrates accepts that the fear-terror emotion can be described by
a number of different words (and there are a lot more, especially in
Homer), but he supposes that they all finally describe and share a common factor, an aversive response to bad or threatening things.[9] He is not
saying that these emotions are identical in every other way. There might
still be ways in which *deos* is not *phobos*. The differences, he says, do not
matter for this particular argument. Throughout the dialogue Socrates
seeks to make the debate manageable and thereby winnable. He prefers
binary oppositions, such that each term has only one opposite (good-
bad, pleasure-pain), and argues against "using a number of terms at
once" (355B). Hence his injunction to Prodicus: "Spare me this distinction of terms" (358B). Simple binaries enable yes-or-no answers: good
or bad, pleasure or pain. But the range of terms that keeps cropping up
complicates any such cut-and-dried reasoning. *Deos* and *phobos*, or
dikaiosune and *sophrosune* (justness, rightness, wisdom, balance), and
their kind are neither fully the same nor fully distinct from each other. To
affirm that a word means only one thing (with one opposite) is to close
off the sort of ambiguity that might suggest one's choice of words as something other than natural and self-evident.

It may be no coincidence that Plato, in a dialogue that belongs to the
foundational canon of the discipline of philosophy itself, chooses the
fear-terror cluster as his test case for examining the play between absolute and inabsolute distinctions. Socrates defends a logic that prefers to

8. *Platonis Protagoras,* 190; *Plato's "Protagoras,"* 205; Patrick Coby, *Socrates and the Sophistic Enlightenment: A Commentary on Plato's "Protagoras"* (Lewisburg, PA: Bucknell University Press, 1987), 166.

9. Robert Zaborowski, *La crainte et le courage dans l'Iliade et l'Odyssee* (Warsaw: Stakroos, 2002), 239–40, isolates forty-three fear-terror words from twenty-two differ-ent families in Homer's poems.

manage clear distinctions, but it also underpins a pedagogical apparatus that seeks to train up Athenian youth into citizenship and accountability, into a shared identity wherein what matters is what is held in common and not what minutely discriminates. Having a simple binary of fear and not fear dissuades us from dwelling on the nuances of feelings and propels us toward actions and decisions. He who restricts such reflections is moving us along to an end, managing our emotions. The same kind of management, though with much more critical consequences, can be traced in the passing over of *horror* (and other terms) in favor of *terror* in the interpellation of 9/11. It is this ideal of management that the *Protagoras* complicates through its sustained immersion in irony and the literary mode, where absolutes cannot survive close inspection and where close inspection slows down the path to action. If fear-terror experiences are among those most likely to disrupt or dangerously reconstruct social solidarity, they are also ones wherein careful critique can inspire disobedience. Differences of degree do matter, and they are not always separable from distinctions of kind. When and how, in English, is fear the same or not the same as dread or terror, and what follows from this? Why can we say "I fear that I cannot help you here" and make a happy sentence but not (with the same sense) "I dread that I cannot help you"? These sentences mean different things, even though *fear* and *dread* can otherwise be used synonymously. If someone wants me to experience terror, it is not in his interest to have me acting like Prodicus, and certainly not to have me laughing in his face.

The exchange between Socrates and Prodicus models the sort of encounter that is always worth having when one feels oneself hurried along into premature agreement about what words mean, and then hurried again into a prescribed response to those hastily assembled terminologies. Victor Klemperer confronted the same phenomenon. So, too, did Thomas Hobbes, writing in the wake of the English Revolution (also called the Civil War or the Great Rebellion) and acutely alarmed by the power of words to move people to critical actions. Near the beginning of *Leviathan*, he writes that "whosoever looketh into himself, and considereth what he does, when he does *think, opine, reason, hope, fear*, &c. and upon what grounds; he shall thereby read and know, what are the thoughts and passions of all other men upon the like occasions."[10] Hobbes channels Socrates here: I may fear one thing and you may fear another, but the "passion" is the same. But who can be sure of this? Later

10. Thomas Hobbes, *Leviathan*, ed. Michael Oakeshott (Oxford, UK: Blackwell, 1946), 6. Hereafter cited with page numbers in the text.

on, Hobbes himself sounds more like a sophist when he argues that fear of invisible powers is called religion when it is "publicly allowed" and superstition when it is not, whereas fear "without the apprehension of why, or what" is called "PANIC TERROR" (35). But could the same thing not also be called anxiety, or just a creepy sensation? Panic terror requires a "throng"; one person's anxiety or fear is amplified into panic terror when surrounded by others, because while someone will "always" have "some apprehension of the cause," others will not. So are these, then, two different passions or emotions, or versions of the same thing? What can we really "read and know" about this question?

Hobbes steers us toward an answer. He famously declares that life can never be "without fear" (39), which is one of the preconditions that inclines us to bond into society (82, 84). It is also the root cause of religion, which is founded upon "anxiety" and "fear" (70). When we get to the sovereign power to whom we give over our independence in exchange for security, the terminology is upgraded: the sovereign (like the god of the King James Bible) has the power of "terror." On three occasions in the first book of *Leviathan* (94, 109, 112), terror is associated with the persuasive apparatus of sovereignty. This is different from the panic terror already defined: it is the certain or possible outcome of a political disposition, an incentive against disobedience. What we fear in the presocial condition is the constant and unpredictable possibility of death or suffering, the life that is "nasty, brutish, and short" (82). What we fear from sovereign power is more measured and infrequent, and mostly or ideally avoidable: the judicial application of irresistible violence to the disobedient subject. The subsumption of anxiety and fear by the state apparatus refigures them as terror. This terror displaces panic terror and is always at the ready. It responds to a predictable outcome from an identifiable and sustained source of power. But it is not easy to implement such univocity by words alone. Hobbes calls into question whether we can indeed pass from reading words to knowing the "thoughts and passions of all other men" (6) when he argues that "the names of such things as affect us" are of "*inconstant* signification" because "all men be not alike affected with the same thing" (24). The same stimulus will or may produce different responses because of the "tincture of our different passions." And if our only access to the original stimulus is by way of words, then we are indeed at sea. Names can thus "never be true grounds of any ratiocination." An example: "One man calleth *wisdom*, what another calleth *fear*." This is an interesting example. If I have a comfortable relation to the state, then I might opt to designate my respect for its punitive powers as wisdom (and wisdom, in this case, would look very like prudence). Conversely, a more cynical view of the social contract might use the word *fear*. Deciding what the words "mean" requires some hypothesis about which tinctures of passion and disposition might be motivating their selection. Assigning the power of terror to the sovereign, and only to the sovereign, simplifies or sidelines the epistemological ambiguities. One man may call wisdom what another calls fear, but the outcome is the same: obedience in the face of absolute authority. That authority needs more than words to do its job.

Darwin Disseminates

Hobbes's unembarrassed avowal of the semantics of state power in relation to physical force has not been comfortably assimilated into a liberal tradition, for which the play of possible idiosyncrasies is generally held to be a good and not a bad thing. Along with this there comes a curiosity about how we balance the sameness in difference that adds up to human nature and how the names we employ might reflect or even construct that nature. Behavioral psychology in the modern era has seemed to promise some solution to these problems by claiming to identify physiological (or, more recently, neurological) indexes telling us just which affect, emotion, or passion (there is a whole literature purporting to distinguish them, or not) is at work, regardless of which words human subjects might assign to them. My brain, for example, may be telling the scientific observer that I am experiencing fear, while I might choose to describe it as wonder or surprise. The exemplary statement of the modern faith in a science of the feelings is Darwin's *The Expression of the Emotions in Man and Animals*, first published in 1872 but subject to some important later revisions. Darwin believes not only in a single human species with some shared universal predispositions but also in a (more limited) continuum between humans and animals: "Even insects express anger, terror, jealousy, and love by their stridulation."[11] The most important emotions are inherited or innate, and, significantly, they can be recognized as such. Darwin had the relatively new technology of the photograph to back him up, whereas his modern successors have an entire neuroscientific apparatus. But was he and are we really at the point of being able to deduce from a person's expression exactly what that person is feeling? The surveillance-security industry certainly likes to think so and has invested

---

11. Charles Darwin, *The Expression of the Emotions in Man and Animals*, 3rd ed., commentary by Paul Ekman (London: HarperCollins, 1998), 347. Hereafter cited with page numbers in the text.

significantly in identifying involuntary facial expressions in people who are nervous or guilty, or who have something to hide. Darwin's follower and editor Paul Ekman has been at the center of the surveillance initiative, and it has many followers and has given rise to much discussion.[12] But can it promise to tell the differences between fear, terror, horror, dread, and anxiety? Or are they all, as Socrates implies, different words for a (more or less intense) single feeling?

Darwin's foundational account is not as simple as I have just made it sound. It is significantly expanded and complicated between the first and third editions (which printed Darwin's final revisions only in 1998). Expression, he claims, is a more accurate index of the feelings than are words, which "may be falsified" (359). But cannot expressions also be falsified? If not, there would be an end to poker games. Can expressions be learned or acquired rather than automatically triggered? Darwin says yes to this. Some innate feelings may further require "practice in the individual, before they are performed in a full and perfect manner; for instance weeping and laughing" (348). They require, that is, a measure of culture to develop them as nature; in invoking performance, Darwin might almost be suggesting that they are theatrical, designed to communicate irrespective of any inner quality. Further, some gestures that appear to be innate can "apparently be learnt like the words of a language" (349). Can terror be learned in this way? Darwin has a complex sense of the balance between culture and nature, and he often makes claims in one place that he seems to retract or qualify in another. He summarizes three principles of expressive behavior. First, movements that have proved useful over time may become habitual, so that they are performed "whether or not of any service, whenever the same desire or sensation is felt, even in a very weak degree" (345). The same signal may thus emanate from different states of feeling, strong or weak: imagined or remembered fear can look the same as immediate fear. Second, gestures may originate in simply doing the opposite, "under the excitement of an opposite frame of mind," as when a dog recognizes its master and switches from an aggressive to a submissive posture. The dog means to indicate a canceling of aggression but not submission in itself: it resorts to a conventional binary. Only the third of Darwin's principles is completely independent of rhetorical or semiotic components: the "direct action of the excited nervous system on the body, independently of the

12. For a comprehensive analysis (and critique), see Ruth Leys, "How Did Fear Become a Scientific Object, and What Kind of Object Is It?" *Representations* 110 (2010): 66–104.

will, and independently, in large part, of habit." Even here there is a qualifier: "in large part." As soon as we are in the realm of habit, even to a small degree, we are operating with conventions, and conventions are the product of an imprecise (or hard to specify) blend of nature and nurture. Much human expression is indeed the result of a combination of inputs, with involuntary responses and "associated habit" working together. Man has a "strong tendency to imitation" (351–52), so that even "extreme terror" might well have some element of "associated habit" governing its expression (82). Horror can produce gestures that "differ in different individuals" (307), while the same muscle responses can be triggered by quite different feelings (300–303). At one point, Darwin writes that "in almost all animals . . . terror causes the body to tremble" (81); then the "dreadful scream of terror" gives way to "utter prostration," which is the signature of "extreme" fear (293). The "shudder" of fear, however, may fail to appear "under the influence of extreme, prostrating terror" (305). Darwin thinks he has devised a graphing of "the diversified expressions of fear, in its gradations from mere attention to a start of surprise, into extreme terror and horror" (308), but he has sown doubt as to whether we can assume any exact recognition of these degrees and distinctions. Fear and astonishment can look the same (290), and rage and fear can both make the hair stand on end (296). It is unclear, moreover, whether we have any "instinctive power of recognizing" such gestures (352). Among twenty-three observers of one of Darwin's photographs of an extreme response, sixteen identified some form of fear or pain, six saw anger, and one, disgust (306). Between fear and pain, there is a good deal of somatic and semantic territory. Even such consensus as there is covers a number of possibilities: how many of the sixteen saw pain, and how many fear? Whatever the place of involuntary expressions in human life, it seems that we can never be sure either that the same gestures signify the same feelings or that we can unambiguously recognize them if they do. In short, Darwin writes, "Very many points in the theory of expression remain inexplicable" (87).

Two important points do, however, emerge from Darwin's work. First, emotions are not to be assumed as spontaneous; they can be trained or learned by imitation. They become theatrical and thereby open to the inauthenticity that has, from Plato onward, been attributed to dramatic performance. One can, for example, be taught to express terror, as, I suggest, many were taught by the media reports of 9/11. Second, emotions may not be recognizable; what looks like terror might actually be wonder. The power of learned or imposed words thus becomes a force for disciplining and schematizing otherwise inscrutable feelings. Whatever you are feeling, we will call it terror. Darwin's insights can bring us around to a Hobbesian scenario whereby the confusion of words and feelings is so radical as to admit legislation of meaning almost as a relief.

But this is not the purpose of Darwin's analysis. His anecdotes and examples come, of course, from the science of his day and from the technology of photography, which some still find to hold the key to human motives and identities through facial recognition systems. But he also resorts on a regular basis to the poets, most often to Homer, Virgil, the Bible, and Shakespeare. Where Socrates (officially) encourages us to be suspicious of the effects of poetry, Darwin, like many earlier theorists of the emotions, regards them as providing decisive citations. But poets use words, not photographs or brain scanners, and words clearly belong to culture and habit. Poetry may be "vague and fanciful" in its delineations of the emotions (83), yet Virgil, Job, and Shakespeare are invoked as examples of Darwin's own observations (292, 295). Words matter.

Darwin's openness to complexity, including the complexity added (or, just as often, simplified) by words, is applauded by Jerome Kagan for never actually leading him to define emotion: "Instead he described with great care a number of involuntary muscular profiles that were presumed to be signs of more than three dozen emotional states."[13] Kagan offers a cogent and skeptical case against the history of reductive explanation founded on a simplified reading of Darwin, a tradition wherein rats and mice (which have no capacity for appraisal that we know of), infants and adults, and humans and animals are all lumped together as part of a project to define emotions simply as involuntary or precognitive gestures open to measurement and exact location in the brain. Kagan finds that the three components of what is called emotion—"brain states, behaviors, and verbal descriptions"—are not in fact commensurable (xii). Or, more exactly, their commensurability is "unknown" (190). Further, the sequencing of emotion components more or less ensures that acts of definition are progressively reductive: "The range of values for most biological reactions is considerably larger than the range for behaviors, and the range for behaviors is larger than the range for words." Obviously, then, "most languages do not contain a sufficient number of terms capable of describing the full variation in an emotional state" (194), either as behavior or as biological value. *Most* here seems too cautious. Given that the functioning of language depends, in its "inherent structure" (195), exactly on its capacity to indicate many different

---

13. Jerome Kagan, *What Is Emotion? History, Measures, and Meanings* (New Haven, CT: Yale University Press, 2007), 17. Hereafter cited with page numbers in the text.

objects or states by relatively few terms, and thus requires supplementary gestures (context, ostension) to eliminate as much ambiguity as possible, it would seem inevitable that variations of inner states would be the most elusive. So it is that the Greek *thumos* "referred to a biological capacity for an intense feeling that could become any one of a number of emotions depending on the setting" (25). According to Kagan, there may even be a materialist explanation of the word-phenomena disjunction in the brain's own structure (10, 31). At the very least we should not "begin our inquiries into emotions with popular words that come packaged with the stamp of authority" (41), especially when those words have as their "primary concern . . . the agent's feeling rather than the provocative setting or the consequences of the state" (59).

These features of the relation between words, behavior, and biological states (which is a disjunction rather than a conjunction) do not affect neurological science alone. If each emotion term (e.g., fear) is in fact a "family of states and not a unitary emotion" (92), there are implications for our description of a whole range of human activities. Translation replaces transparency as the operative means for producing meanings. Obviously, understanding emotions across different cultures becomes a huge question (how do we translate *phobos*?), but even within a single-language culture with a high number of apparently shared conventions it can be difficult or impossible to decide whether one person's fear is the same as another's. Making basic sense, for Kagan, is subject to persuasion and interpellation: "Verbal reports are always modulated by the individual's available vocabulary and his or her estimate of the scientist's purposes and the motivation to please or impress the investigator" (196). The dismay or indifference of many who were unable to summon up feelings of terror after 9/11, notwithstanding the unanimous efforts of politicians and media spokespersons to impose that term as defining both the nature of the attack and the national response to it, may be taken to indicate a healthy awareness among ordinary people of the potential for motivated deception by their leaders, even as it offers reciprocally unsettling evidence of a manufactured unanimity among the media and the elites. In the most general sense, it is a historical subculture that "selects the states that will have salience" (204). So we are *told* that we live in an age of fear, or anxiety, or terror (the recently designated ages have mostly been negative). And within whatever "age" we are supposed to be in, there are those who have an interest in spinning the rhetoric in one direction and those who are committed to contesting it.

The lack of fit that Kagan describes among biological states, behaviors, and words, along with his persuasive account of the paucity of what we often think of as a source of infinite richness—words—suggests that we require a different set of habits for assessing meaning, and especially the meaning of emotion terms. Here we may return to the matter of *deos* and *phobos* in *Protagoras* (358D–E). One commentator finds that Prodicus's preference for *deos* is "defective ... [because it] omits the connotation of painful excitement or disturbance which is essential to the emotion of fear"; a man who is "perfectly composed" cannot be "afraid."[14] After reading Darwin and Kagan, we should doubt that there is anything essential to anything. We must wonder how it is established that *deos* contains nothing of this pain and why we should accept the assumption that the man who looks composed cannot be afraid. We should give up on seeking to essentialize single terms, as if to assume that terror is in every way different from horror or dread or fear. And we should be aware that the very range and flexibility of words, and in particular of words for emotions, allows for and even invites sleight of hand. Horror, as I have said, was notably absent from the roster of circulated terms for describing responses to 9/11, with arguably pernicious consequences.[15] A war on terror was declared against a personification, but it also referenced an emotion, one whereby we would all place ourselves in the position of the about-to-die, without the option for contemplation from a distance. That physical distance, or the imagining of it, is what might have enabled the emergence of critical attention, which the immediacy of terror precludes. The effort to manufacture a national trauma, involving everyone in the primary experience of being in the towers, called for terror, not horror. As I have said, a war on fear, dread, or anxiety would have sounded either familiar or too low key. President Franklin D. Roosevelt delivered a now-famous injunction against fear in his inaugural address of March 4, 1933, telling us that we had nothing to fear except fear itself. What is not so well known is what came next: he went on to paraphrase this fear as "nameless, unreasoning, unjustified terror, which paralyzes needed efforts." He told us, in other words, *not* to give in to terror, lest the "needed efforts" of the economic recovery be put in jeopardy by a fatalistic mass inertia. One can only assume that in 2001 his successor in the White House was setting out to create the very thing that Roosevelt had discouraged.

14. Taylor, *Plato's "Protagoras,"* 205–6.

15. Sandra Silberstein, *War of Words: Language, Politics and 9/11* (London: Routledge, 2002), reports one survivor saying that "it was just absolute, absolute horror, it was horror," which she herself goes on to paraphrase as "an attack of real terror" and as "sights of terror and horror" (65, 74–75). This is how consensus is built.

The questions raised by Darwin and Kagan inform my invocation of the "fear-terror cluster," a phrase intended to capture the baggy, porous, open-to-definition character of such terms. A cluster invokes something that has a visible shape and is set off from other groups or entities while the shape that it does have is neither neat nor absolute: items can be added or taken away. *Fear*, because it is such a common word, can suffice for the low- to middle-intensity end of the range; anxiety and concern are even lower-key terms. *Terror* I take to be the high-intensity end of the scale, a word to be used when maximum rhetorical effect is desired or when an extreme state is indicated. Words move around within the cluster and even come and go across its boundaries, within which they may or may not make it back. So *deinos* to mean "clever" can be tracked to a primary sense of fear (the fearful, the marvelous, the unpredicted, the clever), while "terribly glad you are here" works more obviously as an intensifier by way of antithesis (I am very moved to see you in a positive sense, to the same degree that I am moved by an extremely threatening event). Thinking of key words as members of clusters rather than as single-reference items will allow for a more critical and skeptical (and thus empowering) attitude among those who are used by language even as they themselves make use of it. This means all of us. The way to achieve this is to understand translation not just as what happens when we set out to turn one language into another but as the core procedure (translation without "originals") through which all functioning meanings are established and agreed on. William Reddy has proposed that all emotions are "assemblages of components" rather than single entities and finds that "no one has found a way to probe or measure an emotion directly." Analysis of emotions thus involves a "complexity of translation tasks."[16] When I say *terror*, I am not simply proffering or supposing a specific experience but declining to resort to other options, like *horror*, *dread*, or *fear*. That may be because of an agreed-on best-fit situation, or there may be other motives. Whatever the case, I am making a choice of one among many, just as I do when I translate *phobos* into *fear* or *terror*.

---

16. Reddy, *The Navigation of Feeling*, 12, 31, 94. Before him, William James found that "every one of us, almost, has some personal idiosyncrasy of expression, laughing or sobbing differently from his neighbor, or reddening or growing pale when others do not. We should find a like variation in the objects which excite emotion in different persons." See *The Principles of Psychology*, 3 vols. (Cambridge, MA: Harvard University Press, 1981), 2:1064. In "What Is an Emotion?" James argues that only embodied emotions can be tracked; disembodied emotions are nonentities. See *Mind* 9, no. 34 (April 1884): 188–205.

Thinking through this habit by way of a foreign language sometimes has the virtue of making clearer just how it works. We are more visibly challenged to explain how we decipher *phobos* in relation to *deos* and to the dozens of other cluster members to be found in Homer. Being bewildered has its uses. After the experience of such weighing and measuring, we might be less prone to a simple endorsement of terror as the order of the day.

Homer's Frightening Words

As befits the image (actual or imagined) of a heroic culture, Homer's frightening words are mostly fighting words, and consequently they are most evident in the *Iliad*. Three times in the poem, two personifications of radical threat appear together in the narrative. Their names, capitalized in modern editions, are Deimos and Phobos. Their first appearance presents them as figures on the battlefield, both agents and embodiments of violent feelings generated among the Greeks by Athena and among the Trojans by Ares. They are related to, subject to, or companions of Eris (sister to Ares), often rendered in English as *discord* or *strife*.[17] On their second joint appearance they are figures of figures, icons on Agamemnon's shield, where they feature along with Gorgon (11:37). Eris is involved in the action (11:3), "alone of the gods" in fighting for the Greeks, but not imaged on the shield. Their third appearance is again as embodied agents whom Ares asks to "yoke his horses" (15:119); elsewhere, in Hesiod's *Theogony* (ll. 934–35) they are actually his children (by Kytherea) and fearsome (*deinos*) gods themselves.

What is conjured here in the names of Deimos and Phobos? A. T. Murray translates them on all three occasions as Terror and Rout. For E. V. Rieu, the translator of what is probably the most widely distributed English Homer, they are twice rendered as Terror and Panic, but also once (on Agamemnon's shield) as Panic and Rout.[18] *Deimos*, in other words, appears as both terror and panic, *Phobos* as panic and rout. Chapman, the first English translator and the one who inspired John Keats's famous sonnet, opts for "Terror and Flight" in the first case, "Terror and Feare" in the second, "Feare and Dismay" in the third.[19] Alexander Pope's trans-

---

17. *Iliad*, 4:440. Hereafter cited in A. T. Murray's Loeb edition, *The Iliad* (Cambridge, MA: Harvard University Press, 1960). At 13:299, Phobos is identified as Ares's son; so Eris would be his aunt.

18. *The Iliad*, trans. E. V. Rieu (Harmondsworth, UK: Penguin, 1960), 88, 198, 274.

19. Allardyce Nicoll, ed., *Chapman's Homer: The Iliad* (Princeton, NJ: Princeton University Press, 1998), 105, 216, 301.

lation raises the stakes in the first citation by adding in adjectival inten-sifiers: "Pale Flight and dreadful Terror reign" on the battlefield. But in the second he goes in the opposite direction, as the two figures are col-lapsed into one and diminished:

> Tremendous Gorgon frown'd upon its field,
> And circling terrours fill'd th'expressive shield.[20]

(Thus Wakefield's footnote recommends "fear and terror" for "circling terrours" as closer to what Homer intends). Pope's third coupling has "Fear and Flight" (15:134).

We could go on. The translation of the names *Deimos* and *Phobos* is, like all translation, no simple matter. Homer's *phobos*, whatever it is, may be three or four hundred years earlier than Aristotle's, or more. Knowing how many radical lexical transformations occur, for example, between Chaucer and Shakespeare and between Shakespeare and the present, we would be rash indeed to decide on a definitive rendering of any of the key Homeric terms. Homer, to make things more compli-cated, seems quite fond of effects that modern readers might describe as tautologous. On the battlefield in book 4, the Greek text (Murray trans-lating) has Diomedes's armor clanging "terribly" (*deinon*) at line 420, inspiring "terror" (*deos*) at line 421, and the Greek soldiers advancing partly through "fear" of their commanders (*deidiotes*) at line 431. The Deimos who (or which) appears personified at line 440 has been an-ticipated by cognate-phonetic forms three times in the preceding lines. In book 11, Eris delivers a "terrible" (*deinon*) shout at line 10, and the figure of Gorgon on the shield glares "terribly" *(deinon)* at the beginning of the very line in which Deimos is invoked (36). Put into English, she glares terribly as Terror is "about her."[21] Murray chooses not to disam-biguate, while Rieu opts for giving Gorgon "awe-compelling eyes" (198) as well as for "panic" as the translation of *Deimos*, so there is no *terror* or *terribly* at all in his line.

For anglophone readers, *terror* may crop up or not, depending on the translator. And what is it when it does crop up? Does it disable or enable an active response? Is it single or shared? These questions were of

---

20. *The Iliad of Homer*, ed. Gilbert Wakefield, trans. Alexander Pope, 5 vols. (Lon-don, 1806). Pope's line numbers, like Chapman's, of course stray some distance from the Greek text. These citations are of Pope's books 4:499 and 11:47–48, printed at 2:114 and 3:71.

21. Similarly, at 17:17 Apollo (Phoibos) casts fear (*phobos*) upon the Greeks.

primary concern in the late seventeenth and eighteenth centuries among the scholars and critics engaged in the debate between the so-called ancients and moderns. Pope, roughly speaking, was an ancient; he believed that the fundamental human feelings and experiences were the same for Achilles as they were for us, so what mattered about an original text could be transmitted across time by the efforts of an able translator.[22] The moderns, like Pope's enemy Richard Bentley, took seriously the distortions and transformations of time and place, and argued that any hope of access to original meanings could be tested only after rigorous scholarly acts of recovery. According to the moderns, we cannot make any assumptions that what Achilles is described as feeling is an emotion familiar to or fully shared by us.[23] The fear-terror word cluster in Homer is especially rich and diverse and includes a host of other terms besides *deimos, deos, deinos,* and *phobos.* Emotion words are hard to distinguish one from another: their very logic may well be that they overlap. Then there are questions of a literary sort. Homer did not repeat *deos* and *phobos* in the passages just discussed because no other words were available to him. Quite the opposite. Robert Zaborowski has discovered forty-three terms spread among twenty-two word roots featuring in the fear-terror cluster in Homer's two epics, amounting to 1,052 instances, among which he analyzes something over half.[24] If Homer was deliberately repeating himself for a reason, what was it? And who is the Homer in "Homer": scribe, singer, or redactor?

I give here only the briefest of summary examples from Zaborowski's indispensable work (239–48): *deido* words (including *deos* and *deinos*) are by far the most common fear-terror terms in Homer, with 289 instances (326–27), and the widest ranging. *Aidos* (129 uses) and *kedos* (114 uses) follow.[25] *Phobos* comes in fourth (113 uses); less frequent are such terms as *tromos, tarbos, trein, rigein, stugein, sebas, hazesthai,* and others. Few of these terms appear routinely as single agencies: *aidos* does tend to stand alone, but *phobos* often occurs in company. In other words, most fear-terror words are accompanied by other fear-terror words, so

22. This is also the assumption behind Jonathan Shay, *Achilles in Vietnam: Combat Trauma and the Undoing of Character* (New York: Scribner, 1994).

23. For an overview, see Joseph M. Levine, *The Battle of the Books: History and Literature in the Augustan Age* (Ithaca, NY: Cornell University Press, 1991).

24. Zaborowski, *La crainte et le courage,* 239. Hereafter cited with page numbers in the text. The count would be even higher if his analysis had captured *smerdaleos,* one of the most common of Homer's fear-terror words.

25. These two are not primarily fear-terror words; they signal shame and concern or grief, respectively.

that we have to decide between contrast and replication; sometimes they are set forth as contrasts (*deos* against *aidos*, *thambos* against *deos*), sometimes not. Some usually have physical manifestations, some do not: *tromos* and *phobos* are commonly somatized, while *aidos* and *kedos* are not. *Aidos* can describe a response to the gods; *kedos* does not. No wonder the translators differ so much, both from each other and within their own renderings. Fear-terror words are a lexical minefield or a treasure trove, depending on how you feel about complex data.

There is another Homeric shield, the description of which takes up 130 lines following *Iliad* 18:477 and has been the subject of much attention from scholars and antiquarians: the shield of Achilles. Here, too, there are three personified figures: Eris (strife) again, Kudoimos (panic, tumult, din, confusion), and Ker (fate, death, doom). Although Achilles is not "king of men," he is top dog on the battlefield, which suggests that these three personifications are to be deemed more powerful and fear inducing than those on Agamemnon's shield. But they are only briefly described as elements among the elaborate allegories and cosmologies that Hephaestus fashions upon the shield, and they are further qualified by the foreknowledge of Achilles's death that both the hero himself and his mother, Thetis, proleptically invoke (331–32, 457–58). For all its strength, the shield cannot defend against fate. Images on shields are again extensively discussed by Eteocles in Aeschylus's *Seven against Thebes*. Here the shields are more simply adorned and the allegorical import made easier to grasp. Commenting on the apparel of his seven enemy champions, Eteocles claims to have no fear of mere signs, and thus no fear of Hippomedon's *Phobos*, which at once flashes from his eyes and appears figured on his shield. As it often is in Homer, *phobos* is both image and emotion.

Who feels fear-terror in the *Iliad*? There is no modern state terror. Agamemnon is a king and a chief, but he cannot claim a power comprehensive enough to terrify others into constant submission. Zeus can do this in ruling over the gods (8:8, 15:123), although Eris is still able to run amok (11:74). Humans most appropriately experience fear-terror in the face of the gods, although Achilles is not cowed even by Athena (1:200), and Diomedes is even prepared to engage them in combat (5:286, 817), wounding Ares in battle (5:857). Only the river god Scamander terrifies Achilles (21:248).[26] Horses fear their masters, and Trojans (even Hector) can be terror stricken by the Greeks, but refusal to fear one's enemy is a

26. The one point at which he is "seized with dread" at the sight of Aeneas (20:261) has been deemed textually spurious.

mark of distinction. For all the proliferation of fear-terror terms in the *Iliad*, they designate primarily emotions that the most heroic figures can control, especially in purely human interactions.

In Aristotle, the invocation of fear-terror shifts away from war and into aesthetics. *Deos* compounds do feature in Aristotle, both in the *Rhetoric* and the *Poetics*. For the *Rhetoric*, an argument has been made that *deos* and *phobos* terms are indistinguishable.[27] The most extended discussion of a fear-terror word here is indeed of *phobos*, in book 2 (vv. 1–22, 1382a–1383b). On all but one occasion in this detailed explanation, the *phobos* word group is employed. But in the discussion that pairs pity and fear-terror, *deinos* (the terrible) is used three times (2:viii, 12–13; 1386a), with only one use of a *phobos* word.[28] The Loeb Library translator J. H. Freese renders a contrast between the two words by translating *deinos* as *the terrible* and *phobos* as *fear*. He could as easily have opted to use the same English word for both, or even have inverted his correlation. And it is pity and *phobos* (not *deinos*) that make up the famous pairing in the massively influential discussion of the emotions associated with tragedy in Aristotle's *Poetics*. Here the first two instances refer to *phobos* and *eleos*.[29] This is repeated five times in the major discussion beginning at 1452b.xiii.1 and again at 1453b.xiv.1. *Phrittein* does appear as an alternative to *phobos*, paired with *eleos* at 1453b.xiv.2. And *deinos* appears twice, when Fyfe decides to translate it as "the dreadful" and as "horror" (xiv.6, 13). Seemingly, this dread or horror is not properly at home in tragedy. It is best read as a subspecies of the monstrous or marvelous or wondrous (*to teratodes*), that which, we have just been told, has nothing in common with tragedy.[30] If so, and reading thus, *phobos* and *deinos* have come to mean very different things: the first appropriate to tragedy and compatible with pity; the

27. See David Konstan, *The Emotions of the Ancient Greeks: Studies in Aristotle and Classical Literature* (Toronto: University of Toronto Press, 2006), 153. Konstan here takes issue with the strong distinction between *deos* and *phobos* argued (for Thucydides) by Jacqueline de Romilly (see note 51 in this chapter).

28. *Art of Rhetoric*, trans. J. H. Freese (Cambridge, MA: Harvard University Press, 1982).

29. *Poetics*, trans. W. Hamilton Fyfe (Cambridge, MA: Harvard University Press, 1973), 1449b, vi.2, 1452a, ix, 11. Philip Fisher, *The Vehement Passions* (Princeton, NJ: Princeton University Press, 2002), 132–40, distinguishes three different states: pity, fear, and the more extreme shudder of fear or terror (presumably *phrittein*).

30. Gerald F. Else, *Aristotle's Poetics: The Argument* (Cambridge, MA: Harvard University Press, 1957), 413, makes a clearer contrast between the "horrible" (*deina*) and the "pitiable"; only the second is desired. But on the same page he translates *deinos* (where Fyfe has *horror*) as "the fearful thing," thus reassimilating *deinos* to *phobos* and weakening its negative sense.

second, not so. In the *Rhetoric* they seem more or less interchangeable. Aristotle's presentation of the fear-terror lexicon is thus not without its ambiguities, even as the *Poetics* tilts toward *phobos* as its key term and endorses it as most proper to tragedy.[31] Most modern translators opt for "fear" as the best translation of *phobos*. But the diversified vocabulary of the *Rhetoric*, with *phobos* and *deinos* figuring ambiguously and perhaps undecidably as the same or somewhat different, leaves some open questions about what to say in English.[32] Indeed, at the end of the seventeenth century, *phobos* comes into English for the most part not as *fear* but as *terror*.

The critical translation decisions were made, it seems, in France. While terror and horror originally derive from Latin, they come into English by way of old French, and it is terror (*terreur*) that Rapin includes in his renderings of *phobos*, which is also sometimes *crainte* (causing us to become *craintif*), sometimes *frayeur*, and sometimes *terreur*, accompanied by the onset of the *terrible*. *Horreur* is also in Rapin's lexicon.[33] His English translator renders the options as *fear*, *terror*, and *horror*, and offers both "fear and pity" and "terror and pity" as the crucial dyad.[34] Dacier, coming after Rapin with rather better linguistic credentials, generally prefers *terreur* and *le terrible* (for *phobos* and *to phoberon*).[35] John D. Lyons observes that *crainte* and *terreur* both occur as seventeenth-century translations of *phobos*, the first favored by Corneille, the second by Dacier. *Horreur* is positive for Bossuet but rejected by La Mesnardière; unlike *terreur*, it indicates a rejection of sympathy with the character.[36] *Terreur* is in the mind while *horreur* affects the body; the one allows for contemplative reflection, the other stimulates overpowering revulsion and is thus incompatible with aristocratic decorum. But Lyons suggests that horror cannot be fully banished from the stage and finds in La Mesnardière a sustained effort to "frame horror into an ethically acceptable form"

31. The most recent study is Dana LaCourse Munteanu, *Tragic Pathos: Pity and Fear in Greek Philosophy and Tragedy* (Cambridge: Cambridge University Press, 2012).

32. Thus G. M. A. Grube, *Aristotle on Poetry and Style* (Indianapolis, IN: Bobbs-Merrill, 1983), 12, prefers *fear* for *phobos* only "after some hesitation," noting that the "exact meaning" probably lies "somewhere between fear and terror."

33. René Rapin, *Réflexions sur la poétique d'Aristote, et sur les ouvrages des poètes anciens et modernes* (Paris, 1674), 169–82 (facs. ed.; Hildesheim: Georg Olms, 1973).

34. René Rapin, *Reflexions on Aristotle's Treatise on Poetry* (London, 1674), 103–10.

35. André Dacier, *La Poétique d'Aristote, traduite en francois* (Paris, 1692), 211–16. Corneille, however, in the second of his *Discours de la tragédie* (1660), always uses the pairing of *pitié* with *crainte*.

36. John D. Lyons, *Kingdom of Disorder: The Theory of Tragedy in Classical France* (West Lafayette, IN: Purdue University Press, 1999), 43–82.

(68). At such moments, horror and terror become harder to distinguish. And indeed, *horreur* figures in the works of Racine more frequently than any of its allied cluster terms.[37] A similar ratio is apparent in the early dictionaries, with *horreur* earning more citations than *terreur*.

English-speaking readers were meanwhile being nudged toward *terror* as the common rendering of *phobos*. Thomas Rymer likes "pitty and terror," and John Dennis opts consistently for "terrour" as the partner of "compassion" or "pity."[38] Addison's account of the pleasures of the imagination makes the same decision (*Spectator* no. 418).[39] Dryden's answer to Rymer, written in 1678 but not printed until 1711, univocally renders the Aristotelian pairing as *terror* and *pity*.[40] So, too, at the end of the century, does Henry James Pye, in offering an Aristotle who has hitherto been "almost entirely shut up from the mere English reader." His claim to value accuracy more than elegance leads him to offer *pity* and *terror* instead of *pity* and *fear*, as well as to contrast terror with horror as respectively appropriate and inappropriate to tragedy.[41] By the beginning of the eighteenth century, then, a preference for terror as the English form of *phobos* is beginning to appear, at exactly the moment when, as never before and perhaps since, Aristotle is being transmitted to middle-class audiences.[42] Terror is becoming familiar and domesticated. It figures significantly, for example, in William Smith's influential 1739 translation of Longinus. Here we are dealing with a work composed sometime in the first three hundred years CE, surviving by way of a tenth-century manuscript and often coming into English by

---

37. See Bryant C. Freeman and Alan Batson, eds., *Concordances des Théâtre et des Poesies de Jean Racine*, 2 vols. (Ithaca, NY: Cornell University Press, 1968). *Horreur* or *horreurs* is roughly three times as common as *terreur* or *terreurs*, although the incidence of *horrible* and *terrible* is about equal. *Crainte* is almost as common as *horreur*, while *effroi* and *frayeur* appear about as often as *terreur*.

38. Thomas Rymer, *The Tragedies of the Last Age Considered and Examined* (London, 1678), 95; John Dennis, *The Impartial Critick* (London, 1793), 9–13. Dennis also offers a distinction between terror and horror, finding Dryden guilty of confusing them. Horror is not compatible with pity or compassion and generates "a murmuring, as it were, at Providence" (12).

39. *Spectator* no. 44 is already able to turn theatrical terror into comedy, but Addison also accords "majesty and terror" to Milton's God in no. 333. For Addison and Dennis on terror, see Leslie E. Moore, *Beautiful Sublime: The Making of "Paradise Lost," 1701–1734* (Stanford, CA: Stanford University Press, 1990), 99–103.

40. *"Of Dramatic Poetry" and Other Essays*, ed. George Watson, 2 vols. (London: Dent and Dutton, 1962), 2:210–20.

41. Pye, *The "Poetics" of Aristotle Translated from the Greek* (London, 1788), i, v, 76–78.

42. As noted by J. C. Eade, *Aristotle Anatomised: The Poetics in England, 1674–1781* (Frankfurt: Peter Lang, 1988), 1.

way of Boileau. The *deos-phobos* group is again present in the Greek, and in three out of six cases Smith opts for *terror* as his translation.[43] At three other points a *phobos* word is rendered as "actuated by fear" (57), as "fright" (59), and as "anxiety" (60). But notable here is Smith's propensity for invoking terror in his own voice in his commentary, which he does five times (xiii, 124, 139, 140, 147). So, too, the incidence of *horror* is, in all eleven cases, in his own voice (with one exception, where he cites Phillips's translation of Sappho). It seems that the rhetoric of extreme feeling is being ramped up, in versions of both Aristotle and Longinus, for a readership presumably deemed open to such incentives. Longinus was a rhetorician rather (or more) than a student of human psychology: he was principally interested in what kinds of stylistic devices were best suited to generating certain responses among readers and audiences. Much of his text reads like a guide for speechwriters. What is absent here is the rational and moral component of Aristotle's pity and fear, which were to be experienced only after the spectator had approved the compatibility of those seen suffering on the stage with an exemplary model of the self. Longinus in the eighteenth century came to appeal as the apologist of a heightened passion that was significantly detached from an explicit moral purpose, although some would seek to restore or invent such a purpose. Arguments about the pleasurable component of tragedy, and about what might be meant by that, continued to circulate, but there arose alongside them a much more communicable emphasis on intensity for its own sake and, presumably, for the sake of having a striking effect on others. Terror becomes a key component in persuasive speech and potentially in bullying speech—or perhaps just sheer fun. For William Smith, images of terror can be "grateful and engaging" (124), signs of polite refinement rather than of deep moral curiosity. Later in the century, William Chambers's *A Dissertation on Oriental Gardening* (1772) attributes to Chinese gardeners a distinction between "the pleasing, the terrible, and the surprising," and describes the shades, caverns, and cataracts of human-made landscapes as providing for "scenes of terror."[44] At this point we seem to have come a long way from Aristotle's *phobos*, and even further from the walls of Troy.

43. William Smith, *Dionysius Longinus on the Sublime, Translated from the Greek* (London, 1739), 29, 30, 42. Hereafter cited with page numbers in the text.
44. Cited in Andrew Ashfield and Peter de Bolla, eds., *The Sublime: A Reader in British Eighteenth-Century Aesthetic Theory* (Cambridge: Cambridge University Press, 1996), 268.

The Pleasures of Terror

Homer's use of the fear-terror cluster comes down to us as viscerally immediate, full of blood and guts, although it is hard to be sure that there is absolutely no measure of self-conscious aesthetics in play. In the British eighteenth-century address to terror, aesthetics rules the roost. John Dennis, in his defense of the importance of poetry to religion and of the superior qualities of *Paradise Lost*, still has some sense of the seriousness of terror. It is poetry's capacity to reunite reason and passion, so often at odds, that "causes the Soul to Rejoyce."[45] Dennis makes a distinction between the "vulgar" passions, which everyone experiences, and the "enthusiastick" passions, which are accessible only by meditation upon and contemplation of things "that belong not to common Life" (16). Tragedy has to do with the vulgar (i.e., widely shared) passions, and the common experience of "Compassion and Terror" accordingly appears there (19). Epic poetry, in contrast, is not for everyone, and here a different terror and horror are two of the six "enthusiastic passions" (16) that are not so readily available: "Thousands have no feeling and no notion of them" (18). Because these terrors are not immediate, they can be and are always found mixed with "Admiration," another of the enthusiastic passions. Admiration and terror "give the principal Greatness and Elevation to Poetry" (54; cf. 68–69). Longinus's examples, Dennis contends, also lead to an understanding that religious ideas are the best source of the sublime, even though Longinus never quite says this himself. Ideas are "more terrible as they have more of Religion in them" (89), and nothing is more terrible than an angry god (70). Dennis, it seems, has read his Bible.

But Dennis maintains a distinction that Addison and Kant, among others, will repeat: that "Enthusiastick Terrour . . . proceeds from our reflecting that we are out of Danger at the very time that we see it before us" (86). And yet the enthusiastic passions, terror included, produce "the same Passions that the Objects of those Ideas would raise in us, if they were set before us in the same Light that those ideas give us of them" (17). This seems to say that contemplative terror (of the sort one gets from reading a poem) is the same passion as what we would feel if

---

45. John Dennis, *The Grounds of Criticism in Poetry* (London, 1704), 82. Hereafter cited with page numbers in the text. For accounts of Dennis, see Robert Doran, *The Theory of the Sublime from Longinus to Kant* (Cambridge: Cambridge University Press, 2015), 124–40; and David B. Morris, *The Religious Sublime: Christian Poetry and Critical Tradition in Eighteenth-Century England* (Lexington: University Press of Kentucky, 1972), 47–78.

we were ourselves undergoing the experience that is written about. Because nature has given us a capacity to be terrified by "any thing that threatens approaching evil," it does not matter whether the threat is real or imaginary" (90). Thus, great poets can mimic the effects on the eye and the ear that unmediated (real) terror occasions by imaging violent action and movement, so that objects are "as present to us as if they were really before us," and "we are sensible of the same Passion that we should feel from the things themselves" (92).

Here a question arises. If terror as the most powerful term in the aesthetic of the sublime requires being at a secure distance from actual harm, then what is left in the vocabulary of extreme emotions to describe how we might feel when that harm actually threatens, detached from and preempting any reading experience? Is there something more terrifying than enthusiastic terror? If we designate terror as an idea of violence, aroused as easily by written words as by events, what terms do we have left over for specifying a real experience of radical danger? Presumably the writer can create in the reader something akin to real terror, but the transference goes only one way; whoever is suffering real terror is not thinking about how to write it down. At what point, then, could anyone properly compare the experience of reading about terror (and enjoying the terror of the sublime) to that of actually experiencing extreme threat? Would we, for instance, stand in the path of an avalanche, jump aside, and then pick up a poetic description of an avalanche to conclude that one is much the same as the other? Dennis admits that acts of reading presuppose leisure and distance, being out of the world, so that if we were indeed standing on that mountain with a book in hand, we would not be open to a sublime reading experience because we would be keeping a cautionary eye on the empirical world. In the case of enthusiastic terror—"no Passion is attended with greater Joy" (86)—we can fully imagine ourselves in that world, and in the most exigent circumstances, only when we are not in it. But it does not work the other way round. In the most extreme experiences, there is no sublime. Reading can make us think we are immersed in real experience, but the critical forms of real experience leave no time for reading. Dennis does not say this, but a reader of the poetry of religious terror (e.g., in the Old Testament or in *Paradise Lost*) might thus be able to save his or her soul without having sinned enough to incur the real wrath of God. That reader might feel close enough to the burning pit to behave better in ordinary life. Contemplative reading might, in this way, steer one away from serious trouble; or would it foreclose an experience of real sin of the sort that makes salvation all the more precious? Are we at the point where leisure and distance are beginning to be assumed the property of the genteel classes, who thus invite the stern admonishments of a more demanding religion?

This problem of finding a word for something more terrible than terror as soon as terror is attributed to the aesthetic of the sublime adds another level of complexity to a word already bifurcated between meaning something *in* the world (a terror incarnate) and something that we *feel* about the world. (In Homer, at least as edited, this syndrome appeared, for example, in *phobos* as felt and Phobos as personified). That we might mistake the one for the other, as Dennis and others suggest happens in the more intense kinds of reading, goes to the heart of one of the persistent critiques of literature, the one voiced by Plato and by Rousseau: that it deludes us into thinking that we are in the world of the real, so that we think we know already what the real feels like without ever having sensed it directly. The double demand on literature is that it must signal at once its fictiveness and its verisimilitude. *The Iliad* must make us imagine being on the plains of Troy while also questioning the adequacy of such imagining; many readers will manage only the first response. But the more successful the writing, the less of a distinction we are inclined to make between the fictional and the real. For Plato and Rousseau, this condition threatens the integrity of citizenship itself. After Dennis, who accepts that the terror derived from reading is not the terror faced in life-threatening situations, even though we feel while reading that it is, there still remains a question of terminology: what do you call "real" terror? Perhaps the answer is just that: real terror. Perhaps any perspicuous use of the noun must always require an adjective, a supplement. But however we construe a response or a solution, it cannot be true that the difference does not matter. However immersed we are in reading, it is hard to believe that the onset of the real threat would not remind us of that difference.

Burke takes up this problem in the final section of his 1759 *Inquiry*, in the section devoted to a discussion of the power of words. He grants that words and "natural objects" obviously affect us in different ways.[46] Not only do words not hand over "real" experience, that is, the sensing of real things; they could not work properly if they did. The power of poetry has nothing to do with "raising sensible images" (170) but works "rather by sympathy than imitation" (172). It is passion that is communicated, passion that is common to writer and reader. Burke notes that

---

46. Edmund Burke, *A Philosophical Inquiry into the Origin of our Ideas of the Sublime and Beautiful*, ed. James T. Boulton (Notre Dame: University of Notre Dame Press, 1986), 163. Hereafter cited with page numbers in the text.

there are "many things of a very affecting nature, which can seldom occur in the reality, but the words which represent them often do" (175). So Achilles has killed Hector only once, if at all, but people can write about the event as many times as they care to, and others may read what those people write even more often. What is shareable here is a passion, but not its real object or occasion.

This does not quite solve the problem of terror, however, when terror purports to describe (or prescribe) what people *really* feel. If I have a near-death experience and write about it, you may feel that you are having it, too; but you are not, and when I am writing about it, neither am I. Adam Smith, for one, was well aware that sympathy maintained between persons in this way is something of a fiction: we tell ourselves and others that we "feel their pain," for example, without any way of knowing whether we do, or even whether what they call pain is what we would call pain. The point is to build up sympathy, and so anxious are we to do this that we even tone down our own responses to make it easier for others to sympathize with us. The assumed and/or enacted agreement on the use of words or gestures glosses over possible discontinuities in sensation and emotion. Dennis's argument can work only as long as we restrict the common experience of terror not to what is communicated in words but to what we can agree to assume or accept as communicated, without further inquiry. I can enjoy my reading experience of terror just as long as I do not worry over whether what you have written corresponds at all to what you might have felt or what I might feel on an equivalent occasion, or whether what you have written is what I would have written. For we are in the world of writing, whose enabling condition is that while I am writing (or reading), I am not actually running for my life but imagining (even if I claim to be remembering) what I might have felt if I were. Sympathetic consensus has no necessary or consequential connection to lived events, even as it hopes or seeks to have something (even much) to do with them. It can always be opened to critique, though this does not normally happen with ordinary or habitual interactions. As soon as it is transcribed for others, terror is no longer "simply" terror. This has important implications for anyone claiming to disseminate terror (or anything else) in mimetic forms. My response to someone else's terror could also be described as mere concern, or even indifference. If I am discouraged from thinking about alternatives, then I am probably being manipulated.

A different way of attempting distinctions between the emotions described by fear-terror words can be had by referencing physiological conditions: hair standing on end, blood freezing, bodies trembling, and so on. Here what matters most is what is seen from the outside, not what is surmised as being felt internally. These phenomena can sometimes be adduced for readers or spectators—as in the long-circulated (but probably mythic) anecdotes of women going into premature labor at the sight of Aeschylus's furies (in *Eumenides*)—but they more often serve to set off figures who are being described as embedded in a real-world event from the rest of us reading about it. Many of the fear-terror words in classical epic come with explicitly somatic signifiers. Zaborowski (244) finds that *deos*, *thambos*, *tromos*, and *atuzesthai* are most obviously marked by radical and passive bodily transformations, whereas other words imply a power of response, as when *phobos* (in Homer) is associated with flight. Dryden is particularly attuned to the somatic-psychological distinction in his translation of *The Aeneid*. In comparing his word choices with those of the Loeb translator, who has a flair for melodrama (wherever one could say *fear*, he says *terror*), Dryden emerges as a model of restraint. On several occasions, he boils down Virgil's agglomerations of fear-terror words to simple summaries, for example, where Virgil has *metus* followed by *timor* (at 9:89–90, Dryden compresses to "fill'd with Fear" at 9:104); and where *territat* is followed shortly by *terror* (11:351, 357), Dryden simply offers one word, "fear" (11:545).[47] Not uncommonly the fear-terror word goes untranslated, which has the effect of rendering the English poem emotionally restrained, and thus perhaps more polite, than its Latin original. Dryden also works to register the varieties of meaning that the fear-terror vocabulary allows for. Thus *metus* (1:514) appears not just as *fear* but also as *wonder* (1:723), and *pavor* (2:229) as *amazement* (2:300). But when it is a matter of picking up on the physiological attributes of a response, Dryden follows his original much more faithfully. In book 3, for example, Virgil has Aeneas responding to the portent with an intense bodily reaction: *mihi frigidus horror / membra quatit, gelidusque coit formidine sanguis* (29–30). Dryden follows closely Virgil's doubling of the fear words (*metus*, *formidine*), with the couplet "Mute, and amaz'd, my Hair with Terror stood; / Fear shrunk my sinews, and congeal'd my Blood" (3:40–41). Even when Virgil redoes the physical response a few lines later (ll. 47–48), Dryden follows him (ll. 68–69), and this is the pattern of his whole translation: he is very attentive to somatic manifestations of fear-terror.[48] Notably,

47. Citations are from *The Aeneid*, trans. H. Rushton Fairclough, 2 vols. (Cambridge, MA: Harvard University Press, 1986); and Dryden, ed., *The Works of Virgil*, 3 vols. (London, 1730).

48. See, for example, Virgil at 4:280, 12:867–68 (Fairclough); Dryden at 4:404, 12:1254–55.

in the passage just cited, Virgil's *horror* becomes Dryden's *terror*. In the Latin, *horror* more often indicates a strong somatic response (shivering, bristling hair, and so on), whereas *terror* can be less physically intense.[49] It is often the other way around in English, with *horror* suggesting a greater distance from threat than does *terror* (hence the insistence of the media-political consensus that 9/11 produced terror, not horror; immersion rather than contemplation or critique; an immediate risk to every self rather than a beholding of the suffering of others). Dryden's choice is astute, and his need to make it indicates the instability of the *terror-horror* distinction (apparent, again, in the gothic novel later in the eighteenth century), both as it passes from Latin to English and in its subsequent evolution in English alone.[50]

Dryden's generally reductive representation of Virgil's fear-terror words has the effect of emphasizing those moments in the poem that are marked by extreme physiological symptoms, those moments where he seems to stay very close to his source. The poem in English thus becomes more consistently restrained in its emotional register (as fear-terror words are omitted or read in their weaker versions as anxiety or concern) and relatively more intense when strongly somatic signs do appear. In this way, Dryden sorts out the fear-terror lexicon, consciously or otherwise, establishing a clear hierarchy distinguishing intense from ordinary responses. The previously cited couplet at 3:40–41 is interesting in showing that terror is responsible for Aeneas's hair standing on end while fear shrinks the sinews (a common Homeric image) and congeals the blood. The two words are at once apposites and opposites: the single reaction of the body is parceled out between two agents that have different names but effectively operate to the same end. This is an Englished version of Virgil's doubling, but Virgil's *formidine* is ablative (by, from, or with fear), so that *horror* remains (grammatically) the dominant force. Dryden figures *terror* and *fear* working together, risking the anglophone inference that *fear* is the weaker term (as it generally is) even as it performs much the same work on the body.

At issue here is an important decision about the nature and import of terror; can it be mixed up with other emotions, or should it signify something more restrictive, an all-powerful response that does not leave room

---

49. Ann Radcliffe takes up a similar distinction (see chapter 4 in this volume).

50. Virgil's most common noun in the fear-terror cluster is *metus*, followed by *timor*, although the verb forms *timeo* and *metuo* are more or less equally common. *Terror* and *horror* are less common than their verb forms (*terreo, horreo*), and *pavor* is the rarest of all. See Monroe Nichols Wetmore, ed., *Index Verborum Vergilius* (Hildesheim: Georg Olms, 1961).

for other emotions? Can one feel terror *and* fear or wonder or even joy (as Dennis suggested one could), or is terror better conceived as involving a total sense of imminent danger and destruction that leaves no space for companionate or contrasting feelings? Is the personality reduced to total vulnerability, or can there remain a play between various responses and thus some aesthetic wriggle room? How exactly, if at all, does terror differ from horror, dread, and all the other associated alternatives? And, does our answer to such questions differ according to whether we are speaking of terror as an inner emotion or as an objective agent outside us? I might, for example, refuse to respond to terror personified (as did Eteocles) while finding it impossible to resist terror as an immediate emotion. The one invites, but does not demand, the other. Aristotle, in *Poetics*, is clear that there is room for at least one other emotion: *phobos* always comes paired with pity, and this is because it is contained within a rational calculus wherein one judges the worthiness of the sufferer as a person we can and should identify with: there is no *phobos* generated by the death of a scoundrel.[51] The distance enabled by the space of the theater allows for such openness to seemingly quite different emotions. Dennis, though in a manner not quite so rational, is exuberantly positive that even though we "cannot resist" the power of terror, it is still conformable with other, supplementary emotions; indeed, he proposes that far from being overpowering, terror "scarce ever goes by itself." Like Burke later in the century, he conflates terror with the sublime (finding this in Longinus), and so claims that "terrible Ideas" can "produce a certain Admiration mingled with Astonishment and with Surprize. For the ideas which produce Terrour are necessarily accompanied with Admiration, because every thing that is terrible is great to Him to whom it is terrible; and with Surprize without which Terrour cannot subsist; and with Astonishment, because ev'ry thing which is very terrible is Wonderful and Astonishing."[52] Because Dennis operates on the assumption that real images and written words produce the same effects, he does not, as we have seen, need to discriminate between reading about terror (where we might admire and wonder at the author's skill and style) and living through it; or, rather, being immersed in a terror experience is not on the table here (because we are talking about the sublime), but Dennis writes

51. Somewhat controversially (while attentive to a classical source), Jacquelin de Romilly has argued that Thucydides uses *phobos* as an irrational emotion, with the intellectual, calculative ability residing instead with *deos*. See "La crainte dans l'oeuvre de Thucydide," *Classica et Mediaevalia* 17 (1956): 119–27. So *phobos* signifies defenselessness and *deos* positive action, even useful fear.

52. Dennis, *Grounds of Criticism in Poetry*, 68, 86.

as if it were. The nature of the passion may be the same when, with good writing, "the very Objects themselves are as it were before us" (92), but the degree is quite different. Dennis's "as it were" suggests that we can fool ourselves that we are facing the real; but in the face of the real there is no mediation required or indeed available: if we don't run, we perish. These questions are important when we are told or assumed to experience terror, as if no other emotions are on offer, as we so often were in the aftermath of 9/11.

Burke's famous treatise follows Dennis in presenting an exemplary array of terms in the fear-terror cluster without offering any unambiguous distinctions between them. For him, the sublime may be generated by whatever "is fitted in any sort to excite the ideas of pain, and danger," and the sensations thus excited may be derived from whatever "operates in a manner analogous to terror."[53] Not terror as a thing in itself, notice, but something like it. His extended discussion begins by conflating terror with fear, implicitly rendering the two traditional translations of Aristotle's *phobos* as much the same thing (57). But it is terror that is the "ruling principle" of the sublime, which he goes on to explain thus:

> Several languages bear a strong testimony to the affinity of these ideas [terror and the sublime]. They frequently use the same word, to signify indifferently the modes of astonishment or admiration and those of terror. Θάμβος [*thambos*] is in greek, either fear or wonder; δεινός [*deinos*] is terrible or respectable; αἰδέω, [*aideo*] to reverence or to fear. *Vereor* in latin, is what αἰδέω is in greek. The Romans used the verb *stupeo*, a term which strongly marks the state of an astonished mind, to express the idea either of simple fear, or of astonishment; the word *attonitus* (thunderstruck) is equally expressive of the alliance of these ideas; and do not the french *etonnement*, and the english *astonishment* and *amazement*, point out as clearly the kindred emotions which attend fear and wonder? They who have a more general knowledge of languages, could produce, I make no doubt, many other and equally striking examples. (58)

This passage is of considerable interest for any history of the rhetoric of terror. It is, of course and once again, the sublime that is being described,

---

53. Edmund Burke, *A Philosophical Enquiry into the Origin of our Ideas of the Sublime and Beautiful*, ed. James T. Boulton (Notre Dame, IN: University of Notre Dame Press, 1986), 39. Lowercase nouns are Burke's.

and not unmediated, lived experience. But the etymological-psychological focus brings the two together because the same words describe both. Emotions are at once total and partial. Astonishment carries the charge of being turned to stone, petrified, frozen in time: "That state of the soul, in which all its motions are suspended, with some degree of horror" (57). This suggests a person completely overpowered, but the "some degree of horror" seems to allow space for an imprecise measure, and thus for an astonishment supplemented with horror. In the previous passage, terror (not horror) is described in the same words as denote "astonishment or admiration," which here have a positive (or nonthreatening) application. If the same words describe fear and wonder, and if fear and wonder generate "kindred emotions," then we cannot find a simple way to isolate one from another: all such expressions involve potentially compound affects. Similarly, horror and terror are not clearly distinguished, and each can be experienced along with other emotions; so we find "terror and amazement" and "dread and horror" in Horace and Lucretius (69). Horror can be "delightful" (73), and terror can produce delight "when it does not press too close" (46). If horror can be taken to suggest contemplation at a distance, then here terror, too (in the sublime), is removed from immediate experience and is thus able to generate an emotion that is not exclusive and overpowering: the terror-horror antithesis that will inform Burke's political writings in the 1790s has not yet come into being.

How does terror produce "delight"? Burke is clear that delight is to be distinguished from "positive pleasure": it is "not pleasure, but a sort of delightful horror, a sort of tranquility tinged with terror" (136). Positive pleasure has to do, for example, with the creative and amatory faculties, typified by the beautiful. Delight is a more strenuous experience, and it seems to operate in at least two ways. The first has to do with the positive valence of activity itself, and the second with our common human nature. Tom Furniss has written astutely about Burke's specification of delight as accompanying "the removal of pain or danger" (35). We may remove them ourselves or have them removed for us; either way we are (actual or incipient) agents, which fits well with Burke's stress on the value of activity and labor as keeping us from the "relaxed state of body" that brings about "melancholy" and "dejection" (135). Delight is thus the delight of sheer animal movement, of acting for oneself in putting or keeping terror at a distance, or of being ready to act following the removal of constraint.[54] This will emerge thirty years later in Burke's

54. Tom Furniss, *Edmund Burke's Aesthetic Ideology: Language, Gender and Political Economy in Revolution* (Cambridge: Cambridge University, 1993), 25. Furniss reads

refutation of the French Revolution's claim to deploy the power of terror as, precisely, irresistible, able to cast its enemies into a state of passive despair. Political sovereignty in the 1759 text already has a "connection with terror" (67). While very few can fully resist responding to a dread of the sovereign, it is "young persons little acquainted with the world, and who have not been used to approach men in power," who are "commonly struck with an awe which takes away the free use of their faculties" (67). Burke in 1790 will be acutely concerned that the British not be encouraged to disable themselves in this way, and is accordingly sparing, even after 1793, in affording France the effective power of terror. The compound emotions gathered around the theory of the sublime (fear, terror, dread, horror, and so on), which weaken the force of terror singly conceived even as Burke argues for its role as the dominant emotion, will function after 1789 as ready and able to resist the French state's attempt to arrogate to itself the absolute power of death, which Burke (in 1759) twice refers to as the "king of terrors" (60, 100). Burke's early habit of twinning terror with other, related emotion words suggests the availability of subtle shades of rational comparison and distinction among near synonyms, promising even while withholding the "clear representations" (63) that portend a weakening of the sublime. The Reign of Terror would have carried a lot less conviction if it had been called the Reign of Fear, or Terror, or Horror and/or Dread.

The second source of delight in terror comes from a recognition of our shared human nature. And here, too, the sliding scale or slippery slope imaged in the inabsolute distinctions between words in the fear-terror cluster plays its part. Burke in 1759 is little interested, if at all, in the state of absolute terror: here there would be no place for the sublime. But whereas Kant is adamant that adequate distance is a prerequisite for the disinterested arousal of the protomoral sense (or something analogous to it) in the properly developed individual, who is thus assured of his capacity for transcending given experience, Burke offers a more exclusively sensationalist account in which distance and proximity shift through time without severing person from person (as the moral experience does), instead revealing us as participants in shared sensations ordained as such by our common human nature. Burke thus does not endorse Dennis's strong distinction (implicitly an educational-class distinction), as Kant does, between those who are and are not capable of feeling the sublime. The imagination, as based in the senses, is shared,

---

this work ethic as Burke's contribution to the making of the middle class. It implicitly assumes that one has a choice about how much one works.

though it differs in degree according to habit and natural sensibility (17, 21). This means that the bond between persons is never broken and that the experience of the sublime is open to all, even as it is differently distributed. The "delight" felt in beholding the sufferings of others is not, for Burke, caused by our own immunity (though immunity is required to enjoy it), but by the inherence of sociability itself, the "bond of sympathy" (46) whose operation Kant would later make into the limited, hypothetical universal that is the aesthetic judgment concerning the beautiful. So, for Burke, beholding the sufferings of others elicits pity as part of delight: the delight seems (though he never quite says this) to come from the onset of shared concern, and it reposes in our common nature. Again, this is exemplified in Aristotle's account of the response to tragedy as a compound response, fear-terror (*phobos*) and pity. These emotions always come together, and they can do so precisely because, in the classical drama, one is looking from a distance. Powerful emotions minimize the distance but cannot do away with it. We can feel terror with pity, or with delight, where in direct experience terror alone might overpower us and leave no room for other emotions. The further away the source of terror, the more apt it is to stimulate horror (looking from a distance at an event); the closer it comes, the more potentially terrible it is. The horror-terror distinction is one of degree rather than kind; both may be allied with a measure of "tranquility" (34, 136). This, for Burke as well as for Kant, is the key to the experience of the sublime. But for Burke it is more explicitly theatrical.

Burke's argument was not uncontested. Richard Payne Knight, taking issue with Burke but also implicitly with Dennis, argues that the sublime has nothing to do with terror, because terror is either real and all-powerful or it is nothing, that is, something else.[55] Fear is not sublime or uplifting but humiliating, and to take pleasure in it is as unnatural "as it would be for a man to share in the triumph or the feast of the lion, of which he was himself the victim and the prey" (367). In finding nature sublime, it is power to which we respond, not terror (370). Experiencing that power firsthand can produce only "abject fear" (372). Anyone who does not feel this—and there may be such persons—is not feeling terror. These things are only sublime "in the personifications of poetry" (374). Achilles is sublime to us, but "to the Trojans he was only terrible" (375). Knight is writing after the efflorescence of the gothic novel, whose "terrific and horrific monsters and hobgoblins" (384) he blames

---

55. Knight, *An Analytical Inquiry into the Principles of Taste*, 4th ed. (London, 1808), 338.

on Burke. But his point is telling, in that it attacks the slippage between literature and life that Dennis and Burke appear to condone and even encourage. He further erodes the integrity of terror as a psycho-aesthetic category by invoking the common language, wherein *terrible* and *terribly* were already established as simple emphatics.[56] So a terrible rider is a bad one, but being a terribly good horseman is a good thing; similarly, being damned clever or damned stupid has nothing to do with damnation (376).[57] Samuel Johnson's 1755 *Dictionary* cites one meaning of terrible as "colloquial hyperbole" and glosses terribly as "violently; very much." But his examples still show some connection between terrible and the associations of terror "proper": crying terribly and feeling terrible cold or terrible fear. It seems that the full evolution of *terrible* to indicate, in common use, mere emphasis of any thing or quality, happens (in English) during (or before) the eighteenth century, and it is well under way by the time that the Jacobins are taken to be reinstating a serious understanding of the power of terror.[58] The dilution of *terrible* from *terribilis* to being merely emphatic may be taken to accompany the weakening of terror from its potentially all-conquering place at the top of the fear-terror lexicon to its sharing of space with horror, dread, wonder, astonishment, and the rest, as it did in the uses of *deinos* in classical Greece. Horror is the most significant of the alternatives, since it is a stronger term than astonishment or awe, and also offers itself as a contrast to terror in terms of the distance assumed: horror at seeing another undergoing what to him is terror. But if this distinction is being attempted, it is by no means observed by all, and it is still not consensual. Johnson does not observe any such distinction in describing *horrour* as "terror mixed with detestation." A still weaker sense is that of "gloom; dreariness"; and *horrid*, while signifying "hideous" and "dreadful," also

56. Recall that Socrates (*Protagoras*, 341A–B), commenting on the use of *deinos*, says that this usage is one we should not employ, implying perhaps that people were indeed doing so.

57. Uvedale Price is Knight's target here. Price reasoned that even though *deinos* can mean also "what is excellent, or striking," such a response is still to be attributed to terror, which "is the cause of all that is most striking." See Price, *An Essay on the Picturesque, as Compared with the Sublime and Beautiful*, new ed. (London, 1796), 113.

58. So, too, is the parody of claiming the power of terror, and not only in Addison (*Spectator* 44). In *The Guardian* 143 (August 21, 1713), Steele pokes fun at the "Terrible Club," a group of young men setting out to "strike terror" into their fellow citizens by walking around with long swords. Steele takes this as a sign of their own "apprehensions." In no. 141 (September 26, 1713), he reports that as a result of his satire "the Terrible Club is quite blown up," although he has had offers to employ its members as household ornaments, whereby the "man of terror" might "make a figure in the polite world."

appears in its trivial sense as "unpleasing: in women's cant"—exactly as Austen will use it in *Northanger Abbey*. Notably, *horrible* does not yet have its modern sense as a trivial emphatic (as in "I had a horrible day"), but *terrible* does, with its function as "colloquial hyperbole." It appears that the fear-terror vocabulary is being sorted into usages that are almost those of modern-day speakers, but not quite. It also seems that modern-day uses have not gone any further toward convincing disambiguation.

Johnson indeed records confusion rather than precision all across the fear-terror cluster. The verb *to fear* is thus to dread, to consider with apprehensions of terror, to be afraid of, to live in horror, and to be anxious. The noun *fear* is dread, horror, anxiety, awe, dejection of mind, and terror. *Dread*, in its turn, is fear, terror, affright, horror, and awe. Each term describes the others; Johnson feels no need to record (or indeed suggest) any limits on what can substitute for what, or when and how. If this listing registers mid-eighteenth-century usages, then we can surmise that there are no effective constraints on freedom of movement across the entire spectrum of fear-terror words. Johnson's cited authorities are (as is well known) largely literary, and among them Shakespeare, Milton, Pope, and Dryden are popular. *Horrour*—Johnson's spelling—has (like *anxiety*) a medicalized sense, now lost, perhaps a ghostly residue of the somatic intensities of the classical fear-terror vocabularies. But the general sense is one of fertile imprecision. *Terrour*, as in its modern use, can be either an emotion (fear communicated or received) or the thing that is "the cause of fear." It is both unstable in itself and exchangeable for other allied terms.[59]

Johnson's frequent citations of Shakespeare and Milton, of course, are evidence of the recent emergence of these two writers as the twin Parnassi of English literature. But in the history of the fear-terror cluster in English, both are relatively sparing in their references to extreme emotions. On the evidence of the concordance, Shakespeare uses *terror* or *terrors* forty-one times, *terrible* twenty-eight times, and *terribly* three times. *Horror* or *horrors* occurs nineteen times, *horrible* twenty-four times, and *horribly* twice. *Horrid* appears seventeen times, and *horridly* twice. The active verbal forms horrify and terrify do not occur at all.[60] *Dread* and *dreadful* are more than twice as common as either the

59. The latest *Oxford English Dictionary* (OED) records *horror* from 1382, a hundred years before *terror*. The trivial sense of horror appears only from 1879. *Horrible* appears from 1303 and is already just a "strong intensive" by 1464, and by 1513 clearly a trivial intensifier. *Terrible* is recorded from 1400 and is a trivial intensifier from 1628.

60. Marvin Spevack, ed., *The Harvard Concordance to Shakespeare* (Cambridge, MA: Belknap Press of Harvard University Press, 1974).

horror or terror forms, with *dread* more frequently verbal or adjectival rather than substantive. But all of these terms are far less frequent than fear and its derivatives, which are listed many hundreds of times (though many are, of course, weak senses). Shakespeare, in other words, is not heavily invested in intensifying and diversifying emotion words, seeming for the most part happy enough with the relatively commonplace *fear* as his workhorse, with *dread* as the preferred intensifier. When *horror* and *terror* do occur, they are thus all the more striking. The dominance of *fear* over *terror* is surprisingly consonant with the habits of other Renaissance dramatists, even those known to be adapting the Senecan tradition for the English theater. Heywood's *Thyestes*, a 1560 translation of one of the goriest of Seneca's tragedies, uses *terror* only twice and *horrible* just once; *horror* and *terrible* do not occur at all. *Fear* (with *affright* and *affrayed*) is much more common; *dread* and *dreadful* somewhat more common. The range of fear-terror words in Seneca's Latin is rather wider: *metus* and *timor* dominate, with single instances of (among others) *terror*, *horror*, and *pavor* in their nominal forms.[61] In one passage, dense with extreme emotion words, Seneca's *pavor* and *metus* both come into English as *dred*, and *terror* survives as it is; but the strongly physical sense of *crinis . . . stetit horrores* is rendered descriptively ("my . . . haire . . . standes up") without the word *horror*.[62] At another exemplary moment at the beginning of Act 3 of *Hercules on Oeta*, Seneca packs seven different fear-terror words into seven lines (706–12); the English translator resolves them into three: *feare*, *terrour*, and *dread* (219). The variety, and thus the heady task of making discriminations (or choosing to assume synonymy) in translation, is diminished in the English version.[63]

This reductive tendency in the transmission of Latin into English may be in part attributed to the staged nature of the English plays. It is thought that Seneca's original plays were not performed but read or recited, perhaps even by a single speaker. Since we are thus not shown what is happening, it might have seemed more important to play up the emotional

61. I draw here on Alice Louise Austin, "A Critical Concordance to the *Thyestes* of Seneca" (MA diss., University of Illinois, 1914).

62. Seneca, *Tragedies, II*, ed. and trans. John G. Fitch (Cambridge, MA: Harvard University Press, 2004), ll. 920–69; Thomas Newton, ed., *Seneca: His Tenne Tragedies* (1581); reprint, edited and introduced by T. S. Eliot (Bloomington: Indiana University Press, 1964), 87–88.

63. This appears also to be the pattern in Alexander Nevyle's translation of Seneca's *Oedipus*, which is included in Newton's 1581 edition. By my count, *fear* or *fearful* occurs thirty times, *dread* or *dreadful* fourteen times, but *horror* or *horrible* only six times and *terror* or *terrible* only three times.

vocabulary; we have to be told what someone is feeling because we cannot see it. The Senecan texts are also, in the content of their narration, closer than the English ones to the Aristotelian disdain for spectacle: better to tell than to show. But recitation can also register emotion, so that a purely formal-generic explanation of the differences may not be enough. For some reason, the English range of fear-terror terms is narrower than the Latin, and remains so even in Shakespeare, who does not, for example, use *terrify*, *horrify*, *panic*, *anxiety*, or *anxious*, and uses *horror* and *terror* relatively lightly. Like Shakespeare, Alexander Nevyle (in his 1560 adaptation of Seneca's *Oedipus*) prefers *dread* over *terror*. In Chaucer, *terror* and *terrible* do not appear at all, *drede* again being the favored term. When we come to Milton, horror-terror words show a relative increase when measured against fear words, although *fear* is still much more common, with *dread* still remaining twice as frequent as *terror* or *horror*.[64] All of these findings lead to a perhaps surprising conclusion: that the heyday of *fear* and *terror* in the lexicon of literary English comes not with the blood and guts of the Elizabethan stage in its so-called gothic or barbaric phase but in the age of elegance and decorum taking shape around 1700. It comes, moreover, as a confused and confusing lexicon, wherein *terror* may be accompanied by or substituted for a wide range of fear-terror and associated words, resulting in a weakening of the absolute sense of the term as indicating the highest degree of existential threat. *Terror* comes also as an important word in aesthetics, where it is allied with an experience of pleasure. A pleasurable aesthetics of terror is exactly what was deemed blasphemous in witnessing the collapse of the World Trade Center towers in 2001, but it could not be completely suppressed, not least owing to its updated incarnations in the movie industry. Before Burke and Dennis and their kind, there was another decisive effort to rein in the jumbled semantics of terror, one to which they were perhaps already responding; another effort, much more pervasively distributed, to engineer the common language toward a monolithic and authoritarian usage of the term: the King James Bible.

---

64. Although Milton is quite fond of *horrid*, as in this masterfully compact line from *Paradise Lost*: "Horrid to think, how horrible to feel" (11:465). See William Ingram and Kathleen Swaim, ed., *A Concordance to Milton's English Poetry* (Oxford, UK: Clarendon Press, 1972).

3

Putting Terror into the Fear of God

The King James Bible

The currency of terror as describing an aesthetic experience was well established in English by the early 1700s, in part thanks to a growing propensity to translate Aristotle's *phobos* (paired with *pity* as a constitutive response to tragic drama) as *terror* rather than *fear*. But there is another formative tradition that has contributed to the present state of the common language, which probably owes comparatively little to Aristotle and his kind: translations of the Bible into English. The English Bible, before the relatively recent spate of efforts at user-friendlier versions, usually meant the King James Version or "authorized" version (commonly abbreviated, here and henceforth, as the KJV). But the KJV rested on the shoulders of a number of earlier Bibles (some of which continued to be printed after the first edition of KJV), English and others, whose word choices it variously adopted, adapted, or, in some cases, simply ignored. Historical ironies abound. William Tyndale was strangled and burned at the stake for heresy in 1536, but it is estimated that some 86 percent of the KJV's New Testament and 76 percent of the Old

Testament is based on Tyndale's Bible.[1] The consortium of scholars and clerics convened to do King James's bidding seems to have responded favorably to Tyndale's proclivity for using plain Saxon words to reach ordinary people, even as it took care not to reproduce his antihierarchical *congregation* instead of the mandated *church*.

The Bible, in all its versions, has a lot to say about fear and terror. Corey Robin notes that fear is "the first emotion experienced by a character in it."[2] Newly fallen Adam, when he hides from the face of God at Genesis 3:10, says "I was afraid, because I was naked" (KJV). It is arguable that fear is blurred with shame in the English version; but only after the Fall are Adam and Eve obliged to deal continually with extreme emotions. Most of the English Bibles here opt for *afraid* (Wycliffe has *drede*) as the translation of Vulgate's *timui*, the Greek *phobos* term, and the relatively common Hebrew *yare*. *Terror* is not yet on the scene, but it is on its way. *Terror* is not one of Tyndale's plain Anglo-Saxon words but a Latinate one, which may have come into English by way of Norman French. It is not an important word in English Bible translations before the KJV. Even in the Latin Bible, the fourth-century Vulgate, *terror* is not the favored word for extreme intimidation. Among the various terms describing emotions in the fear-terror cluster, the most common is *timor*, with more than two hundred examples in the noun form alone. *Terror* appears forty-eight times (with twenty-seven uses of *terribilis*, terrible). *Formido* figures thirty-one times, *pavor* more infrequently. Virgil's most commonly used word, *metus*, appears only three times. *Pavor*, in classical Latin, is probably the most extreme state of feeling, the one most closely conforming to our terror.[3] But in three books (Job, Jeremiah, Ezekiel) where the Vulgate uses *pavor* eight times, KJV only once translates it as *terror*: it prefers *fear* (six times), *pain* (twice), and *trembling* (once). On such evidence, one would not predict that the KJV is in the terror business. Indeed, Mikkel Thorup lists fifteen instances of the Vulgate's *terror*, of which only three are taken over by the KJV.[4] And yet in Job alone, the KJV uses *terror* or *terrors* eight times, and only two of these instances are supported by the Vulgate. Earlier English Bibles are far less emphatic. In the 1560 Geneva Bible, only two of these eight cases employ *terror*;

1. Naomi Tadmor, *The Social Universe of the English Bible: Scripture, Society and Culture in Early Modern England* (Cambridge: Cambridge University Press, 2010), 16.

2. Corey Robin, *Fear: The History of a Political Idea* (Oxford: Oxford University Press), 1.

3. *Horror* is much less common in the Vulgate (see note 7 in this chapter).

4. Mikkel Thorup, *An Intellectual History of Terror: War, Violence and the State* (London: Routledge, 2010), 78–80.

the other six prefer *fear*. Where KJV reads *terror* on five occasions in the Pentateuch, Tyndale's 1530 text has *fear* four times and *terrible* only once. The Geneva Bible opts for *fear* all five times. The first KJV use of terror is at Genesis 35:5, "and the terror of God was upon the cities." This comes directly from the Vulgate *terror Dei*, and is the same reading as the 1609–1610 OT Douai-Rheims translation (henceforth DR) published in France by and for Catholics. The corresponding Hebrew *hit-tat* is also a strong word. Septuagint has *phobos*, and Luther *Furcht Gottes*. Other English Bibles come closer to Luther: Tyndale, Matthew (essentially a reprint of Tyndale) Geneva, Coverdale, Bishops, and Great Bibles all have "fear of God." Wycliffe again has *drede*.

At Deuteronomy 32:25, the KJV has an interesting conjunction of external threat with interior emotion: "The sword without, and terror within." Here DR has "fearfulness," while this time it is Luther who opts for the stronger term, *Schrecken*, perhaps himself following the Vulgate's *pavor*. Hebrew has *eymah* (with a range of plausible translations along the fear-terror spectrum), and Septuagint, as before, has *phobos*. Wycliffe's translation, again, has *dread*, and all the other English Bibles (Tyndale, Matthew, Geneva, Coverdale, Bishops, and Great) opt for *fear*. At Leviticus 26:16, the KJV's *terror* is one element of a menu of afflictions God promises for the disobedient: "I will even appoint over you terror, consumption and the burning ague." The key Hebrew word, closest to terror, is different again: *behalah*. DR's "poverty and burning heat" follows the Vulgate's *egestate et ardore*, whereas other English texts opt for a variety of terms: *madness*, *burning* (Wycliffe), *vexations*, *swellings*, and *fevers* (Tyndale, Matthew), *swellings* and *fevers* (Coverdale), *fearfulness* (Geneva, Bishops, Great). The KJV is again notable in its predilection for *terror*, perhaps once again following Luther's relatively strong *Schrecken* rather than the Vulgate's Latin.

We cannot, as I have said, claim hard-and-fast distinctions between the intensities of fear-terror words in any of the languages of the past; indeed, the very functioning of this vocabulary depends on a high level of duplication, overlap, and interchangeability.[5] *Furcht* and *Scheck(en)*, for instance, imply a difference in degree and demonstrativeness, but it is not an unambiguous one, and there are no simple rules of thumb

---

5. Carl Darling Buck, in his very useful *A Dictionary of Selected Synonyms in the Principal Indo-European Languages* (Chicago: University of Chicago Press, 1988), includes only *anxiety* and *fear* from the many words in the fear-terror cluster and inevitably lists only a few among many possible alternatives and affiliates (which are never quite synonyms).

for limiting any of the numerous fear-terror words in Greek, Latin, or Hebrew to single, exclusive meanings. Perhaps early English *dread* denoted just as powerful an emotion as later English *terror*. *Fear*, however, if only by virtue of its relatively commonplace occurrence, might be enough to signify something more ordinary than *terror*, and it is fear that appealed to most of the early English Bible translators (as it did to Shakespeare) when they were faced with a choice of words. The Geneva Bible, the KJV's most widely read competitor, makes use of *terror* only eighteen times to the KJV's forty-five, although it comes a little closer in its liking for *terrible* (thirty-nine times compared to the KJV's fifty-one uses). The KJV is also somewhat in advance of canonical literature in its use of *terrify* or *terrified* (nine times), which is absent in Shakespeare and appears only four times in Milton's poetry (although it also appears in Milton's prose).[6]

Four of these nine uses of *terrify* or *terrified* occur in the KJV New Testament. The God of love and charity, often assumed to be the presiding figure in the Christian texts, still favors bursts of old-time terror, at least as understood by the KJV compilers. The *Oxford English Dictionary* (OED) gives *terrify* as first recorded in 1575, in a translation from Luther, and again in 1578, in a Christian prayer book. On this evidence, the new active verb appealed first to the clerics. Where the KJV NT has *terrify* or *terrified*, Matthew and Geneva range among *fear, fearing, abashed*, and *afraid*. These reflect the Greek *phobein* and the Latin *terrere*. On three of the four occasions the KJV is following DR, but at Luke 24:37, the translators pass over DR's use of *troubled* and opt again for *terrified*. When *terror* appears as a noun (three times) in NT, a similar pattern emerges. At Romans 13:3, both Geneva and Matthew read *fear* where the KJV finds *terror*. Bishops and the Great Bible also use fear words, as does Coverdale. Wycliffe has *dread*, Luther *fürchten*. (DR has "Princes are no fear to the good work," following Vulgate *non*

6. A word of caution here: Online concordances, most centrally the online *Study Bible* (my main source here) with its polyglot array of sources and translations, are an invaluable resource for working on the scriptures, and I am much indebted to them here. (The Study Bible is available at http://studybible.info.) But source texts for the entries (as often in print concordances) are sometimes not specified. DR analogues are especially unreliable, being based on a later edition that has, in some places, used the KJV as a copy text. All critical references I make to DR in the following analysis have been confirmed by comparison with the 1609–1610 OT and the 1589 NT edition produced by William Fulke, which prints parallel texts of DR and the Bishops Bible. The 1602 (revised) Bishops was the (working) copy text for the KJV translators, and where my argument relies on a significant comparison with Bishops, the 1602 text has been used. The KJV citations have been checked against the 1611 first edition.

timori). The KJV is alone here in opting for *terror*. Geneva prefigures the KJV *terror* at 2 Corinthians 5:11, but Matthew and DR again have *fear*, suggesting that the stronger word appeals to KJV's translators wherever they can find a precedent. At 1 Peter 3:14, DR again has *fear*; this time it is the Bishops and Great Bibles that read *terror*, which is what the KJV translators select. (These are all *phobos* words in Greek, *timor* in Vulgate.) Against the trend, the KJV does not pick up a precursor's use of *terror* at 1 Peter 3:6. Here the KJV reads *amazement* for Geneva and Bishops's *terror*; the weaker sense is supported by the other English Bibles' choices of *shadows, disturbance, perturbation,* and *trouble.*

OT uses of *terror* are much more common, as might be expected, and the KJV, as has been said, is ahead of Geneva in its count of (OT) terror words, which stands at forty-two.[7] DR 1609–1610 (OT only), according to a word search, has thirty-five uses in its text (along with another eleven in its marginalia and commentaries, i.e., not the result of translation), and thus comes close to the KJV. The two together suggest a common interest in ramping up the language of extreme emotion. The KJV is especially fond of *terror* and *terrors* in two books of the Bible: Job (nine times) and Ezekiel (twelve). Isaiah has four occurrences but makes heavy use of *terrible* (eleven times). There are interesting coincidences and noncoincidences in the respective uses of *terror* in DR and KJV. One would expect that as the more Latinate of the two, and the one explicitly based on the Vulgate, DR would show a greater inclination to terror than the KJV, but this does not seem to be the case. DR overlaps with only two of the KJV Job's nine uses of *terror* or *terrors* (almost as many as its uses of *fear*), and with none of its three uses of *terrible*. In two places, to be sure, the KJV does not accord with DR's *terror* word (25:2, 37:2). But in three cases, there seems to be no English precursor at all for the KJV's *terror*. One of these is especially notable. At 18:14, KJV has Bildad foretell of the sinner (Job) that "his confidence shall be rooted out of his tabernacle, and it shall bring him to the king of terrors." This is the phrase that Edmund Burke and many others will relish as a phrase describing death. But it is not clear what is meant here (18:11 had threatened that "terrors shall make him afraid on every side"). Geneva and Bishops have "king of fear," and Luther, the closest corresponding text, has *zum Könige*

---

7. Interestingly, *horror* is much less common, with only four uses, along with six instances of *horrible* and two of *horribly*. Even the Vulgate is parsimonious, with ten instances of *horror* and seven of *horribilis*. DR translates the Vulgate's *horror* directly into English on all of these occasions, although it opts for *fearful* and *dreadful*, where Ezekiel twice has *horribilis* (1:18, 1:22). The DR translators do use *horrible* a few times in their commentary but not heavily.

des Schreckens.[8] But DR follows the Vulgate in reading the phrase as a personification and a simile: "Let destruction as a king tread upon him." Coverdale, Matthew, and Great read just "bring him to the king" (closer to the Greek). Again, the KJV prefers the stronger (and more poetic) terminology. The Hebrew *ballalah* corresponds to five of the KJV's *terrors*, suggesting a strong reading of this word by the translators. But Hebrew *pachad* (another, perhaps even stronger, term) appears ten times in Job and is only once translated as *terror* (31:23); elsewhere, it is read as *fear, dread, dominion, thunder.*[9] The appetite for *terror* (nine cases) is thus distinct but not indiscriminate. The KJV translators do refuse some opportunities to pull out all the rhetorical stops and show some flair in varying their vocabulary.

Ezekiel presents an especially interesting case for translators' choices. Of the KJV's twelve uses of *terror* or *terrors* in this book alone, only four agree with DR 1609, and all four are in the formulaic or repetitious section of 32:23–32 where the same afflictions are visited upon different cities one after another. All these cases are supported by strong words in the Vulgate (*terror, pavor, formido*). But in the seven cases where the KJV has *terror*, DR has *fear* or *fearing* in three of them. DR thus produces a more modulated and varied rhetoric in its cumulative assent to God's power.[10] And in six of the seven cases, Luther (1545) uses the fear verb *fürchten*, with terrible power (*schreckliche Gewalt*) only once. Compared with both other translations, the KJV again seems to show an appetite for the higher-intensity word. Indeed, of the five other uses of *terror* in Ezekiel, one (26:17) is not found in any other English Bible, two appear again only in Bishops, and two others only in Bishops and Geneva. Furthermore, Luther uses the strong word (*Schrecken*) in only one of these instances (26:21), and in three of them uses no clearly marked fear-terror word at all. Only one of these five cases is plausibly supported by the Greek or by the Vulgate (*phobos, formidabant* at 26:17).

---

8. Olivétan's 1535 French Bible, the only early French translation I have been able to consult (in online facsimile), has *marcher vers le Roi epouvantable.*

9. Marvin H. Pope, *The Anchor Bible: Job* (New York: Doubleday, 1965), endorses all the KJV's uses of *terror*, including "king of terrors" (whom he identifies as the underworld god Mot), and adds three more where the KJV has *fear* or *dread.* I am not competent to sort out the balance of established KJV precedent and source texts here.

10. In comparing the two Bibles as a whole, there is also distinct evidence of KJV's softening DR's rhetoric, as it did with *Job*'s *pachad.* I count thirteen cases in which KJV OT does *not* repeat DR's uses of *terror.* (But see Thorup, *Intellectual History of Terror,* at note 4 in this chapter). In *Jeremiah* KJV's four cases of *terror* agree with three in DR, but DR has three more where KJV prefers *fear* to *terror.* One of DR's *terror*s that is not in KJV occurs in the NT (Luke 21:11).

The Hebrew may play a role here. No fewer than eight of Ezekiel's terrors are translations of the Hebrew *chittyth*, which is a strong word and
one that occurs nowhere else (in this form) in the Hebrew Bible. Three
of the others correlate with Hebrew *ballahah*, which has a somewhat
weaker signification (alarm, destruction) and is thus here upgraded by
the KJV's translators. In the other case (21:12), the Hebrew reads *magar*
(to be thrown down). We have here an apparently high-intensity Hebrew word being taken to support the English *terror*, which then cap-
tures other (weaker) Hebrew words and often in so doing overrides the
word choices of both Greek and Latin precursors, most other English
Bibles, and Luther. This offers good evidence that at least one translator
among the First Oxford Company (which was assigned Ezekiel) was very
committed to ramping up divine power.

Two books, Job (with nine) and Ezekiel (with twelve), together produce twenty-one (almost half) of the KJV's forty-five uses of *terror*, but
they were not the work of the same primary translators: Job was the
work of the First Cambridge Company, and Ezekiel of the First Oxford
Company. Once again, we can only speculate about how much contact, if any, there was between the two groups and when it might have
happened.[11] The word *terrible*, a relatively familiar English word (OED
from 1430), has fifty-one uses in the KJV, all but one of them in the
OT.[12] At this point, *terrible* does not yet have the function of a simple
intensifier, applicable to almost anything (as in "I had a terrible day at
the office") but is the adjectival form of terror. Ezekiel is once again
interesting here. *Terrible* appears five times, four times as the formulaic "the terrible of the nations." Luther here opts for *die Tyrannen der
Heiden* (tyrants among the heathen). The KJV follows Geneva and Bishops in all four cases. The Vulgate is less emphatic, although the Greek is
stronger. DR 1609 again varies the language, reading "strongest of the
gentiles" (28:7 and 30:11), "the most cruel" (31:12), and "invincible"
(32:12). The fifth KJV case is striking, opting for *terrible* in a case where
the range of other choices is especially broad. Hebrew *yare* (to fear, re-
vere, stand in awe of), one of the most common words in the Bible and
one not easily rendered by any single English word, appears elsewhere

11. Gordon Campbell, *Bible: The Story of the King James Version, 1611–2011* (Oxford: Oxford University Press, 2010), 57, suggests that there might have been consultation between the separate companies. The DR NT was available both in its own editions
(from 1582) and in William Fulke's 1589 parallel text of Bishops and DR.

12. DR 1609–1610 OT uses (Latinate) *terrible* only thirty-six times in its text, but
another twenty-one times in its commentaries and marginalia. This might suggest an
appetite among the DR English editors for the high-intensity word.

as *horribilis* (Vulgate), *schrecklich* (Luther), *dreadful, wonderful,* and *most pure.* Taken together with *terror* and *terrors,* these uses of *terrible* make Ezekiel one of the most rhetorically violent books in the KJV.

Psalms (worked on by the First Cambridge Company) includes ten instances of *terrible,* a fifth of the KJV's count. All of these correspond to Hebrew *yare,* and this seems to be the strongest correlation with any of the source or precursor words. The Vulgate has *terribilis* four times but also *mirabilium, magnalia,* and on three occasions no equivalent at all. Luther uses *schrecklich, wunderlich, Macht,* or nothing. The Greek has *phoberos* seven times and *thaumastos* three times. Among the English Bibles, Geneva and DR are the most common precursors, each with six uses of *terrible;* Bishops has five. In one case, DR is the only sharer (one wonders whether the KJV translators had access to the DR 1609–1610 text in the last stages of their work), and in another case (65:5) there are no English precedents at all.[13] Isaiah (like Ezekiel, the work of the First Oxford Company) uses *terrible* eleven times. Five of these are Hebrew *yare,* the others *ariyts,* a less common word (for, roughly, awe inspiring). Here, the Vulgate refrains from any fear-terror word on six occasions, elsewhere varying, and on nine occasions the Greek uses no equivalent word. Luther, too, is modest here: no fear-terror words appear in five of these eleven lines, and the others vary (*Wunder, greulich*), but *schrecklich* does not appear at all. Emphatically, seven of these eleven KJV *terribles* are unsupported by any other English precursor. Two agree only with Geneva and DR, one with four others (not including Geneva), and one with Geneva only. This last (64:3) is interesting: all other versions except Greek *tromos* stress the miraculous rather than the threatening: *mirabilia, Wunder, wondrous strange, marvelous things.* Isaiah's four uses of terror overlap with only one English version: DR 1609 reads *terrour* at 10:33, following Vulgate. Two of these four translations are based on Hebrew words that each appear only once (here) in the entire Hebrew Bible, although three are *phobos* forms in Greek.

It should now be clear that we do not have definitive evidence for assessing the exact origins of terror choices in the KJV, and we have also seen that it is not the simple consensus term for a closely restricted group of foreign words. There was probably no single reason the various translators did or did not use terror when they did, and it is wholly plausible that each thought that good scholarly criteria were behind many or most

---

13. Given that the KJV companies were using so many Bibles in different languages, it is hard to believe that they would not have taken pains to see what their closest-in-time and leading doctrinal competitors had done in DR 1609–1610.

of the decisions they made. They had, after all, a near monopoly on the national talent pool and many shelves of previous translations in various languages to work with. Why, then, might the consortium of translators have chosen to play up *terror* over good old-fashioned *fear* and *dread*? *Dread* as a noun appears only seven times in the KJV and only twice as a verb; *dreadful* is used eight times. The count for *terror* and *terrible* is forty-five and fifty-one. This contrasts with a roughly contemporary icon of the national language, the collected works of Shakespeare, where *dread* appears fifty-four times (eleven times as a noun, otherwise mostly adjectival) and *dreadful* sixty-eight times, as against forty-one *terrors* and twenty-eight *terribles*.[14] Fear words, of course, are still much the most common among the KJV's (and Shakespeare's) renderings of states of personal anxiety and intimidation, and the samples do not support the idea of a conscious and comprehensive campaign to establish *terror* as inevitably the go-to word for signifying what God inspires in or visits upon the unworthy. Nonetheless, the KJV translators are evidently fonder of terror words than their English precursors; they are moving the index of violence and the response to violence away from fear or dread and toward terror.

Little is known about the exact deliberations of any of the six groups of translators, forty-nine men in all, who divided up the scriptures and sent their separate decisions with two representatives each (twelve in all) to the general meeting, at which the final decisions were to be made. Although the Bishops Bible was used as the working text for revision and was prescribed as the base text in the rules drawn up by Richard Bancroft to guide the translators, the use of other versions was encouraged when they appeared to offer better readings. Indeed, different groups seem to have taken different translations as their preferred models at various times, and even within the same group there is evidence that certain precursors were more favored at some times than others.[15] The Second Oxford Company was entrusted with the first translation or revision of Luke, with its two uses of *terrify*, but the Pauline texts were worked on by the Second Westminster Company. The other two NT uses of *terrify* thus emerged as a happy coincidence, a convergence of scholarly decisions, or the result of a good case made by the one group persuading the committee of the whole, or perhaps as the result of some

---

14. To be sure, the monosyllabic dread may be more useful in metrical language, but Shakespeare was adept enough to choose his words, as he did in having the failing Lear threaten to shore up his kingship with "the terrors of the earth" (II.iv.282).

15. See Olga S. Opfell, *The King James Bible Translators* (Jefferson, NC: McFarland, 1982), for an account of the six groups. Bancroft's rules are reprinted at 139–40.

interim consultation between two or more groups (of the sort which is known to have occurred throughout the process).

It is tempting to suggest (or perhaps to state the obvious) that these scholars and men of the church were also sensitive to ambient social pressures in rendering and revising the English Bible. Naomi Tadmor, for example, has shown in some detail how KJV assimilates a wide range of Hebrew words (in particular) to the single English word *prince*; and Laura Knoppers finds a similar predilection for the word *majesty*.[16] Tadmor does admit that most of the fourteen different Hebrew words Englished as *prince* had already been simplified in the Septuagint's *archon* and the Vulgate's *princeps*. But nothing formally required the KJV's translators to follow either convention. In this case, according to Tadmor's findings (128), the KJV actually reduces DR's use of *prince* or *princes* from 917 to 423, but this count still far exceeds what had appeared in earlier English Bibles. Both the Great and Tyndale-Matthew Bibles have about half of the KJV's count. Tadmor suggests that the consolidation of monarchical authority was very much on the minds of the KJV consortium, and that the same priority is visible elsewhere in the work of Lancelot Andrewes, one of its leaders.[17] And indeed, after the testing experiences of the 1603 succession of James I and the alarms of the 1605 Gunpowder Plot, not to mention the longer-term evolution of nation-state consolidation (whose problems are also represented in Shakespeare's plays) and interfaith rivalries, it might seem unlikely that even the most disinterested scholars could have been immune to concerns about how their decisions might be received by a king who was paying close attention to the new Bible project. In the 1611 Epistle Dedicatory, his translators address him directly as "most dread sovereign" and then invoke his "majesty" eleven times in little more than two pages. Rhetorical emphasis alone was not to prove a sufficient persuader in heading off the turbulence of the 1640s, as Thomas Hobbes would recognize, but it was not for want of effort on the part of the king's translators.

Here it might be useful to look more closely at how *terror* is used in the KJV. It is impossible to claim exact distinctions, because the word

16. See Tadmor, *Social Universe*, 119–64; and Laura L. Knoppers, "Translating Majesty: The King James Bible, John Milton, and the English Revolution," in *The King James Bible and the World It Made*, ed. David Lyle Jeffrey (Waco, TX: Baylor University Press, 2011), 29–48.

17. Gillian Brennan, "Patriotism, Language and Power: English Translations of the Bible, 1520–1580," *History Workshop* 27 (1989): 18–36, suggests that even before the KJV, there was a high level of awareness of how the Bible might be employed to teach, in Thomas Cranmer's words, "subjects obedience, love and dread to their princes" (29).

itself is slippery. In my best judgment, *terror* is deployed as an external agency by God himself on eleven occasions and by others on God's behalf on five more: eighteen times in all. In ten cases, including a number of those in Ezekiel (which is often hard to construe), *terror* describes what is felt by persons within themselves—the internal response to threats from the outside. And on six occasions, *terror* seems to be ambiguously either within or without, or both (e.g., Gen. 35:5, "the terror of God was upon the cities"). Other cases can be hard to categorize. Ezekiel 26:17 is a good example. Here the "terror" of the Tyreans over all who sail the seas is what God is going to destroy. It is terror wielded by the city (state), a worldly power that God will bring down. The implication is that God's powers are of a higher order. But then, at 26:21, God's words to Tyre (via the prophet) promise to "make thee a terror, and thou shalt be no more." Geneva has "bring thee to nothing," and Bishops, the only precursor here, has "I will make thee terrors, and thou shalt be no more." Geneva seems to say that God will create terrors to direct at the city in order to destroy it. But the KJV muddies the waters by rendering *terror* in the singular (with the alternative plural reading added in as a marginal note). This inches toward suggesting that Tyre is the source rather than (or as well as) the object of terror; its example thus becomes a terror to other sinners. The slippage is understandable, given that terror is implicitly all of these things: what God wields, what Tyre feels, and what others see in Tyre's fate.

A similar instability appears at 27:36: "Thou shalt be a terror, and never shalt be any more." At 32:30, it is written of the Zidonians that "with their terror they are ashamed of their might," as if terror is principally what they are feeling within themselves. But at 32:26–27, it is the cities themselves who are (or were) the agents of terror over others. The KJV, as has been said, has chosen *terror* to correspond to the (rare) Hebrew *chittyth* but has scrambled the logic. The editor of the Anchor Bible tidies this up by describing the cities as those "who inspired dread" but then has God take over the power of violence at the end, saying, "I will inspire dread" (32:32).[18] The Anchor version of the promised destruction of Tyre at 26:1–21 is interestingly skewed by the KJV precedent and probably by the ambient political rhetoric of the 1990s. The translation itself does not use *terror*, preferring to distinguish what the city

18. Moshe Greenberg, ed., *The Anchor Bible: Ezekiel 21–37* (New York: Doubleday, 1997), 659–60. But Greenberg admits (668) that the logic and syntax of the Hebrew are notably contorted here. Olivétan's 1535 French Bible uses *terreur* only once (Ezek. 32); *craincte* and *frayeur* are the favored terms.

does (inspire "dread") from what others make of it: they are "horrified" and witness Tyre's (hypothetical) destruction as "a horror."[19] But the Anchor's editor's comment discusses the "ascription of terrorization to Tyre" and the prophet's claim that it "inspired terror" (538). Just as *terror* can be switched from what is beheld to what is felt, so *horror* and *terror* can change places, even as *horror* is used to distinguish what is felt from what is seen.

The ambiguity about where terror resides lends it the appeal of flexibility. Ezekiel 32 may be the product of indecisive or deliberate translation, but the effect is the same: terror seems to be everywhere and to come from everywhere, within and without. If the terror generated by the cities is part of God's plan for their eventual punishment, then God is having it both ways, allowing them to terrorize others in order to elicit a yet greater terror belonging only to him. The beholders or sufferers are doubly threatened.[20] The "king of terrors" at Job 18:14, the line that Burke took to be a figure for death, and which is perhaps the most memorable and often repeated *terror* reference in the KJV, is unclear as to whether Job will be brought to death and/or to the God who holds the power of death. Terror floats in a space between life and death, emotion and personification, torture and termination, and it is all the more rhetorically effective in so doing: the undecidability imprints itself on the restless imagination as a form of haunting. Unfortunately, the paucity of the records pertaining to the decisions made by the KJV translators does not allow for a detailed reassembly of evidence about these decisions. The key manuscript, Bodley 1602, which shows the handwritten emendations made at some point (no one is exactly sure when) by the KJV translator(s) to the Bishops text, remains unedited. Nor would its evidence be conclusive about who decided how and when to opt for *terror* as the appropriate English word.[21] But KJV 1611 arguably demonstrates and performs a claim to authority. Its main text is printed in black letter, which suggests the dignity of an "old" document (although within a year it was also printed in roman). Tyndale had appeared in black letter, as did Matthew 1537 and Bishops 1602.[22] But Geneva 1560 was already

---

19. Again, a rare word in the KJV (see note 7, in this chapter).

20. Ezekiel, we know, is a wishful thinker. Tyre never was destroyed by military action, despite his three efforts at promising just that.

21. See David Norton, *A Textual History of the King James Bible* (Cambridge: Cambridge University Press, 2005), 20–28.

22. So, too, *Book of Common Prayer* and Foxe's *Book of Martyrs*. The first never uses *terror* except in citations of the KJV (after 1662). Even the second is relatively parsimonious, with twenty-seven instances of *terror* or *terrors* in its many (many) pages of

in roman, as was DR 1609. Further, the KJV's preference for archaic vocabulary has been commonly noted; it is judged not to have reproduced the language people spoke, but a more formal and distanced English that would have come across as having an impressive gloss of antiquity.[23] At the same time, it radically reduced the role of paratext as compared to, for example, Geneva 1560 or DR 1609. Its pages look "cleaner," so that the words of the scriptures seem to attest to their own transparency without cross-references, interpolations, and learned discussions. This might also suggest a desire to inhibit too much debate and discussion, of the sort that could lead to doubts about the integrity of the text. By using a dagger to indicate a "literal" translation, the editors suggest that these are rare enough to call for special marking, but there is no reflection on the implied nonliteral status of the rest of the text.[24] Parallel lines are used to indicate an alternative translation into English, and in the margins there appear, as explained in 1618, variations: "Where a Hebrew or Greek word admits of two meanings of a suitable kind, the one was to be expressed in the text, the other in the margin."[25] This might well appear to open the floor to the doubters and debaters, and some surely saw it this way: Thomas Fuller commented forty years later that Catholic detractors thought that printing two possible readings cast doubt on the authority of God's word.[26] The KJV translators' preface makes a virtue of this tactic in claiming (following Augustine) that the "Spirit of God" has left room for a certain play of meaning, "so diversity of signification and sense in the margin, where the text is not so clear, must needs do good" by encouraging the reader "not to conclude or dogmatize." The invitation to enter into the text in a critical spirit is, however, not what it seems. In purporting to present the scripture in such a way that it "may speak like itself" even to "the very vulgar," the KJV translators in fact use very few marginalia for alternative readings, and few, if any, of these present a genuine crux. Job 18:14's "king of terrors," for example, does not indicate any radical doubts about the grammar of the sentence. It could be said, then, that the KJV's use of a mark to indicate a literal translation works to add authority rather than to suggest what a modern reader educated in translation theory would take away: that there is little if anything that could ever qualify as a literal translation. The KJV's

---

trials and tortures; but my count is taken from a searchable later edition and may not be fully reliable.

23. See, e.g., Campbell, *Bible*, 73; Jeffrey, *The King James Bible*, 2.
24. Campbell, *Bible*, 63, describes the editorial markings.
25. Cited in Norton, *Textual History*, 10.
26. See Campbell, *Bible*, 126.

sparsely adorned margins speak for an overall confidence in the integrity of the main text, as do the relatively trivial implications of the variants that are acknowledged there. Despite the lip service paid to a permitted variety of readings, this is not a text designed to stimulate serious debate. In this it is quite unlike DR 1609, or Fulke's 1589 parallel NT text, where the commentary often takes up as much space as (or more than) the "main" text. The KJV instead performs its authority by allowing for the incursion of ambiguity as only ever occasional and always minimal.

In the case of *terror*, the most radical suggestion in any of the KJV marginalia is that an alternative reading might be the plural: *terrors*. *Terror* mostly stands alone and unadorned, as if to endorse its power and authority. Among other English Bibles, only DR 1609 comes even close to the KJV in its recourse to terror words, and it does so with presumably more loyalty to its Latin precursor. I have suggested that the KJV companies had an eye on their major rival's word choice, which they gladly took over in their own efforts to work up the power of God and thereby of the godly head of state. It might also be argued that the inclination to terror words is some sort of response to Puritan sentiments in a text designed to appeal as broadly as possible to a doctrinally divided readership. (Puritanism was not a single doctrine, and the matter of Puritan attitudes to terror, whether God's terror or our own terror of God, is itself a matter of scholarly debate). Perhaps more than one motive was at work in giving the KJV a place in the history of how *terror* came to be a commonplace (and slippery) English word. The KJV is certainly not the only begetter of the orgy of terror talk that broke out after 9/11. But it is the case that after 1611 English readers of the Bible had more of the terror of God before them than ever before. Milton has his Messiah take on the divine mantle of terror in setting about his enemies:

> And into terror changed
> His countenance too severe to be beheld
> And full of wrath bent on his enemies. (*Paradise Lost* VI: 824–26)

Kings and princes have followed suit throughout the modern period. This is surely part of the explanation for how and why a theologian like Jonathan Edwards could come to a notion of just terrors as a proper means of bringing people to God; as such, it is also part of the process whereby Edwards's successors could dial up a war on terror in the name of the nation and implicitly in the name of God. The response to terror, of course, is terror itself: bigger, better, faster. In modern times, it has become commonplace in popular political discussion to attribute terror and terrorism to acts against the state rather than to kings or to the gods whom the kings claimed were behind them. But the KJV's terrors are very much in the hands of the mighty, on the earth and in heaven. They still are. Our own generation's nation-states still possess much of the world's power of terror, which they continue to deploy in ways notably prefigured in the good book as it was retranslated and disseminated with unprecedented thoroughness after 1611.

The Bible Dispersed

The reign of James I was significant for taking up the debates about the divine right of kings, and the Bible sponsored by this particular king surely played its part. If we look simply at Ezekiel, we might conclude that it played something of the fool's role, as none of the terrors there prophesied came to pass in the historical record. Ezekiel, not alone among terrormongers, is all talk. But at Romans 13:3, where the KJV alone among the English Bibles opts for terror as describing the power of the ruler, that ruler is at once specified as the "minister of God" and as such a "revenger" upon those doing evil (13:4). The power of the king, in other words, is delegated by God, and the king's terror is God's terror. The dissemination—or not—of terror in the Bible-inflected literature of the seventeenth century thus needs to be understood, as it was surely understood by Thomas Hobbes, not only in the light of God's unmediated power of violence over sinners but also as the implicit prerogative of God's ministers, whether high or low, over the disobedient. At the same time, the evolution of a literary religiosity (or religiose literature) pressured the fear-terror cluster toward a more secular description of emotions. *Pilgrim's Progress* was among the most widely circulating books of its time, and *terror* or *terrors* does feature here ten times, but in only one instance as far as I can see does it reference the terrors deployed by God as opposed to those felt for various reasons by ourselves. *Terrible* appears only four times, *terrify* only once, and *horror* words are completely absent. In other words, even this monument to popular Puritan sensibility travels relatively lightly on the extreme end of the fear-terror spectrum: fear words are roughly twice as common as terror words.

Things are rather different in another widely read adaptation of the Puritan conversion narrative: Defoe's *Robinson Crusoe*. This foundational English novel records an uncommonly varied list of fear-terror words across a wide spectrum of emotional intensities. There are a number of low-energy words like concern, apprehension, uneasiness, and discomposure, evidence of the measured and rational (and highly articulate) response to challenges so typical of Defoe's prudent protagonist. Notable here is the incidence of *anxiety* (three times) and an *anxious* state of mind (seven times). These are scarce words in previous literature: Milton uses the second only twice and the first not at all; Shakespeare uses neither. There is a precedent in Calvin, however, who deploys a varied vocabulary of extreme emotion, including anxiety.[27] In Defoe, persons are at times also astonished, amazed, and stupefied. But terror compounds are about as common as fear words and fright words, with horror words not far behind. By my count (using an online concordance to supplement a traditional reading of the book), Defoe twice refers to the fear of God and twice to the terrors of God. At the same time, there are a few occasions on which his adverbial use of *terribly* strays toward its modern sense as a mere intensifier while still keeping a toehold on its more literal roots. So we have Crusoe being "terribly frighted" and "terribly surpiz'd," and others being "most terribly scar'd" and "terribly amaz'd."[28] Elsewhere, Crusoe puts the goats into a "terrible Fright" (50). The traditional, strong reading of *terribly* survives by a thread but verges on tautology (as in "terribly frighted") unless read in its weakened sense as a simple emphatic.

Unlike *Pilgrim's Progress*, however, *Robinson Crusoe* is a dramatic narrative, one wherein we are often left hanging over exactly how to read the hero's stories and the far-from-consistent morals he draws from them. Defoe's terrors of God are thus not quite Bunyan's; they are part of Crusoe's back-and-forth meditations about the significance of what happens to him and, sometimes, upon how much he can and cannot get away with on his way to what is, after all, an entirely secular salvation at the end of the novel. Sick with fever while alone on his island, he has a nightmare in which *horror* and *terror* tumble over one another in quick succession (70), but they are functions of the dream, at best ambiguously related to any metaphysical origins. Crusoe's account of the earthquake (64–65), in contrast, is of a waking experience of which the string of fear-terror words seems an entirely convincing record of what we might have felt had we been in his position, but it is dominantly a naturalistic or materialistic description with only the faintest if any intimation of divine agency. Crusoe's command of the fear-terror lexicon, as reflecting

27. See William J. Bouwsma, *John Calvin: A Sixteenth-Century Portrait* (Oxford: Oxford University Press, 1988), 32–48, for a good account of Calvin's understanding of the power of anxiety (Latin *anxietas, solicitudo*; French *angoisse, solicitude*). Calvin was not much given to terror, although his later critics would accuse him of sponsoring a "reign of terror" during the Genevan Reformation.

28. Defoe, *Robinson Crusoe*, ed. Michael Shinagel (New York: W. W. Norton and Co., 1975), 124, 142, 180, 204. Hereafter cited with page numbers in the text.

a world in which responses to threat are various and intense, while causes and effects seem almost impossibly ambiguous, makes him an apt companion to the critics and theorists who were aestheticizing terror in the eighteenth-century adumbration of the sublime.

Defoe's novel does not however fully transpose the fear-terror syndrome into a purely aesthetic or psychological discourse; it still has a very large footprint in the sands of Puritan debate. And here John Bunyan again comes into play, not as the author of a popular classic but of the rather more obscure *A Treatise of the Fear of God* (1679). The word *dreadful* does appear in *Pilgrim's Progress*, and *fear* is not uncommon, most memorably occurring in the figure of Mr. Fearing, who has the right disposition to undergo an awakening but who cannot get beyond his constitutional caution. Nonetheless, *Pilgrim's Progress* is not principally about the terrifying character of God. In the *Treatise*, however, Bunyan devotes a whole book to the importance of fear and trembling to an authentic religious experience. *Fear* describes both God himself, who is "the object of our fear," and the word of God, which is the bearer of that fear to us.[29] For God, Bunyan says, "goeth under this very name himself" (2). His presence is dreadful and terrible, like his name, and our proper worship and service of God are similarly shot through with fear and dread (6). The early sections of the book are marked by a varied vocabulary in which *fear*, *dread*, and *terror* are synonymous, but the exposition evolves into a somewhat more tempered explanation of the differences between godly and ungodly fear. The first, whose groundwork is good, is a "fear of eternal damnation for sin" (16). It is this that motivates us to turn to the word of the Gospel. Ungodly fear is that which is experienced after the word is revealed and is the work of the devil. It is a failure to accept that God's forgiveness is permanent, even as he may continue to administer sharp shocks of fear that temporarily feel like the original fear. Sins committed after our "adoption" should be understood as "the transgression of a child, not of a slave" (22), and we should never forget that we are in God's care. If and when we do forget, then the devil has won our hearts.

Paradoxically, then, after accepting the word of God, we should never fully fear fear itself while also maintaining a "diligent examination of ourselves" (48) in the face of such fears as do arise, testing our faith against them and refusing to fall into despair. Thus, fear is "that tender, sensible, and trembling grace, that keepeth the soul upon its continual

29. *A Treatise on the Fear of God* (1679), https://onlinebooks.library.upenn.edu, 2. Hereafter cited with page numbers in the text.

watch" (67). The original, preadoption fear impels us to God in the first place and is thus always grounded in God's goodness, whereas the post-adoption fears function as a constant measure of self-discipline and right thinking. The will may fail and sins transpire, but they will not be absolute unless we make them so. It may be no accident that the more melodramatic terms *terror* and *dread* become less frequent as Bunyan moves into his calculus of godly and ungodly fears. The startling effect of the opening of the *Treatise* depends not a little on its calling-out the scriptural authority for radical emotional stress, pointing out the "vehemency" with which it is communicated (2). *Terror* and *dread* are good words for this task, and they are heavily used at this point. But as the argument evolves, a more reasoned approach is invited, and Bunyan generates this through his extended analysis of "this word FEAR" (8), the least inflammatory of his available terms. The move from melodrama to repetitive reflection models for us a transition from excitability to understanding, as if to instill an incentive not to fear fear wholly. To avow terror or dread after being "adopted" by God, in Bunyan's argument, would be to regress to a primal and uneducated emotion, one not befitting the assumption of faith. Terror and dread are part of God's plan but are best described more moderately as manageable fear when we understand what that plan is.

In contrast, the predilection of Noah Webster's dictionary for biblical rather than literary sources for *terror* may have been responsive to a more precisely delineated American Puritan tradition embodied in the notion of "legal terrors," one that certainly does not reflect any move from a melodramatic to a lower-key vocabulary. Jonathan Edwards's *Personal Narrative*, written sometime after 1739, is in part the story of coming to terms with terror. His change of heart about thunder and lightning, for example, involves learning to rejoice at what had formerly been a source of mere terror. This can be read as a classic instance of the sublime, in which he works to "fix" himself "in order to view" the storm, presumably at some relatively safe distance.[30] But the strong compulsion to abjection that goes with his awakening, his desire to "lie low before God, as in the dust" (64), suggests that such experiences become the more valuable the more the distance is reduced. What emerges is a doctrine of "legal terror" whereby the first step to conversion requires serious fear and trembling, a

---

30. *Jonathan Edwards: Representative Selections*, ed. Clarence H. Faust and Thomas H. Johnson (New York: Hill and Wang, 1963), 61.

"terrifying sense of God's anger."[31] Not every conversion calls for "great terrors" (166), but many do, albeit that "legal terrors" alone do not complete conversion, which also calls for grace (170). This puts the minister in an awkward spot. How far should he go in "speaking terror to them that are already under great terrors" (389)?[32] As far as he needs to, says Edwards, as long as his purposes are governed by "truth." The more terror, the more light will be "let in" (390). The more desperate the sinner, the more he must be terrified. Comfort can do its proper work only after the regime of terror has been endured; and the suicides that this regimen has inspired should not, Edwards claims, be blamed on the terror but on the unworthiness of the person suffering it. Even if there has been occasional abuse of ministerial privilege, many more have properly come to God by way of terror (394).[33]

Edwards is an enthusiastic adapter, for the rank-and-file minister, of the terror turn taken by the KJV's translators. And before him there was William Perkins, who asserted (like Bunyan) that God prepares men's souls "by bruising them, as if one would break a hard stone to powder," bringing us to faith "with fear and trembling."[34] After him came Benjamin Rush, with a cold-blooded rationale for legal punishment as "exciting terror in the minds of spectators."[35] This is not new in itself; indeed, it is familiar doctrine. Rush's particular genius lies in his calculation of how to maximize terror. He is against the death penalty, for example, in order that the criminal shall have longer to "suffer the reproaches of a guilty conscience" (172). Solitary confinement is particularly useful to this end. Along with this, there are two other ways to "diffuse terror through a community" (151): punishments themselves should be

---

31. *The Works of Jonathan Edwards*, vol. 4, *The Great Awakening*, ed. C. C. Goen (New Haven, CT: Yale University Press, 1972), 164. Hereafter cited with page numbers in the text.

32. Calvin had raised this question about anxiety: if too much incapacitates, how much is enough? See Bouwsma, *John Calvin*, 42–45.

33. Edwards's fiery sermon of 1741, "Sinners in the Hands of an Angry God," actually makes only one verbatim reference to God's "terribleness": see *Jonathan Edwards: Basic Writings* (New York: Signet, 1966), 150–67, esp. 163. But his argument that sinful humans are spared immediate consignment to the pit only by God's arbitrary will, which is always liable to shift without warning or explanation, does fulfil a primary component of the terror experience: extended, radical insecurity through time.

34. *The Works of William Perkins*, ed. Ian Breward (Appleford, UK: Sutton Courtenay Press, 1970), 156, 162.

35. Benjamin Rush, *Essays Literary, Moral and Philosophical, Second Edition* (Philadelphia, 1806), 136. Hereafter cited with page numbers in the text. I owe this and much else here to Colin Dayan, "Legal Terrors," *Representations* 92, no. 1 (2005): 42–80.

fixed by law, but the exact fit between any one crime and its punishment should not be announced, and the duration of a punishment should be fixed by the magistrate without telling the prisoner what that duration happens to be. In this way, the law observes some restraints while ensuring the maximum suffering and uncertainty in the citizen or prisoner: no one knows exactly how he will be punished or for how long. Rush's goal is to prevent crime and reform criminals who have committed it: for the "imagination, when agitated with uncertainty, will seldom fail of connecting the longest duration of punishment, with the smallest crime" (151). In a functional state of terror, people will police themselves.

Edwards and Rush are thus firmly in the terror business; the range of lesser and more nuanced emotions that feature in the narrative of *Robinson Crusoe* are not much at home in the domains of damnation and salvation, sacred and secular. And because *terror* is a term that describes (either or both) what one feels and the thing causing the feeling, terror inspires terror; there is an absolutist, objective dynamic and a closed, subjective, emotional circuit. The terror that is an agent outside the self (God's terror) commands replication as felt terror in the responding person. Implicitly, there is no room for the allied or subsidiary emotions that can accompany terror in the Burkean model of the sublime. Edwards and Rush want to instill the "real" terror that the sublime must keep at a reasonable distance if it is to remain within the sphere of what is aesthetically pleasurable. Two models of terror thus subsist side by side: one absolute, one not. Aristotle, in specifying the coexistence of *phobos* with pity, opts for the inabsolute. But the two kinds of terror share the same word, frequently causing confusion about which is which. Uvedale Price, for example, finds that *Paradise Lost* is "wrought up to a higher pitch of awful terror than any other poem," and here the pressure on aesthetic terror to be taken (or described) as absolute terror is all the greater because this is a poem with an explicitly religious subject matter.[36] It is God's terrors we are reading about. *Macbeth* too, for Price, is a play in which "all is terror" (99), although here the divine agency is murkier. But in *King Lear*, Price finds that the Dover cliff scene raises up "terror" (100), even though the audience is fully aware that there are no cliffs involved and that the whole thing is a deception. The rhetorical lability of terror assists Price in imagining that the spectators experience the scene as if they themselves were Gloucester (who is anyway himself not terrified but eager to die) rather than onlookers watch-

---

36. Uvedale Price, *An Essay on the Picturesque*, 3 vols. (London, 1810), 1:97. Price is defending Burke against his critics.

ing him from a distance. Not the least of the insecurities sponsored by the invocation of terror is that it can seem hard or impossible to know where aesthetic experience stops and existential threat begins.

Updating the Book of Judges: Early Terror Literature

The complex relations between scriptural-theological, aesthetic, and political deployments of the rhetoric of terror take on exemplary form in two versions of stories from the Bible, both adapted from Judges: Milton's *Samson Agonistes* and Rousseau's *The Levite of Ephraim*. Both explore the lineaments of terror before *the* Terror of 1793–1794, and both are gatherings of questions felt as urgent at the time while eerily prescient of a history to come. *Samson*, indeed, has been the subject of a vigorous debate, at once scholarly and public, since the events of September 2001 inspired John Carey to recirculate his longstanding view of the poem as a critique of terrorism in the pages of the *Times Literary Supplement*.[37] Carey's Milton is a poet who would have found "monstrous" the task of following Judges in justifying Samson's act as simply God's righteous will, so he rewrites the Bible to cast doubt on the whole event and to bring out the horror of the observer (and the naive ignorance of the celebrating Israelites) at such wanton destruction. According to Carey, we do not know why Samson acts as he does, but we do know that Milton does not approve of it. To claim as Carey does that the poem has been "usually interpreted" as praising "terrorism" is certainly a misrepresentation of a complex critical debate in place well before 9/11.[38] That said, Milton definitely poses questions about the relation of this Hebraic material to the tradition of classical tragedy invoked in his preface, which sets out to justify the ways of Aristotle to a Bible story,

---

37. "A Work in Praise of Terrorism?" *Times Literary Supplement*, September 6, 2002, 15–16.

38. The debate is too extensive to be properly rehearsed here. For some exemplary positions and summaries of the critical tradition, see Joseph A Wittreich, *Why Milton Matters: A New Preface to His Writings* (New York: Palgrave Macmillan, 2006), 141–93; Stanley Fish, *How Milton Works* (Cambridge, MA: Belknap Press of Harvard University Press, 2001), 391–431; Feisal G. Mohamed, "Confronting Religious Violence: Milton's *Samson Agonistes*," *PMLA* 120, no. 2 (2005): 327–40; Michael Lieb, "'Our Living Dread': The God of *Samson Agonistes*," *Milton Studies XXXIII*, ed. Albert C. Labriola and Michael Lieb (Pittsburgh, PA: University of Pittsburgh Press, 1997); and Linda Gregerson, "Milton and the Tragedy of Nations," *PMLA* 129, no. 4 (2014): 672–87. The most comprehensive survey and bibliography of the debate is Feisal G. Mohamed, *Milton and the Post-Secular Present: Ethics, Politics, Terrorism* (Stanford, CA: Stanford University Press, 2011), 87–126.

and specifically to highlight the categories of "pity and fear, or terror."[39]
Notable here is Milton's provision of two ways to translate *phobos: fear*
or *terror*. Most translators, then as now, have opted for one or the other.
And this is striking because neither the word *terror* nor any of its compound forms occur in the poem, and even *fear* is not used in any strong
theological sense, for example, as God's fear. What is described is horror. Samson compares his sin to the one that earns the "horrid pains" of
the abyss as conceived by "Gentiles" (l. 501), and at the climax of the
action we hear the "horribly loud" shout from the theater (l. 1510). The
messenger then speaks of a "horrid spectacle" (l. 1542) at the "place of
horror" (l. 1550), and then again of the "horrible convulsion" (l. 1649)
of the falling building. These are the responses of persons portrayed as
looking on, from a distance (as indeed Samson looks anachronistically
toward a doctrinal purgatory to come), not those of firsthand emotions.
Milton takes seriously the injunction to keep violence off the stage (doubly so, as the poem is not staged), and puts his readers in the role of bystanders, onlookers hearing the responses of others already themselves
standing at a distance. This is the complete opposite of the injunction
directed by politicians and the media after 9/11: that we should all experience terror, the attribute of total immersion. The double distancing
in *Samson* is arguably an invitation to critical reflection; in being placed
away from immediate contact with the major event, our cooler and more
deliberative responses are encouraged. Milton is indeed less emphatic
than Judges in rendering Samson a coherent tool of God's partiality to
the Israelites. He introduces Samson's death not as a suicide but as a secondary consequence of his vengeance upon the Philistines, "by accident
to himself" (358). And he foregrounds an undecidable attitude in having
the messenger describe Samson thus:

> And eyes fast fixed he stood, as one who prayed,
> Or some great matter in his mind resolved. (ll. 1637–38)

Is this an exclusive *or*—praying or deliberating—or an inclusive *or* with
the meaning of *and*? The messenger cannot choose; nor can we. There
is a world of difference between praying and deliberating if we are to
put ourselves in the way of judging the spiritual integrity of this hitherto
wayward figure, one who is indeed in Judges almost a folkloric ne'er-do-
well. Nor is it clear that either is accurate, given that the *as* can be con-

---

39. *Complete Shorter Poems*, 2nd ed., ed. John Carey (New York: Addison, Wesley,
Longman, 1997), 355.

strued as pure simile: he stood like one who prayed or deliberated. Much about the theological narrative is obscure. Is Samson's change of heart in agreeing to enter the theater (Milton's telling word for the temple here) an index of a cunning plot he has consciously devised, or a response to a divine prompting whose origin and purpose he cannot surmise? What we have is this:

> I begin to feel
> Some rousing motions in me which dispose
> To something extraordinary my thoughts. (ll. 1381–83)

These rousing motions could be the dawning of a rational plan or the promptings of a mind taken over in the Greek manner, enthused by the god's influence, or they could be simply self-delusion. If Samson is enthused, then he is the instrument of a divine plot whose unfolding he cannot foresee. (This is the destiny of Oedipus, whose demise is cited at the start of Milton's poem.) The event would then be the expression of what readers of Benjamin might call the divine (power of) violence, *göttliche Gewalt*, that which comes out of the blue and changes everything while sparing us any responsibility for bringing it about.[40]

So we do not know how conscious—fully, partly, or not at all—Samson might be of his role in a theological settlement and a nation-state prefoundation myth. By extension, we do not know whether he is a hero or a villain in an already-uncertain allegory of life in England after the Restoration, when the poem was published, or indeed during the emergence of parliamentary militancy, when some think that the poem might have been written. Milton does depart from Judges in suggesting that only the Philistine elite die in the rubble: "The vulgar only scaped who stood without" (l. 1659). These are those who did not have "seats" (ll. 1607–10) and who were compelled to stand in the open. If this is what Milton meant, then "all her sons" who die at line 1558 must describe only the governing class, excluding the common people. Samson and/or God's act, then, becomes a targeted assassination, more in line with the current rhetoric of drone warfare apologias than with the mass destruction practiced by, for example, high-altitude bombing, or, indeed, the avenging tribes of Judah elsewhere in Judges. That there is much we cannot know for sure about Samson seems to be the poem's message, just as there is much we cannot see for ourselves. This accords with the

---

40. This is close to Michael Lieb's argument in "'Our Living Dread'" (16). A more skeptical reading of divine violence concludes the present chapter.

nonappearance of terror in the narrative, although Milton was quite capable of deploying terror as among God's weapons when he saw the occasion to do so.[41]

The equivalent words for terror, as it happens, are also scarce in Judges. Only once in the Samson story, if I am understanding correctly, is there a strong fear-terror word, and it comes right at the beginning, when God's angelic messenger appears to the wife of Manoah and prophesies a great future for the unborn hero. The KJV has her describing this "man of God" as "terrible" (13:6). The Hebrew root is *yare*, a word that seems to have had as wide a franchise as *phobos* and *deinos*, able to indicate anything from dismay and fear to reverence, awe, and terror.[42] The strong word *pa(c)had*, used ten times in Job, is absent from Judges, where *yare* is used three times as part of a negative injunction, "fear not" (4:18, 6:10, 6:23), and appears twice more as indicating fear of mortal (not divine) powers (6:27, 8:20). In a book in which there is so much destruction of one sort or another, the only occurrence of *yare* in relation to a divine terror is indeed in the Samson story, but it refers not to the reported violence of various sorts but to Manoah's wife's opening account of seeing the angel. God's violence is thus implicitly marked as hidden, or highly mediated, while the agency of the Israelites is foregrounded.

Because this is a book about the dark days in the tribe's history, when there was no king and "every one did that which was right in his own eyes" (21:25), the obscurity of God's agency is appropriate. But he is pulling the strings and engineering events so as to educate the Israelites in the sorts of violence he will require for the furtherance of his campaign to be number one in the competition with the so-designated false gods: thus he wants to "teach them war" (3:2). The Samson of Judges is infused with the "Spirit of the Lord" during his acts of violence (e.g., at 15:14), but he himself seems not to know it as such. Before the destruction of the temple, he does pray to God, but it is vengeance for himself he seeks rather than the furthering of God's plan (16:28). In the Greek manner, the agent does not fully know (or know at all) the source of his actions. Milton's chorus does attribute the killing of the Philistines to "our living dread who dwells / In Silo his bright sanctuary" (ll. 1673–74), and

41. See, e.g., *Paradise Lost* 6:823, on God's terror; and 10:667, on the natural terror that appears after the Fall.

42. Thus Robert Alter, *Ancient Israel: The Former Prophets: Joshua, Judges, Samuel, and Kings* (New York: W. W. Norton and Co., 2013), 175, has "very fearsome"; Robert G. Boling, *The Anchor Bible: Judges* (Garden City, NY: Doubleday, 1975), 217, reads "very awesome." Tyndale and Geneva read "exceeding fearful." Vulgate has *terribilis*.

Michael Lieb has persuasively situated this synonym for God as fully in the spirit of the Hebrew worldview in which Yahweh is habitually imaged as a figure of terror, but it is not clear how much Samson himself knows about this.[43]

It is not easy to resolve the question of what exactly Milton feels, or allows us to feel, about this terror. The vigor of the critical debate on this topic suggests that much still remains to be said. The poem indeed begins with the unexplained: who is it that Samson bids lend his "guiding hand" for a "little longer" (l.1)? Oedipus had his daughter. Here there is no interlocutor and no agent designated in the list of characters as playing this role. It is a fitting opening to a poem that deals so much in the obscuring of agency. Perhaps it is just an exordium to imaginary spectators who must agree to read to the end. Or, if it suggests an address to an invisible God, then it is an unknowing one, spoken without conscious assurance. And if we imagine for ourselves a physical figure on this virtual stage on the page, who is it? Right from the start, authority is obscure, and obscure, too, is the estimate to be made of the righteousness of this most favored nation-to-be, blundering around as it does with random acts of violence committed in the service of a god whose superiority to others is yet to be proved.[44] Whatever Milton's attitude to the early nation-state aspirations of the Israelites might have been—and there may be no clear answer—it is hard not to infer some relation to the condition of England in the period of the Civil War and/or its aftermaths. Again, clarity is not easy to come by. Here it is not about a land before kings but one that is in the process of getting rid of kingship by violent means, and which may or may not (depending on how one dates the poem) have turned back to its restoration. David Loewenstein notes Milton's support for a "state or military form of terror" in both England and Ireland, and his citations indicate a widespread recourse to the rhetoric of holy terror by Cromwell and other contemporaries.[45] But if Samson is an avenging Puritan wielding the power of terror, he seems neither to say nor know it. If it is

43. Lieb, "Our Living Dread" (4–6). Lieb further notes (11) that in elsewhere rendering into Latin a similar name for God, "the fear/dread of Isaac" (i.e., he who causes Isaac to dread), Milton opts for *pavor*.

44. Thus, Gregerson, "Milton and the Tragedy of Nations," finds that "Milton intends to trouble the whole category of chosen nation" (679). The irony whereby *Philistine* is a transliteration of the word that now designates *Palestinian* is more than etymological.

45. David Loewenstein, "*Samson Agonistes* and the Culture of Religious Terror," in *Milton in the Age of Fish: Essays on Authorship, Text, and Terrorism*, ed. Michael Lieb and Albert C. Labriola (Pittsburgh, PA: Duquesne University Press, 2006), 203–28, esp. 208.

the Restoration kingship that Samson contests, he would be a prophet of better days to come. But if it is Charles I whose theater comes tumbling down, those better days have already passed.

One clear animus does however emanate from Milton's poem: Samson's loathing for the women who have seduced him, and perhaps for all women. Judges is explicit enough here, especially when it is assisted by the KJV translation of the Israelite habit of "whoring after other gods" (2:17; cf. 8:27, 33).[46] Samson is consistent in blaming his misfortunes both on women and on the sex drive that leads him to them. Dalila is both his "wife" and his "concubine" (358, and ll. 886, 535). Milton here exploits or reproduces an ambiguity in the Hebrew vocabulary that plays a telling role in the soon-to-come story of the Levite of Ephraim. Nor does the poet clearly endorse his hero's vituperative language when he has the chorus exonerate Dalila from being "unclean" (l. 325) or when Dalila compares herself to the murdering Israelite heroine Jael (l. 989), the subject of another story in Judges. But Samson himself is clear that sexual attraction per se is what has wrought his downfall (ll. 200, 410, 565), and that it is sexual per se seems to register more with him than that it is for women not of his own tribe. Judges delivers a more or less coherent mandate about consorting only with women of one's own kind; Milton's Samson seems more sensitive to the shortcomings of women in general.

Women, notwithstanding the appearance of heroines of the "nation" like Jael and Deborah, suffer horribly in Judges, and never more so than in its final story about the Levite of Ephraim. The central atrocity, the gang-rape murder of the Levite's wife-concubine, indeed has a folkloric, if grisly, component to it, as the woman's body is chopped into twelve pieces for distribution to the tribes of Israel as an incentive to unification and revenge. But the rape and murder itself is starkly described, with nothing of the relief that allegory might be expected to provide. Thus, the narrative argument that the unity of the protonation is established by way of the abused body of an unnamed woman is bleakly straightforward. Straightforward, too, is the ease with which the men construe the atrocity as an offense against hospitality and perhaps property rather than as the hideous sexual murder of an innocent bystander (for there is

---

46. Boling in the *Anchor* (1975) reads "prostituted themselves to other gods"; Alter in *Ancient Israel* (2013) supports "whoring," as had Tyndale and Geneva; and the Vulgate reads *fornicantes*. The consensus is striking, and apt evidence for Mieke Bal's extended argument about Judges as coherently premised on the abjection or extinction of women in *Death and Dissymmetry: The Politics of Coherence in the Book of Judges* (Chicago: University of Chicago Press, 1988).

nothing here of the dignity in the face of the divine obligation accorded earlier to Jephthah's daughter).[47] In this rather extended story—three whole chapters of Judges—there are (in the KJV) no fear-terror words. The absence of a god called terror does not, however, diminish the human appetite for violent destruction, nor Yahweh's encouragement of it: we read of the total destruction of Gibeah, of the death of (biblical) thousands of Israelites and all but a few hundred of the Benjaminites, of the putting to the sword of all of the inhabitants of Jabesh-Gilead except for four hundred virgins, as well as of the forced abduction of the women of Shiloh. Here indeed "every man did that which was right in his own eyes" (21:25).

But there is also the emergence of an alliance politics and a self-regulating protostate judicial apparatus of the sort that might claim the power of terror as a necessary attribute. It is this, among other things, that reappears as a major theme in Rousseau's rewriting of the story. In Judges, it is Yahweh (20:18) who picks the men of Judah to purge the bad elements from among the tribes and to destroy the men of Gibeah who have offended the Levite. But it is the Israelites themselves who spare the remnants of the offending tribe, devise a way to keep them reproducing, and punish the stay-at-home men of Jabesh-Gilead (whose survival, oddly, does not seem to be such a matter of concern). One way to read all of this is as a fable of the emergence of self-governance, with Yahweh playing a secondary, supportive role rather than acting always as prime mover. Whether or not this ordering of the tribes points inevitably toward the kingship that will historically emerge is not clear. It could also be construed as an experiment in republicanism. On three occasions in Judges (20:1, 8, 11), the Israelites are described as becoming "as one man" in their response to the outrage at Gibeah. But there is no mention of this unification movement as the result of God's contrivance: it is described as seemingly autonomous. We may assume that God is not far away, but he is not, except at the low points of the ensuing battle, present "in person" in the way God so often is at critical moments in the lives of his followers. The story, for long stretches, gives the appearance that humankind is acting on its own instincts.

---

47. For a reading of the Levite in the context of hospitality culture, see my *Romanticism and the Question of the Stranger* (Chicago: University of Chicago Press, 2013), 236–49. A short profile of the tip of the critical and scholarly iceberg underlying this narrative can be gained from the footnotes to Herbert Marks's superb edition of *The English Bible* (New York: W. W. Norton and Co., 2012). Mieke Bal's *Death and Dissymmetry* is again central here.

Rousseau writes a story in which Yahweh plays an even smaller role, one essentially consigned to giving assurances during the battle between the Israelites and the Benjaminites. He is entirely absent from the conclusion, an invention of Rousseau's own, in which the daughters of Shiloh "decide their fate for themselves" after the Shiloh elders have shamed the abductors into ceding to their "judgment."[48] But the women do not quite decide for themselves. They agree to accept their abductors as husbands, only after a somewhat wheedling plea by one of the fathers, who puts himself in the role that might have fallen to Yahweh himself: "For I have counseled everything that has been done" (365). The exemplary daughter who gives up her betrothed to save the future of the Benjaminite tribe is also giving way to the imperative to spare her father from "opprobrium" among his "brothers." Meanwhile, her betrothed commits himself to becoming a sort of reborn Samson, a "Nazarene of the Lord" (365), a role for which he seems rather better prepared than the wayward superman whose story comes (in Judges) just before his own. Rousseau concludes, rather more emphatically than his biblical precursor, that this resolution shows that "there are still virtues in Israel" (365).

Rousseau's ending stages a republic of virtue, but one in which the key role is still played by the patriarch, whose only personal sacrifice appears to be the pleasure of having Elmacin (the about-to-be Nazarene) for a son-in-law. Others, especially the young women, give up rather more to preserve the unity of the protostate. At least the appalling violence against women upon which the whole narrative rests has been softened into a marriage of consent, however coercive that consent may be. But there is a prescience running through the narrative that, for readers after 1794, inevitably seems to portend the Jacobin protostate's embrace of the power of terror in the cause of political unity.[49] Rousseau's opening lines invoke the "sacred anger of virtue," of "terrible" punishments, of "fear" of punishing crimes, of "horror" and of a "horrible act" (352–53). This is not at all offset by Rousseau's invention of a strongly affec-

---

48. Jean-Jacques Rousseau, *Essay on the Origin of Languages and Writings Related to Music*, ed. and trans. John T. Scott (Hanover, NH: University Press of New England, 1998), 364. For an account of the changes Rousseau makes to the Judges story, see Thomas M. Kavanagh, *Writing the Truth: Authority and Desire in Rousseau* (Berkeley: University of California Press, 1987), discussion starting at 103.

49. See Carol Blum, *Rousseau and the Republic of Virtue: The Language of Politics in the French Revolution* (Ithaca, NY: Cornell University Press, 1990), 132, on the emergence of the "man of virtue" in Rousseau's story; and the fine account in Caroline Weber, *Terror and Its Discontents: Suspect Words in Revolutionary France* (Minneapolis: University of Minnesota Press, 2003), 43–54.

tionate, romantic bond between the Levite and his wife-concubine.[50] Indeed, this bond serves rather to emphasize the stoic virtue of the Levite in giving over his beloved to the rapists, "without saying a single word to her, without raising his eyes to her" (358), and his subsequent extinction of all the softer emotions into "fury" (359), which then transforms into the "cold and sure valor" of the Israelites (361) operating (as in Judges) "like a single man" (359). Especially striking is the description of the motives of the Jabesh-Gileadites in refusing to join the alliance: they are guilty of "perjury and desertion of the common cause" because of their "unjust pity" (363). Pity, normally a virtue, must take second place when virtue demands. The gentler inclinations are out of place when the state requires organized violence. Rousseau employs far more fear-terror words than the author of Judges: the word *terror* (*terreur*) occurs four times, along with *fear* (both *peur* and *crainte*), *horror*, and *fright*. The account of the Israelites deploying the "exterminating sword" (*glaive exterminateur*) of divine vengeance (361) in the cause of restoring (or creating) virtue as national unity speaks a language that would become very familiar by 1794. When Saint-Just announces that "the pity that people display for crime is a glaring sign of betrayal, in a republic that can only be based on inflexibility," he is advising a policy of fear-terror without pity.[51] There are to be no mixed or companionate emotions, and implicitly there is to be no aesthetic distance of the sort that maintains the possibility of the Aristotelian spectator having two distinguishable feelings. The judgment for terror puts the agent in the place of God: terror is what God inspires, and what God is. Whatever doubts are to be raised by Milton's depiction of Samson appear to have been dispersed: the representative of the people now claims the power of divine violence.

Violence without Terror: Walter Benjamin

For readers embedded in Judeo-Christian culture, the Homeric heroes can sometimes seem to belong to a more innocent and enabling world. Zeus, the most powerful of the gods, is distractible and thus not always fully vigilant. One can be assisted or impeded by a god or goddess, and

---

50. Here he clearly differs from the KJV reading that says the woman "played the whore" (19:2), as if she might thereby almost deserve what happened to her. Rousseau describes her return to her father as the result of boredom, leaving us to guess why she was bored.

51. Cited in Weber, *Terror and Its Discontents*, 84. See Weber (98–112) also for an account of the Terror as an incarnation of the homosocial abjection of women prefigured in Rousseau's *Levite*.

the stakes can be matters of life and death, but the odds are unpredictable and are as likely to affect one's enemies as oneself. Where there are
many gods, offending one can earn the patronage of another. There is
little in Homer's world to associate the gods with anything more complex than sheer power. There exists no fully developed metaphysic of
justice, and human failure seems not to involve radical self-abnegation
or spiritual despair about an afterlife. There is no "soul" to be consumed
in a burning pit through eternity.

The evolution of Yahweh from a local volcano god to the figure rendered in the modern Christian tradition as "Lord God" leads to higher
stakes and to an enhanced power of terror governing both this world
and the next. The terrors of Ezekiel are dispersed in ways that confuse
agent and victim, God and man, but the KJV still emerges with a new
emphasis on the union between divine and earthly power, and on the
power of that power. Thus aided, both absolute monarchy and parliamentary government can avail themselves of a scriptural language that
readily associates the power of the state with the violent justice of God.
But what kind of violence is divine violence, and what is its relation to
terror? Ezekiel suggests a direct correspondence: God has the power of
terror, God is terror, and our terror is of God as well as of well-armed
earthly kingdoms. Judges piles up so much violence because God is apparently prompting the Israelites to a more restraining kingship and a
limitation on terror. Walter Benjamin's much-discussed "Critique of Violence" (*Zur Kritik der Gewalt*) implies exactly the opposite: that divine
violence is free of terror.

Benjamin is good at crafting charismatically opaque phrases that
have inspired his readers into intense and creative interpretations of
what the master might have meant and what can be made of him. Divine violence is one of the most puzzling. The whole effort of Benjamin's
argument is to explore or imagine the possibility of a form of violence
(*Gewalt*) that is somehow uncontaminated by the alliance between the
law and the state. In the world that we have, these combine as monopo-
lists of the power of violence, and as such are emanations of a culture in
which there seems to be no place to turn, because to remove one institutional embodiment is merely to put another in its place. Revolutionary
violence, insofar as it sets out to replace one set of forms or doctrines by
another, is merely continuing a dismal cycle of coercive governance. Divine violence (*göttliche Gewalt*) is conceived as breaking this circle by
being completely unencumbered with outcomes or agendas; it is pure
means, carrying with it no past and designating no future. It happens
all at once, in a flash, and stands outside time; it thus appeals as one of

those "figures of suddenness" that Sue Zemka notices as preoccupying so much contemporary criticism.[52] It relies on peremptory shock and awe but not on the sustained temporality of terror. It is also bloodless.

It is not hard to see what is appealing about this paradigm: it seems to promise the possibility of radical change without error or guilt, perhaps without critical agency, and certainly without the depressing prospect of a revolutionary present that is destined simply to repeat the sins of an authoritarian past. We really might, it seems, ponder and hope for the eruption of a completely new world with the prospect of radically new beginnings, and all of this without bloodshed. Who would not be interested in that? The moment of Benjamin's essay was a heady one: three years after the end of the Great War, violence in the streets, economic collapse, and hyperinflation, but also a recent and successful Russian Revolution and the brief emergence of localized socialist governments across Germany. Any onset of divine violence would be a world-changing event in which terror, in all or most of its senses, would have no place; terror, as usually understood, depends on temporal duration, on dominating the minds and hearts of human beings, whether for days and years or just for a few unbearable moments. Terror is all about fearing for a future according to evidence of what has happened in the past. Without the drama of anticipation and retrospection, the violence of terror would be simply fate: that which happens. Benjamin's attempt to devise a model of divine violence that is radically uncontingent is also—although he does not develop this point—an imagining of critical historical change without terror. It is thus seemingly at odds with the tradition appealing to the terror of god and it is, of course, no simple matter.[53]

Benjamin's *Gewalt* does not just denote violence: it can also be turned into English as authority, power, force, or might.[54] Two of these senses

52. *Time and the Moment in Victorian Literature and Society* (Cambridge: Cambridge University Press, 2012), 224. Zemka finds that "the trope of the moment has become a predictable discursive figure, almost a fallback position, or maybe a safe place to hide" (225). I share her sense that we are here facing "a retreat behind a certain type of mystification" (14), one that Benjamin surely invites in his essay.

53. See Mark Juergensmeyer, *Terror in the Mind of God: The Global Rise of Religious Violence* (Berkeley: University of California Press, 2003). Benjamin is also implicitly contesting Trotsky's earlier case justifying terror(ism) as a weapon in the hands of the party (though not as a merely individual gesture) in its war against the state. But neither does he endorse Kautsky's argument calling for a wholly peaceful evolution for socialism: divine violence stands between (and aside from) both these positions.

54. It rather complicates things that the most recent, comprehensive, and inevitably authorized translation of Benjamin's work, the four-volume *Selected Writings*, simply reprints Edmund Jephcott's 1978 text, where *Gewalt* is rendered both as *force* and as *violence*. I use this (critically) as the source for my citations: see Benjamin's "Critique of

can be combined in translating *Gewalt* as power of violence, whether exercised or not. This is what is possessed, for example, by the (military) state in the daily exercise of its administrative rituals. But Benjamin's two examples, one from the Greek classics and the other from the Hebrew Bible, both involve the spectacular exercise of power, not merely its prospective presence. Niobe is turned to stone and her children slaughtered, and Korah and his followers are swallowed up by the earth. Violence would indeed seem to be the best English equivalent for Benjamin's *Gewalt*, but it cannot shake itself completely free from its cognates and alternates, to the point that one critic at least has found significance in the refusal of a simple discrimination between power and violence.[55]

Göttliche (translated as *divine*) might seem to be something merely descriptive of an act performed by gods, whether good, bad, or indifferent. But when Benjamin goes on to indicate his approval of divine violence, above all in its relation to the establishment of justice, it seems clear that he does not intend neutrality here. Divine violence is not teleological and does not have as its purpose any purpose at all: it is pure means, purely immediate.[56] Most of all, it does not put into place any

---

Violence," 236–52. The German is taken from Rolf Tiedemann and Herman Schweppenhäuser, eds., *Walter Benjamin: Gesammelte Schriften, 2:1* (Frankfurt: Suhrkamp, 1999), 179–204.

55. Beatrice Hansen, *Critique of Violence: Between Poststructuralism and Critical Theory* (London: Routledge, 2000), 16–30, esp. 20. Similarly, Benjamin's opening distinction between law and justice, upon which the whole essay depends, is less absolute in German, which reads *Recht* and *Gerechtigkeit*. An important resource here is Étienne Balibar, "Reflections on *Gewalt*," *Historical Materialism* 17 (2009): 99–125. Balibar notes that Engels's 1895 essay "The Role of Force in History" also uses *Gewalt* in its title and as a term that is ambiguous: "It refers, at the same time, to the negation of law and justice and to their realisation or the assumption of responsibility for them by an institution (generally the state)" (101). The force-violence distinction matters all the more because one of Benjamin's avowed sources, Georges Sorel's 1908 *Reflections on Violence,* trans. T. E. Hulme and J. Roth (London: Collier-Macmillan, 1950), relies on a clear contrast between force and violence (171, 175). The same contrast is deployed as a judgmental category by Sergio Cotta, *Why Violence? A Philosophical Interpretation,* trans. Giovanni Gullace (Gainesville: University Press of Florida, 1985). Seeking to oppose what he sees as a rising respect for and tolerance of violence, Cotta proposes force as a respectable alternative, one compatible with value (55) and one able to resist passion (66). Hannah Arendt makes a critical distinction between power and violence. Power has need of numbers, whereas violence requires only implements; violence can be maintained only if it has power behind it. See "On Violence," in *Crises of the Republic*, esp. 142–48. The 1970 German translation of Arendt's essay stresses the importance of the distinction in going by the title *Macht und Gewalt*.

56. Werner Hamacher, "Affirmative, Strike: Benjamin's Critique of Violence," in *Walter Benjamin's Philosophy: Destruction and Experience,* ed. Andrew Benjamin and

law. Benjamin's examples are not particularly perspicuous. Niobe sees
her children killed and finds herself turned to stone because she has dared
to challenge the gods with the claim that she is as deserving of worship as
they are. This is a mere manifestation of the being (*Dasein*) of the gods:
they do it because they can. But it involves the imposition or marking
out (*Markstein*, the boundary stone) of the distinction between men and
gods, and is as such, he says, "mythic," because it brings to light a law.
How exactly the message here sent by the gods is a law, and what the
law might be, is not clear. But true divine violence is never mythic. Benjamin offers as a contrast the story of the destruction of Korah and his
company in Numbers 16. In this episode of mass slaughter—some going
alive into the pit, others burned to cinders, and, in a second day of destruction, many more fatally stricken with the plague—Benjamin finds
something different, a different kind of divine violence, "pure power
[*Gewalt*] over all life for the sake of the living," something that does not
simply punish but "expiates" (250). Quite how and why Benjamin finds
the biblical Yahweh so much more worthy of approval than the Greek
gods is not easy to understand. Surely Niobe's fate is just as efficient a
warning to (and expiation of) mere humanity as is Korah's. Korah and his
company, like Niobe, challenge the presumption of an exclusive god-
liness, claiming to be just as worthy of doing God's work as Moses is. To
be sure, the death of Niobe's children is not wrapped up in the language
of sacrifice, but it leads to a similar conclusion: know your place and
stay there. Why is Yahweh's violence not also a boundary stone leading
to a law? In a second distinction, Benjamin makes much of the idea that
divine violence is unbloody, *unblutige*, while the children of Niobe go
to a bloody death (*blutige Tod*—the English translation misses this by
reading simply "cruel death" [248]). Here it seems that Benjamin takes
blood to be the index of mere life, the sign of the physiological economy
at its most basic, the attribute of the normal. Are the three kinds of death
in the Korah story deemed to be without blood because they happen
so fast that there is no time for blood to be spilled?[57] Ovid's account

---

Peter Osborne (London: Routledge, 1994), 110–38, coins the term *afformative* to make
clear that we are not here talking about the performative: nothing happens, nothing is
brought into being. In 1842, Marx himself recommended embodying the power of communism in theory rather than in practice, because only "theoretical elaboration" cannot
be defeated by military means: see Gareth Stedman Jones, *Karl Marx: Greatness and Illusion* (Cambridge, MA: Belknap Press of Harvard University Press, 2016), 142.

    57. For an extended discussion (and a comprehensive bibliography) of this pas-
sage on blood, see Gil Anidjar, *Blood: A Critique of Christianity* (New York: Columbia

(*Metamorphoses* 6:145ff.) does make clear that the children take time in their dying. As an evaluation of suffering, this might seem sophistical: how do we choose between dying by Apollo's arrow or being burned to a cinder? But as a semiotic binary, it makes sense. One happens within ordinary time, the time taken for the body to be pierced and for blood to flow; the other happens outside time, in a flash, *schlagend*. At one moment the victims are alive, then suddenly they are dead.

But Benjamin's contrast between Greek and Judaic gods can still seem somewhat contrived. How are Korah's people removed from the sphere of the law where mythic (divine) violence (for Benjamin) always remains? They presumably do not know that they are offending in a way that is not merely contingent; hence their reasoning that they are just as good as Moses. Neither, apparently, did Niobe. But Benjamin implies that the Judaic god functions at a more elevated level than the Greek gods and acts to some greater end. This all seems to depend on the inscription of the language of sacrifice, which divine violence "accepts" (*nimmt*) rather than "demands" (*fordert*). But in what sense is Yahweh's act not also a demand? Is it because Korah's people seem to be willing to put themselves to the test, thereby signaling obedience to something higher than themselves, some kind of emergent principle, whereas Niobe has no self-conscious commitment to discovering who she should worship and how? She is interested only in being worshipped herself. But is she not part of an effort to establish or enact a (culture-building) ritual, as the men of Korah, with their incense-bearing censers also appear to be?

The followers of Moses and Korah are competing for who is most worthy of worshipping god. Moses's inside edge must come from faith, not knowledge (or else it would be gratuitous cruelty on his part), but it appears that there is room for only one faction in the tent of the almighty. (This principle of schism is a constant feature of the Hebrew Bible.) The stories are not as manageable as Benjamin seems to want them to be; they do not rest easily in the role of merely illustrative episodes of a clearly intended distinction but push against the limits he tries

---

University Press, 2014), 1–13. Jacques Derrida's indispensable reading of Benjamin's essay also takes up the question of how blood relates to respect for the living: see Jacques Derrida, *Acts of Religion*, ed. Gil Anidjar (New York: Routledge, 2002), 258–98, esp. 288. Where blood is shed, Derrida says, the living are not respected. The absence of blood appears as an incentive to the living to think beyond the conditions for merely being alive. This difficult part of Benjamin's exposition is well addressed by Judith Butler, "Critique, Coercion and Sacred Life in Benjamin's 'Critique of Violence,'" in *Political Theologies: Public Religions in a Post-Secular World*, ed. Hent de Vries and Lawrence E. Sullivan (New York: Fordham University Press, 2006), 201–20.

to impose upon them: no wonder he defers to the apologetic claim that things "cannot be shown in detail" (250). But let us grant nonetheless the importance to Benjamin of the distinction itself, that between a law-destroying and a law-preserving violence, where only the first is completely different from anything embodied in normal life within the legal and/or military state. We are to understand that Yahweh's violence, on Moses's behalf and his own, has nothing to do with establishing a law and is thus untainted by the paradox that governs all efforts to enact natural or positive law, which has resulted only in the replacement of one set of masters by another. (This includes, implicitly, the Jacobin terror). The appeal of this is almost irresistible in the light of the wreckage strewn across the records of history.

Along with the Niobe-Korah distinction, Benjamin offers three instances from ordinary life of how divine violence might be thought about. The first is the "conference" (*Unterredung*), the informal and unconstrained but nonviolent exchange of ideas, now most familiar to us as the Habermasian celebration of dialogic communicative action. This has obvious limits (not least that one must question who gets invited to the conference), and Benjamin somewhat sidelines his example by calling it an analogy: pure means (*reine Mittel*) in politics would be an *Analogon* of this feature of private life (245; 193 in German). In other words, the *Unterredung* (which can also be translated as *conversation*, or just *talk*) is not an instance of divine violence but simply an example of how something can be nonviolent: we should not, then, get carried away with organizing conferences in the hope that divine violence will descend upon us. In the same way, human rage (*Zorn*) is an example of how a gesture can be without ends, can appear simply as a *Manifestation* (248). But that does not mean that every angry man is a vehicle for divine violence.[58] These examples are offered to help us think about divine violence, but they are not embodiments of it.

The second instance comes by way of Sorel and carries more weight: the proletarian general strike, insofar as it is a call for sheer inaction, for the stopping of all purposive work without specific demands for improved working conditions (in which it differs from the political general strike), is also an expression of pure means. This is a very appealing example in that it does clearly embody a public sphere that most of us would take to be political, in the sense that it is operative beyond

---

58. Rage (*Zorn*) is the guiding thread in Peter Sloterdijk's *Rage and Time: A Psychopolitical Investigation,* trans. Mario Wenning (New York: Columbia University Press, 2012). "For the raging person, as for the happy person, time does not exist" (60).

the coteries of small-group behavior. The price to be paid, though, is that it cannot be political (as Benjamin understands the term) because it must not ask for defined remedies or improvements. That, precisely, would take it out of the sphere of pure means, and it is at this point that Benjamin comes close to anarchism. It also, we may now say, approximates him to the Occupy movement, which deliberately refrained from the publication of manifestos, although it has not yet been able to claim the status of a general event. Those who complained that Occupy could not be taken seriously because it did not publish a set of demands miss the point that, had it done so, it would have lost any relation (however wishful) to what Benjamin calls divine violence and initiated a relation to the state of the sort that divine violence forbids.

But there is a third example, one it took me many readings to catch on to (and one ignored by most readers), so little emphasis is it given in the essay's compacted final pages.[59] Following directly on from the Niobe and Korah passages, Benjamin proposes that one "sanctioned manifestation" (250) of divine violence is the violence of education. The word is in each case *Gewalt*. So a "manifestation" of *göttliche Gewalt* is *erzieherische Gewalt*.[60] This may have passed with too little comment in the anglophone world because the translator chooses to render *Gewalt* here, and unusually, not as violence but as power. Perhaps he does so because it is so much easier to accept the idea of education as a divine power; it is rather more challenging to think of education as divine violence. Benjamin is here taking over Schiller's word, in his formative treatise of 1794, on the aesthetic education of men, *Über die Ästhetische Erziehung des Menschen*. And Schiller, too, in his refutation of the short-term utilitarianism that he saw embodied in ill-advised efforts to turn the ideas of the French Revolution into immediate political practice, was also arguing for (aesthetic) education as pure means. What, then, is Benjamin doing in using the same word, *Gewalt*, for education's good and permitted effects as he uses for the Greek and Hebrew gods in their spectacular and wholly violent destruction of those who have not signed up for the message? This can be finessed only by arguing for a gentler translation of *Gewalt*, along the lines mentioned earlier: hence *power*, or *authority*, or some such word. But the word is still *Gewalt* and cannot (in a text of this density) fail to invoke or evoke enacted violence. The English translation fails to ask the question

---

59. Howard Eiland, "Deconstruction of Violence," *boundary* 2 44, no. 4 (2017): 113–40, does take up the question of "educative violence" (115) and endorses my sense that few others have done so.

60. *Gesammelte Schriften* 2:1, 200.

in the abrupt way that it is clearly asked in the German. Are we, as educators in the Schillerian mold, being endowed with divine violence?

Perhaps it depends on how one construes the one as a "sanctioned manifestation" of the other (250). Benjamin does not make this easy to follow by using a non-Germanic word, *Manifestation*. We are sent back, and not for the first time with this word in this essay, to the borrowed opacity of a foreign term, one whose claim to philosophical authority comes at the expense of demotic contextualization. There is a long history in German (and not only in German) of debating the function of foreign terms (the case of Kant is exemplary) as markers of the demands (or failures) of philosophy, as that which somehow decides that it must resort to untranslatables (in the sense of not needing translation, of being universal). So what kind of a manifestation is *Manifestation*?[61] The adjective is *geheiligten*, more than a little biblical (precious and time honored but also sacred, sacrosanct, hallowed), as is perhaps fitting for capturing the *religiose* aspiration of the humanist pedagogical tradition. This reference to education is a very brief interpolation—perhaps too rebarbative and undecidable to be handled any other way—before Benjamin moves on to insist that divine violence (like education) is not in its essence about miracles carried out by gods but occurs in a moment of bloodless expiation and in the absence of all lawmaking. How is education involved in expiation, in atonement? And anyway, what is the force of *entsühnend*? Who, in Numbers, is atoning to whom for what? Humans are freed from the guilt of mere life and of the law, we are told. What is destroyed, *vernichtend*, is only the worldly dimension of life, never the soul (*Seele*). There is, then, something beyond the life of this world, something metaphysical and indeed theological, certainly something here that does not sit comfortably with any effort to turn Benjamin into a Marxist. Has Benjamin stumbled into the German ideology, and once again, as in the camera obscura, turned things on their heads, turned earth into an emanation of heaven?

The last two pages of the essay on violence answer fewer questions than they raise. We are told that the (sacred) injunction against taking the life of another is not to be questioned, but yet it becomes irrelevant once the deed (*Tat*) is completed, as if it were after all possible and

---

61. In the fragment from 1919–1920 on "World and Time," *Selected Writings* (1:226–27), Benjamin discusses *göttliche Gewalt* (here translated as "divine power") in relation to its *Manifestation*, which is "first and last, in language, sacred language above all." Here the divine can be *gewaltlos oder gewaltig,* which the translator renders (confusingly) as "with force or without."

even pardonable to kill. Benjamin's terminology is challenging: the commandment is not a hard and fast philosophical principle but a *Richtschnur*, a guide or mason's line, a rough template for behavior and one that can be modified as needed. Who, then, decides on when and how to abandon the guideline? Here we enter into a sort of Kierkegaardian vacuum: there are those who have sometimes to "wrestle with it in solitude and, in exceptional cases, to take on themselves the responsibility of ignoring it" (250). The "exceptional" cases are *ungeheuren*, monstrous, grotesque. Thus, says Benjamin, the Jewish law accepts that one can kill in self-defense (he does not mention Abraham). There is no absolute sanctity of life, not least because life without justice is worth little. Here Benjamin would seem implicitly to support the *geistige Terrorist* who makes exactly that case, that mere life is no life.[62] He disagrees with those who think that the sacredness of life derives from the fact of life alone, but he does accept that we cannot entertain the idea of the complete nonexistence of the species. Here he starts another hare, not to be chased down, about why some of us might entertain at all the dogma of the sacredness of (mere) life.

Benjamin's final point: while the "breaking of this cycle" of mythic forms by divine violence is the principle upon which any hope for a new historical epoch is founded, we cannot expect to read back through history to ascertain when it might have happened in the past. It is not available as an element of any specific historiography: the expiatory, atoning power, or force (*Kraft*) of violence is invisible to us (*nicht zutage liegt*). It could have been there in a war, or in an episode of crowd violence, but it cannot be tracked there even after the event and certainly not ever proclaimed in advance. Could it have been there in the French Revolution, or perhaps just in some of its constitutive moments: perhaps in the crowd's "divine judgment" (*Gottesgericht*) on a criminal (252)? It may be named as governing (*waltende*) events, but it cannot be seen or identified. Calling it anything is, then, it seems, a leap of faith. Calling it useful would appear to be a betrayal of the principle of pure means without ends. It may be that such an event is without terror only because it is completely without visible attributes altogether. So what is it?

The question may indeed seem to invite a less-than-complex response, of the sort typified in Terry Eagleton's summation of Benjamin's negative view of history as "turning our eyes instead to the Messiah who by tinkering a little with the cosmos here and there will succeed in trans-

---

62. *Gesammelte Schriften* 2:1, 201.

forming everything at a stroke."[63] Even Derrida, after an indubitably complex engagement with Benjamin's essay, pronounces it "too Heideggerian, too messianico-Marxist or archeo-eschatological for me"; more cautiously, Judith Butler confesses to a struggle to hold together the theological and the political.[64] Is it really the case that only the gods, or perhaps God, can save us? Does Benjamin implicitly endorse the positions of Schiller and Matthew Arnold, that if we think we are working for specific revolutionary changes, we are by definition getting it wrong, that we should go home and be patient, applying force until right is ready? Is this nothing more than new wine in old bottles? At least one attentive reader of Benjamin thinks not. Slavoj Žižek asks whether we might not "fearlessly identify divine violence with positively existing historical phenomena, thus avoiding any obscurantist mystification."[65] The project here is "an endorsement of emancipatory violence" (206), an effort to justify "revolutionary terror" as divine violence (199). To make this work, Žižek has to reintroduce the temporal dimension that Benjamin has erased, the passing of time that allows for terror to operate. He also has to put back into play an element of knowledge, which Benjamin also displaced, whereby that which is for the observer merely "an outburst of violence can be divine *for those engaged in it*" (200, italics mine). Disregarding the "guideline" forbidding the killing of others thus becomes a matter of conviction rather than a sheer, uninformed risk, even though it remains something enacted without reference to the "big Other." Indeed, it is a sign of the impotence of the big Other or God (201). It is not, however, an "anarchic explosion" (201).

For Benjamin, I think, it is anarchic explosion: there is no other thing it could be if the criterion of pure means is to be respected. It also cannot have a knowledge component, although it is fair to say that Benjamin's account of taking the risk is hard to imagine without having some empirical-historical possibilities in mind. But to make divine violence into a helpful analytic for past history and present-future prospects, Žižek has to refuse or finesse some of its author's injunctions, refusing

63. Terry Eagleton, *Sweet Violence: The Idea of the Tragic* (Oxford, UK: Blackwell, 2003), 61.

64. Derrida, *Acts of Religion*, 298; Butler, "Critique, Coercion, and Sacred Life," 204. In a powerful reading of Derrida's work, Martin Hägglund has argued that it is always founded in a commitment to "temporal finitude" that is absolute: nothing can eliminate "the spacing of time." See *Radical Atheism: Derrida and the Time of Life* (Stanford, CA: Stanford University Press, 2008), 2, 28.

65. Slavoj Žižek, *Violence: Six Sideways Reflections* (New York: Picador, 2008), 197.

to remain outside time and glossing the question of the guideline by re-lating it to knowledge, to an envisaged outcome. Robespierre and Lenin (and to some degree Mao) are his favored examples of the emancipatory violence (terror) deserving vindication. Robespierre did indeed declare that the people throw thunderbolts instead of handing down sentences (202), but this was part of a specific rhetorical case against the trial of the king; the Jacobin terror did hand down sentences, however peremptory, precisely because it sought state recognition as the dispenser of the power of death; it had a clear end to follow its means. The case of Lenin is less clear cut. Lenin did not, as Žižek sees it, either know or claim to know what he was doing; he simply felt the need (rather like Samson) to act, the need not to ask for a guarantee, the overpowering need to bring down the old order. That this same Lenin who precipitated the revolution also felt the later need to slow it down only makes the case stronger; that magic moment of absolute rupture stands alone, unmarked by what came before or after. In this it differs from the *Blitz* (flash of lightning) that Hegel, with the French Revolution in mind, described in section 11 of the *Phenomenology* as illuminating the features of a new world "all at once." There is no ready-to-hand new world, born as if by magic and laid out before our eyes without any effort having been expended or any time passing. But there is an intimation of something that is not the present, or rather that is a present quite different from the past and has no clear future. In his account of Lenin, Žižek writes of this moment as one in which the utopian future is neither fully present nor seen in the distance, yet wherein we are "allowed to act *as if*" a future is somehow "there to be seized" even if it is not.[66] This happens "as if by Grace" and evokes neither wager nor prediction. It is however a kind of (empty) knowledge, or substitute for knowledge, an "immediate index of its own truth" (260). Ends give way to means as "freedom becomes an end in it-self, caught in its own paroxysm" (271).

One can, of course, entertain a spirit of paradox here. It could be said, for instance, that it does not matter what Lenin or Robespierre said or thought they were doing, even to the point of vanguardist delu-sion, because what really matters (is proved to have mattered) is simply what happened. But that is still to decide, against Benjamin's apparent

---

66. V. I. Lenin, *Revolution at the Gates: Selected Writings from February to October 1917*, ed. with introduction and afterword by Slavoj Žižek (London: Verso, 2004), 259. The topic is taken up again in *In Defense of Lost Causes, Second Edition* (London: Verso, 2009), 463–88. Here the case for "actual" popular violence as divine is expanded on, and the Lenin-Stalin contrast is parsed as one between divine and mythic violence.

injunction, that the incursion of divine violence is knowable to some-body after the fact. Benjamin's absolute refusal of such recognition does seem to sanctify the moment of divine violence as truly not of this world and open to influencing this world in ways we cannot possibly know. It seems to suggest that, even if we think we know what we are doing and why, we cannot be the agents of justice, only the unwitting clearers of the ground, conduits of a power whose divinity is indexed by remaining un-known and unseen: an invisible god.

It seems, then, that Benjamin's divine violence is not at all analo-gous to a moment of conversion, a brief hiatus between one state of personal being and another. It opens the possibility for justice but is in-different to the life of the single subject. In this respect, it is the exact op-posite of the Pauline event, the light from heaven that also comes with a voice, an imperative to the pursuit of outcomes: go to Damascus and await instructions. And yet there has been an effort to assimilate Paul and Benjamin under the rubric of messianism, and even to propose Paul as a prefiguring of the Leninist disruption. Alain Badiou reads him as exemplary of the "militant figure" and of "extreme dispositions," one whose experiences render him outside the law and beyond "the remit of knowledge."[67] The Pauline break has "no bearing on the explicit con-tent of the doctrine" but is a "formal" condition, a "pure event" detached from affiliation with world or community; it is in this sense that Paul is "not a philosopher" (107–8). Badiou appears to endorse the conflation of formal disruption with a politics, albeit the politics of possibility, without doctrinal definition.[68] A less politicized Paul preoccupies Gior-gio Agamben, who brings him much closer to Benjamin by way of the paradigm of *désoeuvrement*, the "inoperative" (beyond utility or end).[69] For Agamben, the Pauline texts are literally and historically messianic, a case he makes with some care and attention. Messianic power finds its

67. Alain Badiou, *Saint Paul: The Foundation of Universalism*, trans. Ray Brassier (Stanford, CA: Stanford University Press, 2003), 2, 5, 45. The Lenin comparison appears at least twice (2, 31).

68. Elsewhere, Badiou defines a "genuine event" as instanced only by a "void" marked by "absolute neutrality of being." It must persist as unnameable, lest it descend into evil. The naming of the other as a nothingness in order to ensure one's own sub-stance (the Nazi deviation) is only the simulacrum of the event, and it is this that pro-duces terror. See *Ethics: An Essay on the Understanding of Evil*, trans. Peter Hallward (London: Verso, 2001), 73, 77, 86. Like Žižek, Badiou relates the true event to grace: a "laicized grace" (123).

69. Giorgio Agamben, *The Time That Remains: A Commentary on the Letter to the Romans*, trans. Patricia Dailey (Stanford, CA: Stanford University Press, 2005), 101, 110–11.

expression in "weakness" (136). This weakness is explained as an odd blend of the active and the passive, whereby Agamben works for a strict correspondence with some of Benjamin's accounts of divine violence: "This is the remnant of potentiality that is not consumed in the act, but is conserved in it each time and dwells there . . . it cannot be accumulated in any form of knowledge or dogma, and if it cannot impose itself as a law, it does not follow that it is passive or inert. To the contrary, it acts in its own weakness, rendering the world of law inoperative, in de-creating or dismantling the states of fact or of law, making them freely available for use" (137). Acting in weakness, electing weakness as an expression of not working, fits the profile of the proletarian general strike: making possible a change by unmaking what is given. But that is not the thrust of Agamben's argument (145), which takes us not to Lenin but to an important section of the *Arcades* project, where Benjamin writes about the image (*Bild*) in its relation to historical time.[70] What matters, he suggests, is not what the image has to tell us about times past—the cultural historical register of what we once were—but its coming into the present, which it does all at once, in a flash (*blitzhaft*), in a moment that is described as "perilous" (*gefährlich*). Like the light from heaven, or the onset of divine violence, this moment—the famous *Jetztzeit*—is one of recognition, something previously reposing inertly in the record springs to life owing to its expressing something urgent about the present.

Thus we return to the question of reading, the question that lies suspended in Benjamin's essay, where it has lain waiting for recovery without receiving any commentary that I have so far found in my (admittedly limited, largely anglophone) survey of the critical literature. For this image, be it print or painting or sculpture, can be (in the wider sense) only seen or read. Whether by days or by centuries, it preexists, waiting for someone to come along and notice it. Benjamin's word is striking: images acquire "legibility" (*Lesbarkeit*) only at a "particular time." *Particular* translates *bestimmt*: determined and by determinate conditions. The image is the image "that is read" (*das gelesene Bild*), and reading is dangerous (*gefährlich*). Only later, in the famous theses "On the Concept of History," which adapt and reformulate these thoughts, does this "danger" become that of slipping back into social-democratic gradualism. Here it is more unhinged and unpredictable: not just reader beware, but beware the reader. Reading tells us who and where we are without our knowing anything about it, or us, until we read. The form of the read-

70. *The Arcades Project*, trans. Howard Eiland and Kevin McLaughlin (Cambridge, MA: Belknap Press of Harvard University Press, 1999), 462–63.

ing moment is messianic, but because it is a form of address, and generates address in the "now of its recognizability," we are sent back into
the world. So the *Unterredung*, the conference or conversation of the
essay on violence, may not be so small scale and quietist (some would
say Habermasian) after all, to the degree that it is based on reading, on
the apprehension of the image for now-time. No wonder, then, that it is
Derrida who is one of the few to pick up on the place of reading in Benjamin's essay and asks the question, "Is this deconstruction?" There is,
he writes, "something of the general strike [he must mean the proletarian general strike], and thus of the revolutionary situation, in every reading that initiates something new and that remains unreadable in regard
to established canons and norms of reading."[71] Many proud academics
might prefer to stop right there. Not Derrida. This is and is not deconstruction. It is only part of deconstruction, the thought of which puts
together acknowledging this could-be revolutionary situation with the
awareness that "it is within the academy that it has been developed"
(272). In other words—and this is a familiar Derridean paradox—there
is no pure means without ends, no flash of recognition without before
and after, no proletarian without political strike, no founding without
preserving violence, no divine without mythic violence. Deconstruction,
Derrida says, is the practice of realizing this and "also the thought *of* this
differential contamination—and the thought *taken by* the necessity of
this contamination" (272). He thus disputes (even as he has been associated with) the power of theory as sheer terror proposed by Bruno Bauer
in a letter of 1841: "The terrorism of true theory must clear the field."[72]
Things are not so simple.

Is there a last word? And if there is, is this it? Surrealists, anarchists,
and members of Occupy would surely say not; or perhaps, yes and no.
For us scholars, insofar as we seek to propose that our work in the library and the classroom might be forces for significant positive change
(and there are, of course, other kinds of activism on offer), the road
ahead might seem lonely and slow. Very few, if any, among us are likely
to become that little old lady who started that great big war. The pressure placed on any attempt to make reading and teaching the core of a
revolutionary change, or any change (and it was, of course, thus theorized by Godwin and Paine and other Enlightenment figures), is huge.
It fulfills a deeply held fantasy, that of creating a new and better world
and doing so without bloodshed. The young Coleridge set out to work

71. Derrida, *Acts of Religion*, 271.
72. Cited in Stedman Jones, *Karl Marx*, 98.

for exactly this, describing his grand effort to "place Liberty on her seat with bloodless hands."[73] Before him Edmund Burke, all too aware that the violent history of British politics could hardly be denied, sought to explain it by invoking a seemingly nonhuman agency similar to divine violence, a "first and supreme necessity only, a necessity that is not chosen but chooses, a necessity paramount to deliberation, that admits no discussion, and demands no evidence."[74] Any change brought about by Rousseau's general will always requires a legislator, and in this (along with its emphasis on the vote) it differs from Benjamin's divine violence. But Rousseau sought to give his legislator the cleanest possible hands by insisting that he never be given executive power: whoever makes the law should never be allowed to apply it. So important is this principle that the incursion of a deity has often been faked to impress citizens with the sublime justice of the laws.

No divine violence, says Benjamin, can produce bloodshed; but this is hardly an empirical directive, because it would be absurd to claim, for example, that (actually) burying people alive is ethically superior to shedding their blood. All human violence takes time, while all pure or divine violence is outside time. This alone makes it unseeable and unknowable. It is without terror, but it does nothing to explain the continued presence of terror in the world.[75] There is in Benjamin's model absolutely no payoff, as far as I can see, for acting in the world as a motivated human agent. So it is strange indeed that the case of teaching appears as it does in the argument, where it is understandable partly as a traditional, Schillerian wise passiveness, but also as *göttliche Gewalt*, as a potentially explosive, time-destroying event whose effect must be unknown to its agent—people like us—even as it changes the world forever. What conditions for thinking allowed Benjamin this idea almost one hundred years ago? Can it exist for us as anything other than a grandiose fantasy of possible self-importance? Can we see a space around classroom and podium for the incursion of a divine violence? Has it happened, perhaps, while you are reading these lines? Can we send out not only sparks of inextinguishable thought (Shelley's words) but also sparks that will fuel a revolutionary fire? The question seems especially acute at a time when

73. Samuel Taylor Coleridge, *Lectures 1795: On Politics and Religion*, ed. Lewis Patton and Peter Mann (Princeton, NJ: Princeton University Press, 1971), 17.

74. *The Writings and Speeches of Edmund Burke*, ed. L. G. Mitchell (Oxford, UK: Clarendon Press, 1989), 7:147.

75. Judith Butler, *Parting Ways: Jewishness and the Critique of Zionism* (New York: Columbia University Press, 2013), 95–96, cites another short work of Benjamin's that describes the last judgment as drowning out the cry of terror.

the humanist academy is showing a new curiosity about passive or even inert (and emphatically nonaggressive) affects as critical to our collective efforts. This trend, admirable in its aspiration to minimal ecological harm but perhaps also deriving from Adorno's negative response to the student movement of the 1960s as "pseudo-activity," should concern us. It would be easy enough to deploy Benjamin, too, as a supporter of the school of doing nothing. He wrote his essay in the ambience of a defeated and demilitarized Germany, though also in the knowledge of a violent Russian Revolution. Our besetting conditions include a morally bankrupt global neoliberalism that has completely refused any redistribution of wealth and an appalling refugee crisis, for which the major long-term perpetrator, the United States, acknowledges no responsibility and offers no response. Who could *not* wish for some bloodless divine violence to set the world on a different course; who could *not* wish that the impulse might come out of (or, better said, pass through) his or her classroom? And who could *not* wish that the world of Judges, and the legacies it has helped sponsor, were less appallingly violent than they are?

4

From Terror to *the* Terror

Terror and the French Revolution

By the end of 1794, something remarkable had happened
to the word *terror*: it had become firmly identified with Jacobin control of the French Revolution under the rubric of
the Terror. The emotion or freestanding personification
of extreme fear that under various names in various languages had been roaming Western rhetoric for centuries
as one among a cluster of near-synonymous and imperfectly
distinguished cognates had, for the first time, come to be
anchored in a specific historical formation characterizing
a unique moment in the conduct of a state. Cities had been
sacked and civilians put to the sword, but never before
had any political body been able to lay claim to the power
of terror in a manner so absolute that it could be said to
have created an autonomous, nonhuman agent operating
according to its own abstract laws, seemingly as remote
from human oversight as the stars and planets. For believ-
ers, extreme terrors had always been claimed as God's terrors, even when they were deploying those terrors themselves, as Cromwell, for example, did in Ireland. Or they
were the property of kings and princes who wielded terror
in order to cause terror, sometimes in God's name and
sometimes not. But the Jacobin Terror has passed into history as something more: a monstrous death machine so

demanding that its human creators could not keep up with its demands for sacrifice, compelling them at first to reduce the legal apparatus inhibiting the supply of victims to an absolute minimum, and finally obliging them, when everyone else had been executed, to forfeit their own lives.[1]

Or so we have been led to believe by the more melodramatic among the mythmakers of the French Revolution in contemplating what Carlyle called "this new amazing Thing," this "most remarkable transaction in these last thousand years," this "black precipitous Abyss; whither all things have been long tending."[2] As far as I know, there is no evidence at all of any of the Jacobins referring to their moment in history as *the* Terror. Indeed, careful work by Annie Geffroy on the rhetoric of terror words suggests that we have here yet another case of history as written by the winners. The words *terrorisme*, *terroriste*, and *terroriser* come into use only in the later months of 1794, after Thermidor, in other words, after the fall of the Robespierre faction. *Terreur* occurs more than fifty times before 1789 as a translation of Aristotle's *phobos* (although Corneille, as we have seen, at least in his critical dissertation, preferred *crainte*).[3] When Robespierre invokes "la terreur" in February 1794 as "prompt, severe, inflexible justice," it is at the beginning of a sentence, and thus he does not, given the demands of French grammar, clearly stress the definite article: it is better translated as *terror* rather than as *the terror*.[4] Vergniaud invokes terror as an agency in the name of the law (and not just of monarchs and gods) in March 1792 and repeats it in March 1793. In August of the same year, Danton also associates terror with the dagger (*le glaive*) of the law, and it would be declared "the order of the day" by the end of that month.[5] As the strong arm of virtue (for Robespierre and Saint-Just), terror was indeed being imaged both as a legal power and as a distinct entity governing both its victims and

---

1. On the Terror described as a thermodynamic system in Hugo, see Pierre St. Amand, "Hot Terror: *Quatrevingt-treize*," *SubStance* 27, no. 2 (1998): 61–72. Hannah Arendt, *The Origins of Totalitarianism*, 461–68, also stresses the imagined autonomy of (total) terror as an agency of nature, a constant motion utterly indifferent to individuals and absorbing both victims and perpetrators.

2. Thomas Carlyle, *The French Revolution: A History*, 3 vols. (London: Chapman and Hall, 1889), 3:171–74.

3. Annie Geffroy, "Terreur et terrorisme: Les mots en héritage, du néologisme au concept," in *La Vendée: Après la terreur, la reconstruction*, ed. Alain Gérard (Paris: Perrin, 1997), 144–61, esp. 147.

4. And it is indeed thus translated in Maximilien Robespierre, *Virtue and Terror*, ed. Jean Ducange, trans. John Howe, introduction by Slavoj Žižek (London: Verso, 2007), 115.

5. Geffroy, "Terreur et terrorisme," 149–50.

its deployers, an abstraction with an agency all of its own. But it is only after the fall of the Robespierrists in July 1794 that *the Terror* comes into focus as a term for describing a period in history that is supposed to be over. By 1798, the supplement to the *Dictionnaire de l'Académie* lists *terrorisme* for the first time as *système de terreur* or *régime de terreur*: the reign of terror. From there it is but a short step to popular acceptance of something called the Terror.[6]

Geffroy (153) finds no instance of either *terrorisme* or *terroriste* before September 1794: the terms come into use as derogatory references to the fallen Jacobins, and by the end of the year are in popular use, along with "the terror." François-Noël Babeuf keeps the term alive as describing the new government's continuing intimidation of the populist movement, but it is more frequently invoked as unique to Jacobinism, and as such, according to some historians, its emergence confirms the essential logic of the entire revolution.[7] The existence of two terrors, the red and the white, the first that of 1793–1794 and the second that of the Thermidorean response, became rhetorically familiar only in the 1830s;[8] the second of these has never become comparably familiar in the popular imagination. After the second "Red Terror" of 1917, terror would again become dominantly an attribute of the communist state, and then (after the Nazi phenomenon) of absolutist states in general. After 1945, no European state, and certainly not the United States, would acknowledge its own participation in terror regimes, a sleight of hand made possible by (mostly but not always) displacing the site of terror to other parts of the world, principally the decolonizing countries.

The French Revolution also saw the reinvention of an older but hitherto defunct verb, *terrifier*, and the invention of another, *terroriser* (*terrorifier* was also floated but did not survive).[9] New terror words came into both English (*terrorism*, *terrorist*) and German (*Terror, Terrorist, Terrorismus*) at the same time in the middle 1790s. But was terror

---

6. Geffroy, "Terreur et terrorisme," 147.

7. The most influential modern exponent of this view has been François Furet; it has most recently been contested in Jonathan Israel, *Revolutionary Ideas: An Intellectual History of the French Revolution from the Rights of Man to Robespierre* (Princeton, NJ: Princeton University Press, 2014). There is a detailed history of the post–Jacobin Terror in Howard G. Brown, *Ending the French Revolution: Violence, Justice, and Repression from the Terror to Napoleon* (Charlottesville: University of Virginia Press, 2006).

8. Geffroy, "Terreur et terrorisme," 157.

9. Geffroy, "Terreur et terrorisme," 157. *Terrify* exists in English from the late sixteenth century and appears eight times in the KJV, but it does not occur in Shakespeare. Milton's poetry uses it four times. See the discussion in chapter 3.

really "the order of the day" after September 1793? Recent scholarship has cast this familiar truth into doubt, as it appears that the Convention never actually published the proclamation.[10] Nonetheless, the term appears to have been taken up into popular usage. Annie Jourdan, whose recent work (using up-to-date search engines) I am here drawing on, finds a plethora of precedents before 1793 for the use of *terreur* in both positive and negative senses: positive in aesthetic, political, and even legal contexts; negative as the strategy of those one does not like or support. From 1790, the monarchist *Ami du roi* is accusing the revolutionaries of "reigning by terror," well before terror is taken up (reluctantly or not) as a positive attribute by the revolutionaries themselves.[11] Each side of the political divide appears to have accused the other of resorting inappropriately to terror well before Robespierre and Saint-Just opted to project it as a positive, purgative force.[12] And then, according to Jourdan (63–67), they did so much less emphatically than the latter-day myths would suggest. Saint-Just reinforces Robespierre's advocacy of justice, probity, and virtue as more important than terror.[13] The image of the Terror that we still sustain is the result of the rhetoric of the Thermidorean reaction, which began one day after the fall of Robespierre when Barère spoke of the "system of the Terror."[14]

10. See Annie Jourdan, "Les discours de la terreur à l'époque révolutionnaire (1776–1798): Étude comparative sur une notion ambiguë," *French Historical Studies* 36, no. 1 (2013): 51–81, esp. 52. Jourdan cites the work of Jean-Clément Martin (published in 2006) and attributes the "order of the day" phrase to Danton. The latest account is Timothy Tackett, *The Coming of the Terror in the French Revolution* (Cambridge, MA: Harvard University Press, 2015), 303, which observes that the "order of the day" phrase became a commonplace without being "formally decreed."

11. Jourdan, "Les discours de la terreur," 59–60: "ils ne veulent régner que par la terreur."

12. Indeed, in his very last speech in July 1794, Robespierre accused his enemies of spreading "the system of terror and slander." See George Armstrong Kelly, "Conceptual Sources of the Terror," *Eighteenth-Century Studies* 14, no. 1 (1980): 18–36, esp. 36.

13. Marie-Hélène Huet, *Mourning Glory: The Will of the French Revolution* (Philadelphia: University of Pennsylvania Press, 1997), notes the "consistent desire for moderation" that goes along with Saint-Just's invocations of "inflexible justice" (91). She finds that terror is not, for him, the tool of virtue but its antithesis, the sign of its failure (93). See also Dan Edelstein, *The Terror of Natural Right: Republicanism, the Cult of Nature, and the French Revolution* (Chicago: University of Chicago Press, 2009), 220, 227–28. Timothy Tackett, "Interpreting the Terror," *French Historical Studies* 24, no. 4 (2001): 569–78, also comments on "the long reticence of the revolutionary leadership under the Constituent Assembly to embrace terror or terrorlike activities, even in the face of growing counterrevolutionary threats" (577).

14. See Bronisław Baczko, "The Terror before the Terror? Conditions of Possibility, Logic of Realization," in *The French Revolution and the Creation of Modern Political Culture*, vol. 4, *The Terror*, ed. Keith Michael Baker (Bingley, UK: Emerald Group Publishing, 1994), 19–38, esp. 37n8.

Terrorisme is recorded for the first time in August 1794; *terroriste*, as if by prescient irony, on September 11.[15]

Needless to say, none of this diminishes the terror-inducing functions, for those living through it, of the period now commonly called the Terror, commencing in September 1793 (or, some say, six months earlier) and ending with the fall of Robespierre in July 1794.[16] After the Law of Suspects (September 17, 1793), it no longer sufficed to be merely innocent: one had to actively demonstrate commitment to the revolution. The Law of 22 Prairial (June 10, 1794) subsequently confirmed a culture of universal surveillance and denunciation and sped up the process of conviction to the point where merely to be under suspicion was felt to be (and often was) paramount to a death sentence. But this nine-month period of exceptional fear-inducing legislation (and paralegislation) was not the result of a coherent and consistent ideology of the sort that some historians have seen as the essence of the revolution itself. To propose anything definitive about the Terror is, of course, to take sides in a very long-standing and public debate, and one with very clear consequences for the conduct of politics and counterpolitics in the present.[17] But a good deal of recent scholarship suggests that the recourse to the spectacle of intensified public executions was a largely unanticipated and short-term response to coalescences of military and economic emergencies. Nor, according to Jourdan, was terror ever avowed as the primary agent of political transformation; that task was allotted to justice and to virtue. The Terror, for all its continuing grasp on the political imagination of Euro-American political discourse, was the retrospective creation of those who defeated the Jacobins and who sought to ensure that their memory would be forever disparaged by rendering them cruel in unique and world-changing ways.[18]

But if the mythic status of the Jacobin (and thereby French) Terror has proved a persuasive one, political terror itself was not new. George

15. Jourdan, "Les discours de la terreur," 68.

16. The last and most intense weeks of this period are sometimes called "the Great Terror," a term that Robert Conquest would take over for his influential history of Stalinism.

17. The bibliography here is immense and still growing. Recent summaries can be found, e.g., in Tackett, *The Coming of the Terror*, and Marisa Linton, *Choosing Terror: Virtue, Friendship and Authenticity in the French Revolution* (Oxford: Oxford University Press, 2013), 8–11.

18. Bronisław Baczko, *Ending the Terror: The French Revolution after Robespierre*, trans. Michael Petherem (Cambridge: Cambridge University Press, 1994), gives an account of the post-Thermidor trials (136–84), which argues that much of the so-called evidence of various outrages was not historically founded, even though it became the stuff of history.

Armstrong Kelly finds much evidence of *terreur* being identified as an attribute of arbitrary government under the old regime. In the writings of Malesherbes, especially, in the 1760s and 1770s, terror is what is generated by the culture of unpredictability around taxation and customs, and the production of *lettres de cachet*.[19] This is mostly not the terror of death, although imprisonment without trial could amount to that: Malesherbes is not responding to the spectacle of the guillotine, which had not yet been adopted as the approved method of execution. But such "terror" does embody the power of the state to generate perpetual anxiety or fear by virtue of its own very existence, sustaining a radical uncertainty about whether and how the laws will be applied, and to whom. One need not be an avowed enemy of the state to fall victim to its whims. Kings and nations were of course supposed to be terrible to their enemies, and Ronald Schechter has assembled a good deal of evidence for the power of terror as a traditionally desired and respected feature of kingship and thus of national well-being. Whether French, English, Prussian, or Swedish, kings were admired for being able to generate terror—sometimes merely by the mentions of their names. Military heroes sought similar authority. The coronation oath of Louis XIV called upon the king to be the *pavor, terror et formido* of the enemies of his nation.[20] In the light of this set of inherited expectations, the Jacobin claim to the power of terror is simply an effort to tap into the list of expectations applicable to a newly emergent (albeit now republican) state. Not to possess the power of terror would indeed be to confess failure as a state. To flaunt the power of terror is to affirm the integrity of the nation; it is in this spirit that nine ships of the Royal Navy (from 1696 to 1916) have borne the name HMS *Terror* (one of them went on the ill-fated Franklin expedition in 1845).[21]

19. Kelly, "Conceptual Sources of the Terror," 26–29.

20. Ronald Schechter, "The Terror of Their Enemies: Reflections on a Trope in Eighteenth-Century Historiography," *Historical Reflections/Reflexions historiques* 36, no. 1 (2010): 53–75, esp. 59.

21. The larger history of terror terms is surveyed in some detail by Rudolf Walther, "Terror, Terrorismus," in *Geschichtliche Grundbegriffe*, ed. Otto Bruner et al., 6:323–444. The dominant political and juridical German equivalent before 1789 is *Schreckung*, e.g., as a translation of the *territio* in Roman law (325–36). Until well into the nineteenth century, German generally prefers *das Schrecken* (from 1794) as a translation of *terreur* (364). Although *Terror* and *Terrorismus* do appear from the mid-1790s, there is an early preference (modified in later years) for such terms as *Schreckensystem*, *Schreckenzeit*, and *Schreckenherrschaft* to designate the critical nominalizations of terror (354–55).

The tradition of the state (mostly monarchical) laying claim to the power of terror would seem to be the most likely immediate source of the Jacobin rhetoric, hesitant as it seems to have been. *Terreur* came into French from Latin in the thirteenth century, and by 1736 it was being disambiguated from *peur* and *frayeur* by a criterion of intensity: we feel *peur* at what is sudden and immediate, *frayeur* at dangers that are more striking and "thought upon" (*réfléchie*), and *terreur* at what assaults (*abat*) our spirit.[22] Montesquieu identified fear (*crainte*) and *ter-reur* as the recourses of despotic governments that have no better ways to preserve order,[23] and it is this insight that Malesherbes develops in his critique of the monarchy and that Holbach applies to a critique of the Catholic Church.[24] But state power, as Schechter has shown, still plausibly claimed the right to terrorize its enemies, and it is easy enough to extend the concept of the enemy to domestic as well as foreign factions. Just as Louis XIV was sworn to be a terror to his foes, so, too, Marat, as early as 1790 (and thus well before Danton in 1793), threatened a *terreur salutaire* on behalf of the people against the enemies of the constitution, abroad and at home.[25] So, if terror (then as now) was mostly invoked to describe what one's enemies practiced, it was also available as the righteous recourse of the good governor to respond to states of exception.[26] Few adopted the Hobbesian position that terror is the core principle of government itself, but equally few renounced it completely; among those who did were, consistently or not, some of the major players in the French Revolution.[27]

22. Gerd van den Heuvel, "Terreur, Terroriste, Terrorisme," in *Handbuch politisch-sozialer Grundbegriffe in Frankreich, 1680–1820* (Munich: Oldenbourg, 1985), 3:89–321, esp. 90.

23. van den Heuvel, "Terreur, Terroriste, Terrorisme," 94–95.

24. van den Heuvel, "Terreur, Terroriste, Terrorisme," 96. For Montesquieu's view of terror as best suited to despotism, see *The Spirit of the Laws*, trans. Thomas Nugent, 2 vols. (London, 1750), vi.9. Monarchies and republics should operate with "honor and virtue" as their "spring." It is not clear, in either French or English, whether the logic is inclusive or sequential, i.e., whether each requires both honor and virtue, or the one without the other. For their republic, Saint-Just and Robespierre prefer virtue.

25. van den Heuvel, "Terreur, Terroriste, Terrorisme," 99.

26. This is argued as legitimating the Jacobin view of terror in Sophie Wahnich, *In Defence of the Terror: Liberty or Death in the French Revolution*, trans. David Fernbach (London: Verso, 2012). Dan Edelstein, *The Terror of Natural Right*, 19, argues that 78 percent of the victims of the Terror were designated as outlaws ("hors de la loi"), a category he sees as being conflated with enemies of the species (*hostis humani generis*) according to natural right.

27. Hobbes is clear that justice without terror is ineffectual: see *Leviathan*, 94, 109.

The case for regarding the Terror as the fulfillment of the innate logic of the Revolution is also undermined by looking at the identifications with classical culture that were so prominent before 1795. If terror were part of at least a conscious logic (and there is little evidence of the Jacobins not going public with their plans), one would expect instances of classical "terror"—like knowing one would be put to the sword if conquered after resisting the Romans—to be adduced as justifications for latter-day political success. But Harold T. Parker's *The Cult of Antiquity and the French Revolutionaries*, still the most exhaustive study of its topic, does not find this to be the case. Tracing the revolutionaries' invocations of the classics "from the high school to the guillotine,"[28] Parker notes repeated references to a rather narrow canon of texts taught in the schools, generally more republican than imperialist, and more Latin than Greek. The debate about republican government became more prominent after September 1792, with more allusions to classical precedents (19). Robespierre, Billaud-Varenne, and Saint-Just admire especially the discipline and judicial severity of Lycurgus (155ff.) but do not invoke his name directly or in any justificatory way in relation to the Terror (a term they never used). The Spartan model (via Plutarch) so dear to Saint-Just focused mainly on culture and education rather than coercive politics. And Desmoulins, writing against recourse to terror, produces Tacitus as an ironic mask employed to expose the violence of the Jacobins, nothing less than a model of critique.[29] Terror, especially in the form of panic terror, was indeed evident in classical accounts of various civil wars— Annie Jourdan counts sixteen uses of the term in the first volume of Marmontel's translation of Lucan—but not as a term of approbation.[30]

28. Harold T. Parker, *The Cult of Antiquity and the French Revolutionaries: A Study in the Development of the Revolutionary Spirit* (Chicago: University of Chicago Press, 1937), 8. Hereafter cited with page numbers in the text.

29. Parker, *Cult of Antiquity*, 148–52. For an extended analysis of Desmoulins, see Caroline Weber, *Terror and Its Discontents*, 115–70.

30. Jourdan, "Les discours de la terreur," 55. Marisa Linton, "The Man of Virtue: The Role of Antiquity in the Political Trajectory of L. A. Saint-Just," *French History* 24, no. 3 (2010): 393–419, makes a different case, that Saint-Just at least was directly supported in his resort to violence by his image of Roman republican heroes. But in an earlier essay on Robespierre, Linton concludes that "the linking of virtue and terror appears to have been without precedent." See her "Robespierre's Political Principles," in *Robespierre*, ed. Colin Haydon and William Doyle (Cambridge: Cambridge University Press, 1999), 37– 53, esp. 50. Brown, *Ending the French Revolution*, 127, notes two seventeenth-century prototypes linking force with justice or authority, whereas Robespierre will pair terror with virtue.

If there was no reference to the Terror before Thermidor, was there any mention of a "reign of terror" before 1794? Yes and no, it seems. I have found no evidence that the phrase "dates back to antiquity," as Linton says it does.[31] The *Oxford English Dictionary* (OED) does correctly find the phrase in John Farell's English translation of D'Ivernois dating from 1784 (*Merriam-Webster* records it only in 1798); and Malesherbes almost got there in 1770 in advising the king that it would be useless to "reign by terror."[32] As has been said, Jourdan notes versions of the phrase circulating in the royalist pamphlet *L'Ami du roi* as early as 1790, where it is of course negatively ascribed to the revolutionaries, as it was by Burke around the same time.[33] So it is at least plausible that the reign of terror was from the start part of the rhetoric of the revolution's opponents, even before they coined *the* Terror. The to-and-froing of terror attributions is nicely imaged in a speech by Vergniaud in March 1792, in which he threatens to turn the terror issuing from the royal palace back upon it in the name of the law.[34] But after Thermidor, this tradition of selectively claiming and disclaiming the power of terror was largely forgotten, generating the sort of amnesia that figured again after September 11, 2001, when both terror and terrorism were definitively attributed to al-Qaeda and only to al-Qaeda, and implicitly denied (notwithstanding the earlier shock-and-awe policy statement discussed in chapter 1) as forming any part of the war-making practices of the United States. Not everyone, however, agreed to turn a blind eye to the "white" terror of Thermidor. Babeuf, as has been noted, was alive to the new government's violent repression of popular movements. By 1797, Benjamin Constant was making a distinction between terror when "reduced to a system and justified in this form" and the spontaneous occurrence of terrorism, however "ferocious and brutal."[35] The terrorism of isolated acts may and will continue to exist, but terror, he declares, must never again be institutionalized as a continuous practice, as it had been by the Jacobins. Constant's concerns are close to those voiced earlier by Malesherbes (in 1770), and it is indeed a new "royalist terror" that he is opposing, one directed at the now powerless remnants of the Jacobin faction (167). The suggestion is that

31. Marisa Linton, *Choosing Terror: Virtue, Friendship and Authenticity in the French Revolution* (Oxford: Oxford University Press, 2013), 11.

32. Kelly, "Conceptual Sources of the Terror," 27.

33. Jourdan, "Les discours de la terreur," 59–62.

34. Cited in Linton, *Choosing Terror*, 114–15.

35. Benjamin Constant, *Des effets de la terreur*, ed. Philippe Raynaud (Paris: Flammarion, 1988), 166.

terror had been part of a state system and could easily become so again, if it had not become so already. Far too many modern commentators assume that Constant's arguments have simply won the day.

Constant's formulation anticipates the distinction that mattered so much in the debates about the Benghazi attacks of September 2012: that between spontaneous (or at least occasional) violence and "terror" as the emanation of policy and premeditation. If you are charged with defending people against spontaneous violence, then you are less culpable for failing than you would be if you had missed the signals of rationally devised plots and conspiracies. And if you are perpetrating such violence, or are sympathetic to it, you are correspondingly less responsible (and blameworthy) for its destructive effects than you would be if you were planning to repeat them as a matter of routine. What has appalled so many commentators on the so-called Jacobin Terror is its appearance of routinization. Here is David Andress, a historian of the violence now almost universally known under the name of the "September Massacres"' of 1792: "It is easy to come to terms with the idea of irrational carnage carried out by sadistic mobs: such acts fit neatly into the concept of a radically 'different', almost subhuman crowd, safely distanced from the self-image of the observer. Far less comfortable is the realisation that bloody murder could be committed by upright citizens in the name of their country's freedom."[36] Andress here suggests that it is not just the image of the enemy other that is at stake; it is also the image of the self. To enact deliberative violence associates it with the more esteemed attributes of our species: reason, foresight, and self-control. Our best selves are thus contaminated by our worst instincts. Spontaneous violence is a momentary loss of control, which seems less culpable. There is a long tradition wherein violence, especially fatal violence, is the more excusable when it is least deliberative, making it more palatable (for instance, as a crime of passion) and less punishable. For similar reasons, torture is held to be more inhumane than a brief outburst of rage. Theorists of revolution and of terror have often reflected this conventional understanding in seeking either to attribute or to displace blame for radical change. That is one reason the debate about the Terror has been so divisive: it offers a choice between the Jacobins as demonic in their reason or as desperate in their passions. Sometimes they have been described as both at once, a doubly demonic image of the terrorist.

36. David Andress, *The Terror: The Merciless War for Freedom in Revolutionary France* (New York: Farrar, Straus, and Giroux, 2005), 111–12.

The metaphorical appeal of the malignant Jacobin has proved a powerful one, and it brings with it a touchstone reference to terror. Thus, for Bishop Martin Spalding, writing a polemical nineteenth-century pro-Catholic version of the history of the Reformation, Calvin is a Jacobin before his time, "cool and calculating," "cold and repulsive," and "inexorable in his anger."[37] By Spalding's account, "Calvin's reign in Geneva was truly a reign of terror" (383). Even otherwise responsible historians can get carried away with the power of the example and its hold over the tradition. Timothy Tackett's recent *The Coming of the Terror in the French Revolution* repeatedly announces the proleptic presence whose emergence it is supposed to be explaining. Thus it is that the "wave of fear" sweeping the countryside in the summer of 1789 is said to have generated "terror" among the people,[38] although these events have actually been nominated as the Grande Peur (Great Fear). Tackett writes a chapter on the so-called September Massacres under the rubric of "the First Terror."[39] On the other side of the channel, British radicals attempted to taint Pitt with his own "reign of terror" on behalf of the establishment.[40] The Terror, it seems, cannot wait to be born, and born again.

Burke in 1790

In the light of the recent enthusiasm for terror talk, it is all the more striking that Edmund Burke's famously influential writings on the French

37. M. J. Spalding, *The History of the Protestant Reformation in Germany and Switzerland, Fourth Edition*, 2 vols. (Baltimore: John Murphy, 1875), 373.

38. Tackett, *Coming of the Terror*, 58.

39. Tackett, *Coming of the Terror*, 192–216. The term is actually smuggled into the narrative much earlier (e.g., 113). Georges Lefebvre wrote the foundational book on the disturbances of summer 1789 under the title of *La Grande Peur*: see *The Great Fear of 1789: Rural Panic in Revolutionary France*, trans. Joan White (London: New Left Books, 1973). I have been so far unable to discover who first used this phrase, and when, but it appears to be another retroactive naming. I am grateful to David Wagner for information on the descriptions of summer 1789. Between the Great Fear and the Great Terror there were at least two capitalized massacres (the Champs de Mars and the September).

40. See Kenneth R. Johnston, *Unusual Suspects: Pitt's Reign of Alarm and the Lost Generation of the 1790s* (Oxford: Oxford University Press, 2013), xvi–xvii. Thomas Pringle, writing about the Cape Colony in 1824, accused Lord Charles Somerset of instituting a "Cape 'Reign of Terror.'" See his *Narrative of a Residence in South Africa,* ed. A. M. Lewin Robinson (Cape Town: C. Struik, 1966), 186. Again, Somerset "absolutely paralyzed the mass of the community with terror" (197). C. M. H. Clark, *A History of Australia*, vol. 1, *From the Earliest Times to the Age of MacQuarrie* (Melbourne: Melbourne University Press, 1962), finds that early British Australia was also "a society whose first principle was subordination and whose agent was terror" (247).

Revolution were not in the habit of stressing the presence of a demonic terror as the key to the logic of republican history. We have seen that in his 1759 *Inquiry* terror was indeed Burke's key term holding together the various elements of the aesthetic of the sublime, and one might thus have predicted that his 1790 *Reflections on the Revolution in France*, and even more so his writings after the Jacobin hegemony, would resort to *terror* as the privileged term for describing current and recent events. But this is not the case. A word search of the first edition of the *Reflections* produces only eight uses of *terror* or *terrors*. Among these, three are obviously subjective, describing what is felt by persons in distress, and at least three are objective, personifying the power of terror as an agent in the world. One of the objective invocations is actually almost positive, when the English regicides are described as "men of great civil, and great military talents, and if the terror, the ornament of their age."[41] Burke might have had no incentive to play up the role of terror in 1790, three or four years before the existence of what came to be called the Terror. But he is well aware of the implications of using the term. Thus he refers tellingly to an attempt by the National Assembly to "array itself in all its terrors, and to call forth all its majesty" (8:260), clearly understanding terror as an attribute of the established state that he very much hopes the revolutionaries will not be able to create or maintain. Majesty and terror belong in the hands of monarchs, not those of the people. What is appropriate for us to feel is the Aristotelian "terror and pity" at the spectacle of the demise of the French king and his ruling elites (132). This puts the spectator of history at a distance from the events, beholding what is happening across the Channel and being "purified" by the experience. In the spirit of such relatively distant contemplation—as with the sublime, near enough to be affecting but far enough away to be safe—we find that the word *horror* is more than twice as common as terror in the *Reflections*, and on all but one occasion it describes what we are to feel from a position of detachment. Burke already seems to understand the need to keep the Revolution at arm's length, inviting us to be appalled and disgusted but not directly threatened. Fully half of his uses of *horror* couple it with some other emotion: scorn and horror, disgust and horror, shame and horror, horror and alarm, indignation and horror. The affective economy of *horror* allows for sharing the space with other affiliated or contrasting emotions; terror is more likely to take over completely, edging out any allies or competitors. In this respect, Burke seems to have moved on from his more eclectic and inclusive use of *ter-*

41. *Writings and Speeches*, 8:99.

ror in the *Inquiry*. The power of terror may well be what the new French government would like to claim, as the signature of its consolidated status, and that is exactly what Burke wishes to deny it. Analogously, when he uses the word *terrible*, it is almost exclusively as a simple intensifier, with no recollection of its Latin origin.

Burke's chronicling of the development of the Revolution through the 1790s is similarly parsimonious in its attributions of terror to the French government and correspondingly precise in its understanding of why that matters. In his 1791 *Letter to a Member of the National Assembly*, Burke contends that what the Assembly claims to be a policy of terror is really just mere "force": implicitly, it should not be accorded the dignity of a meditated and rationally apportioned use of purposive intimidation.[42] In the 1793 *Remarks on the Policy of the Allies*, he images the Jacobins as merely "wild savage minds" whose hope of rendering themselves "terrible" depends on energy alone, detached from morals, probity, and prudence.[43] They are capable of governing only "in a state of the utmost confusion," and their deploying of fear and terror as the means of raising and guaranteeing loans and business transactions has no historical precedent and therefore no credibility.[44] In *A Letter to a Noble Lord* (1796), terror goes unmentioned within a hyperbolic denunciation of these "revolution harpies . . . sprung from night and hell."[45] In one of his last works, the *Letters on the Proposals for Peace with the Regicide Directory of France*, the analysis of terror and the reasons for denying it to the revolution become clear. Here Burke talks up France, in language that comes close to that of Blake's prophetic books, as a "monster of a State"[46] whose claim to be a "scourge and terror" to its enemies must come as a surprise: France has become a "vast, tremendous, unformed spectre, in a far more terrific guise than any which ever yet have overpowered the imagination, and subdued the fortitude of man."[47] Terrific, but still a specter that can only lay claim to terror. The power of this "hideous phantom" (9:191) to intimidate its enemies is exactly what must be contested. Given a situation in which France is "too much dreaded," Burke is anxious to steer his readers away from "irrational fear" of the enemy (9:191). So instead of unpredictable, overemotive

42. *Writings and Speeches*, 8:319.
43. *Writings and Speeches*, 8:480.
44. *Writings and Speeches*, 8:499.
45. *The Writings and Speeches of Edmund Burke*, ed. R. B. McDowell (Oxford, UK: Clarendon Press, 1991), 9:156.
46. *Writings and Speeches*, 9:196.
47. *Writings and Speeches*, 9:190–91.

responses to the "first impressions of rage or terror" (9:197), he seeks to encourage a steady resistance and a faith in the powers of the British state's "sober apprehension" and "masculine spirit" (9:191, 192). This involves not acceding to the claims of the French state to wield the power of terror over its enemies, as the rhetoricians of the revolution had been claiming to do from the start.[48] The motley, anarchist rabble whom Burke sees as running France are vilified as sexually and economically profligate, at once cruel and cold and hot and passionate, but they are above all characterized by a "systematick unsociability" (9:257), not the collective single-mindedness that a successful deployment of the power of terror might signal as the property of a unified state. Such unity was an aspiration of the Terror, and it seems that Burke understands this in refusing to concede the formal power of judicial death that the Jacobins sought to possess and to demonstrate (indeed, to possess by demonstrating). Monstrosity and theatricality are his two major rhetorical resources for describing France; one suggests unnatural and threatening intensity, the other a contrived event in which people dress up to deceive others about who they really are. They are at once outside the order of nature and fools. But they do not generate terror. And since we British have "emerged from our first terrors" (9:337), we must be sure not to give way to them again. One way to help in that process is to avoid privileging the term itself.[49] This assists Burke in his task of persuading his readers that France is not so much a "State" as a "Faction" (9:264).

This faction is, however, transnational. The French disease is something whose "spirit lies deep in the corruption of our common nature" (9:265): it has the capacity to emerge as an enemy from within. (The political analogue was the much-invoked Illuminati network that was said to be secretly embedded all over Europe.) If we were to call this disease by the name of *terror*, we would be aptly encompassing both its external and internal qualities: the terror we feel at the sight of terror itself. This is not something Burke is eager to do. Effective resistance to France depends on not according it the objective power of terror, and thereby on not allowing it to arouse a subjective feeling of terror in us. France has "terrified" Europe and promises to remove "terror" if we dutifully sue for peace (9:50,

---

48. Here my understanding differs from that of Ronald Paulson, *Representations of Revolution (1789–1820)* (New Haven, CT: Yale University Press, 1983), 71, for whom Burke really is invested in stimulating terror.

49. Again, in *Remarks on the Policy of the Allies*, Burke had deplored the effects of fear and terror on the European economy, a sphere in which "the least appearance of force" ought to be supposed "totally destructive" (*Writings and Speeches*, 8:499).

51), and in so doing it has produced a new word: *terrorist* (9:89, 90). But Burke seeks to demystify terror, to put it at a distance and to preempt its capacity to enter into the mind of the British subject and act upon him or her from within. Thus, throughout his unfinished letter on the regicide peace, as we have seen to be the case in his *Reflections* of 1790, he makes noticeable use of the word *horror* in places where one might expect to find *terror*. Burke himself, in 1759, had been significantly responsible for running these terms together as meaning much the same thing. But here, near the end of his life, horror is preferred.[50] Horror, again, is the word one uses to indicate a strong adverse reaction to something one sees before one's eyes, something out in the world and not fully in the mind. *Terror*, conversely, is notoriously labile in its signification of either an externally embodied force or an internal response to it. Sometimes it is both, sometimes one cannot be sure which is which. One may look with horror upon an enemy's deeds, but one had best not admit to feeling terror, as terror allows what is outside to conspire with what is inside and to double and redouble its force, leaving us radically uncertain about what is outside and what is within us, and thus, in Burke's terms, unmanned.

Burke's last writings are brilliantly responsive to the complexities of the *terror-horror* distinction as they seek to shore up British resolve without underestimating the power of the enemy, who has to appear forceful enough to be a serious threat without being so forceful as to inspire awe, inertia, and despair. This is what lies behind his earlier (1791) distinction between terror and mere force (8:319). France wants to claim the power of the former while in fact exercising only the vagaries of the latter. Burke is more careful here than many of the political commentators who followed him: Barruel's *Memoirs* invokes the "reign of terror" as both a specific event and as a general feature of the revolution, along with describing "fear and terror" as the crucial component of the initiation rituals of the Illuminati.[51] Barruel's fourth, final volume gives a detailed account of the Freemasons and Illuminati who induct their members by careful use of "terror" (4:356, 374), which runs along with his account of the deployment of terror by the revolutionary state: what is learned through secret rites is broadcast as government policy. Here again there is a conflation of subjective and objective terror, wherein one visits on others a form of what one has oneself endured in order to

---

50. For examples, see *Writings and Speeches*, 9:68, 77, 101, 102, 105, 109, 115.

51. *Memoirs Illustrating the History of Jacobinism: A Translation from the French of the Abbé Barruel*, 4 vols. (London, 1797–1798), 1:189, 2:98, 3:75.

be found worthy of membership of the ruling elite.[52] Even Barruel and Robison are relatively restrained when compared to *The Anti-Jacobin Review*, whose authors do indeed invoke terror (along with the new term *terrorist*) with almost the regularity of a gothic novel.

Novel Terrors

The fastidious distrust and critique of terror talk that informs Burke's writings in the 1790s thus did not impede his more melodramatic contemporaries from a looser rhetoric in which terror was a hot-button polemical attribute of the French enemy, and as such an admitted threat to Britain. Burke's earlier *Philosophical Inquiry* had made the case for terror in the aesthetic sphere as a pleasurably positive thing, but his later work made it clear that this was not to be confused with real-world claims about political power. Hence the French were either denied the power of terror altogether or exposed as practitioners of a merely aesthetic event, a spectacle, which always leaves the beholder in his or her right mind. In the properly aesthetic sphere of fiction, the influence of the early Burke is palpable and was as such summoned to judgment by Richard Payne Knight in his critique of the fashion for "all sorts of terrific and horrific monsters and hobgoblins" evident all over the fine arts productions of his time.[53] The novels of Ann Radcliffe appear to replicate exactly the confused affective vocabulary that Burke's early work had displayed. Her first novel, *The Castles of Athlin and Dunbayne* (1789), records, by my count, more than forty uses of *horror* and *terror*, often densely gathered together, and the two are often synonymous or indistinguishable. Both horror and terror can be "silent"; and in a sentence like "every nerve thrilled with horror at the touch, and he started back in an agony of terror," the terms seem to be interchangeable.[54] When "gleams of horror" emanate from an altar (43), horror is a personified thing rather than or as well as a state of feeling, and it straddles the same range of objective and subjective as does terror. When Alleyn is overtaken with "the horrors of darkness, silence, and despair" (26), horror

---

52. John Robison's *Proofs of a Conspiracy Against All the Religions and Governments of Europe* (London, 1797) at once accuses the Illuminati of wrongly identifying terror with the monarchies while admitting that the excesses of (Catholic) priestcraft have included misrepresenting God to mankind by way of "vain terrors" (240).

53. Knight, *Analytical Inquiry*, 384.

54. Ann Radcliffe, *The Castles of Athlin and Dunbayne*, ed. Alison Milbank (Oxford: Oxford University Press, 1995), 87, 102, 28. Hereafter cited with page numbers in the text.

is not something seen at a distance but precisely not seen. Osbert's heart is "chilled . . . almost to horror" (49), invoking the condition of petrifaction often also associated with terror.[55] And when Mary and the Countess undergo "the horrors of a lengthened suspense" (68), their experience is decidedly internal, once again disrupting the connection between horror and something seen at a distance. It is rare to see Radcliffe introducing gradations and clear distinctions, as she does, for instance, in the following sentence: "He remained for some time in a silent dread not wholly unpleasing, but which was soon heightened to a degree of terror not to be endured" (6). More commonly, fear-terror cluster words tumble over and into one another without any clues toward desynonymization. There is an art to this, one presumably intended to scramble the reader's feelings into a state of pleasurable confusion of the sort that so appealed to Catherine Morland and Isabella Thorpe in *Northanger Abbey*. But this same confusion can operate, Burke's later work suggests, in the service of a political agenda whose aim is to befuddle us out of any confidence in our own judgment and unsettle our command of place and space. Such a state might well contribute to the pleasures of the gothic novel, but it is not a source for establishing a patriotic consensus.

Similarly adept confusions govern another of Radcliffe's novels in its deployment of fear-terror words. *A Sicilian Romance* (1790) couples terror with astonishment and surprise, in the manner of the early Burke, but there is also an occasion where "terror now usurped the place of every other interest," suggesting its propensity to take over completely the mind and body of the person affected.[56] A few years later, in *The Italian* (1797), *terror* appears coupled with *grief, amazement, dismay, pity*, and *astonishment* (twice).[57] Notable here, however, is Radcliffe's relative preference for other terms in the fear-terror cluster. Her uses of both *anxiety* and *horror* significantly outnumber those of *terror*, and in one telling sequence of thrills and chills when the hero is about to face the Inquisition (196–98), *horror* appears three times and *horrible* twice, with not a single instance of *terror*.[58] One might speculate that Radcliffe is by this point,

55. Cf. "petrified with horror" (103) and "freeze her heart to horror" (44).
56. *A Sicilian Romance*, ed. Alison Milbank (Oxford: Oxford University Press, 1993), 9, 10, 41.
57. *The Italian*, ed. Frederick Garber (Oxford: Oxford University Press, 1981), 61, 178, 213, 223, 319, 380.
58. A word search produces a count of thirty-four *terrors* as against fifty-five *horrors* and fifty-three *anxieties*, with *dread* or *dreadful* showing up forty-one times. The much more commonplace *fear* shows up only 110 times (with 21 for *fearful*). Given the regularity of *fear* in ordinary language along with its overlap with purely conventional language ("I fear that you may be getting bored with numbers"), it seems that Radcliffe

three years after the fall of the Jacobins, turning away from an overindulgence in the very word she had done so much to publicize. Her final novel, *Gaston de Blondeville,* published in 1826 but written twenty years earlier, has almost nothing of *terror* and only slightly more of *horror.* Late in her career, she stages an explicit meditation on these two words in her dialogue "On the Supernatural in Poetry," intended as the prologue to *Gaston* but published separately in 1826. Here the two protagonists debate the differences between *terror* and *horror* as they impinge on readers' responses to the ghosts in *Hamlet* and *Macbeth.* The first play, it is said, generates the authentic Burkean sublime, the second, only an inferior interest that involves more of horror than terror, leading one interlocutor to assert that "terror and horror are so far opposite, that the first expands the soul, and awakens the faculties to a high degree of life, while the other contracts, freezes, and nearly annihilates them."[59] Horror is determinate and clear: we see what we see, which aligns it with the spectacle as denigrated by La Mesnardière as that which appeals only to vulgar taste. Terror functions through obscurity, leaving the mind room to expatiate. Thus horror cannot be a source of the sublime while terror can. But if there is room for imagination, does this make terror more or less threatening than horror? If it is horror that takes away the power to act and be energized, is terror then the more sublime, only because it is safer, more in accord with self-preservation?[60] The preponderance of *horror* over *ter-*

---

commits heavily to the stronger terms in the fear-terror cluster, but not so much to *terror.* Between *A Sicilian Romance* and *The Italian* are two other novels, *The Romance of the Forest* (1792) and *The Mysteries of Udolpho* (1794). In each, *terror* is about twice as common as *horror,* although the gap is close in the final volume of each novel, and in *Udolpho*'s fourth volume *horror* actually overtakes *terror.* We might suppose that the closer we get to the end of the story, the more *terror* is explained away and put aside. In *The Italian,* there is a slightly different pattern, with both *terror* and *horror* appearing about twice as often in the second and third volumes as they do in the first. For comparison, *horror* and *terror* run roughly neck and neck in Parsons's *The Castle of Wolfenbach* (1793) and Brown's *Wieland* (1798).

59. "On the Supernatural in Poetry," *New Monthly Magazine* 16, no. 1 (1826): 145–52, reprinted in E. J. Clery and Robert Miles, eds., *Gothic Documents: A Sourcebook, 1700–1820* (Manchester: Manchester University Press, 2000), 163–72, esp. 168–69.

60. Adriana Cavarero, *Horrorism: Naming Contemporary Violence,* trans. William McCuaig (New York: Columbia University Press, 2011), 7, also proposes that horror produces paralysis, a state of "feeling frozen," but allows it the feeling of "repugnance," which seems to imply some self-control. Terror, in contrast, "moves bodies, drives them into motion" (5). Terror is thus less disabling than horror. But there are many instances where these attributes seem to be inverted. Talal Asad, *On Suicide Bombing* (New York: Columbia University Press, 2007), 65–96, specifies horror rather than terror as the primary response to witnessing extreme violence. He finds that horror is a "state of being" with "no object" (68); others have said just the same about terror.

ror in *The Italian* could, in light of this distinction, be taken to indicate Radcliffe's effort to bring her readers as close as she can to the point of extreme discomfort, beyond the self-control always implicit in the terror-based Burkean sublime. Her dialogue appears to prefer *terror* to *horror*, and Hamlet's ghost over Banquo's, as the superior aesthetic stimulant. If the point of reading or spectating is to be roused and enlivened, then terror is the preferred emotion. But if the aim is to produce something more radically threatening, horror works better.[61]

It thus seems that Radcliffe finds in the early Burke's recommendation of terror in the aesthetic sphere exactly the quality that the later Burke desires to arouse in British citizens facing the French Revolution's claim to terror: a (masculinized) freedom of response.[62] But Burke comes to accept that the capturing of terror talk by the political sphere brings with it exactly the threat of "near annihilation" that Radcliffe finds in horror. Political terror is designed to freeze, contract, and disable the enemy and to inhibit resistance, and it must thus be refused. The problem with using the word *terror* is that it is often unclear or ambiguous in both kind and degree: is it political or aesthetic, and in whose sense of political and aesthetic? What happens when we read about political terror or behold it from a distance; does that make it properly aesthetic? Can terror at a distance work to erase the safety net and bring us into the realm of unmediated emotion?[63] Can terror, in Radcliffe's (1826) sense, collapse into horror? Can the terms even be persuasively disambiguated when there is a clearly apparent countertendency in both common and specialized language to employ terror and horror as interchangeable, or indeed to propose terror instead of horror as the emotion best described as freezing and disabling those who experience it?[64] That seems to be the pattern in Horace Walpole's *The Castle of Otranto*, generally taken as the foundational

61. Stephen King, *Danse Macabre* (New York: Gallery Books, 2010), has also pondered the distinction: "I recognize terror as the finest emotion . . . and so I will try to terrorize the reader. But if I find I cannot terrify him/her, I will try to horrify; and if I find I cannot horrify, I'll go for the gross-out. I'm not proud" (25–26).

62. Thus Charles Brockden Brown, *Wieland; or, The Transformation*, ed. Emory Elliott (Oxford: Oxford University Press, 2009), 203: "Terror enables us to perform incredible feats."

63. See Charles Maturin, *Melmoth the Wanderer*, ed. Alethea Hayter (Harmondsworth, UK: Penguin Books, 1977), 345: "The drama of terror has the irresistible power of converting its audience into its victims."

64. Thus Helen Maria Williams, in *Letters Containing a Sketch of the Politics of France, from the Thirty-First of May, 1793, until the Twenty-Eighth of July, 1794*, 2 vols. (London, 1795), describes herself or others as "petrified" by both horror (1:218, 2:9) and terror (2:4). Williams is one of the earliest users of *terrorism* in English (2:42). But even as she is critical of the Jacobins, she accuses the Vendée royalist rebellion of

book for eighteenth-century gothic fiction. First published in 1764, that is to say, quite soon after Burke's treatise on the sublime, the author promises a watered-down Aristotelian pairing of pity and terror not as a moral or physiological experience but simply as way of preventing "the story from ever languishing" and of keeping up "a constant vicissitude of interesting passions."[65] But the vicissitudes seem to be somewhat disciplined. By my count, every use of *terror* (all ten of them) can be taken to conform either to the idea of anticipatory emotion—imagining that which is to come but has not yet fully arrived—or to describe an all-possessing intensity of immediate response. The emotion can be compound, as in "terror and amazement" (74, 134), but in no case is *terror* used as an objectified personification, as a thing outside the self that causes inner terror. There is no proleptic analogue, in other words, to the Terror. Walpole is rather more sparing in his use of *horror* (only six times) but also consistent in how he uses it. One instance clearly indicates contemplation at a distance—"the horror of the spectacle" (75)—and the others do not conflict with this even though they are less explicit (74, 80, 81, 83, 135). Walpole thus observes a rough working distinction between *horror* and *terror*, almost as if he is bringing order into a rhetoric that Burke's early work had scrambled and that Radcliffe would scramble all over again. *Horror* implies either a safer distance or a lesser intensity than *terror*, and neither is personified as an emotion-inducing agent.[66]

The same pattern emerges in Eliza Parsons's *The Castle of Wolfenbach*, published in 1793 during the heyday of the market for gothic fiction, and one of the novels picked out for satirical attention in *Northanger Abbey*. *Horror* and *terror* both appear regularly, each somewhere close to twenty times. Most occurrences of *horror* involve a relatively distant seeing, indexing a strong emotional response but not one that is related to an immediate physical threat to the person involved. One can show horror or cry out with it, or experience it as the result of thought, so the distance factor is not absolute, and in at least one case a character is "overwhelmed" with it.[67] So there is some overlap with the domain of terror,

---

seeking to reappropriate the "avenging terrors of sacerdotal and aristocratical rage" (1:116).

65. Horace Walpole, *The Castle of Otranto and The Mysterious Mother*, ed. Frederick S. Frank (Peterborough, ON: Broadview Press, 2003), 60.

66. A similar logic governs the language of *The Mysterious Mother*, which, perhaps appropriately for a drama and despite its invoking of "terror and pity" (251, 254), makes more use of *horror* (at something beheld or contemplated) than of *terror*.

67. Eliza Parsons, *The Castle of Wolfenbach*, ed. Diane Long Hoeveler (Kansas City, MO: Valancourt Books, 2007), 77.

just as there is in Burke. But there is a high count of "distance" usages, indicating a spectacle beheld in relative safety. *Terror* tends to denote a more extreme and physically immediate sensation. At times, the two are used together and in distinguishable ways. So, Matilda's heart is "beating with terror" before she turns "with horror from the scene" (27). Then the "terror of her mind" gives her "the most horrible ideas" (28). Madame La Roche suffers "agonizing terrors" that are then "realized beyond whatever I could conceive of horror" (97). Again, one character's "scene of horror" is explained by another as designed to produce "terror and fright" (150). In each case (and although the "fright" seems superfluous), *horror* implies some separation of space or time, whereas *terror* suggests immersion and petrified inertia. The energizing component theorized by Radcliffe and implied in Burke's *Inquiry* appears to be absent.

Godwin's *Caleb Williams* is a more explicitly political novel, wherein one might expect an interest in terror as a descriptor of state power rather than of merely interpersonal emotions. Indeed, in the preface to the second printing of 1795, Godwin refers to the time of the original (1794) publication as one when "terror was the order of the day."[68] He means the terror accompanying Pitt's repressions and the treason trials, and he thus conjoins Pitt with Robespierre in an analogy that was relatively common among the radicals of the 1790s. But that terror is embodied in powerful individuals, Falkland and Tyrrel, who, while they may hate each other, are equally overbearing in their manipulation and execution of the laws of the land. The personal is thus the form of the political: what pertains here is not the indifferent, virtue-based process envisaged by the Jacobins but an individually biased application of power that claims the law as its rationale while being driven by explicit self-interest. Of the thirty-one (by my count) uses of *terror* or *terrors*, eighteen designate a subjective response, an emotion; nine specify an objectively personified agent; and four are mixed or ambiguous. Terror as an objective entity (as in *the* Terror) thus figures more commonly here than it does in Walpole, Radcliffe, or Parsons; more than a third of Godwin's terrors are personified agents. But the borders are permeable. Tyrrel and Falkland both generate terror for others and experience it in themselves (20, 43, 89, 112, 151). And when Caleb faces down Falkland with the observation that he is "wearing out the springs of terror" (294), Caleb can be taken to refer both to the objective terror that Falkland deploys and to his own capacity to experience it. Like his precursors,

---

68. William Godwin, *Things as They Are; or, the Adventures of Caleb Williams*, ed. Maurice Hindle (London: Penguin Books, 1987), 4.

Godwin uses *terror* slightly more commonly than *horror*, but the more frequently objective weighting he accords it suggests that we are right to describe Caleb Williams as a "Jacobin'" novel instead of or as well as a gothic one. Godwin is notably interested in (though not supportive of) the terror that appears before us as the power of the state or of its embodied representatives.

A comparable emphasis on terror as an objective figure, an agent with the power of terror, is apparent in the work of William Blake, where the vocabulary of the fear-terror cluster is very prominent. But whereas Godwin only specifies objective terror as specific to the British state and thus wholly negative, Blake is more complex. In the early, unpublished poem *The French Revolution* (1791), terror and the terrible are the property of the French monarchy, tools deployed to intimidate the people, and overcoming terror is the task of the new democracy. But the "new born terror" who emerges at the end of *The Marriage of Heaven and Hell* and who is identified as Orc in *America* (1793) indicates that the power of terror has been appropriated by the new republic and is available for use against the monarchy and its defenders, and is as such even a source of "rejoicing."[69] This explicitly liberating terror does not emerge as clearly in *The Book of Urizen* (1794), but it is there in *Europe* (also 1794). Terror in the unpublished *The Four Zoas* (1797) again has both liberating and repressive incarnations. In *Milton*, printed ten years after the Jacobin Terror, although still within the ambience of Britain's own repressive regime considered by some as itself a "terror," the same dialectic is evident, as it is again in *Jerusalem*, where terror tends to function as a volatile entity or emotion subject to whoever is speaking or feeling but readily convertible to pity and love. Blake is unusual in preserving a faith in the purgative function of terror as an agent of revolutionary creativity, but of course his work was expensive to purchase, expressed in complex allegory, and significantly unread. Even the *Songs* achieved only minimal circulation, although two of the three occurrences of *terror* or *terrors* there (most famously in "The Tyger") are pretty clearly referenced in political terms.[70]

Nonetheless, Blake is remarkable for the persistence with which he introduced terror as a labile and dialectical agent or emotion with an inherent energy for transformation and regeneration. The "deadly terrors" of "The Tyger" that may or may not be grasped are at once those of the observers who are in awe of the creature's power of death and those of

---

69. *The Complete Poetry and Prose of William Blake*, ed. David V. Erdman (Berkeley: University of California Press, 1982), 25.

70. On "The Tyger," see Paulson, *Representations of Revolution*, 97–102.

the creature itself as it senses its eternal energies being encased in fallen form, framed in a "symmetry" that is fearful in both senses of the word: causing and experiencing fear. Presenting terror as neither absolute in itself nor constant through time seems to ally Blake with Robespierre and Saint-Just, for whom terror was envisaged as a means to an end and always in critical liaison with virtue. This is different from the terror I have described in novels like *The Castle of Otranto* and *The Castle of Wolfenbach*, where terror is distinguished from horror as immediacy is from distance. Blake's terror moves in and out of and through his pro-tagonists, a shareable experience often indicative of coming transfor-mations when not frozen hard in Urizenic form. Blake turns to the fear-terror cluster as part of an emotional complex in which only fixed form itself is ultimately negative. Unlike Radcliffe's jumbled affects and emo-tions, Blake's terrors are highly consequential events with clear social-political implications.

In contrast, Wordsworth is remarkably chaste in his use of terror. Re-calling his visit to the "fierce metropolis" of Paris in 1792, just after the September Massacres, Wordsworth resorts (in the climactic tenth book of *The Prelude*) to a relatively sober vocabulary of "fear" and "dread."[71] Terror is invoked but only as the emotion felt by the foreigners invading France who had "shrunk from sight of their own task, and fled / In ter-ror" (10:19–20). The young republic here inspires terror in its enemies, which is more or less in line with the self-descriptions of the French them-selves, and indeed of the Robespierre faction, for whom terror was the outward companion of virtue. The 1850 text mentions that after Robe-spierre's downfall "Terror had ceased" (11:2), but that is the sum total of Wordsworth's usage of the word in his most densely attentive account of events leading up to and including the Terror occupying the months between August 1793 and July 1794. Robespierre's violence is attrib-uted not to innate evil but to "clumsy desperation" (1805, 10:546). Un-like the modern historian François Furet and his followers, Wordsworth does not suggest that the Terror is a culmination of the necessary logic of the French Revolution, and thus the sinister truth behind its claim to democratic ideals, but rather a deviation from a trajectory established in 1789 and restored to its proper direction after the fall of the Montagne. He thus delivers a strong endorsement of the philosophical Enlighten-ment as the core of the revolution, a view recently endorsed once again by Jonathan Israel's *Revolutionary Ideas*. In this view, the Terror is not

71. *The Prelude: 1799, 1805, 1850*, ed. Jonathan Wordsworth, Stephen Gill, and M. H. Abrams (New York: W. W. Norton and Co., 1979), 10:8, 63, 66 (1805 text).

only not the product of the inner logic of 1789; it is an absolute deviation from it: its populist (and hypocritical) claim to enact the will of the
people involved an anti-intellectualism entirely at odds with the Word-
sworthian (and rationalist) faith in "the virtue of one paramount mind"
(10:179) as able in principle to provide a "solid birthright to the state"
along the lines devised by "ancient lawgivers" (10:186, 188).

It is important to notice these carefully modulated judgments, because Wordsworth is often on the record as something of a turncoat on
these matters. But his core position here is that the Terror did not turn
him against the revolution; that would come later, with the invasion of
Switzerland and the rise of Napoleon. Wordsworth is here distancing
himself, retrospectively, of course, from the patriotic hysteria in Britain
in the mid-1790s. If he was committed to a faith in a single "paramount
mind" to come, whoever that might be, as the best hope for setting
French politics in positive directions, he is not in the business, yet, of demonizing Robespierre. He is rather more in the business in fact of demonizing William Pitt, thereby adding his voice to those who found Britain significantly responsible for bringing on the Terror in France.[72] And
it is entirely characteristic of this most self-conscious of writers that he
would understand and confess to the mediated nature of his responses to
events that he did not, after all, witness himself. Recall that, at the sight
of the drowned man of Esthwaite, the poet invokes the power of books,
the "shining streams / Of fairyland, the forests of romance" (5:476–77),
as what protected him from trauma, whether immediate or recollected.
Reading about something prepared him for the sight of death and softened its effects. (This is, famously, one of Rousseau's arguments against
literature itself.)[73] So, too, in Paris in 1792, the poet avers that whatever
he felt of immediate "dread," something more and perhaps something
other "was conjured up from tragic fictions / And mournful calendars of
true history" (10:66–68). He had, in other words, been reading about it,
and that reading influenced his feelings to the point that he could not say
what portion of them, if any, might have derived from his own punctual

72. See Nicholas Roe, "Imagining Robespierre," in *Coleridge's Imagination: Essays
in Memory of Pete Laver*, ed. Richard Gravil, Lucy Newlyn, and Nicholas Roe (Cambridge: Cambridge University Press, 1985), 171–78. This was also Coleridge's position
in 1795: see *Lectures, 1795*, 72–74. Gregory Dart, *Rousseau, Robespierre and English Romanticism* (Cambridge: Cambridge University Press, 1999), 163–208, makes a
strong case for Wordsworth's consistent sympathy with some components of the Jacobin
platform.

73. In lines Wordsworth added in 1816, the man has "a spectre shape / Of terror"
(450–51); terror, too, can be controlled by propaedeutic reading.

experience. This blend of being there and living in print occasions a further act of citation:

> And in such way I wrought upon myself,
> Until I seemed to hear a voice that cried
> To the whole city, "Sleep no more!" (10:75–77)

He seems to hear the voice. The quotation from *Macbeth* is also a citation of Helen Maria Williams citing the same play in the same context: hence doubly literary.[74] Here the regicide king hears a voice that is not his own but yet comes from within himself, a voice that enunciates a conscience as well as a judgment from outside, or at least a fear of detection. Macbeth also wrought upon himself and imagined hearing the broadcast of a general warning. Wordsworth's "ghastly visions" (10:374) keep him from sleep and cause him to imagine that he, too, is implicated and perhaps even guilty, pleading before "unjust tribunals"—whether for others or for himself, for French or British, we are not told—and sensing "treachery and desertion" within his "own soul" (10:377–80). Importantly and typically, he does not blame others to the exclusion of blaming himself; in this "brain confounded" (10:378), self and other are intermixed. The victim also betrays himself. Wordsworth claims a traumatic afterlife "through months, through years" (10:370) but does not exonerate himself from responsibility for it. The soul is here negated as an internal sanctum impervious to outside influence; it is not the thing to which one turns to endure the world's temptations and assaults, the repository of theological or ontological freedom, but a vulnerable entity open to threats from others and from one's own self. The soul is affective and impressed upon by outside circumstances.

"I wrought upon myself / Until I seemed to hear a voice"—perhaps only another British poet would have seemed to hear this particular voice reminding him that killing a king was a significant moment in Britain's own history, with the trauma of 1649 anticipated in a medieval Scottish regicide written about in 1606 for the first Stuart monarch. Citing Macbeth's speech bizarrely places Wordsworth himself in the position of the regicide who is also the usurping monarch. There are no simple identities in this autobiographical drama of affiliations and distinctions. So too when the calm of remote rural England is disturbed by the welcome news of Robespierre's death, which Wordsworth gets

---

74. Helen Maria Williams, *Letters*, 1:3; 2:18. The context is not quite the same: Williams is writing about the Terror of 1794, not the September Massacres.

thirdhand from a traveler's report of a newspaper item while crossing Leven Sands, the political joy is soon succeeded by the story of the visit to the grave of his beloved teacher William Taylor at Cartmel Priory. Taylor is remembered as having predicted that his own "head will soon lie low" (10:501), thereby invoking not only the general mortality that will overtake us all but also the very specific fall of heads—"head after head, and never heads enough" (10:335)—in Robespierre's Paris. The pairing is at once a contrast and a comparison. Taylor's death at age thirty-two was not caused by a revolution, but it was hardly the image of a conventional life span; so, too, the many young people who went to the guillotine, like Madame Roland (at thirty-nine), Danton (at thirty-five), Desmoulins (thirty-four), or Robespierre himself (thirty-six). Saint-Just was twenty-seven when he was executed, three years older than William Wordsworth. France was not a country for old men; to be young was very heaven only for some. Taylor's death avers that even nonrevolutionary Britain could not assure anyone of the proverbial three score and ten years of life.

What might it mean that terror is so sparsely employed in this poet's vocabulary? When it does occur, it is almost always a property of nature or of the mind, a subjective emotion rather than an objective agent. Cambridge, of all places, not Paris, is the place that is recalled as generating "terror and dismay" (8:660), thanks to its display of "guilt and wretchedness" (8:558). The dream of the Arab, which is a nightmare of the flooding of the earth, generates "terror" (5:137), but a sleepless night in revolutionary Paris does not.[75] In refusing the melodrama of terror reportage, Wordsworth is surely turning his back on the purple prose of the anti-Jacobin media, as well as on the chosen vocabulary of those gothic novels he had pronounced to be all too popular. But in relocating terror along the notoriously placid banks of the Cam, he suggests that there is no escape from threatening and disabling emotions, no sure respite to be found in the middle counties of England (or indeed in the remoter parts of the Lake District), which Austen's Henry Tilney would, in *Northanger Abbey*, pronounce (ambiguously) as free of terror and horror. Terror and horror, in other words, cannot be sectored off as the property of the foreigner or the enemy other.

---

75. An interesting exception occurs in the eighth of the "Sonnets upon the Punishment of Death," where Wordsworth affirms that the state may plant "well-measured terrors in the road / Of wrongful acts," including the death penalty. See *Sonnet Series and Itinerary Poems, 1820–1845*, ed. Geoffrey Jackson (Ithaca, NY: Cornell University Press, 2004), 873.

A comedic version of this apprehensiveness shows up in the contribution of an anonymous author to the *Monthly Magazine* in 1797. Here the human habit of imitation is invoked as explaining the transformation of Robespierre's "SYSTEM OF TERROR" into a "revolution" in novel writing.[76] The British novel has given up on its traditional attention to "human life and manners" in favor of melodrama and fearmongering. But along with the disapproval there is laughter, as if to suggest that what has proved all too real for the French can be adopted by the British as nothing more than the source of a good read. The more there is of the laughable, the less there is of true terror. At the same time, given this principle of imitation, the exporting of terror from the aesthetic sphere back into real life can perhaps never be wholly discounted. Those who, like Godwin, felt that they were living under Pitt's "reign of terror" might have taken the point.

The relation of fictional terror to the historical moment is certainly made direct enough in the Marquis de Sade's essay of 1800, where violence in the novel is seen as the "necessary offspring of the revolutionary upheaval which affected the whole of Europe."[77] Where real events are so bloody and brutal, fiction can innovate only by turning to the supernatural, disguising as metaphysical the hideous circumstances of ordinary life. But the history of fiction is never a simple reflection of the historical headlines. Critics and scholars of the gothic novel have been well aware that there is no single gothic, that the genre was well established before 1789 and that it continued well beyond the 1790s in forms that were not directly, if at all, responsive to the events of 1793–1794. Angela Wright, for example, attributes the anti-French tendency of the prerevolutionary gothic to the legacy of the Seven Years' War and to the embarrassing need to cover up the degree to which British writers and translators were plagiarizing French prototypes. Anti-Catholic sentiment persists into the 1790s, when it is able to conjoin itself (however implausibly) with anti-Jacobinism, France being the only required common factor.[78] E. J. Clery has broadly related the popularity of the supernatural to the development of market capitalism, a process well

76. "The Terrorist System of Novel-Writing," *Monthly Magazine* 4, no. 21 (August 1797): 102–4, reprinted in *Gothic Readings: The First Wave, 1764–1840,* ed. Rictor Norton (Leicester: Leicester University Press, 2000), 299–302.

77. Marquis de Sade, *The Crimes of Love: Heroic and Tragic Tales, Preceded by an Essay on Novels,* trans. David Coward (Oxford: Oxford University Press, 2005), 13.

78. Angela Wright, *Britain, France and the Gothic, 1764–1820: The Import of Terror* (Cambridge: Cambridge University Press, 2013).

under way long before the French Revolution.[79] And Joseph Crawford has argued for the formative influence of Collins's "Ode to Fear" and other earlier eighteenth-century poems on what came to be known as the gothic.[80] All of these and most other scholars nevertheless recognize a redirection or reinvention of the genre sometime between 1794 and 1797, with *terror* becoming more and more the order of the printing press. But it was not always political terror. Ghosts are not Jacobins, and few if any wind-blown tapestries or iron chests concealed a Robespierre behind or within them. The British stage was more welcoming to supernatural than to political terror. "Monk" Lewis's *The Castle Spectre* was a runaway success, while scripts that directly represented events in France, like Inchbald's *The Massacre* or Coleridge and Southey's *The Fall of Robespierre*, were never even performed. Perhaps the explicit theatricality of the French Terror and its analogues left too little for the dramatist to do; perhaps there was insufficient opportunity to generate a self-protecting complexity on a subject so thoroughly polemicized. The Jacobin Terror was, as befits its associations with a culture of transparency, incontrovertibly public, committed to displaying itself in the light of day. Many of the novels and plays that were popular in the 1790s—and Radcliffe's novels are perfect examples—take place in darkness and in secret places. This affiliates them as much or more with the culture of the old regime than with that of the revolution. It was under the monarchy that persons mysteriously disappeared and found themselves locked away for years upon years in the Bastille.[81] Novelists could have things both ways by playing into the strong popular conviction that the French Revolution was the product of secret plotting, for example, by the brotherhood of the Illuminati. Peter Will's translation of *Horrid Mysteries* (1796) is one of a number of such novels, offering a "serious warning to all those that listen to the seducing voice of secret, corresponding, and other Societies of a similar nature," but secrecy is also very much the property of the priests, powerful barons, and kings whom the revolution supplanted, as it is in Radcliffe's novels.[82] There was nothing secret about

79. E. J. Clery, *The Rise of Supernatural Fiction, 1762–1800* (Cambridge: Cambridge University Press, 1995).

80. Joseph Crawford, *Gothic Fiction and the Invention of Terrorism: The Politics and Aesthetics of Fear in the Age of the Reign of Terror* (London: Bloomsbury, 2013), 13–22.

81. One of the most famously scandalous among gothic novels, Matthew Lewis's *The Monk* is at heart an enlightened attack on hierarchy, patriarchal power, and religious superstition.

82. Carl Grosse, *Horrid Mysteries*, trans. Peter Will (London: Folio Press, 1968), xviii. *Horrid* here is apparently a new word in a main title. The British Library online

the guillotine; it did its work in full view of the public, promptly, imper-
sonally, and completely without mystery or superstition.

Terror at a Distance

Of course, the relations between fiction and historiographical representations of all kinds, from popular newspapers to official histories, were
and have always been interactive. Joseph Crawford puts it well: "Fiction
and non-fiction drew upon one another in an evolutionary symbiosis"
or "feedback loop."[83] Carlyle's history of the revolution is itself almost
as novelistic as the novel that Dickens based on it. Not all of the novelists of the 1790s were anti-Jacobin or purposively apolitical, but there
were very few explicitly prorevolutionary novels, and there have been few
since.[84] But neither is there a significant tradition of merely polemical negation of the revolution and its terrors. Comparing two now-canonized
novels published in 1814, at which point the wars with France were felt
to be over (even though there was to be a last-gasp, second ending at
Waterloo), we find that the rhetoric of terror is not melodramatically deployed in either case. Austen and Scott tend to be seen now as affiliated
with conservative social and political values; at least, they are not usually
deemed to have been social radicals. But neither *Waverley* nor *Persuasion*, Scott's first novel and Austen's last, shows any interest in recalling
Jacobin terror. *Persuasion* is very careful in its distinction between terror and horror, and it is horror that is deemed appropriate for describing
the characters' reactions to Louisa's climactic fall from the pier at Lyme,
three times during the incident itself, and twice more when it is being recollected.[85] Even the Aristotelian couplet is rendered, unusually and comi-
cally, as "pity and horror" (62). Only once does terror impinge, when

---

catalog shows nine cases before 1800 in which it is part of a subtitle. Most of these are
narratives of murder and abuse, although it is thus used in one eighteenth-century printing of Foxe's *Book of Martyrs*. The use of *horrid* as a serious intensifier was already
having to work against its coexistence as a mere emphatic, as in Pepys's "horrid shame"
(OED, 1666).

83. Crawford, *Gothic Fiction*, 41, 72.

84. For a good account of the positive responses, covert and otherwise, by women
writers, see Adriana Craciun, *British Women Writers and the French Revolution: Citizens of the World* (London: Palgrave, 2005). Craciun describes, among other things, a
complex female response to Robespierre. See also Gregory Dart, *Rousseau, Robespierre
and English Romanticism*.

85. Jane Austen, *Persuasion*, ed. Gillian Beer (New York: Penguin, 2003), 102
(twice), 104, 173, 227. There is also one occurrence of *horror* in the trivial sense: Lady
Russell's "horror" of impudence (27).

it describes the feelings of those obligated to give the senior Musgraves the bad news of their daughter's accident (105). Austen preserves horror here for what is seen to happen to another, and terror for what one feels oneself, in a delicate and minimal but nonetheless emphatic departure from both the diction of the gothic novel and the polemical address to the French Revolution (for terror here is entirely internal to individuals).[86]

Scott's *Waverley* was a publishing sensation, whereas Austen's novel failed to sell out its first edition, but Scott's popularity was not dependent on melodramatic terror talk. Along with a few uses of terror as hypothetical, imaginary, romantic-emotional (concern for another), and trivial, more than half (i.e., eight) of Scott's uses of the word are in describing actual or prospective military violence, whether affirmed or denied. The Highlands clans seek to generate terror to intimidate their neighbors, and opposing armies try to terrorize each other. But Scott's final and most telling use comes when Fergus Mac-Ivor mounts the scaffold, "smiling disdainfully as he gazed around upon this apparatus of terror."[87] If an allusion to the guillotine is intended or elicited, then we are reminded that terror remains above all part of the machinery of the state, in this case the British state as it dispatches one of the leaders of the 1745 Jacobite (not Jacobin) rebellion. We are reminded that the Hanoverians on the British throne were as ready to deploy the power of terror as their French enemies would be some fifty years later. And when Fergus's head is placed above the gate of the city of Carlisle, we are also reminded that the enacting of terror as a spectacle was by no means original to the Jacobins in 1794. Indeed, there were no officially sanctioned severed heads on the ramparts of Paris in 1794: this was the sort of spectacle that the guillotine was intended to preclude.

Among the various writers who learned the techniques of the historical novel from Scott was the even more prolific Balzac, whose first suc-

---

86. In *Mansfield Park*, it is the shy and inexperienced Fanny Price who feels "constant terror of something or other" in wandering around the big house into which she finds herself adopted, who can laugh at the terrors she used to have when riding the pony, but who continues to feel terror at the approach of her uncle, Mary, or Henry Crawford, or of the letter she fears will spoil her happiness. See *Mansfield Park*, ed. Kathryn Sutherland (New York: Penguin, 2003), 15, 27, 288, 330, 370, 371. In other words, what mostly causes terror is the prospect of being bullied or hectored. Sir Thomas is another version of General Tilney, the patriarchal authority in *Northanger Abbey*, who mistreats the heroine and who demonstrates the gothic father figure as all too present in a novel that is supposedly setting out (if only according to Henry) to show that such figures are not to be found in the middle counties of England. *Horror* and *horrible*, meanwhile, are appropriately the words used (four times) to describe Fanny's reaction to the evidence of Maria Bertram's adultery (409–10).

87. Sir Walter Scott, *Waverley*, ed. P. D. Garside (New York: Penguin, 2011), 350.

cessful novel published under his own name was set in the 1790s: *Les Chouans*, first published in 1829 and significantly revised in 1834 and 1845. The events here imagined occur not during the main royalist rebellion in the west of France, which took place south of the Loire in 1791–1793 in La Vendée, but as part of a later outbreak in 1799, at the beginning of Bonaparte's consulate. The guerrilla movement in Brittany, known as the Chouannerie, was mostly defeated by 1796, so that Balzac is here taking up a little-known revival of a cause already defeated once and about to be defeated again. In *Waverley*, Scott, too, had told the story of a lost cause, and one that he was, for all his respect and affection for the best parts of the disappearing feudal culture of the Highlands, mostly glad to consign to a vanished past. Balzac's Breton peasants share with Scott's Highlanders (and Cooper's American Indians, another influence) the attributes of a primitive, often barbaric remnant of a social order whose survival into the modern age seems remarkable and residual. But they are also the bearers of a historically lost cause that Balzac, like Scott, partly admires without definitively supporting. The Chouannerie have their integrity and their dignity, brutal as they may be at times, even as the royalist nobles who command them are, with the one exception of the hero himself, not admirable people. The servants of the republic also include a variety of types, some admired and some despised. The honest soldier Hulot, decently devoted to his country, may be the most fully vindicated character in the novel, while the sinister Corontin, working on the same side for the security service, is certainly the least so. Balzac's even-handedness does not fully negate the royalist sympathies attributed to him, but no more does it fully support them.[88] Both sides carry out executions. That carried out by the Chouans against an informer has about it a certain transparency and formality, and in taking the form of decapitation with an ax it reproduces the traditional manner of death reserved for the nobles, here deployed against a peasant farmer. It is still atrocious and causes the widow Babette to enlist her son in the republican army, and thus to join in the cause of the historical future. But the death plotted by Corontin, the agent of that future, is completely cynical and depends purely on lying and deception. No untainted political or civil ideal is traceable in the lineaments of this historical

---

88. Lukács, in *The Historical Novel*, locates Scott's special genius in his perception of history as carried out through the agency of ordinary people; before him, Engels credits Balzac with the intelligence to go against his own legitimism and to speak with "undisguised admiration" of his "bitterest political antagonists" as embodying the energies of an emergent history. See *Marx, Engels: On Literature and Art*, ed. Lee Baxandall and Stefan Morawski (New York: International General, 1973), 116–17.

moment, happening just before the republic itself is indeed about to be reborn as an empire. There is a balance of good and evil and an avoidance of moral absolutes. And it is notable that Balzac completely avoids any melodramatic recollections of the Terror as any sort of key to or core of the republican identity. It is intimated just once, in a conversation between the two lovers, when the Marquis of Montauran observes that "in the times of terror we live in" people form and dissolve emotional bonds very quickly, because each moment may be their last. But even here there is no capitalization, and this terror is still a thing of the present, not just the past.[89] Almost all the novel's other uses of *terror* (*terreur*) describe extreme personal emotions wrought by threatening circumstances or radical feelings of concern. It is indeed the Breton guerrillas who have the greater opportunity to appear "terrible," as they are generally the antagonists (e.g., 71, 73), because the successors of the republicans of 1794 are for most of the novel on the defensive; but history is known throughout to be on their side. In this way, both White and Red Terrors are kept out of the novel's rhetorical reach.[90] Balzac's interest is in the drama of guerrilla warfare and radical human feeling, not in the apparatus of spectacular violence, whether enacted by the state or against it.

Alexandre Dumas confronted the Terror and its genealogies much more directly when he wrote, between 1845 and 1855, five novels about the revolutionary period. The first to be written, *The Knight of Maison-Rouge*, opens in March 1793, when the Girondins are about to be deposed and arrested, giving Parisians "an overwhelming feeling that something unfamiliar and terrible was about to happen."[91] Like some latter-day historians, Dumas readily employs *terror* and *the terrible* as proleptic rhetoric for the Terror that is to come, soon enough indeed but only named as such after July 1794. In the language of the novel, it comes on May 31, 1793, with the fall of the Girondins, marking the moment when "the Terror came rushing down from the top of the Mountain like a torrent" (100). But it has been already "ushered in" by the law condemning returning émigrés to death (47), and it saturates all the events portrayed in the narrative. It takes form as insistent repetition: Osselin's

89. *The Chouans*, trans. Marion Ayton Crawford (Harmondsworth, UK: Penguin, 1972), 151. The diction is consistent in all three editions of the novel. See *Les Chouans*, ed. Maurice Regard (Paris: Garnier, 1964), 138. Regard lists all the variants.

90. In the French edition (Regard), see 71, 73. There is generally rather less of *terror* in the French than in the English, which sometimes translates both *terreur* and *effroi* as *terror*, and *épouvanté* as *terrified*.

91. Alexandre Dumas, *The Knight of Maison-Rouge*, trans. Julie Rose (New York: Random House, 2003), 7.

"terrible" decree is the "terrible law" that ushers in "the Terror" (47).[92] Dumas opts for the early dating of the Terror, which is here nominated as defining the thirteen-month period ending in July 1794. But because the story ends in October 1793, with the execution of Marie Antoinette, it never engages narratively with what is often called the "great" Terror. Nor does Dumas take this up again: the four other novels set during the revolution all chronicle earlier events. Terror is diffused across Parisian society as a general emotion to which all are vulnerable; even though personal terror is not exclusively rendered as the product of political action, it often is so. It is embodied in the figure of the man of the people more than in that of the guillotine itself, for it is the violence and executive power of the people that is most chilling in this climate of universal suspicion. In this book, as in all five of the Marie-Antoinette novels, it is the uncontrollable and unpredictable power of the Parisian crowd that inspires some of Dumas's most scaremongering language. And yet, on her way to the scaffold, Marie Antoinette is still able to recapture some of the power of terror previously associated with the monarchy and supposedly henceforth denied it: "She took the pride of her courage to such heights as to strike terror into the hearts of all those who looked upon her" (355).[93]

The second novel in the series describes events that are chronologically earlier. *Joseph Balsamo* is a gothic conspiracy narrative in which the man who will become Count Cagliostro, and who is possessed of eternal life, arrives in France as the agent of a radical brotherhood whose destiny is to assist in overturning the royalist state. The real Cagliostro was an Italian imposter and occultist supposedly connected with Egyptian Freemasonry and imprisoned in the Bastille for his perceived involvement in the diamond necklace affair, the scandal that Dumas explores fictionally in *The Queen's Necklace* (1849). Terror and horror figure prominently in the rhetoric of the novel, but at this point in history they are largely within the ambience of the supernatural and of the hypnotic powers that Balsamo employs in his passage through French society, high and low. Fear (or terror) of the Parisian crowd is again vividly transcribed, as it is yet again in *The Queen's Necklace*, when Marie Antoinette and her companion go out disguised among the people; but so, too, are the negative attributes of a decaying and corrupt aristocracy.

92. The vocabulary is the same in French: see *Le Chevalier de Maison-Rouge*, 2 vols. (Paris: Conard, 1934), 1:162.
93. The French is slightly more circumspect: "d'imprimer aux assistants des idées de terreur" (2:206).

Balsamo's own republican sympathies are made clear, but he remains a man of shifting affiliations.

In *Taking the Bastile*, Dumas does however fictionalize the other major moment of the revolution, the events of July 14, 1789, and it is here that Lukács's case for the historical novel as recording the critical contributions of ordinary people is perhaps most fully supported. Much of the action is seen through and carried by the career of the seriocomic figure of Ange Pitou, a rural oddball who plays a critical role in the storming of the Bastille and who matures into an exemplary man of the people. (The French title of the novel takes his name: *Ange Pitou*). The course of history is here governed not just by the decisions of the high and mighty but also by the "invisible hand" of chance coincidence and minor details.[94] Hitherto anonymous individuals, like the upright farmer Billot, appear as agents in a process that they do not control but that is also critically enabled by their actions. Billot is on a personal errand to Paris when he is caught up in a crowd and apparently deprived of his freedom of choice: "In the thick of the throng, all personal liberty was at an end . . . we wish what the crowd wishes, we do what it does" (108). But it is Billot who gives, anonymously, the all-important order to fire on the German dragoons (116), who subsequently summons the people to the Bastille (147), and who comes to embody and enact a power that is beyond any one person: "The crowd . . . recognized in this man one of their own class . . . they followed him, still increasing like the waves of the incoming tide" (150). Historical figures like Marat and Desmoulins do figure in Dumas's narrative, and the workings of Balsamo/Cagliostro continue behind closed doors to prod France toward its republican future, but the novel's major focus is on the historically decisive interplay between ordinary people and the Parisian crowd. The crowd, finally, cannot be controlled, and it is capable of terrible cruelty and violence. Sometimes it can be persuaded, as it is when Pitou argues against the burning of the Bastille archives (206); at other times, nothing will stop it, as is the case in the assassinations of De Launay and De Flesselles (212–16), and of Foulon (406).

As in the other Marie-Antoinette novels, Dumas concentrates some of his most emotive writing on the crowd, the massed human agent of historical transformation. It is both feared and admired, critiqued and applauded. It is the collective outcome of decades of poverty and starvation, and the agent of brutal revenge. It often responds to exemplary figures like Billot and Pitou, but it can also go its own way against their

94. *Taking the Bastile* [*sic*] (New York: Collier, 1910), 196.

best advice. Notably, it is both the sponsor and the sufferer of a terror that is pervasive throughout Paris and beyond being exclusively in the power of any one person or faction. Thus it is the target of the "terror and death" dealt out by the German dragoons (113), and yet at the moment of its greatest triumph it continues to feel its own "terror" at the sight of the Bastille (181, 192). To the same degree, it possesses the power of terror over others. Dumas's English translator however exaggerates the equivalence of both terrors by frequently translating *effroi* and *effrayé* as *terror* and *terrified* (e.g., 164, 183–84). Assuming that Dumas is taking care with his choice of words, we can surmise that he is seeking to minimize the association between the Parisian crowd and the specific incidence of *terreur*. The crowd is radically threatening and violent (actually or incipiently) but is not at this point fully a proleptic figure of the Terror, which was indeed arguably staged to keep power from the people. And yet the shared possession by both sides of the power of extreme fear-terror effects, wherein agents and recipients change places with bewildering speed, each a terror to the other, suggests that although the personification of the Terror has yet to take historical form (which for Dumas, as we have seen, happens in May 1793), its energies are described as fully evident from the earliest days of the revolution. The implication is that radical fear and anxiety are endemic to the old regime as well as to its successor, and the cumulative effect of Dumas's various but pervasive rhetorical deployments of fear-terror terms is to draw attention away from the Jacobin moment as anything more than an example of a much more widely dispersed culture of violence and intimidation.[95]

The Return of the Medusa

At critical moments in Dumas's *Taking the Bastile*, a crowd that is made up of human beings is described as something inhuman, something monstrous yet beguiling. When two streams of people are approaching the Bastille along converging boulevards, they are "like an immense

---

95. In *The Whites and the Blues* (1867), Dumas does set out to chronicle the events from December 1793 through the close of 1795, but he is notably parsimonious in his account of the "great" Terror of June–July 1794, which occupies little more than a page at the start of the second part of the first volume. The narrative dwells on the early months of terror in Strasbourg in 1793, where the city is on the front line and under military law. It offers a balanced portrait of Saint-Just, who is the most principled of the three patrons of the guillotine. It then skips ahead to October 1795, when Napoleon saves the Convention from the reactionary sections. Dumas is explicit in his support of the Jacobins as the agents of the true revolution, although he never explicitly endorses the Terror.

serpent . . . refulgent with luminous scales" (177). Outside the Hotel de Ville, the crowd is "like an enormous boa" that "intwined its enormous folds around the group" (213). The masses become as one, and the one is a snake, that creature whose literary renderings have so often combined the beauty of the angelic with the dangers of the demonic, and whose availability as an icon of eternal self-renewal has made it a favorite figure for revolutionary energy. The coming together of human and serpent form is also what marks the figure of Medusa, invoked in this novel by Bailly as the analogue of the severed head of Foulon atop a pikestaff after his hanging *à la lanterne*: "that head appeared to him to be the head of the Medusa of ancient days" (409). That head, as is well known, has the power to turn to stone all who gaze upon it, and its power is retained even after it is lopped from the body by Perseus. It thus figures the persistence of the power of terror (and/or horror) after the apparent death of the living body. The old regime is ending, but its capacity to generate terror persists even in its defeat, just as the new world order is marked by a violent inheritance from the old.

The mythic Medusa, whose story is told in Ovid's *Metamorphoses* (4:770) and who is figured in Homer, in the company of *deos* and *phobos*, as ornamenting both the aegis of Athena and the shield of Agamemnon (*Iliad*, 5:739–44; 11:36–40), was a woman. Why, then, might she come to mind as the prototype of a dead man? Why does the already-dead Foulon, who was the agent of the old regime, strike Bailly as the agent of future deaths, as Medusa herself? Is Medusa the avenging people, the living snake in the streets, or their victim? How can she be both the energy of a future to come, as the body of the republic, and the icon of what is passing out of history, the apparatus of the monarchy? The Medusa appears to be out of time or for all time, at once the power of death and the lifeless form it creates. The victim of Medusa is . . . Medusa. The dead head creates more death around it, as it takes on the power of petrification that caused its own destruction. Robespierre described the head of Louis XVI as a Medusa's head for the other European monarchs, but not only monarchs were vulnerable.[96] Villeneuve's famous image of the severed head of Louis XVI, often seen as a Medusa image, shows Louis's head turned to the side, his eyes at best half open and certainly not looking at us, as if to preclude the possibility of our being turned to stone.[97] But the power remains an immanent power,

---

96. See Weber, *Terror and Its Discontents*, 67.

97. The image has been widely reproduced, for example by Caroline Weber, *Terror and Its Discontents*, 38.

able to disseminate more death. The Gorgon appears again in Dickens's novel of 1859, *A Tale of Two Cities*, this time invoked as the agent of an already-petrified landscape—"a stony business altogether"—where the faces of men and animals, blushing blood-red in the early morning sun, look out blankly at the visitor to the country house of Monsieur the Marquis, Charles Darnay's evil uncle. The Gorgon returns to claim one more life, the Marquis himself, "the stone face for which it had waited through about two hundred years."[98] Here it is the agent of the people's revenge, and in particular that of a woman who has been raped (as Medusa was in Ovid's telling of her story), and of a child who has been killed.[99] Violence begets violence, as the monstrosity of the Medusa figure marks both male and female agents, and both supporters and opponents of the revolution. The conservative commentators on the revolution, Burke famously among them, were quick to attribute the most radical violence of the streets to women, who became, like the besotted worshipers of Dionysus, abandoned and unsexed (or hypersexed).[100] But the crowd is beyond mere gendering; there is no choice among identities. Dickens's crowd is like Dumas's, capable of both tenderness and joy in unpredictable succession, and it is invoked throughout the novel as both that which is present and that which is always still to come, whether in Paris or in London, its spectral incarnations haunting the future as long as that future fails to enact justice and humanity. For Dickens is surprisingly even-handed about revolutionary violence, which he always recognizes as the outcome of a world organized for the benefit of the few at the expense of the many, and cruel in spite of the many. If the crowd loses its capacity for pity, it is because none has been shown it. Even more than Dumas, who mixes into his narrative a good few of the major historical figures of the times, Dickens's novel is about ordinary people. It is completely devoid of any of the well-known names usually attached (often in

98. Charles Dickens, *A Tale of Two Cities*, ed. Richard Maxwell (New York: Penguin, 2003), 123, 132, 134.

99. Madame Defarge is a modern Medusa turning the tables on Perseus in hacking off the head of the governor of the Bastille (229).

100. On the journalistic "monstering" of Robespierre as a feminized Sphinx-Medusa figure, see Marie-Hélène Huet, *Mourning Glory: The Will of the French Revolution* (Philadelphia: University of Pennsylvania Press, 1997), 150–61. British radicals around the time of Peterloo printed newspapers titled *The Gorgon* (1818–1819) and *The Medusa, or Penny Politician* (1819–1820). Perhaps the conflation of divinity, violence, and the female is bound to subsist as ultimately beyond discursive discipline. A foundational study of this question is Neil Hertz, "Medusa's Head," in his *The End of the Line: Essays on Psychoanalysis and the Sublime* (New York: Columbia University Press, 1985), 161–215.

demonized forms) to the history of the Revolution. For him, a wine mer-
chant and his wife are far more important to the story than any among
the Jacobin or Girondin elites. Tellingly, Dickens's account of the Terror
is written entirely without mention of Robespierre.

In large part, it is at the same time devoid of the rhetoric of terror.
Searchable texts indicate only nine uses of *terror* or *terrors* in the entire novel, and of these no more than three explicitly reference conditions in France, and none is rendered as *the* Terror.[101] Dickens, even
more than Balzac and Dumas, seems to want to avoid the most ready-to-
hand of all terminologies for describing the events of 1793–1794. Terror is employed on three occasions in connection with the experience of
Dr. Manette's mental breakdown (39, 212, 356) and once at the spectacle of Sydney Carton's trial in London (67). The old regime, then, is, by
a whisker, more frequently a cause of terror than the revolution that replaced it. Dickens's word choice is impeccable and suggests that he was
far more than the mere liberal reformer he is often taken to be. There is
never any doubt about the ultimate reason for the violence of the revolution: "The frightful moral disorder, born of unspeakable suffering, in-
tolerable oppression, and heartless indifference, smote equally without
distinction" (360). Dwelling on the Terror, or on the rhetoric of terror in
general, would have aligned the novel too easily with the counterrevolutionary camp, which is not where Dickens meant to go. Sydney Carton's
final, imagined thoughts before his death on the scaffold are of a brighter
future when evil shall have worn itself out (389). This he shares with the
Defarges, whose acceptance of their fate in not seeing the arrival of the
better days for which they are working is less poetic but no less deeply
felt (185–86). Both agents and victims of the revolution, in other words,
share a belief in a better world to come and a hope that their lives will
have contributed something to bringing that world into being. Even the
innocent seamstress who goes to the scaffold along with Sydney Carton
professes herself "not unwilling to die" if it will contribute to the Republic's efforts on behalf of the poor (368). That she cannot see how this
could be the case makes her largeness of mind, and the force of the history that flows through it, only all the more remarkable.

The same admiration for the power of the revolution appears in
Ninety-Three, Victor Hugo's last novel, published in 1874. Like Balzac,
Hugo takes the rebellion in La Vendée as his subject, but he focuses
on the major campaigns of 1793 rather than on the last-ditch events of
1796–1799. The novel's commitment to the power of the people as the

---

101. See Dickens, *A Tale of Two Cities*, 243, 284, 324.

emanation of an irresistible historical force inevitably reflects on the recent demise of the Paris Commune. Like Balzac, Hugo portrays the Breton peasants as residual primitives, but not without their dignity, and as participants in an inevitably lost cause which yet creates "a scar which is a glory," thus partaking of the very glory (*gloire*) that the Republic claimed for itself.[102] In the war of "the local mind against the central mind" (203), Hugo's sympathies are principally with the second, but there is an even-handedness in his narrative. The ruthless royalist Lantenac and the ultrarepublican Cimourdin are birds of a feather, both determined to exercise standards of absolute justice (familiarly associated with the likes of Saint-Just and Robespierre) that seem to others cruel and inhuman. But both have their moments of heroic retraction, Lantenac as he saves the peasant children from the burning tower, and Cimourdin as he commits suicide at the moment of Gauvain's execution. Both, in other words, sacrifice their lives for a principle and for a progressive cause: the survival of the young and the future of the revolution. The fervent republican Gauvain, to be sure, morally trumps Lantenac when he saves his life (and when Lantenac allows him to do so), but like Dickens's characters he sees in his own death nothing that will impede the better earthly life to come: "Under a scaffolding of barbarism, a temple of civilization is building" (393).

Like Dickens and Balzac, Hugo is parsimonious in his invocations of both terror and the Terror. As in the case of Dumas, the English translation wildly overrepresents the words *terror* and *terrible* by conflating a number of French words under a single English word. When Marat appears in English as "the terror of the terrible" (141), the French reads *redouté des redoutables* (155), and on numerous occasions *redoutable* is rendered in English as "terrible." Where the English text reads "Below crouched Terror, which can be noble" (165), the French reads *épouvante*, not *terreur*, and certainly not *Terreur* (181). French *épouvante* becomes English *terror* on a number of occasions, and *épouvantable* is frequently translated as terrible: so, too, *affreux*, *effrayant*, and *formidable*. Not for the first or only time, the English-speaking reader is glutted with terror and the Terror while the French original is relatively restrained in its usages. Which is not to say that Hugo shies away from the word: he does not. He does not conceal the fact that terror is an attribute of the Republic (e.g., 237), but neither does he accept the idea that terror is the

102. *Ninety-Three* (1900 trans., rpt.) (Rock Island, IL: Necropolis Press, 2012), 186. The French text is cited from *Oeuvres complètes: Quatre-vingt-treize* (Givors, France: André Martel, 1954), 204.

invention of the Revolution. The administrations of Louis XIV and of the Directorate are much the same, *deux terrorismes* (121), predictably translated as "two reigns of terror" (107). The terror of 1793 learned its habits "from the parliaments of France and the Inquisition of Spain" (357). And in the vicious fighting in the west of France, terror (*terreur*) answered to terror (197). The ruined feudal tower and the guillotine are equally a source of terror and horror; but the times have changed, and so, too, for the better, have the causes in which such violence is being deployed.

Medusa also appears again in Hugo's novel, in her special role as the image of revolutionary violence, but violence in a good cause. She is the "frightful apocalypse" pushed into the background by the "carnival smoke" of Thermidor (109), and the image that Cimourdin wishes to have on the buckler of his sword (111). Most powerfully, she is born again in the figure of Michelle Fléchard, the Breton peasant whose three children are about to be burned alive in the tower of la Tourgue:

> This figure was no longer Michelle Fléchard; it was Medusa [*Gorgone*]. The wretched are terrible [*les misérables sont les formidables*].... She rose like a power from the grave; her cry was like that of a wild beast, and her gestures like those of a goddess; her face ... seemed like a mask of flame. Nothing could be more sovereign [*souverain*] than the lightning from her eyes; her eyes flashed lightning on the fire. (346–47, 382)

It is this irresistible power that causes Lantenac to abandon his escape and to rescue the children, as if the force of the revolutionary moment itself overcomes him and allows him to rediscover his humanity. Terror and beauty come together, in an outburst of as-if-divine violence that is also a principle of survival and creation. Earlier in the novel, Hugo has made his case for the revolution as an inhuman force, a "will power belonging to all and belonging to none" that must carry all before it, a "miraculous wind" (again as if divine violence) coming from "above" in the form of an "idea, indomitable and boundless, which blew from the height of heaven into the darkness below" (176). The Rousseauvian general will demands its place in history as inevitably progressive: "The wind came from the mouth of the people and was the breath of God" (177). That said, the rights and wrongs of particular events are not held to be of ultimate significance: "In the presence of these climacteric catastrophes which destroy and give life to civilization, one hesitates to judge the details" (177). As Gauvain affirms at the end of his life, "The visible work is cruel, the invisible work is sublime" (393). This is a much more emphatic vindication of terror and the Terror than can be found in the speeches of St. Just or Robespierre, even though they are commonly associated with this same conviction. It comes hard on the heels of a failed second revolution in Paris, and it still looks to a better future: *ça ira.* To deal with the numbers marked for death after the defeat of the communards, the guillotine was deemed too slow, and so they used firing squads.[103]

According to Geroud (64–65), there were apparently earlier schemes afoot to deploy multiple-blade machines to speed up the rate of execution. But the presiding image of the guillotine after 1792 is of a solitary icon of mechanized execution, separating heads from bodies with perfect and impersonal efficiency. In significant ways, it makes a spectacle out of the antispectacular.[104] The infamous torture of Damiens lasted hours, whereas the guillotine delivers death in an instant. What there is to see is the unseeable, the instant passage from life to death, from something to nothing. There is little or no room for human error, and no reasonable curiosity about how long the prisoner will take to die. The only suspense to be pondered was whether the severed head continued to live for a brief moment and, in some sense, after its detachment from the body. As Sydney Carton tells his companion on the scaffold: "They will be rapid."[105] As befits the near-complete automation of this putting to death, the spectators are also frequently represented as deprived of motion, sitting still or contained by rows of uniformed soldiery observing military discipline.[106] There is nothing here of the traditionally riotous and unpredictable behavior of the crowds that witnessed hangings and tortures. Even the knitting, which has passed into political folklore as the mark of supremely callous indifference on the part of revolutionary women, is transcribed by Dickens as a far more meaningful act, a secret record of the misdeeds of the old regime kept by Madame Defarge (like Philomel) as a project of judgment to come. Her knitting is a register of "the steadfastness of fate" (117). And when practiced by others, it is to be read as a compulsive distraction embraced by starving people: "The mechanical work was a mechanical substitute for eating and drinking;

103. See Daniel Geroud, *Guillotine: Its Legend and Lore* (New York: Blast Books, 1992).

104. Daniel Arasse, *The Guillotine and the Terror*, trans. Christopher Miller (New York: Penguin, 1989), 35–36.

105. *A Tale of Two Cities*, 388.

106. See the various prints collected in David Bindman, ed., *The Shadow of the Guillotine: Britain and the French Revolution* (London: British Museum, 1989).

the hands moved for the jaws and the digestive apparatus; if the bony fingers had been still, the stomachs would have been more famine-pinched" (193). Wordsworth, too, registers this in his memory of the "hunger-bitten girl" encountered in France, "busy knitting in a heartless mood / Of solitude" and, as such, emblematic of what it was the Revolution was hoping to put right.[107] That the same compensatory routine still happens for Dickens in front of the scaffold, with the women "never faltering or pausing in their work" (387), signals the ongoing persistence of hunger and starvation and the revolution's failure to bring economic redistribution: much of the social turbulence of the revolutionary years was to be the result of scarce or unaffordable food for the people.[108] Mechanical, mindless behavior, the more salutary the more mindless, knitting in the face of death, corresponds to the automation of death itself, another way of routinizing the passage of time, and thus of disciplining the people through the stupefying repetition, "head after head, and never heads enough."[109] The more blood spilled, the less food needed: an attempted substitution of appetites. Dr. Manette's life in the Bastille was similarly made bearable (or at least survivable) by compulsive behavior, the "dull mechanical" making of shoes,[110] a habit he cannot fully break even after he is set free. Before and after 1789, various kinds of cruelty and deprivation compel people to radical coping mechanisms.

It is thus all the more striking that the revolutionary crowd has not been petrified, reduced to passive inertia, and that it remains the unpredictably animate and energetic agent of critical action. Dickens is often less positive about this than Dumas, and his representation of the crowds in London and Paris before and after the revolution, and of the crowds always still threatening to come, is more demonic and melodramatic. The "baffled blue flies" in search of "carrion" on the streets of London (82), the "monster" crowds of the Gordon Riots in 1780 (162) and of the September Massacres in Paris, are incarnations of terrible violence, actual or potential. But they are also capable of drastic changes of mood and moments of joy and celebration, as when Manette is fêted in the streets (296). What all these moments have in common is the capacity

---

107. *The Prelude* (1805), 9:517–18.

108. George Rudé, *The Crowd in the French Revolution* (Oxford: Oxford University Press, 1967), suggests that the Jacobins lost power because they lost the support of the crowd by imposing wage limits and other sanctions. The Terror would thus have been not the embodiment of a popular thirst for violence so much as an effort to intimidate the people by a display of the power of the state.

109. *The Prelude* (1805), 10:335.

110. *A Tale of Two Cities*, 42.

for bonding, for making one out of many, for imaging something like the general will. The crowds of the 1790s were not yet those of the "industrial" working class so feared by the establishment fifty or so years later, and whose "petrifaction" function would be identified by Sartre as "the profound meaning of the myth of Medusa."[111] The activists of the 1790s were artisans and masters of workshops (or wineshops, like Defarge), not (or not principally) the *lumpenproletariat* made famous in Marx's account. But when they were written about retrospectively, as by Dickens and Dumas, they were inevitably associated with the crowds that were, by the 1840s and 1850s, no longer still to come but already upon the scene. The urgency of their needs and demands could suggest only that the revolution itself remained unfinished and still to be decided.

This chapter's account of various fictional responses to the French Revolution, and in particular to the Terror and to the rhetoric it generated by recoding the vocabulary of the fear-terror cluster after the events of 1793–1794, is, of course, far from complete. It would surely be possible to produce a list of relatively popular literary works that were quite willing to reproduce the more lurid and polemical dismissals of the French as violent and inhuman monsters unworthy of any defense whatsoever before the tribunal of history. Trollope's *La Vendée* (1850), the first half of which is a picaresque homage to the royalist elites, generally presents republican violence as brutal and royalist combatants as chivalrous throwbacks unwilling to murder or mistreat their enemies. But Trollope mostly stays away from terror talk in favor of finding things "horrid," even in the extended fictional depiction of Robespierre himself that figures in the novel.[112] And he complicates the mapping of his affiliations by presenting the republican General Santerre as a complex and humane figure with a genuine commitment to the people, whereas the loyalist peasants of the *Petite Vendée* are cruel and ruthless. In almost all the writers I have been discussing, whether in the displaced, imaginary scenarios of the gothic novel or in those stories given historical place and time in the events of the revolution itself, there appears to have been a remarkable attentiveness to the fear-terror vocabulary and a common effort to avoid identifying with the reductive potential of repetitive terror talk. In this respect, some of the often-disdained Minerva Press authors seem to have been almost as sensitive to word choices as are the likes of Balzac and Dickens. For different reasons, Edmund Burke chose not to characterize the revolution,

111. Cited in *The Medusa Reader*, ed. Marjorie Garber and Nancy J. Vickers (New York: Routledge, 2003), 92.

112. He does, however, deploy the phrase "reign of terror" at least four times.

much as he despised it, as the emanation of a logical and efficient practice of terror: to have done so would have accorded the Republic the power and status it wished to claim, like the monarchy it replaced, of a traditional state apparatus. Burke had no wish to assist in the Jacobin effort at frightening the British out of their manliness and courage. Balzac, Dickens, Dumas, and Hugo had other motives. They wished to keep alive the democratic project of the revolution as either the actual tendency of history or its utopian ideal; in neither case did they have an interest in demonizing its servants. The gothic novelists by and large tend to imagine the power of terror and violence as residing either directly with the state or with its patriarchal analogues, the barons and prioresses shuttered in their castles and convents where they try hard to keep the younger generation immured forever, unable to reproduce or to challenge their power. Where terror is deployed, it is entirely in the hands of the old regime: it is not a tool available to or desired by those who are working against it. It seems fair to say that none of the writers here discussed subscribe to the myth that terror is always a "red" terror, or that it is the privileged resort of those who have an interest in opposing the state by violence. Quite the opposite: the Jacobin terror is either explained as precisely a version of state terror, or as a brief departure from an otherwise progressive energy, a violent but brief cleansing of the stables. At the very end of his life, Alexandre Dumas was persuaded to write a novel aimed at awakening France to the dangers of Prussian expansionism in the mid-1860s. It appeared in 1867 under the title of *La terreur prussienne*. It was translated into English in 1915, under the pressure of another urgent concern about the role of Germany in another European war. Dumas's purpose (like his translator's) is polemical, and the major narrative event is the Prussian occupation of Frankfurt in 1866–1867, which was "rightly called *the Prussian Terror at Frankfort*."[113] Dumas is unremitting in his condemnation of the Prussian generals and of Bismarck; but for all the propagandist agenda, the novel remains notably even-handed in its disposition of heroism, shared more or less equally among a Frenchman, an Austrian, and an officer serving Prussia. Terror here has become thoroughly metaphorical and quite detached from its associations with Jacobin Paris: it describes military occupation, financial exploitation, and everyday cruelty of the sort practiced by many armies before and after. Above all, terror is firmly identified as a power in the service of the state. The process whereby it would become the rhetorical property of antistate organizations had not as yet seriously begun.

113. *The Prussian Terror*, trans. R. S. Garnett (London: Stanley Paul, 1915), 214.

Meanwhile, the Gorgon has had another recent reincarnation on the political scene, and there is no question as to whose power of terror it now represents. In December 2010, a "revolutionary" combat intelligence system called "Gorgon Stare" made its debut over Afghanistan.[114] The mythic name has replaced the more cumbersome locution "Wide Area Airborne Surveillance System." Gorgon Stare never blinks; no data can pass unnoticed.[115] What was in the 1790s an icon of the power of the people as well as of the monarchy resisting that power has now been subsumed into the United-States-controlled global targeted assassination program. Those on the receiving end have little or no chance of counter-violence. The Medusa stares only one way. As if to add insult to injury, the figurative description of the apparatus intended to allow "U.S. forces to overwhelm enemy defense with favorable cost-exchange ratios" now embraces the language of the "swarm," the coalition of the many into one that had characterized Dumas's and Dickens's descriptions of the dangerous and volatile behavior of the people as the crowd.[116] This swarm will not blink or waver, and will increasingly function by artificial rather than human intelligence, bypassing human error but also human correction. As it happens, Gorgon Stare seems to have had a dismal record so far, and looks like one more case of corporate profiteering without competitive bidding or competent oversight.[117] But the ambition it represents shows no signs of going away, and the dream of absolute surveillance and instant destructive power (at no human cost to the possessor) continues to be desired and developed. In earlier times, the Gorgon imaged what was most feared in the urban crowd, its apparently autonomous and irresistible force. Now it is chiefly deployed by the state: the stare of the Gorgon no longer threatens Monsieur the Marquis, just those who threaten him and his kind. But there is no absolute guarantee that this will always, everywhere, be the case. The Medusa is never more alive than when dead.

114. http://www.globalsecurity.org/intell/systems/gorgon-state.htm (accessed April 22, 2013).

115. Steve Coll, in *New Yorker*, November 24, 2014, titles his essay on drone warfare "The Unblinking Stare."

116. Robert O. Work and Shawn Brimley, *20YY: Preparing for War in the Robotic Age* (Washington, DC: Center for a New American Security, 2014), 28–29.

117. See Andrew Cockburn, *Kill Chain: The Rise of the High-Tech Assassins* (New York: Henry Holt, 2015), 182–88.

5

Terror against the State

Dostoevsky, Dynamite, and the Supernatural

In Dickens, Balzac, Dumas, and Hugo, as well as in the British gothic novels of the 1790s and in the more emotionally restrained novels of Scott and Austen, there appears to be a notable reluctance to emblematize the French Revolution as the exemplary and inevitable bearer of terror, a monstrosity dispensing a criminal and inhuman violence. None of these authors goes so far as to celebrate the lethal violence of 1793–1794 as the necessary instrument of an emergent state facing a state of exception, but most make an effort to imagine the excesses of the guillotine as embedded in long-standing as well as short-term historical conditions that preclude attributions of a purely idiosyncratic or historically exceptional cruelty. Even Carlyle, who is more given than most to the hyperbolic mode of writing history, and who anticipates Arendt in projecting totalitarian terror as an autonomous agency enveloping both victims and perpetrators, holds on to a connection between radical violence and the years of poverty and oppression that preceded it. In short, these writers do not seem mesmerized by the specter of the Terror. Many of them do however seem very apprehensive of the crowd, of masses of people acting together in ways that seem unpredictable and uncontrollable. That same prospect of mass agency, according to one explanation of the Terror, was exactly what motivated the Jacobins to project their own control of the power of violence by way of highly visible state-administered executions. The crowd can sometimes be persuaded to spend its violence in the service of the state, as it was (though this was far from uncontested) in the mass conscription that produced the armies of the revolution and forged them into such a powerful military force. But it can also turn against the state, as it was seen to have done in the storming of the Bastille and in the early phases of the revolution while the king remained in office. The slow or negligible pace of economic reform after 1789 meant that the volatility of the crowd would always be a condition of political life, especially in the urban centers and above all in Paris. No revolutionary party was able to solve the endemic problems of poverty and food supply, and a hungry crowd was not to be imagined as being kept in its place forever, even by a government it seemed to endorse.[1]

Increasingly throughout the nineteenth century, violent terror would come to be projected as something likely to be directed against the state rather than deployed by it. The first historically significant bomb, in the modern sense, was exploded on Christmas Eve 1800, when Napoleon and his entourage narrowly escaped being blown up by a pile of gunpowder and scrap iron hidden in a cart: an improvised explosive device, or IED, in current parlance.[2] Terrorism, which began life (in 1794) as a term describing (and disparaging) the servants of the republic, would become more and more the marker of those acting against it. Indeed, in current popular usage, the identification of terrorism with the activities of the state itself has almost disappeared outside of limited countercultural subgroups and specialists. By the end of the century, the media image of the terrorist was of a figure with a pistol or a box of dynamite acting either alone or on behalf of some below-the-radar anarchist or liberationist group. What is often most striking here is the lack of connection between the individual or group and any larger social whole sub-

1. For an account of the ongoing occurrences of crowd-based civil disobedience after the fall of the Jacobins, see Brown, *Ending the French Revolution*.

2. See Rand Mirante, *Medusa's Head: The Rise and Survival of Joseph Fouché, Inventor of the Modern Police State* (Bloomington, IN: Archway Publishing, 2014), xv–xix. See also Brown, *Ending the Revolution*, 316–18. The so-called *machine infernale* was planted by royalists but was used as a pretext for executing or imprisoning a range of enemies of the consulate.

stantial enough to be thought of as "the people."[3] The terrorist emerges from the crowd but does not speak for it or represent it. One way to read this would be as antirevolutionary wish fulfillment: society remains too complex and fragmented to compose anything like a crowd, a body capable of unified agency and radical effect. Gestures against the state are thus merely idiosyncratic and bound to fail; they can never command the consent of the majority. Terror against the state thus lacks conviction and remains a series of one-off events incapable of generating historical crisis. Fear of the crowd thereby takes the form of denying the crowd's existence as a historically critical mass. At the same time, the exposure of the "terrorist" as finally unable to change the world leaves open a narrative space for at least partial sympathy with an ideal fictionally ensconced as purely utopian. Or, alternatively, that same utopian aspiration can be marked negatively as the dangerous delusion of an unhinged mind. Numbers are not everything. The exemplary appeal of the Narodnaya Volya for future generations far exceeded its numbers or the historical success of its plans. With a core group of only a few hundred across the whole of Russia, and lasting only three or four years, it did manage the assassination of the tsar. And it had some moral authority in asserting that targeted terrorism should prevail, with bystanders being kept out of the line of violence.[4] Much of its rhetoric is at most moderately terroristic, and it often came to function as a sort of moral yardstick for approvable social activism thereafter. But there were other options for fictional exploration, including those at play in Dostoevsky's pre-Narodnaya novel of 1873, variously translated into English as *The Possessed*, *The Devils*, and *Demons*.

We know that the novel had its origins in Dostoevsky's effort to transcribe the story of Sergei Nachaev's murder of a fellow nihilist in 1869 and that many of its characters are intended as representations of contemporary writers and political activists: the novel is something of a roman à clef.[5] The world described does not however have the coherence of

3. The Irish Fenian movement came closest but was often disparaged as being funded from America.

4. See Astrid von Borcke, "Violence and Terror in Russian Revolutionary Populism: The *Narodnaya Volya*, 1879–83," in *Social Protest, Violence and Terror in Nineteenth-and Twentieth-Century Europe*, ed. Wolfang J. Mommsen and Gerhard Hirschfeld (London: Macmillan, 1982), 48–62.

5. See Gudrun Braunsperger, "Sergey Nechaev and Dostoevsky's *Devils*: The Literary Answer to Terrorism in Nineteenth-Century Russia," in *Literature and Terrorism: Comparative Perspectives*, ed. Michael C. Frank and Eva Gruber (Amsterdam: Rodopi, 2012), 27–39.

the Lukácsian historical novel: there is no emergent historical formation embodied in the life stories of ordinary people, or indeed of any social group. Dostoevsky's Russia is a place marked by hyperirritability, idiosyncrasy for its own sake, and a seemingly uncontrollable unconscious, where a slavish respect for foreign cultures sits beside an equally extreme loathing of strange manners. This is admirably described by Bakhtin as an instance of the "polyphonic novel" wherein "souls and spirits" do not merge but coexist, often violently, in contested social space.[6] Here opinions are emphatically delivered not so much with the aim of achieving social consensus as to "convince the speaker himself" (261). The range of idiolects on display, each one marking a particular character, can never come together as a common language. Thus the vocabulary of emotional extremes remains at best minimally interpersonal or otherwise entirely solipsistic. Fear-terror responses happen between individuals or within single minds; nothing ignites the masses. Dostoevsky's would-be revolutionaries are neither latter-day Robespierres nor pan-European secret conspirators akin to Barruel's imagined Illuminati. They are just confused and uptight young men without either coherent doctrine or significant effect. The favored fear-terror word is *strakh*, which seems to have a set of options for English translation that covers almost the entire range of the fear-terror spectrum, from mere *dismay* and *anxiety* all the way to *terror* and *trembling*.[7] The choices made by the translators are interesting. The two most recent tend to choose the weaker possibilities (*fright, alarm, fear*), as if to tamp down or limit the extreme carnivalesque hyperbole latent in so many of the novel's encounters. It is the first English translator, Constance Garnett, who makes heavy and consistent use of *terror* in the same places.[8] Garnett, publishing in 1913, is working at the end of the period of "dynamite" fiction. She knew Conrad and was intimate with a number of radical Russian exiles. *Terror* was a term of her times. But no amount of semantic hyperbole can realign the social dynamic of the novel, which constantly inhibits any transition between individual and larger communal emotions.

6. Mikhail Bakhtin, *Problems of Dostoevsky's Poetics*, trans. Caryl Emerson (Minneapolis: University of Minnesota Press, 1984), 26, 178.

7. Lacan comments on the term: see *Anxiety: The Seminars of Jacques Lacan, Book X*, ed. Jacques-Alain Miller (Cambridge: Polity, 2014), 158, 170.

8. See, among many examples, *The Possessed*, trans. Constance Garnett (1913; rpt. New York: Barnes and Noble, 2005), 95, 98, 116; *Demons*, trans. Richard Pevear and Larissa Volokhonsky (New York: Random House, 1994), 91, 96, 115; *Demons*, trans. Robert A. Maguire (London: Penguin, 2008), 101, 106, 128. I am very grateful to Michael Holquist for information about Dostoevsky and his translators.

There are exceptions, to be sure: Garnett has "panic terror" afflict at least "the society of the town" (609) at the discovery of Shatov's murder.[9] But the perpetrator has vanished, and the murder itself has minimal political motivations, being carried out principally as a bonding ritual designed to keep together the members of the radical quintet in preparation for a future critical moment that may never come. Here Dostoevsky makes interesting use of the specter of Shpigulin's workmen, a factory labor force that is frequently invoked by others as a likely source of riot and revolution but who themselves never appear in the novel, except at one point when they assemble in a group of seventy to present their case to the masters. At this moment the narrative is taken over by reports of urban legends and of melodramatic newspaper stories about "a rebellion which threatened to shake the foundations of the state" (Garnett, 436). But little or nothing is offered by the narrator in the way of exact information, and it is clear that whatever happens is not serious enough to disrupt the fête that takes place on the following day. If there has been a revolution, he and his fellow townspeople must have missed it.

For all of these reasons, it is hard to endorse André Glucksmann's proposal of a direct connection between Dostoevsky's novel and the events of 9/11.[10] An important development in the evolution of modern terror was in process at the time of the novel's publication, but Dostoevsky, who died in 1881, seems to have just missed it: the invention of dynamite, patented by Alfred Nobel in 1867. Dynamite was quickly disseminated for military and industrial uses, along with efforts to restrict access and control its transportation.[11] It was available to the Fenian Brotherhood for its bombing campaign in Britain between 1881 and 1885, and it had come to sponsor both urban legends about mysterious terror weapons and anarchist optimism about easy access to the power of violence. Among the first writers to respond in fiction to the new terrorist economy (along with Zola in *Germinal*) were Robert Louis and Fanny Van der Grift Stevenson, and the mode is principally comic. In *The Dynamiter* (1885), *terror* and *horror* do indeed feature in the story, but neither word carries any serious charge, either historical or fictional.[12] Three down-on-their-luck

9. Maguire has "mystical fear" (675); Pevear and Volokhonsky read "almost mystical sense of fear" (609).

10. See the addendum to Garnett, trans. *The Possessed*, 720.

11. See John Merriman, *The Dynamite Club: How a Bombing in Fin-de-Siècle Paris Ignited the Age of Modern Terror* (Boston: Houghton Mifflin, 2009), 72–78.

12. For a brief account, see Michael C. Frank, "Plots on London: Terrorism in Turn-of-the-Century British Fiction," in *Literature and Terrorism*, ed. Michael C. Frank and Eva Gruber (Amsterdam: Rodopi, 2012), 41–65, esp. 51–57.

young Englishmen set out to have adventures, encountering an Irish terrorist and his shape-shifting young female ally, but the dynamite either
fails to go off or explodes without critical harm, except at the point where
it blows up the terrorist himself. Along the way there is an entirely fab-
ricated side story of the Mormons of Utah as dispensers of terror and
violence on a worldwide scale (the role assigned in the 1790s to the Illuminati). Mormon gothic appears again two years later in Conan Doyle's
A Study in Scarlet, this time as a "true" part of the plot, where it has
the effect of undermining the popular press's attribution of the central
murder to the familiar European "political refugees and revolutionists,"
an attribution seen here as an effort at "admonishing the government
and advocating a closer watch over foreigners in England."[13] Here, too,
the socialist-anarchist-Fenian presence is displaced in favor of a Mormon
"more formidable machinery" (88) whose reach appears to be global but
corresponds to no historical circumstances whatsoever.

What is the effect of this? Doyle, like the Stevensons, projects London
as a dangerous and complex place within which all sorts of threats are
lurking unseen, especially in the bland anonymity of the suburbs. Watson calls London "that great cesspool into which all the loungers and
idlers of the Empire are irresistibly drained" (8). For the Stevensons it
is "the Bagdad of the West" characterized by mysterious "city deserts"
whose streets are in broad daylight are "secret as in the blackest night
of January."[14] Much of the time (as in Stevenson's better-known story
of Jekyll and Hyde) the secret of what is behind all those ordinary and
identical closed doors remains apolitical, partaking more of the gothic
supernatural than of revolutionary politics; terror and horror are on almost every page, but they have minimal or highly displaced relations to
the historical "terrorist" subculture. Henry James, in *The Princess Casamassima* (1886), is much more direct, identifying a political cell located
in London and run by a German exile, but there is again no reference
to the Fenians, who were in fact the only group that actually detonated
bombs in Britain at the time. Nor is James in the business of whipping up
fervor against foreigners by stepping up terror talk. The term *terrorist*
never appears and *terror* hardly ever: Lady Aurora is in fact in "terror"
of her own upper-class culture and not of those working against it.[15]
James, as one might predict, is much more interested in the nuances of

13. Arthur Conan Doyle, *A Study in Scarlet* (London: Penguin Group, 2001), 50.

14. Robert Louis Stevenson and Fanny Van der Grift Stevenson, *The Dynamiter*
(New York: International Book Company, n.d.), 1, 7, 44.

15. Henry James, *The Princess Casamassima* (London: Penguin, 1987), 44.

individual psyches and in the intricacies of personal relationships and loyalties than in making clear pronouncements about violent revolution. But he is interested in the consent or co-option of a young mind by the romance of revolution in the cause of social justice. Hyacinth, visiting Paris, registers the "magnificent energy" of the revolution (rather than its "turpitude and horror"), but it makes him not want to die (393). That he does so and by his own hand suggests that the impulse to revolutionary agency is too overdetermined by personal conflicts and confused motivations to emerge as a serious historical force, even though the novel is published shortly after a well-known series of Fenian assassinations and dynamite attacks, including several in London itself.

When Edmund Burke held back from according the power of terror to the Jacobin state, he was motivated (or so I have suggested in chapter 4) by a determination not to allow the foreign enemy a credible basis for undermining the British national morale: terror is effective only when one believes in its power. Something similar may have been happening in the relative silence about the Irish situation in late nineteenth-century fiction. Mary Elizabeth Braddon's short story of 1893, "The Dulminster Dynamiter," blends a tale of English provincial life with the "infernal machine" made possible by dynamite, but order is implacably preserved when the bomb in the cathedral turns out to have been planted by the Dean himself, in a state of mental distraction.[16] It does not go off, but had it done so, it would have caused little damage, being poorly built. The accompanying illustrations however show the destruction that might have happened if it had been a better bomb and had actually exploded. Image and text do not correspond, but Braddon can have things both ways: in a world where explosives are readily available, the danger is real, even in the most improbable places, and disaster could have followed. At the same time the culture of normalcy wins out, and life goes on as usual. The builder of the bomb is no Fenian but a deranged minister of the Church of England. At a time when "the air of the Senate and the Law Courts seemed full of terror" (470), terror is tamed or at least deferred.

Barbara Melchiori has pondered the significant question of why "the Fenian bombs of fact became the anarchist bombs of fiction."[17] She

16. M. E. Braddon, "The Dulminster Dynamiter," *Pall Mall Magazine* 1 (May–Oct 1893), 469–82.

17. Barbara Arnett Melchiori, *Terrorism in Late Victorian London* (London: Croom Helm, 1985), 10. Melchiori offers a detailed survey of novels about terrorism; some do address the Irish question, but most do not. Trollope's last novel, *The Land-Leaguers* (1883), takes as its topic the Irish land wars of 1879–1882 and does include an assassination, but only twice uses the word *terror*, in both cases describing emotions, not

suggests a desire to keep the Irish question out of fiction altogether, along with a reciprocal concern about the onset of class warfare as the more likely agent of a long-term violence in British society. And indeed the Fenian campaign was, by modern standards, none too efficient. The Clerkenwell prison explosion of 1867 took twelve lives, using gunpowder. But the main Fenian bombing campaign of 1881–1885, using dynamite, seems to have occasioned only one fatality: a seven-year-old bystander was killed in the Salford explosion of 1881.[18] Many were injured and property was damaged, but there appears to have been no further loss of life. Whether this was a function of incompetence (many of the bombs indeed failed to detonate), policy, or luck, is hard to determine: one of the three bombs that went off on Dynamite Saturday (January 24, 1885) did explode at peak visiting time in the Tower of London, but there were no fatalities.[19] There is at least some historical rationale for the incompetence that marks the Stevensons' portrayal of terrorism. Dynamite ignition technology was relatively new and far from perfect. At the same time the socialists, who (unlike the nihilists) did not carry out assassinations or plant bombs (as did the anarchists) were by the close of the 1880s perceived as the most credible opponents of the establishment. Socialism and anarchism were commonly conflated and readily identifiable with foreign exiles coming to London; they were not usually seen as Fenian causes. Neil Whelehan notes that "existing studies on the Fenian dynamiters agree that 'terrorist' was a term they never applied to themselves. Neither did others apply it to them."[20] Only much later did the Irish nationalists come to be called terrorists.

---

personifications. It makes no use at all of the words *terrorist* or *terrorism*. I rely here on a searchable text of *The Land-Leaguers*, new ed. (London: Chatto and Windus, 1884), published online by the University of Toronto Robarts Library (call no. AAR-753), https://archive.org/details/landleaguersootroluoft.

18. See Frank, "Plots on London," 56. The number of fatalities is not clear from the sources I have consulted, but it seems certainly well below the Clerkenwell figure.

19. Frank, "Plots on London," 21. For good accounts of terrorism in London in this period, see Antony Taylor, *London's Burning: Pulp Fiction, the Politics of Terrorism and the Destruction of the Capital in British Popular Culture, 1840–2005* (London: Bloomsbury, 2012), 46–74; and Gerry Kearns, "Bare Life, Political Violence, and the Territorial Structure of Britain and Ireland," in *Violent Geographies: Fear, Terror, and Political Violence*, ed. Derek Gregory and Allan Pred (New York: Routledge, 2007), 7–35. Kearns (22) notes that, in the 1880s, *The Times* published 976 articles on terrorism, with Ireland featuring in 824 of them.

20. Niall Whelehan, *The Dynamiters: Irish Nationalism and Political Violence in the Wider World, 1867–1900* (Cambridge: Cambridge University Pres, 2012), 25. Thorup, *An Intellectual History of Terrorism*, 103, agrees with this judgment. Elizabeth Carolyn Miller

The Fenians are also absent from Joseph Conrad's two classic novels about terrorism, *The Secret Agent* (1907) and *Under Western Eyes* (1911). The first is a fictionalized version of the single anarchist explosion that had taken place in London, in 1894, in which the would-be bomber (and no one else) was himself blown up. Conrad's self-nominated terrorists are a grotesque bunch, physically repellent and mentally deranged, the effect of which is not so much to denigrate the cause of the social justice that they might claim to espouse (though they hardly do) as to undermine their own sincerity: they are shams and poseurs who generate not pity and fear but "pity and contempt."[21] These terrorists do not disseminate terror: they are unwitting players in a plot laid by Verloc as a double agent working for the Russians, who wish to stage a dynamite event—albeit something that "need not be especially sanguinary" (24)—to push the British into a more restrictive policy on the immigration of Russian radicals. Here the British police are remarkably competent (as they are not in the Sherlock Holmes stories, for example), knowing as they do that the explosion is "no part of any general scheme" (122), and the British politicians do not take the bait: no clampdown ensues (even though it is historically the case that a newly restrictive Aliens Act had been passed in 1905). Conrad seems to have every confidence in the establishment as both liberal and sensible. And his anti-Russian streak conforms not only to his inherited Polish identity but also to the foreign policy of his adopted country, for which the Russian state, and not its exiled radicals, is the main enemy. Thus it is a telling detail that the power of terror is not possessed by the anarchists but by the state itself in its ability to execute criminals. Winnie Verloc is terrified by the gallows, and Ossipon by Winnie herself as a woman with the power of violence, but no

---

argues that the Irish in particular were perhaps ignored because they were less threatening than the alternatives, being vigorously masculine and working for their own nation state rather than seeking to alter the existing order of things from inside. See Miller, "Exile London: Anarchism, Immigration and Xenophobia in Late-Victorian London," in *Fear, Loathing, and Victorian Xenophobia*, ed. Marlene Tromp, Maria K. Bachman, and Heidi Kaufman (Columbus: Ohio State University Press, 2013), 269–85. Miller's earlier *Framed: The New Woman Criminal in British Culture at the Fin de Siècle* (Ann Arbor: University of Michigan Press, 2008) discusses "dynamite" fiction in some detail as a response to the perceived feminization of culture, with mindless violence operating alongside mindless consumerism. Suffragette theory itself involved approval of a measure of "secret and healthy terror": see Alex Houen, *Terrorism and Modern Literature: From Joseph Conrad to Ciaran Carson* (Oxford: Oxford University Press, 2002), 126.

21. Conrad, *The Secret Agent* (London: Penguin, 2007), 248.

one is terrified by terrorists.²² The revolution that looms as terrifying for
Ossipon is one of gender, not politics. The bizarre figure of the "Professor" who walks the streets with his hand on a rubber ball in his trouser
pocket that will trigger a suicide bomb is also, not coincidentally, promising to explode his own masculinity.

Anti-Russian sentiment is even more apparent in *Under Western Eyes*,
where Conrad employs a narrator who often reminds his reader that the
narrative is "not a story of the West of Europe" to project Russia as an
anthropological oddity that no Englishman could be expected to under-
stand.²³ Although an explosion is reported early in the novel as causing
"terror" among the bystanders (17), the "terroristic wilderness" (316)
here chronicled is largely of the mind (as it so often is in Dostoevsky).
Although few positive claims are made for the ideals of the revolutionaries, there is no support whatsoever for the integrity of the state they wish
to destroy. But the wider historical context of violence against the state is
only minimally signaled to provide a vague backdrop to the interpersonal
and psychological dramas in which Conrad is most interested. Haldin,
who makes the classic defense of terrorism as much less violent than the
statist oppression it opposes (19), disappears early in the novel, whose
principal focus is on the career of the man who betrays him and on his
interactions with those who still believe in the cause. To be a Russian, it
seems, is to be faced with living life between a rock and a hard place.

At least one novel of the times does take up the task of giving terrorism a sympathetically human face: Frank Harris's *The Bomb* (1909).
Without entirely justifying radical violence, Harris's narrator describes
the conditions that produced the Chicago Haymarket bombing of 1886
as largely the responsibility of the state: xenophobia, police corruption,
brutal antilabor repression and procapitalist newspaper reports suggest
a world not so very different from Conrad's Russia. The man charged
with the bombing, Louis Lingg, did not throw the bomb; he blows himself up in prison having made sure that he does not kill anyone else in so
doing. Only the single American among the seven accused garners any
popular sympathy among a population driven by hatred of foreigners:
Harris's aim is to establish the moral integrity of those foreigners, socialists and anarchists as they are, and of Lingg especially. Modern American culture, according to the narrator (who is the real bomb thrower) is

22. Conrad, *The Secret Agent*, 212, 230–31, 234–45, 244.
23. *Under Western Eyes* (London: Penguin, 2007), 23. For accounts of Conrad's
analysis of terrorism, see Houen, *Terrorism and Modern Literature*, 34–92; and Miller,
Framed, 149–222.

nothing more than an "organized swindle." He writes an article on police behavior called "The Reign of Terror in Chicago," but no one will publish it.[24] Terror is deployed as a one-off event by the workers but is an ongoing policy on the part of the state apparatus.

Harris's novel is very much an outlier in its explicit sympathy for those driven to radical violence and in its clear condemnation of the capitalist state, and in this it appears to be very different from what we find in James or Conrad. But even Conrad is no defender of statist privilege when it happens to be Russian. British liberalism is the idealized alternative, and its tolerance is sacred enough that even the exiled anarchists are welcome under its umbrella. If the state is to be endorsed, it must be the right sort of state. Cosmopolitan tolerance and competent policing keep Conrad's Britain safe, and the one bombing incident that does occur, and that is the historical basis for the plot of *The Secret Agent,* is for Conrad an unfortunate accident and the result of a (foreign) state-manufactured plot. Making the state itself (whether Russia or Britain) the covert instigator of so-called terrorist violence performs a function very like that enacted by modern conspiracy theory: if it is always "the government" that is secretly pulling the strings (Pearl Harbor, the Kennedy assassinations, 9/11), then there is no real threat from the outside. A perverse form of xenophobia governs this kind of thinking: no one but ourselves could possibly pull off such events. Avowed distrust of the state bizarrely endorses the state's power and self-sufficiency. This phenomenon appears in G. K. Chesterton's novel of 1907, *The Man Who Was Thursday.* Here there is a whole group of supposed anarchists plotting dark deeds of destruction, and each one turns out to be an undercover policeman. The whole story is presented as a nightmare and is protoallegorical, putting it at some remove from a referential history. Thus it does not seem overtly cynical about the state's determination to vindicate its own authority by inventing enemies that do not exist. The book is friendly to the police and gives the impression that such hypervigilance is indeed a sign of the security of those it aims to protect. At the same time it generates a disturbing uncertainty about what is real and what is imagined.

Terror talk is much more explicit in Arthur Machen's short story "The Terror," first serialized in 1916 as "The Great Terror."[25] The story describes how, in the middle of the Great War, strange and unexplained killings begin to occur all over England. The newspapers keep quiet and

24. Frank Harris, *The Bomb* (Portland, OR: Feral House, 1996), 49, 170.
25. Arthur Machen, *The White People and Other Weird Stories* (London: Penguin, 2011), 372.

all sorts of speculations are let loose: many suspect the secret operations of German agents and secret weapons. The population finds itself living under a "reign of terror" (304), but it is one that has no political or even human resolution: the narrator's opinion is that there has been a revolt among the animals, who rise up violently as a result of the loss of human authority and control apparent in the conduct of the war. It is not a moral protest that is suggested, and there is no alternative moral order to be seen in the profile of these acts of violence. The animal revolution appears more an attempt to fill the power vacuum created by the abdication of the "king" of creation (356). The animal kingdom thus becomes an instance of the threat from below, always latent unless kept in check: "They may rise again" (357). But much of Machen's rhetoric comments critically on the cooperation of the politicians and the mass media in keeping people in the dark; although the state is not finally deemed to be the origin of the terror, it is not much respected or applauded. The threat carried in the supernatural is rendered the more mysterious by the state's failure to describe or control it in ways that its citizens find convincing or adequate.

Machen's story belongs in a tradition of supernatural terror that was just as popular at the end of the nineteenth century as was the dynamite narrative. Supernatural terror tends to be presented as harder to contain. For all its fanciful exoticism, it also can and does carry a historical-political charge. Richard Marsh's *The Beetle* (1897) records a sophisticated understanding of the statist culture of blaming the victim by disavowing the state's own reliance on the power of terror. Here it is the British who claim vulnerability to terror while themselves dishing it out whenever and wherever it is felt useful. Marsh tells the story of a magical man-woman, insect-human devotee of the Egyptian cult of Isis who arrives in London to avenge an earlier erotic involvement with an upright Englishman, thereby cutting a swathe through the progressive and scientific subculture of the metropolis in a gender-bending spree of magic and mesmerism. It is the alien beetle, the exotic-demonic eastern sorceress, who earns the single attribution of the term *terrorism* in the book, when Paul Lessingham begs the detective to protect him from her.[26] And it is the feeling of "terror" generated by the beetle that the various characters repeatedly invoke. Terror, again, is here the declared property of

---

26. Richard Marsh, *The Beetle*, ed. Julian Wolfreys (Peterborough, ON: Broadview Press, 2004), 251. For an account of the gender politics of the novel, see Kelly Hurley, *Sexuality, Materialism and Degeneration at the Fin de Siècle* (Cambridge: Cambridge University Press, 1996), 124–41.

the enemy other. But there are odd occasions when the beetle feels terror instead of causing it, for instance, when it encounters the electrical apparatus in Sydney Atherton's laboratory, where its own terror is mentioned three times in quick succession (145). We might by this point have noticed also the "terror" ascribed to the cat who was about to be suffocated in an experiment to demonstrate the power of "Atherton's Magic Vapour" (136). But we should not miss the clear narrative that describes Atherton's progress on this ultimate terror weapon, the gas bomb that, he promises, will give his country an absolute military superiority over its enemies. The powers of the individual "terrorist" beetle are relatively circumscribed even as they have radical effects on a few chosen targets; they cannot affect the "hundred thousand men—quite possibly more" (137) whom Sydney imagines destroying with a single bomb.

Sydney (like Alfred Nobel) is naive or corrupt enough to imagine that his invention will contribute to world peace, because once it is known that Britain possesses it, no one will ever start another war. But there was already a heady international competition under way in the development of the poison gases that would feature so destructively on the Western Front. Nor did the contemporary record suggest that the British state was at all invested in bringing about an end to war. Quite the opposite. Since 1881 Britain had been fighting against the Mahdists in the Sudan; Khartoum (and General Gordon) fell to the enemy in 1885. It took until 1896, the year before the novel's publication, for Kitchener to reconquer the Sudan, and he did so principally because he deployed the latest weapon of mass destruction, the Maxim gun, which would soon kill so many on both sides in the Great War of 1914–1918. Marsh plays up Sydney Atherton as a naive optimist who justified his interest in weapons of mass destruction in a world that the novelist and his readers could hardly have failed to acknowledge as critically driven by terror deployed on behalf of the British state. This is not precisely right or left terror, but it is definitely white terror in that it is exercised by a European colonial power to defeat a national liberation movement, and an Islamist one at that. In the light of all this, the terrorism deployed by the beetle seems distinctly limited in its effects.

There is another, clever turn in Marsh's plot. The beetle and her captive (a woman dressed as a man) escape by express train. The rescuers follow in another train, a "special." Modern technology—the train and the telegram—is what makes this adventure possible, but time is tight, and the rescuers have to travel at breakneck speed in hopes of catching the express. The experience of the journey is frightening, "as if we were being pursued by a legion of shrieking, bellowing, raging demons"

(315). So the pursuers are being terrified by the speed and noise of the train while they are chasing the agent of another attributed terror. And indeed train travel, even at ordinary speeds, was widely reported in the nineteenth century as a major source of stress and trauma.[27] In Marsh's novel the good guys do catch up, but only because the express is itself wrecked in an accident, leaving some dead and some "half-frenzied" survivors (318). The rescue of the heroine and the (at least temporary) defeat of the beetle is enabled by the catastrophic misfunction of the very technology that makes rescue possible, in a prescient example of what we now recognize as the autoimmunity syndrome, whereby healthy organisms generate threats to their own existence and actually contribute to nourishing them.[28] The target is indeed located and eliminated but only by way of the death and injury of numbers of innocent bystanders.

In another famous novel published in 1897, Bram Stoker's *Dracula*, the source of terror is again located in the foreign supernatural. Humans and animals alike sense the terror generated by the vampire, which is at one point called a "scheme of terror," as if it were the result of a deliberate policy.[29] There have been many hypotheses about who or what Count Dracula represents, but what governs them all is the observation that to work his will he must first be invited into the houses of his victims and made welcome as a guest.[30] The vulnerability of a protected space is thus a function of the host-guest convention prescribing hospitality: making the stranger welcome proves an inadvisable and dangerous thing to do. In Guy Boothby's *Pharos the Egyptian* (1898) the threat is once again of Egyptian origin. Boothby fashions a dazzling version of the "mummy's curse" narrative, in which the vengeance of the violated foreign land takes double form, in the figure of Pharos and in the plague whose dissemination across Europe he controls by making the English narrator himself the vehicle of contagion. This is another autoimmunity

27. See Wolfgang Schivelbusch, *The Railway Journey: The Industrialization of Time and Space in the Nineteenth Century* (Berkeley: University of California Press, 1987), 134–49.

28. See Borradori, *Philosophy in a Time of Terror*; and Roberto Esposito, *Bios: Biopolitics and Philosophy*, trans. Timothy Campbell (Minneapolis: University of Minnesota Press, 2008). On a lighter note (but is it lighter?), Senator Lindsey Graham reportedly criticized President's Obama's speech of May 2013 as follows: "This is the most tone-deaf President I ever could imagine, making such a speech at a time when our homeland is trying to be attacked literally every day." See Peter Baker, "In Terror Shift Obama Took a Long Path," *New York Times*, May 28, 2013, A1, A3.

29. Bram Stoker, *Dracula*, ed. Nina Auerbach and David J. Skal (New York: W. W. Norton and Co., 1997), 239.

30. Stoker, *Dracula*, 211, 264.

parable which indexes not only the desecration of Egyptian tombs but the occupation of Cairo by the British (in 1882) and the ensuing Suez Canal convention: the narrator specifically notes the presence of an army of occupation.[31] Like *The Beetle*, this story is about the empire fighting back, although it turns out that the ancient Egyptian gods are just toward an avenger who is himself sacrilegious and is punished accordingly with his own onset of the "terror" he has caused in others (chapter 21). Equilibrium returns and the homeland is safe once more.

It is safe only in one of the two endings of Bram Stoker's contribution to Egyptian gothic, *The Jewel of Seven Stars* (1903). In the first ending, the resuscitated mummy creates death and destruction, after inducing in the narrator an internal "state of terrorism," of being "in constant dread of some unknown danger which may come at any time and in any form."[32] The final, anticipatory terror of the narrator is reflected in the "fixed eyes of unspeakable terror" in the dead victims' faces (244). H. G. Wells's short story of 1895, "The Stolen Bacillus," returns to the anarchist plot to describe how London is saved from a terrorist-generated cholera epidemic only by the quick thinking of a scientist. In Wells's magisterial *The War of the Worlds* (1898), it is earth's natural bacteria that are the single saving force sparing the planet's being permanently conquered by the Martians, against whom the new Maxim guns are useless. In *The War in the Air* (1908) it is the global lust for empire that reduces Britain to a primitive agrarian economy that must begin again the progress of modernization after admitting the need for a life-saving counter violence against the worst that is in human nature.

There are many other novels of the late nineteenth-century that imagine the imminent demise of Britain and its empire resulting from human, biological, or supernatural invasion, and they constitute a collective address to (and exploitation of) terror, whether as a politically motivated policy or as a human response to the supernatural or extraterrestrial. The political agents may be either those operating against the state (anarchists, for example) or those states (Germany, the imagined Asian alliance) that are rivals in the scramble for empire and global domination. The Fenians, empirically unignorable dispensers of political violence, are barely mentioned. This may be a form of nationalist insouciance, whereby the known and relatively limited Irish threat cannot

---

31. *Pharos the Egyptian*, chapter 10. The story was published serially in *The Windsor Magazine,* June–December 1898.
32. Bram Stoker, *The Jewel of Seven Stars*, ed. Kate Hebblethwaite (London: Penguin, 2008), 227.

be parlayed into convincing terror fiction, where the stakes have to be higher.[33] But the threat posed by European anarchists must have seemed even slighter. Marsh and Boothby make their Egyptians into supernatural time travelers to compensate for the completely minimal empirical threat to the homeland offered by any actual Egyptian; and Wells making his Martians outgun the British army and its Maxim guns disavows and displaces a real-world situation in which lightly armed colonized peoples were being ruthlessly mown down by modern British weaponry.

Although these things are going on in the novel, there is another development in the rhetoric of terror, which comes to be specified as a desirable end for a properly intense experience of art itself. Burke's theory of the sublime, along with the gothic novel and its afterlife in Poe and others, had already made clear the aesthetic potential for a managed recitation, for willing readers, of terror experiences, and this tradition has been more or less continuous since, emerging again, for example, in Karlheinz Stockhausen's infamous remark about the falling towers on 9/11 as "the greatest work of art ever."[34] Chesterton, in *The Man Who Was Thursday*, has his "anarchic poet" Lucien Gregory make the case, in identifying him as the real "villain" of the story:

> The man who throws a bomb is an artist, because he prefers a great moment to everything. He sees how much more valuable is one burst of blazing light, one peal of perfect thunder, than the mere common bodies of a few shapeless policemen. An artist disregards all Governments, abolishes all conventions. The poet delights in disorder only.[35]

In Isabel Meredith's *A Girl among the Anarchists* (1903), the anarchist newspaper is called *The Bomb* (later, *The Tocsin*), as if the power of print could replicate the power of dynamite. Between 1900 and 1905 the journal *Iskra* (Spark) was published in Leipzig and smuggled into Russia: Lenin, in London, was involved for its first three years. Wyndham Lewis's short-lived (1914–1915) periodical was named *Blast*, an English

33. There were to be sure *some* fictional representations of Irish terrorism; see Houen, *Terrorism and Modern Literature*, 21–33, and my remarks earlier in this chapter.

34. Exactly what he said and how he said it have been disputed and discussed ever since. He also offered a weaker explanation whereby the effect of shock and disruption that the terrorists achieved is what art should also strive for—a more conventional and acceptable analogy.

35. *The Annotated Thursday: G. K. Chesterton's "The Man Who Was Thursday,"* ed. Martin Gardner (San Francisco: Ignatius Press, 1999), 38, 39, 277.

version of the 1909 *Futurist Manifesto's* worship of violence, speed, and the machine. Metaphors of explosive power also featured in the titles of German avant-garde publications such as *Die Aktion* (1911–1932) and *Der Sturm* (1910–1932), the second begetting associated lectures called *Sturmabende* and occasional publications called *Sturmbücher*. Here aesthetic radicalism shares semantic territory with German fascism, whose popular anti-Semitic newspaper later went by the name of *Der Stürmer*. Left and right are competing for the same radical conflation of print and transformative real-life power, while violence itself, the terrible beauty that Yeats sees in Ireland in 1916, takes on aesthetic appeal. As late as 1924, well after the monstrous violence of the Great War, Breton would compare the surrealist act to firing "a volley shot into a crowd."[36] What gets muddled here is the distinction between explosive violence as an analogy for and an instance of the desired effects of art and literature. Art thus conceived is not strictly productive of terror, because its effect is punctilious, instant and unrepeatable, a moment of shock and awe that is more akin to Benjamin's divine violence, something transformative but without remainder, a change of state. Nonetheless it is the instruments of terror(ism) that are invoked as most apt for describing art's aspirations, and while it is one thing to hope that art might have a world-changing power, it is quite another to suggest that it turn into high explosives. The aesthetic appeal of dynamite as providing the spectacle of falling buildings (with no loss of life) is troubling enough, but by 1914 (if not before) it would have been impossible not to connect explosive weaponry with the annihilation of human bodies. Fascists and some futurists appear to have been quite comfortable with this conjunction.

Perhaps the identification of the word or the image with dynamite inadvertently signals the degree to which actual "terrorist" violence was so often enacted against overwhelming odds. In the case of the bomb thrower, those odds were apparent in the sheer power of violence embodied in the modern nation-state, which terrorism could hope to disrupt only occasionally unless it had behind it (which it seldom if ever did) the support of the irresistible masses who could be expected to rise up and reinvent a state of their own. Perhaps only the supernatural could be imagined as the agent of a comprehensive and enduring terror able to compete with the state itself in its possession of the power of violence. Even as terrorism is becoming the property of the state's antagonists,

36. See Houen, *Terrorism and Modern Literature*, 93, and, more extensively, *The Violent Muse: Violence and the Artistic Imagination in Europe, 1910–1939*, ed. Jana Howlett and Rod Mengham (Manchester: Manchester University Press, 1994).

the most powerful images of terror enforcement in the twentieth century remain attached to the state itself. D. H. Lawrence's *Kangaroo*
(1923), an odd mélange of fiction, autobiography, and political commentary, records a "reign of terror" in Britain during World War One
that afflicted anyone not fully supportive of the war effort.[37] Hans Fal-
lada's books transcribe the terror of life under the Nazi state; Orwell's
1984 and Koestler's *Darkness at Noon* do the same for other times and
places. Doris Lessing's five novel sequence *Children of Violence* images
a world completely pervaded, at every level from the family to the state,
by fear and terror, and it is clear that the primary agent here is the state
in both its global wars and its colonialist regimes. Any political radical
taking to terrorism must face almost overwhelming odds in the state's
command of terror itself. For the aesthetic radical, the odds were stacked
in favor of a mass media seen as wholly corrupt and coopted by national
and international vested interests that bound together a political and
economic consortium that controlled the dissemination of ideology and
the regimen of taste. Artist and bomb thrower share a common enemy
and a common desire to bring about a new world order. The possess-
ors of "illegal" dynamite were subject to prosecution and punishment;
so, too, the authors and publishers of radical ideas. The history of both
becomes more visibly entwined in the late nineteenth-century than ever
before, not least because both regard mass culture as largely hostile to
any true culture of the masses as well as to the critical potential of radical elites. As the words *terror* and *terrorism* become commonplace,
notwithstanding the fastidious distance from terror talk maintained by
novelists like James and Conrad, they cease to describe anything precise
or doctrinally specific. Nihilists, anarchists, and socialists all become
"terrorists," whether in Russia, Germany, Britain, or elsewhere. To perform or threaten violence is to become a terrorist, however ineffectual
that violence may prove to be and however little of verifiable terror it produces.[38] Meanwhile, terrorist actions against the Nazi state and occupation were quite reasonably described as resistance, whereas resistance
to the Soviet empire (East Germany, Hungary, Czechoslovakia) largely
took rhetorical form as national-patriotic movements or courageous individual actions. Historically, terror and terrorism figured in early (1948)
settler-colonial (Jewish) state formation in Israel and on both sides of the

---

37. D. H. Lawrence, *Kangaroo* (London: Heinemann, 1964), 216, 253.

38. For specimen surveys, see Mommsen and Hirschfeld, *Social Violence, Protest and
Terror*; and Walter Laqueur, *A History of Terrorism* (New Brunswick, NJ: Transaction
Publishers, 2012).

anticolonial struggle in Algeria; but in the later twentieth century it was once again resistance to state and colonial power that came to be most commonly called terrorism, most vividly embodied in the mainstream and mediatized Western imagination by the Palestinians, the Irish Republican Army (IRA), the Black Panthers, and the various liberationist-revolutionary movements in Africa, Asia, and Central and South America. The more charismatic figures (Che Guevara, Leila Khaled, Bobby Seale, Daniel Ortega, Steven Biko) were heroes among the young and the left inclined and demons in the eyes of others. Very few who ended up on the winning side managed a transition to power over the state without seeming to lose the moral authority they had while opposing it: Nelson Mandela may stand alone in this respect. For all the soul-searching that the Black Power and (to a lesser extent) American Indian movements set going in some American souls, their causes were all too readily racialized (and, moreover, relatively nonviolent), to sustain widespread and long-term majority attention, let alone support. Opposition to apartheid in South Africa took on literary forms from the very beginning, and South African writers continue to explore both the apartheid era itself and the implications of its partial (legal but not economic) dismantling. And in Europe the antistate movements of the 1960s did produce one movement (or conflation of movements) that garnered a national and international literary response that did not fade away when its initial "terrorist" actions were consigned to history: Baader-Meinhof, also known as the Rote Armee Fraktion (RAF).

Our Terrorists Are Us

The literary representation of the Baader-Meinhof movement has not been dominantly negative or simply judgmental. German antigovernment radicalism in the 1970s had a lot going for it. Nazism and Stalinism had not left the state per se with a good name, and postwar Germany in particular was widely recognized as not having fully come to terms with the *Hitlerzeit*. American economic and cultural support was managed by a bureaucratic class full of former Nazi party members, and American war making in Vietnam (especially) was in itself the object of a worldwide protest movement. It was perhaps too early for the man in the street to suggest (or at least publish) that the bombing of Dresden and Hamburg shared a visible criminality with the bombing of Hanoi, but in Germany both the homeland state and the two competing superstates were morally compromised and mutually embroiled. For ten years (1967–1977) the Baader-Meinhof group made headlines, the background to which is still being explored and reinterpreted.[39] It has also generated a considerable output of fiction and film. According to Julian Preece, part of the appeal of these events is a function of the relative vagueness of the movement's agenda, making it a "blank screen" for the projection of all sorts of plots and possibilities.[40] Most of these, according to Preece, pass lightly over the fatal violence and the Palestinian-Israeli involvements, allowing for the terrorists to be seen as romantic outlaws who are also insiders, and to function as proxies for a larger cycle of national mourning that could not be explicitly avowed (166). They are also comfortably open, in their citations of the likes of Heine and Hölderlin, to the companionship of the national classics (93). To a remarkable degree, terrorists are us, our siblings, and our children, whose dissatisfactions with the postwar settlement are understandable and even admired. In Heinrich Böll's *The Lost Honor of Katherina Blum* (1974), the true enemies of the people are the popular press with its appetite for sensation and blackmail, and the reactionaries who fund it. In the same author's *The Safety Net* (1979) the successful capitalist open to being targeted by terrorists himself believes that "socialism must come."[41] War profiteers mingle with well-intentioned liberals in a world where even the best families contain their social radicals and occasional terrorists. Violence against the ruling economic class fizzles out in this novel, where the irritations and inconveniences generated by the surveillance state constitute more of an affliction than terrorism itself.[42] Böll writes a reconciliation novel in which the errant "terrorist" daughter gives herself up before causing critical harm and returns to a world that is, at least below the level of the bureaucratic state, more than a little forgiving.

Walter Abish's *How German Is It*, also first published in 1979 (in English), is not so consoling as it embeds its terrorist narrative in a whole-culture analysis of a Germany still attempting to cope with the legacies of the Nazi years: "Lots of people around with all kinds of scars."[43] Characters shift between uneasy repetition and refutation of a past that they

39. The standard history is Stefan Aust, *Baader-Meinhof: The Inside Story of the RAF*. First published in 1985, this book is now in its third, revised edition, trans. Anthea Bell (Oxford: Oxford University Press, 2009).

40. Julian Preece, *Baader-Meinhoff and the Novel: Narratives of the Nation, Fantasies of the Revolution, 1970–2010* (Basingstoke, UK: Palgrave-Macmillan, 2012), 2. Preece offers an indispensable survey of both translated and German-only books.

41. *The Safety Net*, trans. Leila Vennewitz (New York: Melville House, 1981), 323.

42. The English translation loses the rather more sinister implication of the German title, *Fürsorgliche Belagerung*.

43. *How German Is It / Wie Deutsch Ist Es* (New York: New Directions, 1980), 73. The title appears to be a statement as much as a question.

know only imperfectly and through the screens of individual repressions and social misinformation: "Why this curious predilection for leather?" (3). The "hero" lives in a town named after a prominent philosopher who is clearly Heidegger (by a different name) and located next to a wartime extermination-concentration camp that most prefer to forget or disown but that is kept alive by one man's obsessive effort at an exact scale model and by the discovery of a mass grave during a roadworks project. The main protagonist, Ulrich Hargenau, appears to have informed on his terrorist wife's companions (inadvertently or not), facilitating their imprisonment, and continues to be ambiguously involved with persons who may be working for or against the state. Relatively pointless and sometimes fatal acts of destruction (culminating in the blowing up of a bridge to the East Frisian Islands) occur without coherent purpose or effect. Where *The Safety Net* chronicles efforts at restoring some level of social harmony, Abish's novel is edgy and obscure, withholding both exculpation and full disclosure. Nothing is quite as it seems. The last scene reports Ulrich, under hypnosis, raising his arm in a Nazi salute. Ulrich is a writer (*haargenau*: spot on, precise, meticulous), and he is at work on a manuscript about his experiences with the terrorist movement. Abish suggests, indeed, that this writer is far from being in a position to offer any insights into the forces at work in contemporary Germany. But the weight of judgment falls equally on those profiting from and those opposing the new Germany; there seem to be no heroes or heroines on either side.

Similarly complex attitudes and affiliations register in Eva Demski's *Deadalive* (1984), much of which describes life in the middle ground lived by supporters of radical causes who are not committed fully or clearly enough to be immune from surveillance by both sides. Helmut Krausser's more recent *Eros* (2006) refigures some of Abish's themes, but this time the writer is paid lavishly by a multimillionaire to produce a biography (in the form of a novel to be published after his death) and thus rigorously disbarred (but can this ever work?) from writing about himself. The millionaire, Alexander von Brücken, born in 1930, weaves a narrative that is inevitably both revealing and deceiving, and his offer of openness is constantly qualified by admonitions about what can and cannot be said. His urge for commemoration—"I want you to be harsh but just, and please don't spare me"—is offset by his long-serving assistant's cynicism about the desire for "*a work of art*. It's his way of justifying the whole business, retrospectively."[44] The story Alexander tells is (like Ulrich Hargenau's) one of a touching but disturbing erotic obsession, one that leads him for entirely personal reasons into radical circles. He drifts into the 1967 student demonstration at which Benno Ohnesorg was killed and observes that "for the first time ordinary people, who so far have looked down on the students, begin to feel sympathy for them, share their feelings" (195). He confesses that "sometimes my thinking was of necessity left-wing, without my really realizing" (314). And, like the characters in *The Safety Net*, he comes to find that the major consequence of the emergence of radical terrorism is the massive expansion of the police state (214). He is sympathetic enough to the radical cause (or to Sophie, his obsession) to propose that he pretend to be kidnapped for a hefty ransom, as if to enact the Schleyer affair as harmless theater.[45]

Krausser ends the novel with a strong hint that the story Alexander has told is far from the whole truth, suggesting that his father was in fact a strong supporter of the Nazis, and not the somewhat unworldly aesthete described in the memoir. As a bridge (*Brücke*) between factions and between generations, Alexander represents an economically buoyant Germany that cannot settle with either its past or its present. Like Abish, whose book he seems to follow closely, Krausser implies that the past is the present. The terrorism of the 1970s is thus embedded in a much longer history for which it is not responsible, and which it seems compelled to repeat even as it seeks to enact reparation. But the repetition of violence against the state is a mere footnote to the violence enacted by the state in the Hitler years; the power of terror that the radicals seek to claim is far less convincing than what has been imposed by the Nazis, many of whom continue to prosper in the new Germany. Historical inertia, and the continued presence of state policing power, make clear that the RAF and their kind are both latecomers and inevitably on the losing side. Opposition to the Nazis inside Germany had been a failure; the conscious internationalism of the new radicals, and their place in a worldwide culture of radical idealism, seemed to give them more credibility, especially when they claimed to be themselves agents of denazification. At the same time their doctrinally eclectic statements made them readily exploitable by a rampant tabloid press whipping up popular paranoia in the good old cause of selling newspapers.

Baader-Meinhof continues to generate fictional interpretation. Bernhard Schlink's 2008 novella *The Weekend*, inspired by the debate about

45. See Preese, *Baader-Meinhoff and the Novel*, 97. Hanns Martin Schleyer was kidnapped and murdered by the RAF in 1977. Sophie is not an RAF member but belongs to a similar group.

whether to release the last terrorists still in prison, rehearses a coming to terms with the past plot apropos of both radical violence and the legacies of a preunification Germany. The terror syndrome is somewhat awkwardly updated by having Marko, a member of the current radical community (whose extent is never specified but is not presented as a serious alternative), articulate his approval of the 9/11 attacks as bringing about "good things" that otherwise would not have happened: "Sometimes the world needs a shock to come to its senses."[46] There is no sign that any meaningful coalition of German radicals with al-Qaeda or any other group is likely to materialize, although one person writes a story that imagines that her long-disappeared partner was carrying a suitcase that guided the planes to the World Trade Center. The German president's pardoning of the three remaining prisoners is enacted with the aim of showing that "German terrorism and the tensions and fractures in society that it provoked were passed" (201). At the same time, in a story where every character says his or her piece, the case for necessary violence is not wholly dismissable: "The fact that it is no longer chic to speak of oppression, alienation and disenfranchisement doesn't mean they've gone away" (195). The radical terrorism that one of the older characters recalls only as a "sickness" (81) is for the young Marko very much a living ideal. Schlink does not endorse his view, but no others are endorsed either.

Few of the late twentieth-century European terrorist fictions go as far as Nanni Balestrini's *The Unseen* (1987) in emphasizing the disproportionate excess of state violence in countering the radical threat, although there are elements of this in Böll's *The Safety Net* and in a number of the films made in Germany about the RAF phenomenon. At the other end of the spectrum, Doris Lessing's *The Good Terrorist* (1985) seems best read as a critical satire of the bourgeois revolutionary aspiration, though one not without some sympathy for the damaged young people who fall for it.[47] There is little sympathy here for the cause for which violence is projected (the IRA), and the analysis of the mind of the would-be terrorist is mounted very much from a distance. In this respect the novel is a far cry from Lessing's earlier address to the African situation in *The Grass Is Singing* (1950), an intense exploration of the settler-colonial experience in

46. Bernhard Schlink, *The Weekend*, trans. Shaun Whiteside (New York: Vintage International, 2011), 55.

47. See Margaret Scanlan, *Plotting Terror: Novelists and Terrorists in Contemporary Fiction* (Charlottesville: University of Virginia Press, 2001), 75–91; and, for this and other novels about British radicals, Taylor, *London's Burning*, 130–56.

Southern Rhodesia (now Zimbabwe) through the lives of unprospering white farmers despised by their more affluent racial peers and at the same time engaging their black workers in an implacable master-slave confrontation in which death takes the place of any Hegelian reconciliation. Although "terrorist" acts do not take place in the novel, the brutality of race relations suggests that they are looming and that the explosion of radical violence can be only a matter of time. If it does not overtly justify that violence, it also suggests that it might not be an implausible or unreasonable recourse. A similar tolerance of or openness to imagining violence shows up in Nadine Gordimer's *A World of Strangers* (1958), where the powder keg that is South Africa is seen through the eyes of an English visitor whose liberal inclinations make it hard for him to fathom the racial gulfs that beset society and that are engaged (historically) in destroying the Sophiatown community whose subculture is to him so immensely attractive. Before Sharpeville (1960) the apartheid state had not fully or publicly revealed itself as a terror state, nor had the African National Congress abandoned its policy of nonviolent resistance. It was thus possible for Lessing and Gordimer to imagine that the violence of extreme racial segregation might not lead inevitably to terrorist violence on the streets. After Sharpeville this changes, and the dynamics of that change are the subject of an exhaustive imaginary chronicle by André Brink, *An Act of Terror* (1991). Brink's novel is a tour de force that imagines not only the recent history of South Africa up to and including Mandela's release from prison but also the entire history of the Boer colonization, told by way of a supplement on the history of the Landman family. As the novel's title announces, the matter of terror is not sidelined. No one is clearer than Brink about the relation between the terrorism of the radicals and the terror deployed by the state. As one movement member, under torture, puts it to his interrogator: "What you choose to call the State of Emergency" is nothing less than "terror."[48] The main (Afrikaner) protagonist's mother tells the police that she is "not sure who the real terrorists are" (194). The surveillance state and its ruthless executors kill off all the young women who are working against them and as many men as they can manage. What makes the activists so sympathetic is not only the justice of their cause, which by the 1980s has become well known all over the world, but also their capacity for strenuous ethical self-reflection on the limits and possibilities of violence itself. The apartheid state only ever had the support of a minority of those living in South Africa and had given rise to a vigorous opposition

48. André Brink, *An Act of Terror* (London: Minerva, 1992), 349.

from the first.[49] It is perhaps this that affords Brink the option for an unin-
hibited representation of the terror state and a clear understanding that its
capacity for fatal violence far exceeds whatever is enacted by those it labels
"terrorists." As Thomas observes, "What strikes me most today is how
remote Dostoevsky's world is from ours" (480).

Meanwhile, in the Northern Hemisphere, 9/11 produced a revived interest in novels about terrorism, with a wide range of attitudes and ap-
proaches, although few of them go as far as their predecessors in defending
or sympathizing, covertly or otherwise, with the case for violence; a safer
and more common response is satire directed at the responses (or lack
thereof) of middle-class Americans.[50] But one writer at least has shown a
career-long interest in terror and terrorism, one that encompasses fictional
responses to both Baader-Meinhof and 9/11: Don DeLillo.

Before and after 9/11: Don DeLillo

In reading through DeLillo's pre-9/11 fiction, a respectable conspiracy
theorist would have little trouble deciding that the novelist had predicted
the whole thing. Many of his novels engage with what we would now
call agencies of terror: crowds, revolutions, chemical explosions, assassinations, and finally 9/11 itself. But DeLillo sticks to the tradition he
inherits from those responding to the French Revolution and its legacies: he is very sparing in his recourse to terror talk and seemingly very
much aware of its contribution to a degraded and ideologically satu-
rated language. At the same time he is strikingly predictive of violent
futures. In *Players* (1977), a group of friends is sitting on a Manhattan
rooftop looking out at a skyline that includes the recently built World
Trade Center (WTC); a few pages later, one of them says "That plane
looks like it's going to hit . . . I was sure it would hit."[51] One member of
the novel's primary couple, Pammy, works there in grief management;
the other, Lyle, at the New York Stock Exchange, where he witnesses

49. In confronting the nature of life under state terror Brink's novel is anticipated by
Alan Paton's *Too Late the Phalarope* (1953), which dramatizes the tortured psyche of an
Afrikaner man who transgresses the immorality laws and repeatedly experiences a "ter-
ror" that is simultaneously of surveillance and discovery and also of guilt and conscience.

50. It is probably no longer feasible to attempt a comprehensive chronicle of novels
responding or alluding to 9/11. But for an impressive interim taxonomy up to 2010, see
Birgit Däwes, *Ground Zero Fiction: History, Memory and Representation in the American 9/11 Novel* (Heidelberg, Germany: Winter Verlag, 2011).

51. Don DeLillo, *Players* (New York: Random House, 1989), 81, 84–85.

a terrorist attack and gets involved in an obscure liaison with a cast of characters that includes radicals, government agents, and double agents. In *Mao II* (1991) the twin towers are "two black latex slabs that consumed the available space."[52] In *Underworld*, written four years after the first (1993) WTC bombing, the narrator senses a "poetic balance" between the outline of the towers and the profile of the Fresh Kills landfill on Staten Island, where the detritus (including some fragments of human remains) of 9/11 would in the future end up.[53] The story looks back to the time when the WTC was under construction, leading to one character's observing that it is a "very terrible thing but you have to look at it" (373). Klara Sax, in a dyspeptic moment that was quite common in those times but has now become almost sacrilegious, sees the twin towers as "a model of behemoth mass production, units that roll identically off the line and end up in your supermarket, stamped with the day's prices" (377–78). One can easily imagine that DeLillo had long had privileged information about the coming destruction of the towers; what he more plausibly possesses is a remarkable grasp of the political, aesthetic, and linguistic dimensions of gargantuan consumer capitalism.

Underworld looks back to a Cold War mentality in which enemies were known quantities and psychic responses were, seen retrospectively, comfortingly predictable, "anchored to the balance of power and the balance of terror" (76). Now, money and violence (Klara again) are everywhere but not in identifiable forms. Cold War clarity appears also in the rhetorical confluence of football and military training that marks *Endzone* (1972). In *White Noise* (1985), first published almost at the very moment of the Bhopal explosion, DeLillo explores responses to an airborne toxic event in the American homeland that elicits a Stockhausen-like appreciation of the conflation of beauty and terror: "It was a terrible thing to see . . . but it was also spectacular, part of the grandness of a sweeping event."[54] But it is in *Mao II* that DeLillo, following Walter Abish and the legacies of the Futurist Manifesto, most thoroughly depicts the relation between art and terror. Here, art (as fiction writing) is presented as buried by the hegemony of consumer culture and as relatively helpless in the face of a world more and more aggregated into crowds, where the premise is a loss or giving over of the individuality that the writer traditionally prizes. Crowds are variously violent and revolutionary (as in the Iranian Revolution of 1979), mindlessly and happily led by the nose (as in the mass wed-

52. *Mao II* (New York: Viking Penguin, 1991), 165.
53. *Underworld* (New York: Simon and Schuster, 1997), 184.
54. *White Noise* (New York: Penguin, 2009), 124.

dings of the Moonies), or tragically endangered (as in Tiananmen Square
and in the Hillsborough stadium disaster of 1989). They are always symptoms of massification, expressions of a willingness to follow a leader (or a
team), and as such they are especially prone to the persuasions of a culture
based on the spectacle, the image, the commodity. They create terror to
the exact degree that they are themselves subject to it: the terror is us. The
hegemony of the graven image over modern culture—"we sleep and eat
the image and pray to it and wear it too" (36)—pressures the writer to a
withdrawal from the world, to a recognition that "the withheld work of
art is the only eloquence left" (67). Bill Gray, the famous writer imagined
in this novel, is thus a recluse, a man who cannot be found, and who does
not publish his work. But in his self-imposed withdrawal from the world
he is not only protesting modern culture but also taking upon himself the
role of god, "playing God's own trick" (37). The writer is thus in a bind,
unable to make his statement without sacrilege or hubris. It is this impasse
that, for Bill, appears to be resolved in the conflation between artist and
terrorist that he explores but finally refuses. Like a terrorist, Bill is near
impossible to find, hidden from sight (27, 30). But writer and terrorist are
in competition, because terrorists have claimed the space previously occupied by novelists in making "raids on human consciousness" (41). They
have created a world in which writers are themselves terrorized—Bill is
paranoid about getting on a plane (41)—even as they themselves wish for
access to the power of terror. So it is that Bill both worships and loathes
his own prose as "bits of human tissue sticking to the page" (28, and again
at 55). He wants to resist the commercial conspiracy "to make writers
harmless" (47), and it is this that leads him to accept an invitation to mingle with terrorists and to stand in for another writer who is held hostage in
Lebanon. For his editor, little is at stake other than the opportunity to engineer a "happy sensation" (99), but Bill is motivated by a sense of shared
purpose, by the possibility that "it's the novelist who has felt affinity for
the violent man who lives in the dark" (130).

Bill thereby has a choice, between the road taken by Dostoevsky,
Conrad, and Lessing, for whom terrorism is a narcissistic disorder, or
that suggested by Harris and Abish, who explore the integrity of dissent
and its affiliations with the artist's vocation. In the long discussion between Bill and George, his contact man with the terrorist Abu Rashid,
Bill contrasts writer and terrorist in a zero-sum game: "What terrorists
gain, novelists lose. The degree to which they influence mass consciousness is the extent of our decline as shapers of sensibility and thought. The
danger they represent equals our own failure to be dangerous" (157). So
minimal is Bill's access to the modern world of image and spectacle that

his books have not even been made into movies (206). But in the face of an invitation to accept the idea of himself becoming a terrorist, Bill refuses at the last minute, giving voice to a "democratic shout" that is still embodied in the novel, and one based not on loud certitudes but on "ambiguities, contradictions, whispers, hints." The failed novel may be nothing more than a "shitpile of hopeless prose," but it is a democratic shitpile, one open for all to see and to pass judgment on (159).

Bill here voices a very traditional defense of literary writing, one articulated in opposition to the modern world by I. A. Richards, by the New Critics, and by many since. His own life ends in limbo, his novel remains in camera (thanks to the devotion of his acolytes), and DeLillo's final portrayal of the terrorist Abu Rashid's place in a world dominated by images seems to include him, too, in its unavoidable contamination, one where there is very little prospect of a "democratic shout" having any effect. Bill's experience of coming close to terrorism sends him back to the old pieties, but the old pieties earn no narrative vindication, although they do of course get an airing in DeLillo's own book and for whoever picks it up and reads it. Ambiguities and whispers may be preserved in good novels, but good novels are drowning in a sea of commodification. Margaret Scanlan, reading *Mao II* as a comment on the Rushdie fatwa, reasonably sees it as exploring "the failures of a romantic conception of writing."[55] The world is now run by other, negatively aestheticized forces, anticipated by and embodied in a human propensity to assemble or be assembled into crowds and to worship spectacular images of heroes.

What, then, might we make of DeLillo's fictional response, in *Falling Man*, to the real-world destruction of those very twin towers which had figured in his earlier work as exemplary cases of what is most to be lamented in contemporary culture: stereotypy, commodification, and spectacle? He can hardly celebrate the violent loss of life that came about on 9/11, but how can he regret the disappearing of that great icon of global capital (and America's control of so much of it) while remaining true to the spirit of critique that had previously cast the World Trade Center as a "behemoth of mass production," a "terrible thing" that must be looked at? His solution is ingenious: the art-terror event is displaced away from the towers themselves, where Stockhausen had left it, and relocated in the figure of the falling man, the man who pretends to be falling to his death to shock (it seems) New Yorkers into a recognition of the real human

---

55. *Plotting Terror*, 34. See also Scanlan's reading (95–107) of Coetzee's *The Master of Petersburg* as an exploration of the relation between artist and terrorist. On Blanchot's equating of literature itself with terror, see Redfield, *Rhetoric of Terror*, 81–86.

lives that ended on 9/11, including that of the man whose documented existence in photographs had been so speedily expunged by the national media in the days after the attacks.[56] The facsimile that is performance art is used to reintroduce the reality that commodified art (the media) has erased from the record. Debates about taste and propriety of the sort that had from the first been based on the hypnotically repeated footage of the towers falling at a distance, over and over again as if for the first time and thus living forever as image and spectacle, now focus on the integrity of the artist who reminds us repeatedly of the fate of the flesh and blood that was destroyed once and forever. The terrible beauty of art in relation to terror and terrorism had, after *Mao II*, already figured again as an inevitable topic in DeLillo's short story based on the April 2002 Museum of Modern Art exhibition of Gerhard Richter's 1988 paintings of the dead figures of the Baader-Meinhof group.[57] Instead of deciding for or against the quality of these paintings (themselves based on photographs) or the propriety of showing them in New York so soon after 9/11, DeLillo fashions a story about two visitors to the gallery who are unable to complete an interpretation but who are haunted by the paintings into repeated visits, visits that then devolve into and intertwine with an abandoned or impeded seduction scene.[58] The man declares himself unmoved by the paintings but returns anyway, perhaps to pursue the woman. The woman, who has refused the man, also returns to find him there once again. The story stages no clear response to an art that is about terrorists; it is more about the effort at response, which the woman is making in good faith but the man probably not. Even with the mediation of art, these visitors struggle to apprehend anything about the terrorists and about what Richter might have felt about them. Both are out of work and have the time to spend in front of the paintings, but what comes out of this is at most a haunting, or otherwise (for the man) an opportunity for a romantic (or purely sexual) encounter. The paintings were done fourteen years earlier, about events taking place twenty-five years before they were made. The distance of time and place seems too wide to overcome.

"Baader-Meinhof" fits with that species of post-9/11 fiction, as evidenced in Claire Messud's *The Emperor's Children* or Jay McInerney's *The Good Life*, which depicts not so much the events themselves as their

56. The sensitivity of this photographic record has not yet diminished. See Tom Junod, "The Falling Man: An Unforgettable Story," *Esquire*, September 9, 2016. DeLillo presumably also draws upon the work of "falling man" artist Kerry Skarbakka.

57. For a good discussion of Richter's paintings, see Alex Danchev, *On Art and War and Terror* (Edinburgh: Edinburgh University Press, 2009), 8–32.

58. Don DeLillo, "Baader-Meinhoff," *New Yorker*, April 1, 2002.

effects on those standing by.[59] Often these are noneffects, and the tone becomes satirical, as if asking what exactly it might take to shock such persons into a serious response, something that would make them pause in their pursuit of wealth and happiness. DeLillo asks that question, too, though not in a satirical way, as neither wealth nor happiness seem to be in the offing for his two protagonists. His characters cannot find a language, either to describe the paintings or to establish a sympathetic understanding with each other. They live, like so many of DeLillo's characters, amid a confusion of tongues. Making sense of this confusion is very much the traditional task of the novelist: eschewing jargon, making it new, adding precision, and taking care to discriminate between near synonyms and to split apart tired general terms: Prodicus's ambition in *Protagoras*, before Socrates moves him aside to make possible the founding of philosophy. DeLillo's novels have however often wondered whether this task is still possible, even as they seem to perform it. In *Endzone*, he tells us (as if echoing Victor Klemperer) that "the problem goes deeper than just saying some crypto-Goebbels in the Pentagon is distorting the language" (85); even sportswriting and broadcasting appeal not least because of their commitment to "elegant gibberish" (113). In *White Noise*, the professor of Hitler studies has not yet learned basic German; his monolingualism is a testimony to our insouciant assumption of anglophone supremacy but one that is ironically challenged by the simple experience of going to the grocery store: "More and more I heard languages I could not identify, much less understand" (40). *Mao II* extensively transcribes the reduced grammar and vocabulary of the Moonies, a "half-language, a set of ready-made terms and empty repetitions" (7): "They chant for one language, one word, for the time when names are lost" (16). This is the antithesis of Bill Gray's ideal of the novel, with its "democratic shout" that records "one thing unlike another, one voice unlike the next" (159). But as we have seen, it is not at all clear that this ideal of literary integrity can sustain itself in the modern world, one where all cities (including New York) are becoming versions of the war-torn Middle East: "Our only language is Beirut" (239).[60]

The oneness of language, whether it be Moonspeak, global English, military-sporting gibberish, or the polyglot assemblage of the city street, asks to be pondered in relation to the oneness of global capital, typified

59. On Messud, see Simpson, "Telling It Like It Isn't," in *Literature after 9/11*, ed. Ann Keniston and Jeanne Follansbee Quinn (London: Routledge, 2008), 209–23.

60. And making sure to drive home this point about oneness and Beirut, DeLillo makes it on at least three other occasions: 146, 173, 176.

by the commodity-spectacle of the World Trade Center, that "model of behemoth mass-production" (*Underworld*, 377). But, for the defender of liberal democracy, like Bill Gray and perhaps Don DeLillo, language is also what can undermine or contest the looming oneness of the world system, a means to "wage a war on totality."[61] At this point it is hard to resist a conjunction between the skyscraping towers that fell on 9/11 and the play between the oneness and multiplicity of languages that has preoccupied DeLillo in so many of his books. It is hard to resist, in other words, some attention to the story of Babel. It is in *Falling Man* that this narrative is most fully adumbrated, without its ever being spelled out and given its name. The novel is full of misnamings, mistranscriptions, and misunderstandings at the level of language and marked also by unmistakable references to impiously tall buildings, evident even in the supposedly trivial world of the poker game, where the master cardplayer Terry Cheng has a phobia about making two piles of chips high enough to topple, and of exactly the same height.[62] But to endorse the Babel myth—the fall of tall towers as God's judgment on an overambitious humanity—would be to endorse precisely the position of the terrorists, those who see themselves as enacting divine justice upon a corrupt Western world. The paradigm must thus remain implicit or uncompleted, latent in the fabric of the novel but never brought to full expression. DeLillo gets across the idea that there is something wrong with those towers without going so far as to celebrate their destruction. Indeed, the confusion of tongues is already with us, before and after their demise, in a scrambling of temporality that mimics the notable (and debated) doubling of references in Genesis, which describes the Babel event not once but twice. The oneness of language that the biblical Shemites possessed is for demographic reasons already unavailable in America. So, too, the monopoly of global trade nominally claimed by the towers (two of them) could only ever have been an aspiration or a false indicator of an absolute hegemony never attained or already lost, even as it has reappeared in the very naming of One World Trade Center: "Behold, the people is

61. These words famously belong to Jean-François Lyotard, *The Postmodern Condition: A Report on Knowledge*, trans. Geoff Bennington and Brian Massumi (Minneapolis: University of Minnesota Press, 1984), 82.

62. *Falling Man* (New York: Scribner, 2007), 128. For a more detailed account of the Babel motif in the novel, see David Simpson, "A Confusion of Tongues," *Reconstruction* 11, no. 2 (2011). On the novel in general, see, among others, Kristiaan Versluys, *Out of the Blue: September 11 and the Novel* (New York: Columbia University Press, 2009), 19–48; and Georgiana Banita, *Plotting Justice: Narrative Ethics and Literary Culture after 9/11* (Lincoln: University of Nebraska Press, 2012), 61–74.

one" (Genesis 11:6). The Babel story is the story of an autoimmune dysfunction: the urge to build the tower is prompted by a fear of loss—"lest we be scattered" (11:4)—but it produces the very punishment for which it is intended to compensate. The Shemites, like Oedipus, are doomed to fail to the precise degree that they struggle to succeed. In Genesis the Shemites incur punishment before the tower is even finished: they abandon it half-built. It does not actually fall but, presumably, decays, a standing reminder of a failed challenge to god. Perhaps a wiser understanding of the myth would have had the WTC forever unbuilt.

Falling Man brings together a number of DeLillo's favorite terror-related topics: the prospect of totality (both terrible and comforting, as in Cold War culture), the confusion of tongues, the art-terror dialectic, and the Baader-Meinhof connection: his character Ernst Hechinger, alias Martin Ridnour, is hiding his own terrorist-leaning past as a member of Kommune One (146)—not the RAF itself but close enough to get him put onto a wanted list in Germany. Martin is an art dealer, and it is the quiet still lives of Giorgio Morandi that provide an aesthetic connection with his lover and her daughter, who sees in the symmetrical, upright forms of Morandi's ordinary objects nothing but images of the towers. It is Martin who provides the Klara Sax critique of America as oneness, world dominating, and who expresses the fantasy of its future irrelevance. DeLillo, as befits the modeler of a better language than the one most of us have already, is very sparing with fear-terror words, even when he is fabricating the experience of being inside the towers when the planes strike. The immediacy of this experience is suggested by disconnection and fragmentary perception, a succession of punctualities, rather than by recourse to any summarizing affect terms like terror and panic. They do occur in the novel, but only as elements of a retrospective account, a remembering of what was felt, but not the experience itself (e.g., 55, 56). One decides later that this was terror, but at the time there was no synthesizing vocabulary, no access to control through language, just the unmediated sequence of senses and perceptions. The language of terror, quite properly, belongs to the bystanders and the rememberers. The falling man's existence in the city, where he is always potentially to be encountered, "trails a collective dread" (33) and provides a foreknowledge in the experience of art that had not been there in reality.

Seeing from a Distance

Displacement is the mode of DeLillo's effort to represent terror in fiction, one that is typified by his general avoidance of the *t*-word itself, by the recourse to a performance artist as the crux of his narrative, and by marking his protagonist's observations of the disaster as it happened by a studied metonymy: a shirt, and not its owner, coming down "out of the high smoke" (4, and again in the novel's last sentences, at page 246). Metonymy is the mode of *Falling Man*, which offers hints of a thematic coherence that it never fully presents. The oneness of languages is not celebrated but offered as an index of a global commodification and confusion that preempts any functioning deliberative democracy of the sort beloved by liberals, but at the same time it hints at a utopian alternative in suggesting that efforts to enforce (or weaponize) differences between the homeland and elsewhere are simply not convincing: we are all in Beirut. What DeLillo does confront directly is the debate about the role of art: Eric Fischl's *Tumbling Woman* sculpture was a notorious talking point after 9/11, as was the photograph of a falling body, by Richard Drew, that was widely critiqued for looking balletic enough to be deplored as an aesthetically refined travesty of an unrepresentable or never-to-be-represented horror. Aesthetic decorum or sheer modesty (and perhaps a measure of political-aesthetic correctness) have deterred most writers from taking on the task of imagining the experience of dying in the towers (though DeLillo does include a third-person report of the death of his character Rumsey). DeLillo's focus is more consistently on the spectatorial quality of 9/11, wherein the repeatability of the falling man performance implacably forces its beholders into the realization that they are not themselves at risk, that they can enjoy (although that is not the word) the privileges of the Burkean sublime, and that they must, as this event keeps happening, ask themselves what a proper response might be, and whether they are capable of it. If they imagine terror, in other words, they are not themselves experiencing it. And it is among them, us, who look on that the awkward ethical questions are generated, and not on behalf of those who themselves dropped from the sky on September 11. If we ascribe terror to ourselves, we are erasing any difference between those who died (or barely survived) and those of us watching from a distance.

DeLillo touches lightly on the imagining of what happened in the final moments inside the towers. In contrast, Frédéric Beigbeder's *Windows on the World* (2003), one of the earliest 9/11 novels, employs its metafictional framing to break all sorts of taboos and to "describe the indescribable" to remind us that "terrorism does not destroy symbols, it hacks people of flesh and blood to pieces."[63] This novel aggressively

63. Frédéric Beigbeder, *Windows on the World*, trans. Frank Wynne (New York: Hyperion, 2004), 55, 167.

contests the culture of religiosity and decorum that developed around the events of 9/11, taking on the flesh and blood in various ways: the "human torches" (81), the jumpers (among whom is the narrator and his children), and the extreme end-of-life sex (at 10.15 in the French text) that Beigbeder decided to leave out of the English translation as perhaps too much of a challenge for his American readers.[64]

Another taboo, much weaker but still discernable in the decisions made by those writers who have tried to depict 9/11 in any direct way, concerns the mind of the other, the event as seen through the eyes and minds of the terrorists themselves. It is of course one of the conventional claims of good fiction that it set out to record the varieties of persons and views that make up its world: the murderer as well as the victim, the ordinary person as well as the hero or heroine. DeLillo somewhat has it both ways in putting into his novel a few short chapters in which the actions and meditations of one of the hijackers interrupt the main story. This mostly has the appearance of a sort of sidebar rather than a full rendition of the novel as a "democratic shout," although it ends with a moment of virtuosity at the time of the plane's impact on the tower, when the "he" who is the terrorist slides into the "he" who is the victim in a paragraph that runs together the two in a grammatical commonality (239). Henry James and Frank Harris had indeed fully represented the mind of the terrorist (and not unsympathetically), but with 9/11 the terrorist has become comprehensively racialized: the Islamic fanatic whose mind, if it were to be explored, could reveal only bigotry and obsession. John Updike's *The Terrorist* (2006) tries to work around this by making his central figure a biracial American citizen prone to cultural conflicts that can provide material for deep fiction. But often, such attempts to enter into the mind of the other who is fully other have about them either a dutiful sense that this is what writers must do, or a recourse to stereotypic adventures that may indeed have occurred in the lives of the 9/11 suicide bombers but which have the fictionalized effect of cliché (for example, an obsession with sex that comes from avowed contempt for western women).[65]

Perhaps unsurprisingly, the most complex and fictionally successful attempts to enter and represent the minds and hearts of the other who

---

64. Notably, Beigbeder is also explicit in his invocation of the Babel myth, about which DeLillo is indirect: see 116–17, 135, 231–32.

65. See, among others, Andre Dubus III, *The Garden of Last Days: A Novel* (New York: W. W. Norton and Co., 2008); Aram Schefrin, *Marwan: The Autobiography of a 9/11 Terrorist* (Indianapolis: AuthorHouse, 2007); Slimane Benaïssa, *The Last Night of a Damned Soul: A Novel,* trans. Janice and Daniel Gross (New York: Grove Press, 2004).

is coded as the enemy come from writers whose identity is not primarily Anglo-American. Mohsin Hamid's *The Reluctant Fundamentalist* (2007) adopts the extraordinary strategy of having the entire novel told in the voice of the "other" (which means, of course, that it is extraordinary only to readers steeped in the mainstream literary culture around terrorism). The American dinner companion, who appears to be a CIA agent, never speaks, although his responses are constantly transcribed. The narrator is a Pakistani man who has been educated at Princeton and accepted into the highest echelons of corporate culture, before finding that his life experiences and especially the anti-Muslim disposition of the homeland after 9/11 persuade him to move back to Lahore. Here, his post as a university teacher seems to have involved him in encouraging anti-American activities (including an assassination), so that the man with whom he is having dinner may well have been sent to arrest or kill him. Hamid's eschewal of dialogue would appear to transgress one of the cardinal rules of good novels, that they represent more than one side of a debate. But Changez (the protagonist-narrator) is widely experienced in the ways of his enemy, whose values and priorities come across quite clearly and mostly without recourse to stereotypic formulations. What also comes across is a world that is not obsessed with 9/11 but nonetheless has to endure the consequences of the US response to it, here most clearly typified by the narrowly avoided war between India and Pakistan in 2002. Hamid's story gives no dialogic space to the American, who thereby is made other to the one who is himself, in American eyes, the other. It is as if a balance is being righted, or perhaps inverted. In the intimation that the American might be a secret agent, and that he might even be at risk in this foreign place, there is a turning of the tables, a switch in who commands the power of terror. The implacable reasonableness of the narrative voice works to persuade us that there is a certain justice in this turn around; a case to be made. It is contingent, not for the long term, but it is there.

The still ongoing India-Pakistan crisis, or series of crises, is also at the center of Salman Rushdie's *Shalimar the Clown* (2005), a novel whose dazzling use of magic-realist tropes does nothing to diminish its eloquent and precise address to the political-historical details of the Kashmir situation and its claim to wider attention. Here, the life of the Kashmiri "radical" assassin is transcribed in massive detail, along with that of his victim, a retired American spymaster, and the complex local and national cultures that provide a long-durational context for this single, sensationalized event. Covering a history that stretches from World War Two to the late 1990s (and occasionally beyond), that transcribes numerous

varieties of terror and terrorism including those of the French resistance to the German occupation in the 1940s, Rushdie's world is one in
which the sheer fullness of motive and description overpowers any rhetoric that would simply invoke terror talk as any adequate explanation
of anything. Some might contest his projection of a tolerant, intereth-
nic Kashmir village life as a historically credible ideal, or his insistence
that in critical ways all political violence is at heart deeply personal; but
for readers obsessed with the spectacle of 9/11 as the only instance of
radical violence now worth thinking about, Rushdie offers a detailed
fictionalized history of the struggles in and over Kashmir and of an enduring murderous exchange that has persisted for more than sixty years.
His record of the bitter strife between Hindu and Muslim (and of individual efforts to overcome it), of the destructive role of India and Pakistan in the lives of Kashmiri communities, and of the nefarious presence
of global powers (especially the United States) in pulling strings above
them both, is a powerful assertion of the complex conditions determin-
ing seemingly singular events. Without ever saying so, it pushes 9/11
to the margin of a world history where it subsists only as one among
many such tragedies that are never to be explained as simply events
unto themselves.

So, too, does *Burnt Shadows*, Kamila Shamsie's 2009 epic, fictional
account of the fortunes of a single family group between the Nagasaki
bomb and the post-9/11 world. Here, too, there is a global history on
display, and it is once again a history molded by the largely ignoble behavior of the American superpower. Without in any sense justifying the
WTC attacks, Shamsie weaves together a history that commences with
the second atomic bomb, the one that seems most gratuitous and most
indicative of the West's insouciance about the lives of nonwhite people,
although in this case it destroyed a city that was the center of Christianity in Japan, a city marked more than most by cosmopolitan culture. The
Sikh hero of Michael Ondaatje's *The English Patient* (1992)—a novel to
which Shamsie explicitly alludes—had felt his life change with the Hiroshima bomb, as he realized that the people for whom he was fighting
had no regard for the lives of Asians. Shamsie's characters learn the
same lesson. Across three generations, and in various places—Nagasaki,
Delhi, Istanbul, Karachi, and New York—a group of characters whose
lives are composed of multiethnic and polyglot identities are buffeted
against the seemingly irresistible effects of racialized violence and mono-
lingual triumphalism: state terror. World War Two, the horribly destructive 1947 partition of India, the wars in Afghanistan and the worldwide interventions of the CIA—all lead up to a conclusion whereby the

brown-faced linguistic genius Raza Ashraf is arrested as a reputed terrorist. After 9/11, the multilingual melting pot of New York City has become a site of persecution for Arabs and Muslims, and the democratic openness (Bill Gray's "democratic shout") cherished by Harry Burton, the exemplary American, as the last hope for "justice," has collapsed into a bastion of paranoid homeland security.[66]

Shamsie, Rushdie, and Hamid are all identifiable as "postcolonial" novelists, writing in English but from sites of multilingual and multiethnic complexity that invite and enable them to register the details of a history of domination (whether imperial or neoliberal-economic) that fully embeds those whom we might otherwise see as radical terrorists in a world that is not of their own making, one that misunderstands and mistreats them with breathtaking condescension. It is not just that these authors record the "claims" of the other; they devote hundreds of pages to the lifeworlds that are all too often unnoticed and undiscussed in the rhetoric around terror and terrorism. These lifeworlds are not islands of residual ethnicity but sites where all sorts of personal affiliations and loyalties cross geographical and linguistic borders; they are icons of cosmopolitanism, but one that seems only able to survive if it is left alone by the West and seen as unimportant to the West's self-interest. An incipient multiracial society is similarly explored in two novels by Nadine Gordimer, one written before and one after the end of political apartheid. In *July's People* (1981) Gordimer imagines an ongoing violent revolution in which South Africa is the site of a full-scale civil war. Old loyalties allow a white family to hide in the village of their former domestic servant, the masters now living at the behest of the slaves. At first the story seems to be a celebration of personal ties overcoming racial and class affiliations, but it is more than that. All sorts of stresses emerge, making it impossible for the adults to create a functional postracial microsociety: the wounds and the habits go too deep. Only the children appear to be able to model a new start and to implement the host-guest relation in nondisruptive ways. It is not simply the West as other that interferes in this process but the West that is in Africa already.

But this is not Gordimer's last word. In *The Pickup* (2001), notwithstanding all the problems of postapartheid South Africa and its tardiness in areas of social and economic redress, she does imagine a new generation for which matters of race are not beyond negotiation and solution.

66. Kamila Shamsie, *Burnt Shadows* (New York: Picador, 2009), 175. Hiroko's first experience of pre-9/11 New York seems like a homecoming: "Nothing foreign about foreignness in this city" (295).

This is a world in which the avowed ethic (whatever the residual realities) is "to be open with strangers" and to "encounters."[67] Julie is a liberal white girl whose family lives in considerable luxury; the stranger, Abdu, is a Muslim illegal immigrant from a country "well known to have a high rating as a place of origin from which immigrants were undesirable" (140), a place her father calls "one of the worst, poorest and most backward of Third World Countries" (98). After variously tense interactions Adbu is marked for deportation and Julie goes with him, to a place where she becomes "as strange to herself as she was to them" (117). After a slow and difficult cultural immersion she develops meaningful relationships with the women and children of Abdu's family, so much so that when he himself at last (with help from her influential family) gets his visa to enter the United States, she decides to remain behind. This is not exactly a happy ending, not least because it reenacts the separation of husbands and wives that the South African apartheid economy enforced in its labor laws (and which has by no means disappeared with the end of apartheid itself). But this time it represents a choice, a choice on Julie's part to abide with the other, and a perhaps less positive choice by Abdu to become the other in a place that almost certainly will fail to make him welcome. Moreover the self-other dynamic plays out across what is perhaps the most toxically politicized (as well as gendered and racialized) barrier in today's world, that between white-Christian (women) and brown-Muslim (men). Late in her life, and with some faith in the capacity of young South Africans to not simply imagine but enact a better attitude to strangers, Gordimer here creates a person who goes as far as she can toward not simply tolerating but becoming the other.

And yet an enlightened individual act does not in itself make a new society, nor does Gordimer pretend that it does. Julie's is an exemplary decision that displaces the project of opening up South African society as she relocates herself elsewhere, to a place where few, if any, could be expected to follow. As a fictionalized event it does, however, suggest what may be necessary: a willingness to give up on what one knows, on feeling comfortable, on being in place, on identity itself. In Shamsie's and Rushdie's novels, a project of global cosmopolitanism is made explicit, but it fails, and global history looks like a destructive force determined to erase all many-faceted lives in the cause of world domination: one superpower, one language, one economy. In *The Pickup* there is not even an imagining of anything beyond a private and personal decision, which may be why it is able to subsist and survive. It is a small beginning indeed, but

67. Nadine Gordimer, *The Pickup* (London: Bloomsbury, 2001), 10.

one that is in sympathy with the widespread call for active heterogeneity and transnationality that writers and critics have been expressing for
at least a generation. Stephen Clingman offers an apt summary of this
commitment to a fiction that embodies our "provisional, transnational
space" where protocols have yet to be established and where we are in
"the space of navigation."[68] Making a priority of this kind of writing
goes against the long-term nationalist project of the novel itself, which,
as Srinivas Aravamudan has argued, has been familiarized for three
centuries as a "national realist enclosure" at odds with transnational
affiliations and diminishing or displacing the significance of foreigners
and strangers.[69] The national enclosure syndrome is what encourages
terror talk to flourish. A key fictional item in its literary establishment
was the body of a woman: Samuel Richardson's Pamela. Gordimer's
The Pickup presents the woman, Julie, as its exemplary hope, and as
such it accords with an all-too-often marginalized set of voices in international feminism that has from the start resisted any cooptation by
the national-patriotic enclosers, most of whom are men. The editors of
one representative publication are notably careful in their summary of
what the events of 9/11 brought about: "They caused widespread sorrow and suffering, fear and panic."[70] All of these, but not terror. How
much healthier the debate would be if there were more attention to sorrow and suffering, even to fear and panic, rather than simply to terror.

But despite the recent and spectacular electoral events in Britain and
the United States, it is worth remembering that patriotic aggression was
not the only alternative available after 9/11, and that February 2003 saw
a worldwide public peace movement bringing more people out onto the
streets than anything ever before. It would be hard to imagine any more
visible evidence of a road not taken, any more persuasive sign of a global
desire for a language not fixated on terror as the primary attribute of the
enemy other. For the time being at least, that option has been sidelined;
if we are to remember and recover it in our pedagogy and in our writing
of history, it will perhaps be most readily found in "minority" writers,
in global feminism, and in the global English novel and in what is not yet

---

68. Stephen Clingman, *The Grammar of Identity: Transnational Fiction and the
Nature of the Boundary* (Oxford: Oxford University Press, 2009), 26. Earlier work by
Homi Bhabha, Paul Gilroy, Gayatri Spivak and others was important in establishing this
priority.

69. Srinivas Aravamudan, *Enlightenment Orientalism: Resisting the Rise of the
Novel* (Chicago: University of Chicago Press, 2012), 24.

70. *Terror Counter-Terror: Women Speak Out*, ed. Ammu Joseph and Kalpana
Sharma (London: Zed Books, 2003), xi.

global English, accessible only in the commitment to translation in all of
its bafflements and complexities. This chapter perhaps exposes a disciplinary idealism in its focus on the novel, and on the novel's capacity to
engage with the lives of others in ways that go beyond the friend-enemy
dichotomy. It is a truism that good literature is supposed to do this, and
I am uncomfortably aware of falling back into a traditional endorsement
or even a comfort zone. Plenty of not-so-good literature can surely be
produced by way of counterexamples. We might here recall the fragility
of Benjamin's case for education as a positive instance of divine violence,
a transformative moment that erupts without terror. But surely the appeal to the best fiction as a yardstick for critical reflection (and critical
philology) should not require an apology. It may not be bedtime reading
in the White House or the Pentagon, or among the makers of the popular media, but there is no absolute obstacle preventing it becoming so.
Above all, we are there reminded, efficiently and even pleasurably, albeit
with the shadow of pleasure that exists in representations of pain, that
terror and terrorism are not simply the property of those who are not us.
In my final chapter I turn to the philosophers, and to another critical la-
cuna in anglophone culture, one that has in its own way made possible
the hegemony of terror talk.

6

Being in Terror, Being as Terror

Subject to Terror: Sartre, Hegel, Kojève

In the first volume of his *Critique of Dialectical Reason*, first published in 1960, Jean-Paul Sartre offered a dazzling reinterpretation of the relation between terror and the French Revolution. Before and indeed since, the discussion among historians has tended to highlight the question of whether the events of 1793–1794, and especially of 1794, were the consummation of the inner logic of the revolution, and thus inevitable and necessary, or rather the outcome of a short-term crisis, bringing about one-time events that were a regrettable deviation from the revolution's fundamental identity. The inevitable, polemical context of this decision often has to do with some or other advisory address to one's own generation about the turn to violence: does all aspiration for revolutionary change instigate a process that must end in radical terror, or could one hope for positive outcomes unmarked by rivers of blood? The same question animates Benjamin's essay on violence and the ongoing debates about it.

Sartre's book models and arguably consummates an important shift in the project of doing philosophy after Kant—one begun by Hegel—in that it attempts a full integration of philosophy and history. Kant's three great *Critiques* had purposefully sought to exclude anthropology, history, and politics to clear a space for the disinterested contemplation of the workings of the mind: epistemological, ethical, and aesthetic. Not surprisingly, this involved a theorization of disinterest itself. No sooner was the project published than a call came, most vigorously from Hegel, to put philosophy back into the world from which Kant had tried to detach it, and the tug of war has continued ever since, not least over the matter of disinterest. Is it ever possible, and if so, for whom and under what conditions?

If it is fair to say, *pace* the aspirations of some analytical philosophers and a number of philosophy departments, that the place of (and the wreckage that is) history cannot easily be ignored by anyone seeking to make sense of human experience and the human mind, then Sartre's book should remain required reading. On the matter of terror, it articulates a remarkable position. The debate about the special place of *the* Terror of 1793–1794 is entirely secondary, because for Sartre the encounter with terror is built into all modern experiences of subjectivity. We must say modern, because we should not assume that there is any absolute experience of subjectivity that preexists one's situation in place and time. What typifies the modern, in Sartre's account, is our involvement with collectivities, not out of choice but by contingent necessity; even solitary life can be thought in only an awareness of groups, the most visible of which are class and race. Thus, it is no accident that his ideas take both form and expression in the light of the Algerian crisis and that they reflect on a long modern tradition of collective efforts at social change (1848, 1870, 1917) whose initial coming into being occurred with the French Revolution.

Bluntly put, for Sartre one encounters terror whenever one participates in a group whose emergence is implicated in or directed toward radical change. Predictably, there is the terror that the state deploys to punish or discourage those whose interests conflict with its own: state terror. But there is another terror, reciprocally related to the first: the terror that the group exerts to preserve its own solidarity. The first terror, state terror, was in play at the storming of the Bastille, an event that Sartre reads as "purely defensive," an effort to "repulse a threat."[1] The crowd was motivated by a felt need to arm itself against an imminent incursion by the army into the city, not by an urge to make some symbolic gesture against the old regime. So, although the crowd may have terrified the garrison, it was itself subject to terror. As the revolutionary process continued, in-

---

1. Jean-Paul Sartre, *Critique of Dialectical Reason I: Theory of Practical Ensembles*, trans. Alan Sheridan-Smith (London: Verso, 1982), 389.

volved groups felt an urgent need to consolidate their own identities by enforcing a pledge, one that committed their members to a group loyalty punishable by death. As fear of the enemy without becomes intermittent or relatively remote, terror of the group itself is intensified and provides the mechanism of the group's own solidarity. This is the pairing that Sartre calls "fraternity-terror" (430, 523). Because the group is produced as a "non-existent totality" (583) the urge to integration is all the stronger, as if the pledge is all that holds things together. The internal terror of the group cannot persist without some degree of threatened terror from the outside, but it remains primary to the degree that the external threat can be invented or imagined even if it is no longer there. (Reciprocally, state terror assumes or invents the existence of terror groups). Terror is thereby the principal feature of the experience of the self in groups. The experience of the self is, indeed, one of terror—at one's own capacity for traitorous behavior and at the punishment that would follow.[2]

This schema allows Sartre to discuss terror in the French Revolution without mentioning the name of Robespierre, and indeed with only the briefest account of what historians before and since have insisted on calling *the* Terror.[3] Sartre attributes *the* Terror to the behavior of the Girondins in leading France into war and in advancing the interests of the bourgeoisie within a divided Convention. The key mechanism is competitive group pledging and purging, which replaced a "quasi-structured heterogeneity" with a "diffuse heterogeneity" (593) whereby every subgroup is other to another subgroup and, finally, to itself: "everyone is Other in the Other" (596). For this reason "Terror is *never* a system based on the will of a minority; it is the reappearance—in specific circumstances—of the fundamental group relation as an inter-human relation; subsequently, differentiation may or may not create a specialised

---

2. The positive binding function of terror in the modern radical republic is also the topic of Jacques Lezra's *Wild Materialism*. In military-state discipline, it has of course long been received practice to render soldiers more frightened of their own officers than of the enemy, so that their capacity to spread terror depends on their being themselves terrified.

3. See 591–99. Sartre may be being mischievous in constantly capitalizing terror as *la Terreur* when he is deliberately not referring to *the* Terror of 1794. Or he may be intending to accord it some dignity as a primary term, as he does with *l'Autre*, the Other. It does not help that in the first edition (which the English translation follows) the pairing *fraternité-terreur* is always lower case, nor that he also uses lower case *terreur* on some occasions later in the text. See *Critique de la raison dialectique* (Paris: Gallimard, 1960), e.g., 448, 520, 567. In the second volume of this work, published much later, the revolution under inspection is the Russian Revolution, and there is a more direct reckoning with the figure of Stalin as both embodying and "deviating" the historical process.

organ whose function is to govern according to terror" (598). Notable here is the phrase "fundamental group relation." By his own logic, Sartre would accept that this fundamental element might remain inactive or dormant in low-stress situations. But the modern world, with its incremental consolidation of groups defined by class and race, is not routinely low stress. Colonialist settlers in particular are always and everywhere aware of the terror of the other because they must "maintain themselves by force and against the colonised," so that "*everyone is in danger in the Other*" (302). Similarly in capitalist society, social man is "Other than himself, conditioned by Others in so far as they are Other than themselves" (309). Class in nineteenth-century France then became not "practical solidarity" but "the absolute unity of destinies brought about by lack of solidarity. Every worker feels himself confirmed in his inertia by the inertia of all the Others" (312). Class identity is enforced by negation and mutual competition, a peculiar version of solidarity.

While Sartre is adamant that there is no "essence of terror" and that its incarnation is always specific and requiring description in a "totalising reconstruction effected by historians" (597), there is yet a "permanent living structure of coercion" (608) in all forms of sovereignty, in other words in all social forms that have evolved beyond the primitive or minimal. Modern class and colonialist formations are thus underpinned by a general principle of sovereignty whereby "the sovereign is produced by terror, and he has to become the agent responsible for it" (624–25). Thus, along with the fraternity-terror dynamic of group life, there is an overarching awareness of sovereign terror. And even beyond and before that, in the earliest stages of social development, "all men are slaves in so far as their life unfolds in the practico-inert field and in so far as this field is always conditioned by scarcity" (331). In societies other than modern ones, there is still a "reciprocal conditioning in alienation" because everyone struggles with scarcity and scarcity tends to generate competition (331–32). In "ancient" slave societies, the Hegelian model indeed pertains, but scarcity also supervenes "*above all* because the cost of a slave tends to constantly increase whereas his productivity constantly tends to decrease" (331). This economic formalism is hardly a full description of historical slave-based societies, and Sartre's emphatic "above all" may indicate his too much protesting a difference from Hegel. Like Hegel, he has constructed a modeling of the role of terror that is at once ontological and historical, although it is not fully phylogenetic except in a limited historical sense according to which the fraternity-terror and sovereign-terror factors increase with the progressive extension of capital and colony.

Indeed, Sartre's terror plays something of the role that fear (*Furcht*) plays in Hegel's account of the master-slave relation, a paradigm that has provided compulsive reading for a whole range of subsequent efforts to theorize both subjectivity and society. Hegel's instatement of history into philosophy is more opaque than Sartre's. In part thanks to the English translation of *Herrschaft und Knechtschaft* as "Lordship and Bondage," feudal Europe is often assumed to be the historical expression of this particular ontological moment which, it is implied, every human subject will pass through in some form, but not always with the same intensity or representational force. Indeed, serfdom was being abolished in the German states only in Hegel's own lifetime: in Baden in 1783, Prussia in 1807 (the year in which Hegel's *Phenomenology* was published), Bavaria in 1808, Hanover in 1831, and so on. In Russia serfdom was in place until 1861; evidence enough that historically persisting serfdom could have figured in Hegel's thinking. Also implicitly referenced is classical slaveholding, which perhaps best fits a narrative that moves on to an account of the emergence of Stoicism and Skepticism, both taking form in ancient Greece. Meanwhile, recent scholarship has enriched the historical reading of Hegel's text by rediscovering his familiarity with German abolitionist literature and with the Haitian Revolution, suggesting that the Caribbean slave economy is also likely to have impinged on his account.[4] To be sure, the scenario of overseeing master and working slave that marks this critical section of the book seems much more likely as a rendering of Caribbean plantation life (or perhaps of classical domestic slavery) than of the more remotely conducted economies of serfdom. Yet it could be said that slavery in some form has never been absent from the historical record, nor is it yet extinct, a recognition that reduces any radical tension between Hegel's historical and ontological paradigms and reasserts his continuing relevance to the modern condition.

At first Hegel's paradigm can seem purely ontological, offering itself as a description of the development of every human subject everywhere, although it is implicitly dependent on making normal the figure of the adult male who can take part in violent struggle. Crucially, coming to self-consciousness occurs simultaneously with and indissolubly from consciousness of the other, in our recognition that exactly the same process is going on, and at the same time, for the other person in our field of vision. Sensing that one's existence depends on recognition at first produces an impulse to a struggle unto death. The other is felt as a threat, as

---

4. See Susan Buck-Morss, *Hegel, Haiti, and Universal History* (Pittsburgh, PA: University of Pittsburgh Press, 2009).

an uncontrollable element of the self that cannot be mastered because it is outside the self. But the struggle unto death must be displaced by the understanding that the death of either self or other is no solution: either one dies oneself and the story ends or one faces a dead other who is no longer capable of conducting the experience of mutual recognition on which the whole dynamic depends. So one learns that life is essential to self-consciousness. But at the moment of the trial by death this solution is not apparent; it is wholly lived as such, and it is this immersion in the death threat that alone offers the experience of freedom: "It is only through staking one's life that freedom is won."[5] Hegel is having things both ways. His ontology allows for an analogy with revolutionary struggle, an immersion in *Freiheit* for the moment, but also generates its passage into negotiated compromise. That part of the single consciousness that aspires to live for and in itself is the Lord (*Herr*); that which recognizes its role as being for another is the slave or serf (*Knecht*).

As soon as this vocabulary, with its unignorable social-historical signification, is introduced, it becomes almost impossible to think this scenario as a purely ontological one. In the classic liberal doctrines defining (and justifying) slavery, it is the conquest of one person by another that creates the culture of slavery, which results from the victor forgoing his right to kill (earned in combat) but maintaining his right to decide the fate of his conquered enemy (and his women and children) in whatever way he sees fit. Slavery, in other words, is life extended at the good grace of another and only for as long as that other chooses. The slave has, in accepting continuing life, given up on all his rights. But he has still, in Hegel's account, experienced a moment of freedom at the point of staking his life in the first place. And as he becomes the executor of the master's life tasks, he deprives that master of the experience of work, of transforming the world in the way that Hegel regards as fundamental to the vocation of all human beings. This moment of self-building, when the slave absorbs himself in work and thus breaks the scopic spell of looking only at the master, is the key to his incipient independence and, bizarrely, establishes his superiority over a master whose desire (for world-changing work) can be fulfilled only in imagination, through seeing the slave as his essential self but a self from which he is implacably alienated, and by his own conquest. At the same time this positive component of slavery is attainable only through the experience of radical and total dread or anxi-

---

5. *Hegel's Phenomenology of Spirit*, trans. A. V. Miller (Oxford: Clarendon Press, 1979), 114. The German text is cited from *Phänomenologie des Geistes,* ed. Gerhard Göhler (Frankfurt: Ullstein Verlag, 1973).

ety (*Angst*). Unlike the master, the slave has fully experienced the fear of death that the defeated party undergoes. His life has hung in the balance, and it still does. This "absolute fear" (*absolute Furcht*), much more intense than merely momentary dread (*Angst*) (119), further intensifies the work experience as of irreplaceable value; what it creates becomes an embodiment of the absolute fear in which the slave works, while at the same time it images the slave's adjustment to the world as one he has made in despite of that fear.

Like Sartre, Hegel insists that self-consciousness builds itself only in the presence of the other, and like Sartre he finds that the process is immanently conditioned by fear-terror (Hegel uses *Furcht* where Sartre has *Terreur*). Subjectivity and fear-terror come together and are implicated in the basic fabric of sociability. This is an important shift from, for example, the world that Rousseau had modeled in his theory of metaphor as a primary element of language in primitive society. Metaphor emerges out of fear in the original social encounter with the other, but that fear is dissipated as soon as the other is seen to be a person like oneself: "As soon as one man was recognized by another as a sentient, thinking Being and similar to himself, the desire or need to communicate his feelings and thoughts to him made him seek the means for doing so."[6] Here the threat of the other is displaced by a more powerful compulsion to communicate; with Hegel, communication does not occur before the struggle unto death. It is tempting to speculate, in the manner of the grand-narrative historians of culture, about why this transition happens when it does. Is the diminishing of unpredictable, interpersonal masculine violence and its incremental appropriation by the state (a view associated with Norbert Elias) responsible for creating a historical psychology that senses the constant possibility of a (state) terror that is all the more preoccupying because it is rarely seen and felt? Is this congruent with the biopolitical bureaucracy theorized by Michel Foucault as so pervasively carceral that there is no need to itemize the French Revolution at all as marking any radical shift in history? Or does the experience of mass warfare and total war that came with the Revolutionary and (especially) Napoleonic Wars scramble the distinction between predictable and unpredictable in ways that forced philosophers to reimagine subjectivity to take new account of radical violence?[7] Should we be thinking, as Sartre is, of the beginnings of class consciousness and the power of the colonial

6. *Essay on the Origins of Language*, 290.
7. See Anders Engberg-Pedersen, *Empire of Chance: The Napoleonic Wars and the Disorder of Things* (Cambridge, MA: Harvard University Press, 2015), which describes

encounter as the model of all possible encounters? All of these conditions, and surely others, may be thought to determine a world in which philosophers feel the need to theorize radical violence, or its imminent prospect, as constitutive of one's being in the world. These are among the circumstances that make it feasible for Thomas Pfau, for example, to propose paranoia, trauma, and melancholy, all implicated in violence, as historically successive "moods" typifying Romanticism from the 1790s onward.[8] For Hegel this violence was also constitutive of the progress of *Geist* through human history: his three examples of world-historical figures are all military generals, and all had careers combining radical world changing with radical violence.[9]

Hegel's most literal references to the phases of the French Revolution come much later in the *Phenomenology*, and it is only there that he uses a term, *Schrecken*, that we might choose to translate most conventionally as *terror*. (He does not use the new word *Terror* that had come into German after 1794). As always the historical sequence is fluid and confusing because it is not strictly or simply a conventional chronology. In the section following the lordship-bondage analysis, skepticism collapses into one the two figures that were "formerly" separate (126), but this locator seems both historical and ahistorical at the same time. Hegel's *früher* (formerly) indicates narrative sequence as well as historical succession, but if we think we are simply in a historical story, then we have to push aside the teasing hints that it is Kant who is repeating Stoicism's return to the "pure universality of thought" and withdrawing from the "bustle of existence," and that Kant, too, could, like the Stoics, only have appeared "in a time of universal fear and bondage, but also a time of universal culture which had raised itself to the level of thought" (121). Hegel's superimposition of ontology upon history makes it famously hard to plot a simply linear narrative, especially if history is given to repeating itself as part of its cunning. But the discussion of "Absolute Freedom and Terror" does follow that of the Enlightenment, and it looks very like Kant once more who is implicated in its damaging turn away from utility and the useful, which is where the self must find its realization instead of in that fixation on "the in-itself" (353), which leads only to an inflexible "cold

---

a passage from warfare conceived in limited and mathematical terms to warfare seen as total and stochastic in its outcomes and procedures.

8. Thomas Pfau, *Romantic Moods: Paranoia, Trauma and Melancholy, 1790–1840* (Baltimore: Johns Hopkins University Press, 2005).

9. Caesar, Alexander, Napoleon. See Engberg-Pedersen, *Empire of Chance*, 54, which takes its title from Hegel's account of the "cunning of history" as operating through the *Reich der Zufälligkeit*.

universality" (359; *kalte Allgemeinheit*) that here enrobes not only the incorruptible man from Arras but also the sage of Königsberg, as well as the Rousseau who gave us the general will.[10] The experiential self-world relation cannot, however, be satisfied by a formal utilitarianism, a separating out of the object world as merely a passive resource for need and desire. This is one of the negative symptoms that has led to *Geist*'s attraction to absolute freedom in the first place. But an aspiration for a universality detached from any empirical embodiment or engagement can take form only as death at its coldest and meanest, which allows Hegel his famous comment on the Terror as being about cutting off the heads of cabbages (360). The fear of death that characterized the master-slave encounter now becomes the terror of death (361; *der Schrecken des Todes*), an experience no longer marked by the face-to-face violence of the struggle unto death but by the industrialized lopping off of one head after another. Hegel affirms that this dead end of self-world interaction, with *Geist* seeming wholly trapped in self-regarding abstraction, would be enough to kick the whole machine back into starting again from the beginning, repeating its entire earlier evolution, including "the fear of the lord and master which has again entered men's hearts" (332), were it not for the "sheer terror of the negative" (362) prompting a scene-changing shift into the moral sphere (363).

So is it the case that, despite the chilling spectacle of terror as *the* Terror, Hegel rescues, by flicking the switch of history, the French Revolution as a good and forward-moving thing? Is this what we might expect from one who was rumored to propose a toast on every Bastille Day? Rebecca Comay notes that the proposed critical transition from terror to morality is the moment "most reviled" by Hegel's critics as a glaring example of the German ideology: a "sublime combination of resignation and opportunism that knows how to turn a profit from the most irreconcilable disaster."[11] But, she goes on to argue, this shift from terror to morality is not at all the solution to *Geist*'s and history's problems because morality takes form only as "the prolongation of terror by other means," with the result that the "blocked promise of the Revolution" is not at all redeemed (93). Kantian morality takes over all the negative features of the Terror, including its vehement subjectivity and total world denial. The passage

10. Although elsewhere it is Fichte, not Kant, whom Hegel associated with Rousseau and with the formation of revolution-inducing ideas: see *Elements of the Philosophy of Right*, ed. Allen W. Wood (Cambridge: Cambridge University Press, 1995), 277.

11. Rebecca Comay, *Mourning Sickness: Hegel and the French Revolution* (Stanford, CA: Stanford University Press, 2011), 81.

from Terror to morality repeats that from lordship-bondage to Stoicism (92). Comay (74) finds throughout Hegel's career a constant vacillation between approving and deploring the Revolution, one that does not index a progressive moment of history but marks an impasse that is always to be, until the end of history itself, repeated. This is to say that the moment of Hegel's own lifetime could look forward only to a resolution some time in a future. The famous proclamation, in the Preface to the *Phenomenology*, of the "birth-time" of a new age (6) at once proposes a "flash" (*Blitz*) that shows up the features or images (*Gebilde*) of a new world, but also is nothing more than a "vague foreboding" (62)—or is it a yet-to-be-determined hunch, *unbestimmte Ahnung*—of what is to come?

It remains the case, therefore, in the present as at the beginning, that where consciousness feels itself to be at home (*bei sich selbst*) it has lost sight of *Geist* (*Phenomenology*, 15). And if the path to absolute knowing is always the path of recollection, a gathering up of *Geist* in all its expressive moments, then the terror-morality transition will be reexperienced not as sublimation (as the official doctrine would imply) but as blockage or dead end. If Comay's reading is correct, the incoming new age does not and cannot overcome terror (the Terror) without reliving it and experiencing its own reorientation. The Terror may not last, but terror never goes away. It presents an ongoing roadblock that demands a diversion but also an ongoing encounter. The modern subject, then, still lives with terror and in terror. Hegel here offers a strong contrast with Kant, because for Hegel there are no bystanders. In *The Conflict of the Faculties* (1798) Kant had recuperated the French Revolution and the Terror by way of an argument analogous to the operation of the aesthetic sublime: even as those involved suffer horribly and in ways that ought to be avoided or regretted, even as no such events are to be encouraged in the German states, and even as a positive response to French events "borders closely" on the risky feeling of "enthusiasm," nonetheless the onlooker approves of the general tendency of the revolution and thereby indicates the presence of a "moral disposition in the human race."[12] This detached judgment is possible only because what is happening is seen from afar, with no personal interests at stake. Hegel, by contrast, brings the moment of terror into an ontological framework, as the property of every human subject. Few of us will undergo a historically enacted terror, but all of us will go through the motions of an experience of both self-

---

12. Immanuel Kant, *Religion and Rational Theology*, ed. and trans. Allen W. Wood and George Di Giovanni (Cambridge: Cambridge University Press, 1996), 302.

consciousness (fear, the master-slave relation) and universality (terror, morality as terror) from which terror cannot be formally set apart.

In offering the Tennis Court Oath as the initiating or exemplifying moment of the Terror, and of a terror that remains for our historical present, Comay assimilates Hegel to the Sartre of the *Critique of Dialectical Reason*. Conventional models of cause and effect do not work well here, but there is a strong conjunction between Rousseau's general will (as theory) and the structure of the oath or pledge (as historical event) that renders the revolutionary trajectory formative of its own time and of continuing urgency for, or presence to, ours. Perhaps Jameson's musical analogy is the better model: Hegelian moments occur as themes and variations, recalling and redoing each other through time.[13] Jameson, like Comay, is anxious to preempt the reading of Hegel's work as simply a "developmental narrative" and thereby an "out-of-date teleology" (1, 4). If there is no "centered and fulfilled subjectivity" (17) to be had, and if the adumbration of absolute spirit is no more than a "provisional halt" (113), then the terror-morality blockage can stand for the "end" of the book (in both senses of end). The early Sartre (the author of *Being and Nothingness*) had taken Hegel somewhat to task for an unearned optimism about the self's efficiency in knowing the other (as displayed in the master-slave encounter), proposing instead that what pertains is always and only a matter of being. No self can know another as the other knows itself, so that in place of any prospectively happy recognition of each by the other we should understand the issue to be one of coexistence without knowledge. Hegel gets credit for dispelling solipsism from the philosophical scene, in that "being-for-others appears as a necessary condition for being-for-myself," but the master-slave moment can never be parsed into one of reciprocity, and what matters about the other is not its life but its objectivity.[14] Thus our manner of coexistence is not founded in recognition but in mere proximity; it is all about functioning, for instance, as a member of a crew, a point clearer to Heidegger than it was to Hegel. For this early Sartre, to be sure, terror is not a governing concept. What figures here is anxiety (*angoisse*) in its Kierkegaardian-Heideggerian mode, that which dominates the subject in its apprehensive attitude to possible futures and to the specific possibility of failing or falling short. But here, too, Sartre calls forth a latent if low-level fear term as underpinning all subjectivity, mostly unseen

13. Fredric Jameson, *The Hegel Variations: On the "Phenomenology of Spirit"* (London: Verso, 2010), 15.

14. Jean-Paul Sartre, *Being and Nothingness: An Essay on Phenomenological Ontology*, trans. Hazel E. Barnes (London: Methuen, 1957), 238, 241.

only because of the speed with which we translate thought into action in the conduct of trivial everyday life. Like terror in the later work, anxiety is of and for the self; when it is directed at something in the world, then it becomes fear (29). Like terror, it is also "consciousness of freedom" (33), but at the price of being aware of a "nothingness" between the self and its essence (35), one that leads us to the position of bad faith.

Angoisse (anxiety) was also a key term for Alexandre Kojève, whose hugely influential lecture courses on Hegel, delivered throughout the 1930s, gave Sartre and many others much more than just a word. Kojève set out to establish a fully atheist Hegel for the history of philosophy, one whose focus on mortality and death was absolute and not to be displaced by Christian ideas about a life after death. There is a kind of life after death, but it is completely metaphorical and historical, consisting in the changes in the world to which one has contributed when alive. Here there is indeed progress, enough so that the master-slave paradigm should not be regarded as part of a permanent ontology. Napoleon's armies and Hegel's philosophy are for Kojève a true end of history, with which everything changes. The French Revolution embodied the turning point because before 1789 the bourgeois intellectual had already fallen out of having any place in the master-slave dialectic. He was neither master nor slave, participating neither in fight and struggle nor in work. With access to citizenship and to military service (this remains a visibly masculine sphere), all of this changed. The internal or self-invented experience of the Terror, whereby the bourgeois devises his own being-toward-death, is replaced by the revolutionary wars and by conscription, which at once provide work and violent struggle and enact the formation of the new state. The Napoleonic (not the Jacobin) state for the first time synthesizes master and slave, in "the *soldier* who *works* and the *worker* who makes *war*." Man finally achieves satisfaction and experiences universality in particularity.[15]

Kojève (voicing Hegel) makes the remarkable case that a great revolution is at its start always bloodless: the old regime dies of its own sick-

---

15. Alexandre Kojève, *Introduction à la lecture de Hegel* (Paris: Gallimard, 1968), 134 (my translation). I have been directed to the importance of Kojève's views on fear-terror by Jonathan Strauss, *Subjects of Terror: Nerval, Hegel, and the Modern Self* (Stanford, CA: Stanford University Press, 1998), 54–64. Many of Kojève's most important theorizations of being-toward-death are not included in the edited English translation of the lectures, which were first published in French in 1947 but were well known and well attended when they were first delivered. It is worth recalling that Lukács's work on the historical novel also dates from the early 1930s and also relies upon the phenomenon of mass conscription in the French armies.

ness, publicized by the thinkers of the Enlightenment (166).[16] The Terror works to educate mankind (by its own energies) into its own nothingness and accords it the freedom to create the new state. Before this moment the master-slave paradigm has remained largely intact and operative (except, recently, for the bourgeois intellectual). And what governs the slave's consciousness is anxiety, *angoisse*, indeed an absolute anxiety (*angoisse absolue*) as opposed to some or other simple fear (*seulement quelque peur*).[17] Anxiety about and toward death is a necessary but not sufficient condition for the slave's liberation, for which it inaugurates only the possibility (67).[18] Kojève lectured at length in 1933–1934 on the idea of death in Hegel (see 620–75). It is here that the atheist, world-bound Hegel is most fully expounded. To present mankind as subject and not substance is to render him fully temporal and finite; only without God can man be a free, historical individual (631) whose existence is at all points "discursive" (635). To be human is to be able to die and to know how to do it (663). This is what Marx has missed: anxiety and death (137), and thereby the eventually and inevitably bloody nature of revolution: the Terror (675).

Heidegger and Freud: Fear-Terror and the Uncanny

Before both Sartre and Kojève there is Heidegger, whose early *Sein und Zeit* (1927) is, along with the work of Kierkegaard from which it draws, the most famous locus for the place of anxiety in the fear-terror cluster's modeling of the self. Heidegger prefigures the early Sartre in making, at first, little use of anything we might translate strongly as terror: *Erschrecken* figures (as far as I can see) only once in the book, in the company of *Grauen* and *Entsetzen*, but none of these becomes at this point Heidegger's guiding term.[19] *Dasein* is founded in fear (*Furcht*). Fear is not its only disposition, but it is the one that Heidegger chooses here to demonstrate the functioning of "states of mind" (*Befindlichkeit*) in

16. But bloodless *only* at its start: even Marx, he says, failed to understand that revolution is necessarily and essentially bloody (675); it is not Benjaminian divine violence.

17. See 37–39. The English translation renders *angoisse*, oddly, as *terror*. See *Introduction to the Reading of Hegel*, ed. Allan Bloom, trans. James H. Nichols Jr. (Ithaca, NY: Cornell University Press, 1980), 26–29. When Kojève does use *terreur*, as he occasionally does, the English resorts to *dread*.

18. On one occasion Kojève describes this moment as "la Terreur ou l'angoisse (Furcht) du Néant" (204).

19. Heidegger's English translators render *Erschrecken* as alarm and *Entsetzen* as terror. See *Being and Time*, trans. John Macquarrie and Edward Robinson (London: SCM Press, 1962), 181–82. Citations in German are from *Sein und Zeit* (Tübingen: Max Niemeyer Verlag, 2006), which is conventionally indicated by H. So, here, H 142.

general (179, H 140). And fear is of the self itself. It thereby takes on special status in the account of *Dasein*, and it is nested together with other
threat terms, *Angst* and *Sorge*, as constitutive for *Dasein*. *Angst*, which
Heidegger takes over from Kierkegaard (and Sartre from both), becomes
anxiety in English; *Sorge* is harder to carry over.[20] The standard English
translation opts for *care*, but English cannot register the interplaying
concepts available in German. Being-in-the-world is "essentially care"
(*wesenhaft Sorge*), "Being-alongside the ready-to-hand" becomes "concern" (*Besorgen*), and "Being with the Dasein-with of Others" is "solicitude" (*Fürsorge*) (237; H 193). Care for oneself (*Selbstsorge*) would,
however, be a tautology, because *Sorge* is an a priori condition posited in
Being itself, always already there, a "primordial structural totality" (*ur-
sprüngliche Strukturganzheit*) (238; H 193) that is at one with concern
and solicitude, *Besorgen und Fürsorge* (H 194). Deciding to translate
Sorge as care means deciding not to translate it as sorrow, apprehension, fear, concern, trouble, or alarm, among other possibilities. Its ca-
paciousness in the common language accords with its place in Heidegger's schema for the description of *Dasein*. *Besorgen* and *Fürsorge* are
similarly open, commonplace, and available. To exist in the world is to
be absorbed in a world of/as concern, *in der besorgten Welt* (H 172). A
further "methodological" requirement for an exemplary exposition of
Dasein is to be found in *Angst*, anxiety (217; H 182). While fear, which

20. *Sorge* and *Furcht* are for Schiller the first manifestations of man's drive toward
the absolute. They are products of reason but prior to the full development of the personality; they are future oriented but limited to the world of matter and thus must be
left behind. See *On the Aesthetic Education of Man, in a Series of Letters*, ed. and trans.
Elizabeth M. Wilkinson and L. A. Willoughby (Oxford, UK: Clarendon Press, 1967),
175–77. One might reasonably object that it is Kierkegaard and not Heidegger who
deserves recognition as the originator of anxiety as foundational to the modern philosophical tradition, and in strictly historical terms this is indeed the case. It is Kierkegaard
who distinguishes anxiety from fear by its lack of an object, and who connects it to freedom in ways that prefigure both Heidegger and Sartre. The difference is that for Kierkegaard the issue is always also theological. Anxiety is connected to sin and sensuousness
(hence it is stronger in women) and progress beyond it is a religious event. But importantly, anxiety is ontological and thereby foundational. The grasp at faith requires absolute risk, so that existential terror is incurred. One remains time bound at the moment of
yearning to escape it. Kierkegaard uses *Angest* and *Angst* interchangeably for what his
translators render as *anxiety*. For a good account of this syndrome, see Sue Zemka, *Time
and the Moment*, 43–54. Heidegger acknowledges Kierkegaard as having opened up the
"*possibility* of a completely new epoch of philosophy" in his *The Fundamental Concepts
of Metaphysics: World, Finitude, Solitude*, trans. William McNeill and Nicholas Walker
(Bloomington: Indiana University Press, 1995), 150. Kierkegaard's "moment of vision"
(*Augenblick*) shocks us out of the boredom with temporality and restores the sense of
being-toward-death that is the essence of *Dasein*.

is also essential to Dasein, manifests itself as responding to contingent, outer circumstances, or things, anxiety "springs from Dasein itself" and arises from "Being-in-the-world as thrown Being-towards-Death" (*geworfenen Sein zum Tode*) (395; H 344). Being-toward-death is "essentially anxiety" (310), which gives access also to freedom toward death (311). Anxiety makes fear itself possible (230); one has anxiety as a condition of Being-in-the-world as such, and what threatens is "nowhere," and in "nothing ready-to-hand within-the-world" (p. 231). It is a prior disposition: "The *world as world* is disclosed first and foremost by anxiety, as a mode of state-of-mind" (232). Heidegger here displaces a range of other candidates for primary status in producing the world (curiosity, wonder, sympathy, knowledge, vision) with a threat term. In anxiety, *Dasein* must be uncomfortable and resides in the "not-at-home" (*das Un-zuhause*) (233–34; H 188–89). And here Heidegger assimilates anxiety to the Freudian uncanny, *das Unheimliche*, theorized by Freud in 1919 as that which is familiar and unfamiliar at the same time, that which repeats itself, and that which is seen in "the basic state-of-mind of anxiety" (321), mostly covered up in the everyday world but always present (322). The coming to light of *Dasein* to itself is by way of uncanniness. *Dasein* is not at home when it is home.

By 1929–1930, in the lectures now published as the *Fundamental Concepts of Metaphysics*, the doing of philosophy itself has become terrifying (*abschreckend*) in its exposure of the "insurmountable ambiguity of all questioning and being" (21), and *Schrecken* (terror) is cast as the requisite therapy for a generation whose torpidity tolerates even something like the Great War without its "leaving a trace" on self-composure (172).[21] The Kierkegaardian *Augenblick* now initiates terror, which dispels anxiety and boredom as a means to access the essential selfhood. Heidegger calls for a rediscovery, by way of terror, of the "essential oppressiveness" (*Bedrängnis*) without which *Dasein* must remain inauthentic (163–64). At the end of the lectures, terror returns as *Entsetzen*, the means of an encounter with danger that is now our only hope of recovering the "bliss of astonishment" that is philosophy its true form as enthusiasm (366). Subsequent history tempts us to look unkindly upon this plea for "someone capable of instilling terror into our Dasein again" (172), but Heidegger was far from alone in his lamenting the stultifying routines of bourgeois life and bureaucratic culture. By 1935, in a lecture series given from then on and published in 1953 as the *Introduction to Metaphysics*, it is the uncanny that takes over the task of disturbing the complacent subject, in a

21. See Redfield, *Rhetoric of Terror*, 25, 125–26.

way that (uncannily enough) brings us back almost to where we began: it is Heidegger's choice for the German translation of Sophocles's *deinos*. Here there is a yet more explicit reference to the historical state of things, to a "darkening of the world" (*Weltverdüsterung*) and a "disempowering of the spirit" (*Entmachung des Geistes*) enabled by "the flight of the gods, the destruction of the earth, the reduction of human beings to a mass, the preeminence of the mediocre."[22] Communism, liberal democracy, Russia and America, modern technology, the preeminence of mass movements and of the average man—all come under fire as symptoms of the *Wirzeit*, the time of the we (74; H 53). Whether this is Hegel gone mad or Hegel gone bad, and whether or not it explains (or critiques, or justifies) the *Hitlerzeit*, it now seems that the modern self is embedded within a destructive process in which it enables its own further decline. Rectification, if it is possible at all, can come only through a "revolution in our relation to language" (56), one for which the German language joins the Greek as "the most powerful and the most spiritual" (60), one to be carried out by "struggle" (*Kampf*) on the part of "poets, thinkers, and statesmen" (65; H 47).[23] True knowing now involves not just anxiety but, again, a confrontation with terror (*Schrecken*) (120; H 86). Logos itself "needs to use violence (*Gewalt*) in order to fend off glibness and dispersion (*Zerstreuung*) (186; H 133). This is the context in which Heidegger undertakes his reading of the first choral ode of the *Antigone* (ll. 332–75), and translates Sophocles's *polla ta deina kouden anthropou deinoteron pelei* as *Vielfältig das Unheimliche, nichts doch / über den menschen hinaus Unheimlicheres ragend sich regt* (H 112); "Manifold is the uncanny, yet nothing / uncannier than man bestirs itself, rising up beyond him" (156). English translators of the Greek have gone for wondrous or strange as the sense of *deinos* here, but Heidegger's rendering is an apt acknowledgment of the range of the Greek word, with its aura of the terrifying and awe inspiring. The humankind under discussion is a being able to invoke all the senses of *deinos* (including cleverness), and one who always, as the chorus says, in the end "comes to Nothing" (157). Heidegger glosses *deinos* at some length. It names "the terrible" (*das Furchtbare*), as well as the "overwhelming sway (*überwältigenden Waltens*) that induces panicked fear (*panischen Schrecken*), true anxiety (*wahre Angst*),

---

22. *Introduction to Metaphysics*, trans. Gregory Fried and Richard Polt (New Haven, CT: Yale University Press, 2000), 47; *Einführung in die Metaphysik* (Tübingen: Max Niemeyer Verlag, 1953), 34.

23. Here we may recall Benjamin's comments on the power of education as a manifestation of divine (power of) violence.

as well as inwardly reverberating, reticent awe (*Scheu*) and violence, as is appropriate to one who needs himself to use violence (*Gewalt*) (159–60; H 114–15). Humankind is violence doing; it must use violence against what is overwhelming (160), as it leaves what is "homely" (*Heimlichen*) to go into the world "in the direction of the uncanny in the sense of the overwhelming" (161; H 115–16). Natural forces—the sea, the winds—are violent, and call forth violence doing as their overwhelmingness is countered. This happens also in the violence of language, the violence enacted by the creators laying out the paths of a renovated diction by breaking out the unsaid and unthought (*Un-gesagte, Un-gedachte*) (172; H 123). This works by a "shattering" (*Verbrechens*) of the familiar, in a process that knows no "kindness and conciliation" (173–74; H 124–25). This is what the Greeks knew and enacted, and what must presumably be known and enacted once again if humankind is to save itself. *Dasein* is the uncanny, is *deinos* on all fronts: violent, terrifying, wonderful, clever. Something like Benjamin's divine violence reappears here in the power of language itself but as something implicitly more powerful than what can be contained in Benjamin's education (*Erziehung*) or conversation (*Unterredung*).

Heidegger comes back to *deinos* as the uncanny in his 1942 lectures on Hölderlin's poem/hymn *Der Ister*. Now conceding that his translation is itself "violent" (*gewaltsam*) or even in some philological sense "wrong"— which is not at all clear—Heidegger now identifies *to deinon* as "a fundamental word (*Grundwort*) . . . of Greek antiquity itself."[24] It now expresses "the originary unity of the fearful, the powerful, the inhabitual" (*in der ursprünglichen Einheit des Furchtbaren, Gewaltigen, Ungewöhnlichen*, 78) which is what Heidegger wishes to name in and by *das Unheimliche* (64). The powerful invokes the power of violence (*das Gewaltige*) as well as the doing of violence (*das Gewalttätige*), like the *Dasein* of the earlier lectures (63). Hölderlin himself had two tries at translating *deinon*, once as *Ungeheuer* (extraordinary, immense, monstrous) and once as *gewaltige* (violent, powerful, or having the power of violence) (69–70). These qualities belong within the catchment of *deinon*. Heidegger devotes some seventy pages, his entire second lecture, to his reading of the *Antigone* in the light of Hölderlin's reading of Sophocles and counterpoints the German poet's address to the river (Danube) as a homing agent with Antigone's homely-uncanny persona, extending his earlier discussion of the choral ode and

24. Martin Heidegger, *Hölderlin's Hymn "The Ister,"* trans. William McNeill and Julia Davis (Bloomington: Indiana University Press, 1996), 61, 63. German citations are from *Hölderlins Hymne "Der Ister,"* ed. Walter Biemel, 2nd ed. (Frankfurt: Klostermann, 1993), 74, 76.

adding to it a reckoning with Antigone's apparent embrace of the *Unheimliche* at line 96 of the play, *pathein to deinon touto*, glossed as "to take up into my own essence (Wesen) the uncanny that here and now appears" (103). This is, in Heidegger's terms, to bring forth the uncanniness that one already possesses, that makes one what one is, a gesture paralleled by Hölderlin's capacity to encounter the (Greek) foreign, the stranger within the self who is already familiar while remaining strange (49–50).

As it was in 1935, the project of reading here (in 1942) is contextualized within a polemic against "America" and against the overpowering takeover of human experience by bureaucracy and technology, which now exercises a "kind of domination of its own" (44), epitomized in the machine-tool factory where tools are deployed to produce other tools. Delivered before El Alamein or Stalingrad, these remarks would seem to be uninfluenced by any negative sense of the course of Germany's war effort. Nor had the terror bombing of Germany yet reached its later scope and intensity. Heidegger's views are indeed consonant with those expressed in 1935, before the war, and are as such conformable with those later enunciated from the left by the Frankfurt School. His placing of the human subject as a being-toward-death structured by the logic of the uncanny maintains a place for a sense of freedom, one that comes from the full recognition of *Dasein*'s predicament but nonetheless stands within a generally anti-Enlightenment tendency (wherein it is also possible, as we have seen, to place Hegel) that refuses to imagine progress toward more and more peace and happiness as the possible or proper human destiny. If it is not terror per se that throws us into the world as human, the fear and anxiety embedded in the uncanny do yet constitute subjectivity as significantly experienced in the form of what is threatening. The threat is both outside and within, as *Gewalt*, violence and the power of violence, is not only what the subject endures but also what it puts forth in its own worlding, its own disposing of *techne*. Terror and the power of terror work together; one can no longer say that terror is simply an external "it." The first sentence of Horkheimer and Adorno's *Dialectic of Enlightenment* famously summarizes the fantasy that their book will set about dismantling: "Enlightenment, understood in the widest sense as the advance of thought, has always aimed at liberating human beings from fear and installing them as masters. Yet the wholly enlightened earth is radiant with triumphant calamity."[25] The words give themselves

---

25. Max Horkheimer and Theodor W. Adorno, *Dialectic of Enlightenment: Philosophical Fragments*, ed. Gunzelin Schmid Noerr, trans. Edmund Jephcott (Stanford, CA: Stanford University Press, 2002), 1.

away, as they are meant to. Freedom from *Furcht*, when this very thing has been the core of the Heideggerian ontology? Existence *als Herren*, after Hegel and Sartre have turned the tables on mastery itself?[26] Of course it is true to say that not all modern philosophy or social science conducts itself within the vocabulary of the fear-terror cluster. Liberal Anglo-American thought has indeed quite ably managed to avoid the dark side in its analytic and ordinary-language schools, and two major encyclopedias of philosophy in English (the old Macmillan and the newer Stanford) include no entries on fear, dread, anxiety or *Angst*, never mind terror.[27] These are more often the property of what is loosely called Continental philosophy, usually handed over to a specialist or two if it is represented at all in British and American philosophy departments (though it is more at home–and not at home–in literature circles).[28] But Horkheimer and Adorno make terror primary, both in the hypothetical "cry of terror" (*Ruf des Schreckens*) of primeval experience (10–11; Gr 21–22), and yet more so in a here and now dominated by a panic terror (*panische Schrecken*) generated by the awareness of incumbent nuclear war (22; Gr 35), a world wherein "one cannot abolish terror (*Schrecken*) and retain civilization" (180; Gr 227). As late as 1969, the authors declared that although the Nazi terror was by then over, "horror (*Grauen*) has been prolonged" (ix; Gr ix). Civil law has become a "mere instrument of terror (*blosser Terror*) (189; Gr 242). The key, as with Sartre, seems to be in the formation of a "compulsively controlled collectivity," like that made up by rowers in the galleys (29), along with the Enlightenment mathematization of life (67), the culture of sameness, and the reduction of nature to that which must be mastered (149). One can sense here the ghost of Hegel's absolute freedom and terror and see the common ground with Heidegger in the perception of a language which "calculates, designates, betrays, initiates death; it does not express" (209). The culture industry rules us all, under the umbrella of nuclear catastrophe. There seems to be no way out.

Perhaps nowhere is the rift between liberal and neoliberal fantasies of progress and positive self-fashioning on the one hand, and death-directed subjectivity on the other, clearer than in the various deployments of psychoanalysis. The name of Freud encompasses both extremes as it successively

26. German citations (hereafter designated by Gr) are from *Dialektik der Aufklärung* (Frankfurt: Fischer Verlag, 2011), 9.

27. Stanford does have a good entry on *terrorism* but not on the more philosophically complex *terror*.

28. Accordingly, the French-originating *Dictionary of Untranslatables* does have entries for *Anxiety, Care/Sorge, Gewalt*, and *Macht*.

supports both the pleasure principle and the death drive, analysis terminable and interminable, a prospect of healing and accommodation and
an imperative to face up to a life of perpetual pain, deferral and disappointment. Many of the concepts that have become assertoric and cast
in stone in the practice and theoretical evolution of psychoanalysis are
adumbrated in Freud's own writings in a more skeptical and exploratory
way. (In this sense reading Freud is rather like reading Plato or Darwin;
each has generated orthodoxies that are critically reductive). Anxiety
(*Angst*) is a prime example. It figures in Freud's work from at least 1895
onward and goes through a number of shifts of emphasis and indeed basic definitions.[29] It is disambiguated from fear (*Furcht*) in much the same
way as it is by Sartre and Heidegger (and by Kierkegaard), in that it is
not object directed; and from fright or terror (*Schreck*), which is a startled response to unanticipated danger.[30] Angst is of more consistent interest to Freud than either of the other terms and is more of a puzzle. At
first related to incomplete (implicitly male) sex acts (and thus to repression), it is later positioned as elemental to the birth experience, but not in
the form of loss of the mother (of whom the fetus has no concept) but as
an immediate sense of danger. Thus it is not a function of trauma but of
anticipatory threat. It remains ever present to the human being through
all its developmental stages, but it does not emerge with equal intensity
for all. Supervening upon this, and remaining coexistent with it, are all
sorts of neurotic anxieties, which may be attributed to a whole range of
specific causes both real and imaginary. These cannot always (if ever) be
clearly distinguished.[31] Like all affects (for Freud), anxiety is always generated between somatic and psychic determinations: "we are ignorant
of what an affect is" (*SE* 20:132). Whatever the physiological factor,
there always seems to be a "historical" component that brings it to the
surface (133), which leads to methodological confusion, most visibly in
a case where, for instance, castration anxiety leads to a more "undefined
social or moral anxiety" (*Gewissensangst*) (128, 139). As with Darwin
in his study of the emotions, what at first appears instinctual and universal turns out to be open to inflection and even definition by historical or
semiotic variables: language, culture, place, and time. Because anxiety
comes into being as a response to danger situations, "each period of the

29. For a useful editorial summary, see *The Standard Edition of the Complete Psychological Works of Sigmund Freud*, trans. James Strachey and Anna Freud, 21 vols. (London: Hogarth Press, 1966–1974), 20:78–86. For Freud's own summaries of his shifts and
developments, see 132–43, 160–72. Again, see Lezra, *Wild Materialism*, 24–25.

30. *SE* 16:395. See also 20:165 and 18:12–13, where the same distinctions hold.

31. See *SE* 16:404–5.

individual's life has its appropriate determinant of anxiety," all of which can "persist side by side" and recur in ways that may seem circumstantially inappropriate or excessive (142). All of us have a fear-of-danger instinct, but we do not manifest it in the same ways at the same times.[32]

It comes as no surprise to see that many of these kinds of anxiety are invoked in the 1919 essay on the uncanny (*SE* 17:217–56) that became so important to Heidegger among others. In Freud's essay it takes such forms as *Augenangst, Kastrationsangst,* and *Kinderangst,* this last including a fear of silence, solitude, and darkness which most of us have failed to conquer (252). Freud's brief and unelaborated note on the Greek *xenos* as the analogue of *das Unheimliche* serves, as we have seen, to generate numbers of pages a propos of *deinos* in Heidegger's work. Freud's essay has been hugely generative for subsequent theory and need not be further elaborated here.[33] It figures unignorably and familiarly, along with his late elaboration of the death drive, in our current roster of concepts out of which the modern subject must construct itself in and for theory. For now let us return to the remarkable comment Freud makes in 1926: that we do not know what an affect is (*SE* 20:132).

Toward the Contemporary Subject

Fredric Jameson famously implied that he did, if only by way of its disappearance. Following upon "what used to be called the age of anxiety," postmodern culture, writes Jameson, displays a kind of "flatness or depthlessness" that he calls "the waning of affect."[34] Depth models of the subject give way to surface models, liberating us not just from anxiety but "from every other kind of feeling as well, since there is no longer a self present to do the feeling" (15). The feelings that used to be attached to the self now become "free floating and impersonal and tend to be dominated by a peculiar kind of euphoria" (16). It is precisely such free-floatingness that now often gets called affect, which may be distinguished from feelings and emotions by its very lack of relation to deep internal motives or attitudes: there is a whole literature attempting to

---

32. Anxiety (*l'angoisse*) is the topic of Lacan's seminar of 1962–1963, published in French in 2004 and in English in 2014. Lacan offers a major revision whereby anxiety is *not* without an object: it is generated by the object (*petit*) a. For a Lacanian reading that attempts to characterize the entirety of contemporary culture as anxiety driven, see Renata Salecl, *Anxiety* (London: Routledge, 2004).

33. See, for example, Nicholas Royle, *The Uncanny* (New York: Routledge, 2003).

34. Fredric Jameson, *Postmodernism, or, the Cultural Logic of Late Capitalism* (Durham, NC: Duke University Press, 1991), 9–11.

distinguish or identify feelings, passions, emotions and affects. The euphoria of free-floating feelings, independent of acts of judgment or cognition, has to do with a desire to escape from ideology, selfhood, and self-consciousness, whether into a space of hope, a radical opening in colonized space and time, or into a scientific safe-house of autonomous neurological processes of stimulus and response untouched by the mediations of thought and language. We can look at this as a bracing new materialism, a progressive political turn, or explain it as the last desperate refuge of a deluded anarchism or liberalism. At any rate, if affect is or has been on the wane, nothing has impeded the efflorescence of affect theory. Even apathy, so long the bête noire of the masters of industry and for their critics an index of the hegemony of joyless labor, can be made over, in the Stoic tradition, as a "productive force in shaping public life."[35] And once again we are hearing, most recently from Slavoj Žižek (echoing Alain Badiou echoing Engels) that there are times when it is best for the good man to do nothing, and that ours may be one of them. But fear-terror terms, be they feelings, emotions, or affects, have not been left out of the list of prioritized subject identifiers. Publishing the third volume of his *Affect Imagery Consciousness* in the same year as Jameson published his *Postmodernism*, Silvan Tomkins, far from endorsing any waning of affect, set out to intensify the then-current vocabulary by asking for a replacement of anxiety, which he saw as simply "a weasel word, meaning all things to all men," by "the word *terror*, which has not yet lost its affective connotation."[36] Freud's fear-anxiety distinction, common also to Kierkegaard, Heidegger, and Sartre, needs to go, and "terror be recognized as the same affect whether its object is known or not" (494–95). Terror inducers are multiple and complex, and can readily persist well beyond their immediate impact (497) depending on the "type of script" in play (509). The semiotic component matters here as it did for Darwin, and Tomkins accepts also Kagan's distinction between affective response in some physiological sense and our conscious awareness of it (502). Terror is omnipresent, but its "magnification" depends on both social and individual circumstances, to the point that no two persons can ever be presumed to respond to terror in exactly the same way. In short, while there is "plurideterminacy" in script formation (511–12), it is still terror all the way down.

35. Daniel M. Gross, *The Secret History of Emotion: From Aristotle's "Rhetoric" to Modern Brain Science* (Chicago: University of Chicago Press, 2006), 53.
36. Silvan S. Tomkins, *Affect Imagery Consciousness*, vol. 3, *The Negative Affects: Anger and Fear* (New York: Springer, 1991), 494.

By the end of Tomkins's account it is hard not to feel that terror has become as overused as anxiety had been before it. Does it make decisive sense to refer to the bachelor's feelings on the eve of his wedding as "classic terror" (541)? (It might indeed be more apt to apply this syndrome to the bride). Is this the same feeling (or affect) that one feels before the guillotine or during a drone attack? As early as 1962, Tomkins had accepted that there was no consensus on what the primary affects (which for him means primary biological responses) might be; hence his preference, in a prototype of my own employment of the fear-terror cluster, for "joint" names that include high- and low-level versions. What holds these together as one identity with different variations is, for Tomkins, physiological evidence. Thus fear-terror involves "eyes frozen open, pale, cold, sweaty facial trembling, with hair erect."[37] Here again is the Darwin-Ekman paradigm, which once again invites the objection about different affects or emotions generating indistinguishable physical indicators, or indeed none at all.

A quite different terror-anxiety distinction functions in Sianne Ngai's *Ugly Feelings*, where what interests the author are the low-intensity affects that indicate a "suspended" or "obstructed agency" but have not yet reached a life-threatening potential and might therefore fall beneath critical notice.[38] So it is once again anxiety, not terror, that interests her (209–47), and an anxiety she finds to be historically gendered male, castration anxiety being only an extreme example of a tradition that tracks what it calls anxiety (Kierkegaard, Heidegger, and so on) through a set of markedly masculine vectors. So indeed they are and have been; Tomkins's anxious bridegroom is merely the latest in a series of inscriptions of the human subject as a male subject, one who works, fights, and is frightened in visibly gendered ways. What Ngai calls an affect is simply something less intense than an emotion rather than a "formal difference of quality or kind" (27). So anxiety would be an affect, while terror, presumably, is an emotion. But she does not refute the more conventional distinction whereby affect describes what is seen by the third-person observer and emotion is what belongs to the speaker or analysand (25). There is no need here to try to summarize (and certainly not to pass judgment on) the bewildering range of distinctions made by various commentators between feeling, affect, and emotion. But it is worth noting that Ngai's emphasis on the often-overlooked "weak-intentionality"

---

37. *Shame and Its Sisters: A Silvan Tomkins Reader*, ed. Eve Kosofsky Sedgwick and Adam Frank (Durham, NC: Duke University Press, 1995), 74.

38. Sianne Ngai, *Ugly Feelings* (Cambridge, MA: Harvard University Press, 2005), 1, 3.

(22) of the less intense feelings (emotions, affects) stands for a visible trend in contemporary aesthetics that privileges the protoapathetic, passive, or inert dispositions, a trend that is indeed an implicit rebuke of a masculinized grandiosity of response of which terror, especially in its recent militarized versions, would be a prime example.[39] There is here a basis for a principled, gender-based refusal to be terrorized, or to adopt combat and conflict as the definitive subjectifying experiences. This position is analogous to a scrupulous environmentalism that seeks to refrain from world-modifying trespasses in favor of intangible, nondestructive footprints: subject formation need not require Hegelian world-changing work or struggles unto death.

This effort at redirecting attention away from the grandiosity of terror responds to the omnipresence of terms from the fear-terror cluster that can be found all over modern explanations of human subjectivity, especially after the mid-nineteenth-century and especially in what is called "Continental" thought; they are less common in anglophone theory.[40] Descartes, writing in 1649, notably did not include any fear-terror term among his six primary passions. Fear (*la peur*) or terror (*l'épouvante*) are subsidiary and derivative, merely "an excess of timidity, wonder and anxiety (*la crainte*)," wonder alone being primary.[41] By the late nineteenth century it would be hard to imagine some version of fear-terror being absent from the list. Along the way, according to Thomas Dixon, emotions were invented, distinguished from passions, and imagined "as a set of morally disengaged, bodily, non-cognitive and involuntary feelings."[42] There had never, Dixon contends, been any consensus about the numbers of passions nor about the exact distinctions between them (18). Fear (*timor*) was primary for Cicero, and thence for Augustine (40). Whether we call them passions or emotions, fear-terror terms had won their way to the front of the line by the early twentieth century if not before. Jonathan Strauss suggests a beginning event in the "radically negative model of self-understanding" that came after 1794

39. See, again, Gross, *Secret History of the Emotions*; and Anne-Lise François, *Open Secrets: The Literature of Uncounted Experience* (Stanford, CA: Stanford University Press, 2007).

40. Where they can be notably absent, as in Martha Nussbaum's *Upheavals of Thought: The Intelligence of Emotions* (Cambridge: Cambridge University Press, 2001), which sets out to make a positive case for the priority of compassion and barely mentions the fear-terror spectrum.

41. *The Philosophical Writings of Descartes*, trans. John Cottingham et al., 3 vols. (Cambridge: Cambridge University Press, 1985), 1:353, 392.

42. Thomas Dixon, *From Passions to Emotions: The Creation of a Secular Psychological Category* (Cambridge: Cambridge University Press, 2003), 3.

and evolved thereafter into an awareness of "death in its utter emptiness at the heart of subjectivity."[43]

To be sure, it is not always terror that emerges as the preferred focus of the fear-terror cluster. We have seen that Jameson's dismissal of "what used to be called the age of anxiety" may be premature, as the lower-intensity affects (feeling, emotions), anxiety among them, continue to attract critical attention. In Philip Fisher's *The Vehement Passions*, fear is described as holding first place among the passions partly because of its importance to Homer and the Greeks, for whom the mental state of the soldier going into battle was of major concern. The same priority was reflected in classical philosophy, and these precedents alone have been sufficiently formative for subsequent literature and theory, which have regularly returned to them as their own compass points. At the same time, modern thinkers, at least since Hobbes and Hume, have privileged the "template of fear" as primary in the experience of the subject of the modern state.[44] Fisher does draw attention to the massively influential thesis of Albert Hirschman's *The Passions and the Interests*, where avarice comes to the fore as perhaps the one passion that is powerful enough to overcome all the others. In Fisher's own terms, avarice is a good "blocker": its operation suppresses or deflects other passions and entirely possesses the subject. But (and here I depart from Fisher's account) it is likely not powerful enough to overcome terror; no one in the face of a sudden radical threat to life is likely to be found counting his money or searching for more. It can also in itself become the cause of an anxiety about never having enough.

One likely verbal source for "what used to be called the age of anxiety" is Auden's poem of 1947, titled indeed "The Age of Anxiety," which in turn provides a ground bass for Rollo May's widely read *The Meaning of Anxiety*, first published in 1950. Auden, while tilting at some of the familiar and ongoing shortcomings of modern civilization (alienation, anomie), sets his dramatic dialogue during World War Two, wherein "Many have perished; more will" and at a time when we can look forward only to "more deaths / And worse wars."[45] Auden finds that this war has indeed done for our sense of being what Heidegger claimed that the Great War had not done: woken us out of our ontological slumber.

43. *Subjects of Terror*, xii, 23.

44. Philip Fisher, *The Vehement Passions*, 127. Again: "Modern disciplinary interest is largely an interest in the matter of fear" (17).

45. W. H. Auden, *Collected Longer Poems* (New York: Random House, 1969), 266, 269.

But May has very little to say about the war, or indeed about the nuclear threat that succeeded it, relying instead on a thoroughly secularized Kierkegaard and a copiously explicated Freud to propose that what is now the "central problem in psychotherapy" emerging as such in the middle of the nineteenth century, although it remains a "presently uncoordinated field."[46] He thus himself attempts a comprehensive explanation that is at once ontological, psychological, and cultural-historical. May accepts the standard fear-anxiety distinction but argues that anxiety is the primary and more comprehensive threat: fear triggers the subject's "security pattern," but anxiety threatens the pattern itself (191). Thus one *has* a fear but one *is* anxious. The subject-object distinction crumbles, and the self is left in a state of collapse. While the capacity for anxiety is hardwired, the forms it takes are culturally inflected and perhaps even culturally determined. Thus it is that modern humankind is principally made anxious by the demands of "individual competitive success" (153), at least (although this is never explored) in May's postwar America. That same location surely determines his sense of the task before him: to explore how anxiety can be "used constructively" (227).[47]

Fear-Terror in the Cold War

May has surprisingly little to say about the global presence of nuclear weapons as a possible source of first-world anxiety, perhaps because it is not easy to envision routine coping mechanisms, let alone ways in which this anxiety-source can be turned in self-enabling or uplifting directions. And indeed, anxiety was not a major part of the official lexicon with which the civil defense establishment attempted to make bearable the experience of living with the presence of weapons of mass destruction both within and outside the homeland. Neither, perhaps surprisingly for those of us living in the post-9/11 rhetorical climate, was terror. In the wake of World War Two, Joseph Masco has argued, the US government became a "committed affect theorist" to a degree that for

46. Rollo May, *The Meaning of Anxiety* (New York: Ronald Press Co., 1950), v, 16, 18.

47. Anxiety still has a shelf-life and a self-life: Scott Stossel's *My Age of Anxiety: Fear, Hope, Dread and the Search for Peace of Mind* (New York: Random House, 2013) has been marketed as a "national best seller." Stossel notes that "anxiety and its associated disorders represent the most common form of officially classified mental illness in the United States today" (8). He admits to a complexity of causes between body and mind, culture and biology (14), and offers a useful history of efforts at classification.

him renders the 9/11 response very much a repetition of the "launch of the national security state in 1947."[48] But there is a crucial difference, and one that Masco elides, because during the Cold War, remarkably, terror talk is not the order of the day. The civil defense policies extensively publicized and instituted in the 1950s were designed explicitly as population management strategies, and as such they had no interest in encouraging traumatic responses in their citizenry, nor in interpellating a besetting condition of anxiety. Terror and anxiety go largely unmentioned. Cold War emergency rhetoric instead took *panic* as its primary target, and the war on panic was entirely domestic: it is ourselves we must be policing. Federal civil defense administrator Val Peterson, writing in 1953, noted that "in the last five years the use of the word *panic* in the public press has increased by 1,447 per cent."[49] This bracingly precise statistic embodies exactly the spirit of the civil defense initiative: that citizens must be given reliable (or credible) information as a means of restraining the spread of panic itself. The United States, according to Peterson, is not only the strongest nation on earth but also the most panic-prone, as the record "amply demonstrates" (102). Panic is "simply uncontrolled fear" (105), leading to "violent, unreasoning action" (106). But panic can be controlled, not only by the provision of reliable information but also by an education in self-reliance and participatory civic action: the civil defense culture. Hiding under the desk and running for the garden shelter were always going to be hopelessly inadequate defenses against nuclear attack, but habits of preparation and response were designed not so much to save lives as to discipline a population otherwise prone to panic. This may have worked. Peterson's office had declared a year earlier that "sixty-four million adults believe that civil defense is necessary now and would be effective against atomic warfare."[50] Four years earlier, in 1948, the Hopley Report had stressed the importance of reducing "fear and panic," which could "render large groups almost unmanageable"; and once again the tools required were knowledge,

48. Joseph Masco, *The Theater of Operations: National Security Affect from the Cold War to the War on Terror* (Durham, NC: Duke University Press, 2014), 5, 7.

49. Val Peterson, "Panic: The Ultimate Weapon," *Colliers*, August 21, 1953, 99–110, esp. 101. There is an important discussion of this topic in Guy Oakes, *The Imaginary War: Civil Defense and American Cold War Culture* (Oxford: Oxford University Press, 1994), 33–77. See also Jackie Orr, *Panic Diaries: A Genealogy of Panic Disorder* (Durham, NC: Duke University Press, 2006), 79–164. Hobbes had discussed "panic terror" (see chapter 2), as had Horkheimer and Adorno (see above).

50. Federal Civil Defense Administration, *Annual Report for 1952* (Washington, DC: Government Printing Office, 1952), 1.

self-reliance and coordinated community training.[51] Knowledge and understanding are invoked as the means whereby fear can be prevented from turning into panic (101).

In late 1951 an interdisciplinary conference of academics and military personnel convened Project East River, with the aim of producing a report addressing the preparation for nuclear war on the home front.[52] Here the plan was to devise a method for steering American citizens to react within the rational middle of the spectrum running from panic to mere complacency. The techniques it discussed were based on those employed by the United States against its communist enemies, a prophetic version of the feedback loop whereby, more recently, Abu Ghraib–style torture tools were adapted from the endurance training the US and its allies forced on their own soldiers. Again, the word *terror* is much less common than *panic* in this early Cold War literature. Peterson does use it as a loose synonym for *panic* on two or three occasions, but it is *panic* that is the (contested) order of the day: a notable contrast to the language of 9/11.[53] Emotion management in the 1950s (as for Edmund Burke in the 1790s) aims to produce a sense that personal and collective control are effective strategies and pivotal to national security. Fear is not to be disavowed but acknowledged as healthy and constructive: "MAKE FEAR WORK FOR YOU," as Peterson puts it (108). Fear can be the basis for rational decision making (good Aristotelian doctrine, as it happens), while panic prevents it. Avowing and accepting fear to head off panic is the core of civil defense policy. Fear can be addressed and modified; panic cannot.

What might have made panic a more appropriate word here than terror or anxiety? Panic is above all a collective emotion, activating mobs and crowds. Terror, in one of its common uses, suggests something more isolated and subjective, a sense of paralysis in solitude. The greater concern is over an uncontrollable crowd looting, raping and clogging the highways. But terror, too, threatens the essence of the civil defense culture, wherein people act together and for the common good. At this point, the theory holds that panic is the more likely response among the untrained populace, and this is what must be countered. The odd person frozen stiff by terror may seem less of a problem. He or she will not be useful but also will not be likely to be blocking the escape routes and in-

51. *Civil Defense for National Security* (Hopley Report) (Washington, DC: Government Printing Office, 1948), 186.

52. See Oakes, *Imaginary War*, 47–69; Orr, *Panic Diaries*, 98–100.

53. Peterson, "Panic," 101, 105.

terfering with the emergency services. But widespread terror would not be helpful, whether as panic or as inertia. Anxiety might have seemed equally unproductive; insofar as anxiety is psychologically pervasive and lacks a focus, it cannot be turned to positive action, producing only an aimless general bewilderment.

Furthermore, terror was already rhetorically in place as an attributed response to the very existence of nuclear weapons in themselves, a long-term predicament. Panic is Peterson's projected response to an actual attack (or explosion), limited to a particular moment in space and time. His reference to Russia's "arsenal of terror" (105) risks reminding his readers that they themselves live among their own such weapons: indeed, throughout the 1950s, the balance of nuclear power was overwhelmingly in favor of the United States. Prolonged reflection on this fact risks turning people into fatalists, or perhaps into political activists. The belief that one can live on after a nuclear attack also serves the purpose of rendering one's own arsenal of terror less absolutely threatening. Panic is always to come, and as such directs us to a future; terror, if one thinks about it, is already here among us. If the rhetorical task of the state is to persuade its citizens that it can provide and encourage effective security, panic in prospect is more manageable than terror (or anxiety) in place. Mere civic discipline will not wish away the bomb, but it can claim to teach us how to live on after it has exploded.

Interestingly, the concern about panic was not simply supported by such empirical research as existed at the time. Irving Janis's *Air War and Emotional Stress* (1951) sets out the evidence of responses to both conventional bombing (in England, Germany and Japan) and to the A-bomb (in Japan). He admits that the samples are far from scientific, and he is relatively uninterested in the possibilities of culturally inflected or induced behavior. But time and again he makes clear that there has been very little evidence, recorded or reported, of mass panic among any of the populations being bombed. Exodus from the cities was relatively orderly, and often followed by people returning to their homes. He concludes that predictions of "panic and mass hysteria" have "proved to be a myth."[54] This was true of A-bomb survivors as well as of those who went through conventional bombing: Janis finds no significant differences. Nor, he suggests, did civilian morale suffer visibly from either conventional or atomic explosions (59–60). In place of panic, Janis com-

54. Irving Lester Janis, *Air War and Emotional Stress: Psychological Studies of Bombing and Civilian Defense* (New York: McGraw-Hill, 1951), 192.

monly uses the Aristotelian coupling of "fear and/or terror" (along with "acute anxiety") to describe civilian responses to being bombed. But terror here is a short-term experience, not commonly sustained beyond the immediate danger itself. He does, however, agree with Peterson and others that mutual aid and "rational, practical actions" (39) were important to both survival and public order; the difference is that he finds these, and not panic, to have been normative occurrences.

The purported inclination to panic thus becomes Peterson's odd form of American exceptionalism. Precisely because the British, Germans, and Japanese did not panic, Americans undoubtedly will. The insistence on family and community-based self-help that was at the heart of the civil defense initiative is of course deeply familiar in American culture. John Foster Dulles's and George Kennan's concerns about the erosion of the national character as a result of urbanization, consumer culture, and the decline of religion date back to the founding fathers and look forward to such icons of small-town republican idealism as Robert Putnam's year 2000 book *Bowling Alone*. If only we could get to know our neighbors, join teams, volunteer for charitable work, and hash out our political differences in the town-hall meeting, then all will be right again in the heartland.[55] The war is to be won in the hearts and minds of the survivors, not by the power of terror, theirs or ours. Of course, the consequences of nuclear attack were largely discussed in terms of the immediate impact, the blast, and how to survive it. Longer-term radiation damage was barely discussed or limited to affirming the importance of stripping the outer leaves from the lettuce and washing it thoroughly. The massively increased destructive power of the hydrogen bomb compared to the Hiroshima bomb was ignored or finessed. Nuclear war was in this way conventionalized, treated as if it were just a larger version of the nonnuclear bombings of World War Two. For several years the government staged a mock attack on selected cities, Operation Alert, to familiarize the population with a projected routine for getting through and over a nuclear attack. Getting through World War Three became a matter of familiar habit: keep calm and carry on.

There were serious doubts about this policy among important people, but they were kept quiet. By 1955 President Eisenhower himself was voicing reservations about whether the spread of panic could be stopped by emotion management.[56] Staged rehearsals on a national scale were

55. See Oakes, *Imaginary War*, 22–32; Robert D. Putnam, *Bowling Alone: The Collapse and Revival of American Community* (New York: Simon and Schuster, 2000).
56. Oakes, *Imaginary War*, 149–52.

suggesting that responses to nuclear attack could not possibly be as orderly as the civil defense initiative was proposing. And indeed, as far
back as 1938 there had a been a vivid reminder of the difficulties of edu-
cating the population about how to assess what was accurate and inaccu-
rate information: Orson Welles' famous radio broadcast of *The War of
the Worlds* apparently persuaded fully one-sixth of its six million listen-
ers that the Martians really had landed in new Jersey.[57] But terror talk remained sparse. President Kennedy's address to the nation on October 22,
1962, at the height of the Cuban Missile Crisis, does not invoke terror,
although it does speak of weapons of mass destruction. Nor, as far as
I have discovered, does terror figure in any of the headlines in the various *New York Times* articles reporting the evolution of the crisis. It is
similarly absent from that same newspaper's account of the first World
Trade Center bombing of February 1993, which is much more focused
on the botched evacuation procedures. People are described as terrified,
but the personification of terror itself does not stalk the front pages.
Between 1962 and 1993, meanwhile, terrorism had been shifted pretty
comprehensively away from its identification with violence enacted by
the state and had become associated first with Soviet-sponsored activity and thereafter with irrational or evil forces deployed, in the words
of Benjamin Netanyahu, by the forces of barbarism against the forces of
civilization (which mostly meant Israel and the United States).[58]

Looking again at the events of 9/11, could we not surmise that some
of the lessons of the civil defense program were indeed still very much in
place? Normal and rational responses were immediately triggered. Hos-
pitals set up blood drives for the injured who did not show up; workers
filed dutifully up and down stairs, some remembering that they had done
it all before in the WTC bombing of 1993. Told to stay put or even to
return to their offices instead of leaving the buildings, many had at first
no idea of what was happening above and below them. The whole experience was (as reported) orderly and communal, with the able helping
the unable. There seemed, until the towers collapsed, to be little panic.
A bit more panic might indeed have saved more lives, among them many
firefighters who were sent back into the building to fight the flames. Even
after the WTC site turned to a heap of rubble, the physical evidence of

---

57. See Joanna Bourke, *Fear, a Cultural History* (Emeryville, CA: Shoemaker and
Hoard, 2006), 178–88. Orr, *Panic Diaries,* 33–77, offers interesting speculations about
the mutual investments of commercial radio and military-academic research in the stag-
ing of this event.

58. See Lisa Stampnitzky, *Disciplining Terror: How Experts Invented "Terrorism"*
(Cambridge: Cambridge University Press, 2013), 113–14.

the disaster seemed remarkably contained. Most of the visible destruction was within and around the footprints; acres, not square miles, were devastated. Despite the spectacular horror of the day, and the terrible loss of so many lives, the immensity of the damage was bizarrely miniaturized in the evidence that remained: more than two thousand souls and thousands of tons of debris all piled up in one place, as if in a planned detonation (a perception not lost on the conspiracy theorists).

Perhaps civil defense culture also had something to do with the alacrity with which people began to talk of Ground Zero, a term hitherto mostly applied to the sites of nuclear explosions. Like the imagined attacks of the 1950s, 9/11 also left no fallout.[59] It was as if, after all the horror and continuing grief, many survivors could feel that they *had* survived, bloodied but unbowed, and we who looked on could feel even more intact. This was not what our media-political class wanted to have happen. So, at the very moment when so many ordinary citizens managed not to panic, managed to display a determination to carry on, just as Val Peterson and his colleagues might have wished, we witnessed the interpellation from above of terror and war into the common language. Where Peterson sought to inhibit panic, his successors set out to introduce terror. Terror not just in New York, and not just among those directly involved as victims or witnesses, but across the nation and even across the world. It is as if the incentive of the 1950s had been reversed: radical affective response is now to be encouraged, not displaced by self-directed efforts. Instead of being invited to pick up tools and work for a civic future, we were bidden to experience shock and awe, terrified inertia, when time stops (hence all those images of the falling towers cycling through the media over and over again). We were bidden above all to be passive, and to attend to and await the militarized revenge of the world's largest war machine headed toward . . . whatever, someone, somewhere. Perhaps we might even be freed from our deepest fears, our own terrors, and be led into a world of absolute security, absolute homeland. After 2001, our leaders were working toward a passive citizenry; not the can-do communal helpers of Operation Alert, but a traumatized, in-the-dark mass that could be persuaded to approve the most irrational and implausible responses by their government.

Or perhaps the citizenry was imagined as already all too passive and needing to be prompted into violent response. Early studies of witnesses

59. I do not mean to make light of the very real long-term medical effects on many people who survived the first day. Toxic dust has proved a very real source of ongoing harm. But it was not a nuclear event.

to the Hiroshima and Nagasaki bombings had apparently concluded that they were not significantly more demoralized after the events than before, and there is even evidence that some of them had a positive response to the explosions as sheer spectacle. Later, American reactions to the faraway tests of the hydrogen bomb suggested that around half of the population was not significantly worried about having one explode somewhere near them.[60] Certainly 9/11 coverage did its best to play up the appeal of the spectacle, with seemingly endless reruns of the footage of the collapsing towers, but only from a safe distance, and with the images of the falling bodies tastefully brushed away. And along with the interpellation of the aesthetic, initiated only to be at once disavowed as such, there was the interpellation of terror, a demand that one break away from fascination with the visual image to an internal imagining of a nameless but life-threatening external agent. What was missing was the middle ground in which real things happened to real people: the falling bodies of the jumpers, their mangled remains on the sidewalk, the evidence of burning and suffocating bodies inside, and so on. This sphere, which it is tempting to call the empirical or even the real world, was deemed too undecorous to recall or represent (so, too, were the coffins at Dover Air Force Base during the Iraq War), perhaps because it is beyond easily controllable political management. With a few exceptions (Frédéric Beigbeder among them and, to some degree, Don DeLillo), even the novelists have stayed away from this territory. Social solidarity did manifest itself in the immediate wake of 9/11 in such forms as blood donation, volunteerism, informal health support networks, firefighters coming from afar, and so on. But these, like the efflorescence of posters and photos of the missing, were generally not scripted by the media or the politicians. What was scripted was the mélange of spectacle and terror aiming to capture those who were not within live distance of the events, which was most of us. The affective profile was in this way rendered remote from the physical sensations of being at or near the site, rendered as a distant sort of "shock and awe" experience, to borrow the terms of Ullman and Wade's 1996 military policy document that was borrowed again in giving rhetorical zest to the start of the second war against Iraq in 2003 (where it functioned as a euphemism for death and destruction).

    Cold War civil defense culture placed a good deal of emphasis on self-help and helping one's neighbors in small-group collective actions.

---

60. See Orr, *Panic Diaries*, 76–77, 85. Similarly, there was much evidence that the terror bombings of German cities in World War Two did not have the desired effect of weakening morale or bringing about an early end to the war.

This should not of course be taken simply in good faith: as well as operating as a form of domestic discipline, such emphatic localism discouraged any reflection on those global sites where the war was far from cold, where the US and its allies were engaged in the violent suppression of "communism" and aggressively seeking to manage decolonization projects in their own interests. In such places state terror was alive and well, and often acknowledged as such in the military counterinsurgency literature. Nonetheless, civil defense rhetoric was in itself visibly (albeit falsely) rational. The message from the politicians after 9/11 was rather different: we were urged to carry on shopping and to inform on any of our neighbors who were behaving oddly. Political management in the 1950s believed (or pretended) that accurate information and clear knowledge would contribute positively to civilian morale and performance under stress. After 9/11, Americans were instead bidden not to know (hence the famous Rumsfeld analysis) and either given no information (it is all top secret) or lied to (the Iraqi "weapons of mass destruction"). Seeking to impose a state of terror on the population also reversed a long-standing culture of restoration, going back at least as far as the shell-shock victims of the Great War, whereby the job of the state was to heal psychic and physical wounds, not to create them. As far as I know there have been no comprehensive studies of exactly how terrorized or not the nation at large was after 9/11, or for how long. How, after all, do you measure terror? Computing the mentions of terror in the press, as Val Peterson did for panic in 1953, would lead us only into a numerological sublime. It seems possible that this particular management effort was a failure, although it may have done just enough to make possible the war against Iraq; and even here the unprecedented worldwide protests of February 2003 made clear the demographic extent of the dissent. With the onset of Katrina in 2005, any residual faith in the government's capacity (or desire) to protect its citizens from harm was severely challenged, if not shredded. Efforts to package the hurricane as a natural disaster pure and simple were quickly and widely discredited, and efforts at rhetorical management appeared more threadbare than perhaps ever before. Ongoing revelations about the excesses of the national security state at home and abroad (surveillance, drones, and so on) ought to have made it harder to fool most of the people most of the time. But it is far from clear that this is the case. We are in the middle of a publicity campaign for which all news is fake news, and terror talk still pollutes a common language in which genuinely positive political management (gun control, health care, immigration) does not earn majority support among politicians or their electorates. We are still encouraged to be enthralled by the militarization of approved knowledge; nonmilitarized rhetoric remains hard to sell, perhaps even hard to speak. Not so long ago the preferred term for addressing poverty was, after all, *war*: the War on Poverty.

Is there a ray of hope? Janis had noticed another phenomenon among the bombing survivors of World War Two: resentment against their own governments. In Britain, Germany, and Japan, civilians who went through the bombing were dismayed and outraged at the apparent inability of their leaders to protect them. This in turn encouraged a general disrespect for law and order, and thus threatened to become the basis for an unmanageable population.[61] In the aftermath of Katrina the widespread contempt for the Federal Emergency Management Agency was both justified and unignorable. And even within the vociferously managed terror-patriotism after 9/11, dissident voices could be heard, most of all in New York City and among families directly affected, where inefficient radio systems sent emergency workers to avoidable deaths. Val Peterson's success in carrying the Cold War argument about panic, against the apparent evidence of Janis's empirical studies, makes it clear that the goal was always political management. Why were Americans (cowboys aside, according to Peterson) deemed, on dubious or nonexistent evidence, more panic-prone than citizens of other countries, if not to insinuate a management policy?[62] Living as we do in "consent" states, to use Philip Bobbitt's term, where the credibility of a government depends on an ability to protect and secure, the exposure (or suspicion) of massive incompetence erodes the integrity of the ruling orders and questions their very reason for being. Covering up the mess was surely one of the main motives (along with the plot against Iraq) for the dissemination of terror talk, relatively successful after 9/11 but completely impossible as applied to Katrina. The current version of the rational and informed response that the civil defense theory of the 1950s required from its citizens should not be deployed against the prospect of external attack but against the covert and overt manipulations of our own government: not duck and cover but look and uncover. This might be our best chance of escaping from the mind-set (to put it politely) and the persistent rhetoric of militarization, which continues to rely on terror talk.

61. Janis, *Air War and Emotional Stress*, 127–29, 149.

62. In the case of the Orson Welles broadcast, one could argue that once the belief in invasion by someone (Martians or not) was in place, subsequent reactions were entirely rational.

The preceding account of terror and terror talk is intended to encourage and assist our passage beyond coercion and persuasion, whether
self-administered or imposed from outside. We may find it hard to go
along with Benjamin and Heidegger in supposing that education or language alone can embody a divine power of violence that can bring about
a radical new beginning to our world. But we can surely agree, with
Empson, on the duty of doing no harm as in itself a plausible good,
and with Klemperer on the importance of paying critical attention to
"certain expressions" of the sort that lead us astray. This study of mine
aspires to contribute to a coalition of the unwilling, a common cause,
yet to be fully forged, among those who stand against the deceptions of
terror talk both at home and across the world. It is aimed at specialist
readers, for example, those who might take seriously the claim that the
Anglo-American distrust of Continental philosophy (which has a long
history) has contributed to the shroud of unknowing around the concept
of terror. Few even among this group would suggest that a good dose
of Sartre and Heidegger would in itself put an end to popular abuses of
the rhetoric of terror, but it cannot do harm to have these particular expressions circulated more widely. We specialists have to hope for some
contact, somehow, with other and larger groups, for example with some
among the millions of people all over the world who marched against
the invasion of Iraq in 2003. Between the two, between the academic
few and the multilingual millions, there are all sorts of other groups, like
the poets and writers (and their critical interpreters), minority activists,
ecologists, and international feminists who are almost never fully in the
mainstream but whose language is accessible enough that unpredicted
audiences can be imagined for their work. After World War Two, when
the ratio of civilian to military casualties increased so massively, the gendering of the rhetoric of terror ought to have changed radically. It became no longer a matter of exemplary males living the lives of soldiers,
as it had been from Homer to the Great War, but of men, women, and
children facing indiscriminate fatal violence on a massive scale. The succeeding threats of nuclear war and of an ecological catastrophe of planetary proportions (as well as of small-scale random attacks in the street)
further drives home the fear-terror syndrome as a condition of universal
applicability. Perhaps it is this very uncontainability that sponsors the
vague, unembodied, erratic, and desperate recourses to terror talk as a
disciplinary rhetoric among our politicians: only the indescribable can
be imagined as potentially containing the innumerable. In the face of the
forces arrayed against any prospect of nonviolent coexistence, the forces
in whose interest terror talk is regularly deployed, it is hard to imagine

that any critique of language is alone going to change enough of the world to diminish radically the death and suffering that language (in the wrong hands) also assists and justifies. In the aftermath of 9/11, Mahmoud Darwish made a bold statement: "We know that the horizons of the intellect can traverse landscapes of devastation." Perhaps they can, but whom and how many will they carry with them, and how long will it take? The words of his fellow poet and Palestinian Suheir Hammad also bear remembering: "There is death here and there are promises of more."[63] This promise, alas, continues to be fulfilled. In such dark times, one can only hope that the first knowledge can survive and sustain itself against the second.

63. Both Darwish and Hammad are cited from Joseph and Sharma, *Terror Counter-Terror*, 8, 68.

Bibliography

Abish, Walter. *How German Is It/Wie Deutsch Ist Es*. New York: New Directions, 1980.

Agamben, Giorgio. *The Time That Remains: A Commentary on the Letter to the Romans*. Translated by Patricia Dailey. Stanford, CA: Stanford University Press, 2005.

Ahmad, Eqbal. *Confronting Empire: Interviews with David Barsamian*. Cambridge, MA: South End Press, 2000.

Alexander, George, ed. *Western State Terrorism*. Cambridge, UK: Polity, 1991.

Alter, Robert. *Ancient Israel: The Former Prophets: Joshua, Judges, Samuel, and Kings: A Translation with Commentary*. New York: W. W. Norton and Co., 2013.

Andress, David. *The Terror: The Merciless War for Freedom in Revolutionary France*. New York: Farrar, Straus, and Giroux, 2005.

Anidjar, Gil. *Blood: A Critique of Christianity*. New York: Columbia University Press, 2014.

Arasse, Daniel. *The Guillotine and the Terror*. Translated by Christopher Miller. New York: Penguin, 1989.

Aravamudan, Srinivas. *Enlightenment Orientalism: Resisting the Rise of the Novel*. Chicago: University of Chicago Press, 2011.

Arendt, Hannah. "On Violence." In *Crises of the Republic*, 103–98. Orlando, FL: Harcourt Brace and Co., 1972.

———. *The Origins of Totalitarianism*. Orlando, FL: Harcourt, 1976.

Aristotle. *Art of Rhetoric*. Translated by J. H. Freese. Cambridge, MA: Harvard University Press, 1982.

———. *The Poetics of Aristotle: Translated from the Greek with Notes.* Translated by Henry James Pye. London, 1788.

———. *The Poetics.* Translated by W. Hamilton Fyfe. Cambridge, MA: Harvard University Press, 1973.

Asad, Talal. *On Suicide Bombing.* New York: Columbia University Press, 2007.

Ashfield, Andrew, and Peter de Bolla, eds. *The Sublime: A Reader in British Eighteenth-Century Aesthetic Theory.* Cambridge: Cambridge University Press, 1996.

Auden, W. H. *Collected Longer Poems.* New York: Random House, 1969.

Aust, Stefan. *Baader-Meinhof: The Inside Story of the RAF.* 3rd ed. Translated by Anthea Bell. Oxford: Oxford University Press, 2009.

Austen, Jane. *Mansfield Park.* Edited by Kathryn Sutherland. New York: Penguin, 2003.

———. *Persuasion.* Edited by Gillian Beer. New York: Penguin, 2003.

Austin, Alice Louise. "A Critical Concordance to the *Thyestes* of Seneca." MA diss., University of Illinois, 1914.

Baczko, Bronisław. *Ending the Terror: The French Revolution after Robespierre.* Translated by Michael Petherem. Cambridge: Cambridge University Press, 1994.

———. "The Terror before the Terror? Conditions of Possibility, Logic of Realization." In *The French Revolution and the Creation of Modern Political Culture*, vol. 4, *The Terror*, edited by Keith Michael Baker, 19–38. Bingley, UK: Emerald Group, 1994.

Badiou, Alain. *Ethics: An Essay on the Understanding of Evil.* Translated by Peter Hallward. London: Verso, 2001.

———. *Saint Paul: The Foundation of Universalism.* Translated by Ray Brassier. Stanford, CA: Stanford University Press, 2003.

Bakhtin, M. M. *The Dialogic Imagination: Four Essays.* Translated by Caryl Emerson and Michael Holquist. Austin: University of Texas Press, 1981.

———. *Problems of Dostoevsky's Poetics.* Translated by Caryl Emerson. Minneapolis: University of Minnesota Press, 1984.

Bal, Mieke. *Death and Dissymmetry: The Politics of Coherence in the Book of Judges.* Chicago: University of Chicago Press, 1988.

Balibar, Étienne. "Reflections on *Gewalt*." *Historical Materialism* 17 (2009): 99–125.

Balzac, Honoré de. *The Chouans.* Translated by Marion Ayton Crawford. Harmondsworth, UK: Penguin, 1972.

———. *Les chouans.* Edited by Maurice Regard. Paris: Garnier, 1964.

Banita, Georgiana. *Plotting Justice: Narrative Ethics and Literary Culture after 9/11.* Lincoln: University of Nebraska Press, 2012.

Barruel, Augustin. *Memoirs Illustrating the History of Jacobinism: A Translation from the French of the Abbé Barruel.* 4 vols. London, 1797–1798.

Beigbeder, Frédéric. *Windows on the World.* Translated by Frank Wynne. New York: Hyperion, 2004.

Benjamin, Walter. *The Arcades Project.* Translated by Howard Eiland and Kevin McLaughlin. Cambridge, MA: Belknap Press of Harvard University Press, 1999.

———. "Critique of Violence." In *Walter Benjamin: Selected Writings, Volume One, 1913–1926*, edited by Marcus Bullock and Michael W. Jennings, 236–52. Cambridge, MA: Belknap Press of Harvard University Press, 1996.

———. *Walter Benjamin: Gesammelte Schriften 2:1*. Edited by Rolf Tiedemann and Herman Schweppenhäuser. Frankfurt: Suhrkamp, 1999.

Bindman, David, ed. *The Shadow of the Guillotine: Britain and the French Revolution*. London: British Museum, 1989.

Blake, William. *The Complete Poetry and Prose of William Blake*. Edited by David V. Erdman. Berkeley: University of California Press, 1982.

Blum, Carol. *Rousseau and the Republic of Virtue: The Language of Politics in the French Revolution*. Ithaca, NY: Cornell University Press, 1990.

Bobbitt, Philip. *Terror and Consent: The Wars for the Twenty-First Century*. New York: Random House, 2009.

Boling, Robert G., ed. *The Anchor Bible: Judges*. Garden City, NY: Doubleday, 1975.

Böll, Heinrich. *The Safety Net*. Translated by Leila Vennewitz. New York: Melville House, 1981.

Boothby, Guy. *Pharos the Egyptian*. *The Windsor Magazine*, June–December 1898.

Borcke, Astrid von. "Violence and Terror in Russian Revolutionary Populism: The *Narodnaya Volya*, 1879–83." In *Social Protest, Violence and Terror in Nineteenth- and Twentieth-Century Europe*, edited by Wolfgang J. Mommsen and Gerhard Hirschfield, 48–62. London: Macmillan, 1982.

Bourke, Joanna. *Fear: A Cultural History*. Emeryville, CA: Shoemaker and Hoard, 2006.

Bouwsma, William J. *John Calvin: A Sixteenth-Century Portrait*. Oxford: Oxford University Press, 1988.

Braddon, Mary Elizabeth. "The Dulminster Dynamiter." *Pall Mall Magazine* 1 (May–October 1893): 469–82.

Braunsperger, Gudrun. "Sergey Nechaev and Dostoevsky's *Devils*: The Literary Answer to Terrorism in Nineteenth-Century Russia." In *Literature and Terrorism: Comparative Perspectives*, edited by Michael C. Frank and Eva Gruber, 27–39. Amsterdam: Rodopi, 2012.

Brennan, Gillian. "Patriotism, Language and Power: English Translations of the Bible, 1520–1580." *History Workshop* 27 (1989): 18–36.

Brink, André. *An Act of Terror*. London: Minerva, 1992.

Brown, Charles Brockden. *Wieland; or, The Transformation*. Edited by Emory Elliott. Oxford: Oxford University Press, 2009.

Brown, Howard G. *Ending the French Revolution: Violence, Justice, and Repression from the Terror to Napoleon*. Charlottesville: University of Virginia Press, 2006.

Brzezinski, Zbigniew. "Terrorized by 'War on Terror.'" *Washington Post*, March 25, 2007.

Buck, Carl Darling. *A Dictionary of Selected Synonyms in the Principal Indo-European Languages*. Chicago: University of Chicago Press, 1988.

Buck-Morss, Susan. *Hegel, Haiti, and Universal History*. Pittsburgh, PA: University of Pittsburgh Press, 2009.

Bunyan, John. *A Treatise on the Fear of God*. London, 1679.

Burke, Edmund. *A Philosophical Enquiry into the Origin of our Ideas of the Sublime and Beautiful*, edited by James T. Boulton. Notre Dame, IN: University of Notre Dame Press, 1986.

———. *The Writings and Speeches of Edmund Burke, Volume VIII*. Edited by L. G. Mitchell. Oxford, UK: Clarendon Press, 1989.

———. *The Writings and Speeches of Edmund Burke, Volume IX*. Edited by R. B. McDowell. Oxford, UK: Clarendon Press, 1991.

Bush, George W. "Address to the Joint Session of the 107th Congress." September 20, 2001. https://georgewbush-whitehouse.archives.gov/infocus/bushrecord/documents/Selected_Speeches_George_W_Bush.pdf.

Butler, Judith. "Critique, Coercion, and Sacred Life in Benjamin's 'Critique of Violence.'" In *Political Theologies: Public Religions in a Post-Secular World*, edited by Hent de Vries and Lawrence E. Sullivan, 201–20. New York: Fordham University Press, 2006.

———. *Parting Ways: Jewishness and the Critique of Zionism*. New York: Columbia University Press, 2013.

Campbell, Gordon. *Bible: The Story of the King James Version, 1611–2011*. Oxford: Oxford University Press, 2010.

Carey, John. "A Work in Praise of Terrorism? September 11 and Samson Agonistes." *Times Literary Supplement*, September 6, 2002.

Carlyle, Thomas. *The French Revolution: A History*. 3 vols. London: Chapman and Hall, 1889.

Carr, Caleb. *The Lessons of Terror: A History of Warfare Against Civilians*. New York: Random House, 2003.

Cassin, Barbara, ed. *Dictionary of Untranslatables: A Philosophical Lexicon*. Translated by Emily Apter, Jacques Lezra, and Michael Wood. Princeton, NJ: Princeton University Press, 2013.

Cavarero, Adriana. *Horrorism: Naming Contemporary Violence*. Translated by William McCuaig. New York: Columbia University Press, 2007.

Chang, Kenneth. "Simulated Space 'Terror' Offers NASA an Online Following." *New York Times*, July 10, 2012. http://www.nytimes.com/2012/07/11/science/space/seven-minutes-of-terror-video-grabs-online-audience-for-nasa.html.

Chesterton, G. K. *The Annotated Thursday: G. K. Chesterton's Masterpiece, "The Man Who Was Thursday."* Annotated by Martin Gardner. San Francisco, CA: Ignatius Press, 1999.

Civil Defense for National Security: Report to the Secretary of Defense by the Office of Civil Defense Planning, as Prepared and Recommended by . . . Russell J. Hopley, Director. Washington, DC: Government Printing Office, 1948.

Clark, C. M. H. *A History of Australia, Volume 1: From the Earliest Times to the Age of MacQuarrie*. Melbourne: Melbourne University Press, 1962.

Clery, E. J. *The Rise of Supernatural Fiction, 1762–1800*. Cambridge: Cambridge University Press, 1995.

Clery, E. J., and Robert Miles, eds. *Gothic Documents: A Sourcebook, 1700–1820*. Manchester: Manchester University Press, 2000.

Clingman, Stephen. *The Grammar of Identity: Transnational Fiction and the Nature of the Boundary*. Oxford: Oxford University Press, 2009.

Coby, Patrick. *Socrates and the Sophistic Enlightenment: A Commentary on Plato's "Protagoras."* Lewisburg, PA: Bucknell University Press, 1987.

Cockburn, Andrew. *Kill Chain: The Rise of the High-Tech Assassins.* New York: Henry Holt, 2015.

Coleridge, Samuel Taylor. *Lectures 1795: On Politics and Religion.* Edited by Lewis Patton and Peter Mann. Princeton, NJ: Princeton University Press, 1971.

Coll, Steve. "The Unblinking Stare." *New Yorker,* November 24, 2014. https://www.newyorker.com/magazine/2014/11/24/unblinking-stare.

Comay, Rebecca. *Mourning Sickness: Hegel and the French Revolution.* Stanford, CA: Stanford University Press, 2011.

Conrad, Joseph. *The Secret Agent.* New York: Penguin, 2007.

———. *Under Western Eyes.* New York: Penguin, 2007.

Constant, Benjamin. *Les effets de la terreur.* Edited by Philippe Raynaud. Paris: Flammarion, 1988.

Cotta, Sergio. *Why Violence? A Philosophical Interpretation.* Translated by Giovanni Gullace. Gainesville: University Press of Florida, 1985.

Craciun, Adriana. *British Women Writers and the French Revolution: Citizens of the World.* London: Palgrave, 2005.

Crawford, Joseph. *Gothic Fiction and the Invention of Terrorism: The Politics and Aesthetics of Fear in the Age of the Reign of Terror.* London: Bloomsbury, 2013.

Dacier, André. *La Poetique d'Aristote, traduite en françois.* Paris, 1692.

Danchev, Alex. *On Art and War and Terror.* Edinburgh: Edinburgh University Press, 2009.

Dart, Gregory. *Rousseau, Robespierre and English Romanticism.* Cambridge: Cambridge University Press. 1999.

Darwin, Charles. *The Expression of the Emotions in Man and Animals.* 3rd ed. Commentary by Paul Ekman. London: HarperCollins, 1998.

Dass, Sujan, ed. *Black Rebellion: Eyewitness Accounts of Major Slave Revolts.* Atlanta: Two Horizons Press, 2010.

Däwes, Birgit. *Ground Zero Fiction: History, Memory, and Representation in the American 9/11 Novel.* Heidelberg: Universitätsverlag Winter, 2011.

Dayan, Colin. "Legal Terrors." *Representations* 9, no. 21 (2005): 42–80.

de Bolla, Peter. *The Architecture of Concepts: The Historical Formation of Human Rights.* New York: Fordham University Press, 2013.

de Romilly, Jacqueline. "La crainte dans l'oeuvre de Thucydide." *Classica et Mediaevalia* 17 (1956): 119–27.

Defoe, Daniel. *Robinson Crusoe.* Edited by Michael Shinagel. New York: W. W. Norton and Co., 1975.

DeLillo, Don. "Baader-Meinhoff." *New Yorker,* April 1, 2002.

———. *Falling Man.* New York: Scribner, 2007.

———. *Mao II.* New York: Viking Penguin, 1991.

———. *Players.* New York: Random House, 1989.

———. *Underworld.* New York: Simon and Schuster, 1997.

———. *White Noise.* New York: Penguin, 2009.

Dennis, John. *The Grounds of Criticism in Poetry.* London, 1704.

———. *The Impartial Critick.* London, 1793.

Derrida, Jacques. *Dissemination.* Translated by Barbara Johnson. Chicago: University of Chicago Press, 1981.

———. *Acts of Religion.* Edited by Gil Anidjar. New York: Routledge, 2002.

———. *Philosophy in a Time of Terror: Dialogues with Jürgen Habermas and Jacques Derrida.* Edited by Giovanna Borradori. Chicago: University of Chicago Press, 2003.

Descartes, René. *The Philosophical Writings of Descartes.* Translated by John Cottingham, Robert Stoothoff, and Dugald Murdoch. 3 vols. Cambridge: Cambridge University Press, 1985.

Dickens, Charles. *A Tale of Two Cities.* Edited by Richard Maxwell. New York: Penguin, 2003.

Dixon, Thomas. *From Passions to Emotions: The Creation of a Secular Psychological Category.* Cambridge: Cambridge University Press, 2003.

Doran, Robert. *The Theory of the Sublime from Longinus to Kant.* Cambridge: Cambridge University Press, 2015.

Dostoevsky, Fyodor. *Demons.* Translated by Richard Pevear and Larissa Volokhonsky. New York: Random House, 1994.

———. *Demons.* Translated by Robert A. Maguire. New York: Penguin, 2008.

———. *The Possessed.* Translated by Constance Garnett (1913 rpt.). New York: Macmillan, 1913. Reprint, New York: Barnes and Noble, 2005.

Doyle, Arthur Conan. *A Study in Scarlet.* London: Penguin, 2001.

Dryden, John. *"Of Dramatic Poetry" and Other Essays.* Edited by George Watson. 2 vols. London: Dent and Dutton, 1962.

Dumas. Alexandre. *The Knight of Maison-Rouge.* Translated by Julie Rose. New York: Random House, 2003.

———. *Le chevalier de Maison-Rouge.* 2 vols. Paris: Conard, 1934.

———. *The Prussian Terror.* Translated by R. S. Garnett. London: Stanley Paul, 1915.

———. *Taking the Bastile.* New York: Collier, 1910.

Eade, J. C. *Aristotle Anatomized: The "Poetics" in England, 1674–1781.* Frankfurt am Main: Peter Lang, 1988.

Eagleton, Terry. *Sweet Violence: The Idea of the Tragic.* Oxford, UK: Blackwell, 2003.

Edelstein, Dan. *The Terror of Natural Right: Republicanism, the Cult of Nature, and the French Revolution.* Chicago: University of Chicago Press, 2009.

Edwards, Jonathan. *Jonathan Edwards: Basic Writings.* New York: Signet, 1966.

———. *Jonathan Edwards: Representative Selections.* Edited by Clarence H. Faust and Thomas H. Johnson. New York: Hill and Wang, 1963.

———. *The Works of Jonathan Edwards.* Volume 4, *The Great Awakening.* Edited by C. C. Goen. New Haven, CT: Yale University Press, 1972.

Eiland, Howard. "Deconstruction of Violence." *boundary 2* 44, no. 4 (2017): 113–40.

Else, Gerald F. *Aristotle's "Poetics": The Argument.* Cambridge, MA: Harvard University Press, 1957.

Empson, William. *The Structure of Complex Words.* Totowa, NJ: Rowman and Littlefield, 1979.

Engberg-Pedersen, Anders. *Empire of Chance: The Napoleonic Wars and the Disorder of Things*. Cambridge, MA: Harvard University Press, 2015.

Esposito, Roberto. *Bios: Biopolitics and Philosophy*. Translated by Timothy Campbell. Minneapolis: University of Minnesota Press, 2008.

Faludi, Susan. *The Terror Dream: Fear and Fantasy in Post-9/11 America*. New York: Henry Holt, 2007.

Federal Civil Defense Administration. *Annual Report for 1952*. Washington, DC: Government Printing Office, 1952.

Fish, Stanley. *How Milton Works*. Cambridge, MA: Belknap Press of Harvard University Press, 2001.

Fisher, Philip. *The Vehement Passions*. Princeton, NJ: Princeton University Press, 2002.

François, Anne-Lise. *Open Secrets: The Literature of Uncounted Experience*. Stanford, CA: Stanford University Press, 2007.

Frank, Michael C. "Plots on London: Terrorism in Turn-of-the-Century British Fiction." In *Literature and Terrorism: Comparative Perspectives*, edited by Michael C. Frank and Eva Gruber, 41–65. Amsterdam: Rodopi, 2012.

Freeman, Bryant C., and Alan Batson, eds. *Concordances des théâtre et des poesies de Jean Racine*. 2 vols. Ithaca, NY: Cornell University Press, 1968.

Freud, Sigmund. *The Standard Edition of the Complete Psychological Works of Sigmund Freud*. Translated by James Strachey and Anna Freud. 21 vols. London: Hogarth Press, 1966–1974.

Furniss, Tom. *Edmund Burke's Aesthetic Ideology: Language, Gender and Political Economy in Revolution*. Cambridge: Cambridge University Press, 1993.

Garber, Marjorie, and Nancy J. Vickers, eds. *The Medusa Reader*. New York: Routledge, 2003.

Geffroy, Annie. "Terreur et terrorisme: Les mots en héritage, du néologisme au concept." In *La Vendée: Après la terreur, la reconstruction*, edited by Alain Gérard, 144–61. Paris: Perrin, 1997.

George, Alexander, ed. *Western State Terrorism*. Cambridge, UK: Polity, 1991.

Geroud, Daniel. *Guillotine: Its Legend and Lore*. New York: Blast Books, 1992.

Godwin, William. *Things as They Are; or, The Adventures of Caleb Williams*. Edited by Maurice Hindle. London: Penguin Books, 1987.

Gordimer, Nadine. *The Pickup*. London: Bloomsbury, 2001.

———. *A World of Strangers*. London: Victor Gollancz, 1958.

Greenberg, Moshe, ed. *The Anchor Bible: Ezekiel 21–37*. New York: Doubleday, 1997.

Gregerson, Linda. "Milton and the Tragedy of Nations." *PMLA* 129, no. 4 (2014): 672–87.

Gross, Daniel M. *The Secret History of Emotion: From Aristotle's "Rhetoric" to Modern Brain Science*. Chicago: University of Chicago Press, 2006.

Grosse, Carl. *Horrid Mysteries*. Translated by Peter Will. London: Folio Press, 1968.

Grube, G. M. A. *Aristotle on Poetry and Style*. Indianapolis: Bobbs-Merrill, 1983.

Hägglund, Martin. *Radical Atheism: Derrida and the Time of Life*. Stanford, CA: Stanford University Press, 2008.

Hamacher, Werner. "Afformative, Strike: Benjamin's Critique of Violence." In *Walter Benjamin's Philosophy: Destruction and Experience*, edited by Andrew Benjamin and Peter Osborne, 110–38. London: Routledge, 1994.

Hamilton, John T. *Security: Politics, Humanity, and the Philology of Care*. Princeton, NJ: Princeton University Press, 2013.

Hansen, Beatrice. *Critique of Violence: Between Poststructuralism and Critical Theory*. London: Routledge, 2000.

Harris, Frank. *The Bomb*. Portland, OR: Feral House, 1996.

Hegel, G. W. F. von. *Hegel's Phenomenology of Spirit*. Translated by A. V. Miller. Oxford, UK: Clarendon Press, 1979.

———. *Phänomenologie des Geistes*. Edited by Gerhard Göhler. Frankfurt: Ullstein Verlag, 1973.

Heidegger, Martin. *Being and Time*. Translated by John Macquarrie and Edward Robinson. New York: Harper and Row, 1962.

———. *Einführung in die Metaphysik*. Tübingen: Max Niemeyer Verlag, 1953.

———. *The Fundamental Concepts of Metaphysics: World, Finitude, Solitude*. Translated by William McNeil and Nicholas Walker. Bloomington: Indiana University Press, 1995.

———. *Hölderlin's Hymn "The Ister."* Translated by William McNeill and Julia Davis. Bloomington: Indiana University Press, 1996.

———. *Hölderlins Hymne "Der Ister."* Edited by Walter Biemel. 2nd ed. Frankfurt: Klostermann, 1993.

———. *Introduction to Metaphysics*. Trans. Gregory Fried and Richard Polt. New Haven, CT: Yale University Press, 2000.

———. *Sein und Zeit*. Tübingen: Max Niemeyer Verlag, 2006.

Herman, Edward, and Gerry O'Sullivan, eds. *The "Terrorism" Industry: The Experts and Institutions That Shape Our View of Terror*. New York: Pantheon, 1989.

Hertz, Neil. "Medusa's Head." In *The End of the Line: Essays on Psychoanalysis and the Sublime*, 161–215. New York: Columbia University Press, 1985.

Heuser, Beatrice. "The Cultural Revolution in Counter-Insurgency." *Journal of Strategic Studies* 30, no. 1 (2007): 153–71.

Heuser, Ryan, Franco Moretti, and Erik Steiner. "The Emotions of London." Stanford Literary Lab, *Pamphlet 13* (October 2016). https://litlab.stanford.edu/LiteraryLabPamphlet13.pdf.

Hitchens, Christopher. "Wanton Acts of Usage: Terrorism: A Cliché in Search of a Meaning." *Harper's Magazine*, September 1, 1986, 66–70.

Hobbes, Thomas. *Leviathan*. Edited by Michael Oakeshott. Oxford, UK: Blackwell, 1946.

Homer. *The Iliad of Homer*. Edited by Gilbert Wakefield. Translated by Alexander Pope. 5 vols. London, 1806.

———. *The Iliad*. Edited by A.T. Murray. Cambridge, MA: Harvard University Press, 1960.

———. *The Iliad*. Translated by E. V. Rieu. Harmondsworth, UK: Penguin, 1960.

———. *Chapman's Homer: The Iliad*. Edited by Allardyce Nicoll. Princeton, NJ: Princeton University Press, 1998.

Horkheimer, Max, and Theodor Adorno. *Dialectic of Enlightenment: Philosophical Fragments*. Edited by Gunzellin Schmid Noerr. Translated by Edmund Jephcott. Stanford, CA: Stanford University Press, 2002.

———. *Dialektik der Aufklärung*. Frankfurt: Fischer Verlag, 2011.

Houen, Alex. *Terrorism and Modern Literature: From Joseph Conrad to Ciaran Carson*. Oxford: Oxford University Press, 2002.

Howlett, Jana, and Rod Mengham. *The Violent Muse: Violence and the Artistic Imagination in Europe, 1910–1939*. Manchester: Manchester University Press, 1994.

Huet, Marie-Hélène. *Mourning Glory: The Will of the French Revolution*. Philadelphia: University of Pennsylvania Press, 1997.

Hugo, Victor. *Ninety-Three*. 1900 translation. Reprint, Rock Island: Necropolis Press, 2012.

———. *Oeuvres Complètes: Quatre-vingt-treize*. Givors, France: André Martel, 1954.

Hurh, Paul. *American Terror: The Feeling of Thinking in Edwards, Poe, and Melville*. Stanford, CA: Stanford University Press, 2015.

Hurley, Kelly. *Sexuality, Materialism and Degeneration at the Fin de Siècle*. Cambridge: Cambridge University Press, 1996.

Ingram, William, and Kathleen Swaim, eds. *A Concordance to Milton's English Poetry*. Oxford, UK: Clarendon Press, 1972.

Israel, Jonathan. *Revolutionary Ideas: An Intellectual History of the French Revolution from the Rights of Man to Robespierre*. Princeton, NJ: Princeton University Press, 2014.

Jackson, Richard. *Writing the War on Terrorism: Language, Politics and Counter-Terrorism*. Manchester: Manchester University Press, 2005.

James, Henry. *The Princess Casamassima*. London: Penguin, 1987.

James, William. *The Principles of Psychology*. 3 vols. Cambridge, MA: Harvard University Press, 1981.

———. "What Is an Emotion?" *Mind* 9, no. 34 (April 1884): 188–205.

Jameson, Fredric. *The Hegel Variations: On the "Phenomenology of Spirit."* London: Verso, 2010.

———. *Postmodernism: or, the Cultural Logic of Late Capitalism*. Durham, NC: Duke University Press, 1991.

Janis, Irving Lester. *Air War and Emotional Stress: Psychological Studies of Bombing and Civilian Defense*. New York: McGraw-Hill, 1951.

Johnston, Kenneth R. *Unusual Suspects: Pitt's Reign of Alarm and the Lost Generation of the 1790s*. Oxford: Oxford University Press, 2013.

Joseph, Ammu and Kalpana Sharma. *Terror Counter-Terrror: Women Speak Out*. London: Zed Books, 2003.

Jourdan, Annie. "Les discours de la terreur à l'époque révolutionnaire (1776–1798): Étude comparative sur une notion ambiguë." *French Historical Studies* 36, no. 1 (2013): 51–81.

Juergensmeyer, Mark. *Terror in the Mind of God: The Global Rise of Religious Violence*. Berkeley: University of California Press, 2003.

Junod, Tom. "The Falling Man: An Unforgettable Story." *Esquire*, September 9, 2016. http://www.esquire.com/news-politics/a48031/the-falling-man-tom-junod/.

Kagan, Jerome. *What Is Emotion? History, Measures, and Meanings*. New Haven, CT: Yale University Press, 2007.

Kant, Immanuel. *Elements of the Philosophy of Right*. Edited by Allen Wood. Cambridge: Cambridge University Press, 1995.

———. *Religion and Rational Theology*. Edited by Allen W. Wood and George Di Giovanni. Cambridge: Cambridge University Press, 1996.

Kavanagh, Thomas M. *Writing the Truth: Authority and Desire in Rousseau*. Berkeley: University of California Press, 1987.

Kearns, Gerry. "Bare Life, Political Violence, and the Territorial Structure of Britain and Ireland." In *Violent Geographies: Fear, Terror, and Political Violence*, edited by Derek Gregory and Allan Pred, 7–35. New York: Routledge, 2007.

Kelly, George Armstrong. "Conceptual Sources of the Terror." *Eighteenth-Century Studies* 14, no. 1 (1980): 18–36.

King, Stephen. *Danse Macabre*. New York: Gallery Books, 2010.

Kirkpatrick, David D. "Deadly Mix in Benghazi: False Allies, Crude Video." *New York Times*, December 29, 2013.

Kitson, Frank. *Gangs and Counter-Gangs*. London: Barrie and Rockliff, 1960.

———. *Low Intensity Operations: Subversion, Insurgency, Peace-Keeping*. London: Faber and Faber, 1971.

Klein, Naomi. *The Shock Doctrine: The Rise of Disaster Capitalism*. New York: Picador, 2007.

Klemperer, Victor. *The Language of the Third Reich, LTI—Lingua Tertii Imperii: A Philologist's Notebook*. Translated by Martin Brady. London: Athlone Press, 2000.

Knight, Richard Payne. *An Analytical Inquiry into the Principles of Taste*. 4th ed. London, 1808.

Knoppers, Laura L. "Translating Majesty: The King James Bible, John Milton, and the English Revolution." In *The King James Bible and the World It Made*, edited by David Lyle Jeffrey, 29–48. Waco, TX: Baylor University Press, 2011.

Kojève, Alexandre. *Introduction à la lecture de Hegel*. Paris: Gallimard, 1968.

———. *Introduction to the Reading of Hegel*. Compiled by Raymond Queneau. Edited by Allan Bloom. Translated by James H. Nichols Jr. Ithaca, NY: Cornell University Press, 1980.

Konstan, David. *The Emotions of the Ancient Greeks: Studies in Aristotle and Classical Literature*. Toronto: University of Toronto Press, 2006.

Koselleck, Reinhart. *Futures Past: On the Semantics of Historical Time*. Translated by Keith Tribe. New York: Columbia University Press, 2004.

———. *The Practice of Conceptual History: Timing History, Spacing Concepts*. Translated by Todd Samuel Presner, Kerstin Behnke, and Jobst Welge. Stanford, CA: Stanford University Press, 2002.

Krausser, Helmut. *Eros*. Translated by Mike Mitchell. New York: Europa Editions, 2008.

Lacan, Jacques. *Anxiety: The Seminars of Jacques Lacan. Book X*. Edited by Jacques-Alain Miller. Cambridge, UK: Polity, 2014.

Laqueur, Walter. *A History of Terrorism*. New Brunswick, NJ: Transaction Publishers, 2012.

Lawrence, D. H. *Kangaroo*. London: Heinemann, 1964.

Lefebvre, Georges. *The Great Fear of 1789: Rural Panic in Revolutionary France*. Translated by Joan White. London: New Left Books, 1973.

Lenin, V. I. *Revolution at the Gates: A Selection of Writings from February to October 1917*. Edited, with an introduction and afterword, by Slavoj Žižek. London: Verso, 2004.

Lessing, Doris. *The Grass Is Singing*. London: Michael Joseph, 1950.

Levine, Joseph M. *The Battle of the Books: History and Literature in the Augustan Age*. Ithaca, NY: Cornell University Press, 1991.

Leys, Ruth. "How Did Fear Become a Scientific Object, and What Kind of Object Is It?" *Representations* 110 (2010): 66–104.

Lezra, Jacques. *Wild Materialism: The Ethic of Terror and the Modern Republic*. New York: Fordham University Press, 2010.

Lieb, Michael. "'Our Living Dread': The God of *Samson Agonistes*." In *Milton Studies XXXIII*, edited by Albert C. Labriola and Michael Lieb, 3–25. Pittsburgh, PA: University of Pittsburgh Press, 1997.

Linton, Marisa. *Choosing Terror: Virtue, Friendship and Authenticity in the French Revolution*. Oxford: Oxford University Press, 2013.

———. "The Man of Virtue: The Role of Antiquity in the Political Trajectory of L. A. Saint-Just." *French History* 24, no. 3 (2010): 393–419.

———. "Robespierre's Political Principles." In *Robespierre*, edited by Colin Haydon and William Doyle, 37–53. Cambridge: Cambridge University Press, 1999.

Loewenstein, David. "*Samson Agonistes* and the Culture of Religious Terror." In *Milton in the Age of Fish: Essays in Authorship, Text, and Terrorism*, edited by Michael Lieb and Albert C. Labriola, 203–28. Pittsburgh, PA: Duquesne University Press, 2006.

Lyons, John D. *Kingdom of Disorder: The Theory of Tragedy in Classical France*. West Lafayette, IN: Purdue University Press, 1999.

Lyotard, Jean-François. *The Postmodern Condition: A Report on Knowledge*. Translated by Geoff Bennington and Brian Massumi. Minneapolis: University of Minnesota Press, 1984.

Machen, Arthur. *The White People and Other Weird Stories*. London: Penguin, 2011.

Marks, Herbert, ed. *The English Bible, King James Version: The Old Testament, Volume One*. New York: W. W. Norton and Co., 2012.

Marsh, Richard. *The Beetle*. Edited by Julian Wolfreys. Peterborough, ON: Broadview, 2004.

Marx, Karl. *Marx, Engels: On Literature and Art*. Edited by Lee Baxandall and Stefan Morawski. New York: International General, 1973.

Masco, Joseph. *The Theater of Operations: National Security Affect from the Cold War to the War on Terror*. Durham, NC: Duke University Press, 2013.

Maturin, Charles. *Melmoth the Wanderer*. Edited by Alethea Hayter. Harmondsworth, UK: Penguin Books, 1977.

May, Rollo. *The Meaning of Anxiety*. New York: Ronald Press Co., 1950.

Melchiori, Barbara Arnett. *Terrorism in Late Victorian London*. London: Croom Helm, 1985.

Merriman, John. *The Dynamite Club: How a Bombing in Fin-de-Siècle Paris Ignited the Age of Modern Terror*. Boston: Houghton Mifflin, 2009.

Miller, Elizabeth Carolyn. "Exile London: Anarchism, Immigration and Xenophobia in Late-Victorian London." In *Fear, Loathing, and Victorian Xenophobia*, edited by Marlene Tromp, Maria K. Bachman, and Heidi Kauffman, 269–85. Columbus: Ohio State University Press, 2013.

————. *Framed: The New Woman Criminal in British Culture at the Fin de Siècle*. Ann Arbor: University of Michigan Press, 2008.

Milton, John. *Complete Shorter Poems, Second Edition*. Edited by John Carey. New York: Addison, Wesley, Longman, 1997.

Mirante, Rand. *Medusa's Head: The Rise and Survival of Joseph Fouché, Inventor of the Modern Police State*. Bloomington, IN: Archway Publishing, 2014.

Mitchell, W. J. T. *Cloning Terror: The War of Images, 9/11 to the Present*. Chicago: University of Chicago Press, 2011.

Mohamed, Feisal G. "Confronting Religious Violence: Milton's *Samson Agonistes*." *PMLA* 120, no. 2 (2005): 327–340.

————. *Milton and the Post-Secular Present: Ethics, Politics, Terrorism*. Stanford, CA: Stanford University Press, 2011.

Montesquieu, Baron de. *The Spirit of the Laws*. Translated by Thomas Nugent. 2 vols. London, 1750.

Moore, Leslie E. *Beautiful Sublime: The Making of "Paradise Lost," 1701–1734*. Stanford, CA: Stanford University Press, 1990.

Morris, David B. *The Religious Sublime: Christian Poetry and Critical Tradition in Eighteenth-Century England*. Lexington: University Press of Kentucky, 1972.

Munteanu, Dana LaCourse. *Tragic Pathos: Pity and Fear in Greek Philosophy and Tragedy*. Cambridge: Cambridge University Press, 2012.

Ndebele, Njabulo S. *Fine Lines from the Box: Further Thoughts about Our Country*. Compiled by Sam Thlalo Radithlalo. Cape Town: Umuzi, 2007.

Neocleous, Mark. *Critique of Security*. Montreal, QC: McGill-Queen's University Press, 2008.

Netanyahu, Benjamin, ed. *Terrorism: How the West Can Win*. New York: Farrar, Straus, and Giroux, 1986.

Ngai, Sianne. *Ugly Feelings*. Cambridge, MA: Harvard University Press, 2005.

Norton, David. *A Textual History of the King James Bible*. Cambridge: Cambridge University Press, 2005.

Nussbaum, Martha. *Upheavals of Thought: The Intelligence of Emotions*. Cambridge: Cambridge University Press, 2001.

Oakes, Guy. *The Imaginary War: Civil Defense and American Cold War Culture*. New York: Oxford University Press, 1994.

Opfell, Olga S. *The King James Bible Translators*. Jefferson, NC: McFarland, 1982.

Orr, Jackie. *Panic Diaries: A Genealogy of Panic Disorder*. Durham, NC: Duke University Press, 2006.

Parker, Harold T. *The Cult of Antiquity and the French Revolutionaries: A Study in the Development of the Revolutionary Spirit*. Chicago: University of Chicago Press, 1937.

Parsons, Eliza. *The Castle of Wolfenbach*. Edited by Diane Long Hoevaler. Kansas City, MO: Valancourt Books, 2007.

Paton, Alan. *Too Late the Phalarope*. London: Jonathan Cape, 1956.

Paulson, Ronald. *Representations of Revolution (1789–1820)*. New Haven, CT: Yale University Press, 1983.

Perkins, William. *The Works of William Perkins*. Edited by Ian Breward. Appleford, UK: Sutton Courtenay Press, 1970.

Peterson, Val. "Panic: The Ultimate Weapon." *Colliers*, August 21, 1953, 99–110.

Pettersson, Olof, and Vidgis Songe-Møller, eds. *Plato's Protagoras: Essays on the Confrontation of Philosophy and Sophistry*. Cham, Switzerland: Springer International, 2017.

Pfau, Thomas. *Romantic Moods: Paranoia, Trauma and Melancholy, 1790–1840*. Baltimore: Johns Hopkins University Press, 2005.

Plato. *Platonis Protagoras*. Edited by J. Adam and A. M. Adam. Cambridge: Cambridge University Press, 1962.

———. *Plato, "Protagoras."* Translated by C. C. W. Taylor. Rev. ed. Oxford, UK: Clarendon Press, 1991.

———. *Protagoras*. Translated by W. R. M. Lamb. Cambridge, MA: Harvard University Press, 1924.

———. *Republic*. Translated by Paul Shorey. Cambridge, MA: Harvard University Press, 1937.

Pope, Marvin H., ed. *The Anchor Bible: Job*. New York: Doubleday, 1965.

Popkin, Jeremy D., ed. *Facing Racial Revolution: Eyewitness Accounts of the Haitian Insurrection*. Chicago: University of Chicago Press, 2007.

Preece, Julian. *Baader-Meinhof and the Novel: Narratives of the Nation, Fantasies of the Revolution, 1970–2010*. Basingstoke, UK: Palgrave-Macmillan, 2012.

Price, Uvedale. *An Essay on the Picturesque, as Compared with the Sublime and Beautiful*. New ed. London, 1796.

———. *An Essay on the Picturesque, as Compared with the Sublime and Beautiful*. 3 vols. London, 1810.

Pringle, Thomas. *Narrative of a Residence in South Africa*. Edited by A. M. Lewin Robinson. Cape Town: C. Struik, 1966.

Putnam, Robert D. *Bowling Alone: The Collapse and Revival of American Democracy*. New York: Simon and Schuster, 2000.

Radcliffe, Ann. *The Castles of Athlin and Dunbayne*. Edited by Alison Milbank. Oxford: Oxford University Press, 1995.

———. *The Italian*. Edited by Frederick Garber. Oxford: Oxford University Press, 1981.

———. "On the Supernatural in Poetry." *New Monthly Magazine* 16, no. 1 (1826): 145–152.

———. *A Sicilian Romance*. Edited by Alison Milbank. Oxford: Oxford University Press, 1993.

Rapin, René. *Réflexions sur la poétique d'Aristote, et sur les ouvrages des poètes anciens et modernes*. Paris, 1694. Facsimile ed. Hildesheim, Germany: Georg Olms, 1973.

————. *Reflexions on Aristotle's Treatise on Poetry.* London, 1674.

Reddy, William M. *The Navigation of Feeling: A Framework for the History of Emotions.* Cambridge: Cambridge University Press, 2001.

Redfield, Marc. *The Rhetoric of Terror: Reflections on 9/11 and the War on Terror.* New York: Fordham University Press, 2009.

Rediehs, Laura. "Evil." In *Collateral Language: A User's Guide to America's New War,* edited by John Collins and Ross Glover, 65–78. New York: New York University Press, 2002.

Robespierre, Maximilien. *Virtue and Terror.* Edited by Jean Ducange. Translated by John Howe. Introduction by Slavoj Žižek. London: Verso, 2017.

Robin, Corey. *Fear: The History of a Political Idea.* Oxford: Oxford University Press, 2004.

Robison, John. *Proofs of a Conspiracy Against All the Religions and Governments of Europe.* London, 1797.

Roe, Nicholas. "Imagining Robespierre." In *Coleridge's Imagination: Essays in Memory of Pete Laver,* edited by Richard Gravil, Lucy Newlyn, and Nicholas Roe, 171–78. Cambridge: Cambridge University Press, 1985.

Rousseau, Jean-Jacques. *Essay on the Origin of Languages and Writings Related to Music.* Edited and translated by John T. Scott. Hanover, NH: University Press of New England, 1998.

Royle, Nicholas. *The Uncanny.* New York: Routledge, 2003.

Rudé, George. *The Crowd in the French Revolution.* Oxford: Oxford University Press, 1967.

Rush, Benjamin. *Essays Literary, Moral and Philosophical, Second Edition.* Philadelphia, 1806.

Rymer, Thomas. *The Tragedies of the Last Age Considered and Examined.* London, 1678.

Sade, Marquis de. *The Crimes of Love: Heroic and Tragic Tale, Preceded by an Essay on Novels.* Translated by David Coward. Oxford: Oxford University Press, 2005.

Salecl, Renata. *Anxiety.* London: Routledge, 2004.

Sartre, Jean-Paul. *Being and Nothingness: An Essay on Phenomenological Ontology.* Translated by Hazel E. Barnes. London: Methuen, 1957.

————. *Critique de la raison dialectique.* Paris: Gallimard, 1960.

————. *Critique of Dialectical Reason I: Theory of Practical Ensembles.* Translated by Alan Sheridan-Smith. London: Verso, 1982.

Scanlan, Margaret. *Plotting Terror: Novelists and Terrorists in Contemporary Fiction.* Charlottesville: University of Virginia Press, 2001.

Schechter, Ronald. "The Terror of Their Enemies: Reflections on a Trope in Eighteenth-Century Historiography." *Historical Reflections/Réflexions historiques* 36, no. 1 (2010): 53–75.

Schiller, J. C. F. von. *On the Aesthetic Education of Man, in a Series of Letters.* Edited and translated by Elizabeth M. Wilkinson and L. A. Willoughby. Oxford, UK: Clarendon Press, 1967.

Schivelbusch, Wolfgang. *The Railway Journey: The Industrialization of Time and Space in the Nineteenth Century.* Berkeley: University of California Press, 1987.

Schlink, Bernhard. *The Weekend*. Translated by Shaun Whiteside. New York: Vintage International, 2011.

Scott, Sir Walter. *Waverley*. Edited by P. D. Garside. New York: Penguin, 2011.

Seneca. *Seneca, His Tenne Tragedies*. Edited by Thomas Newton (1581). Reprint, edited and introduced by T. S. Eliot. Bloomington: Indiana University Press, 1964.

———. *Tragedies, II*. Edited and translated by John D. Fitch. Cambridge, MA: Harvard University Press, 2004.

Shamsie, Kamila. *Burnt Shadows*. New York: Picador, 2009.

Shay, Jonathan. *Achilles in Vietnam: Combat Trauma and the Undoing of Character*. New York: Scribner, 1994.

Silberstein, Sandra. *War of Words: Language, Politics and 9/11*. London: Routledge, 2002.

Simpson, David. "A Confusion of Tongues." *Reconstruction* 11, no. 2 (2011).

———. *Romanticism and the Question of the Stranger*. Chicago: University of Chicago Press, 2013.

———. "Telling It Like It Isn't." In *Literature after 9/11*, edited by Ann Kenniston and Jeanne Follansbee Quinn, 209–23. London: Routledge, 2008.

Skinner, Quentin. *The Foundations of Modern Political Thought, Volume One: The Renaissance*. Cambridge: Cambridge University Press, 1978.

———. "Language and Social Change." In *The State of the Language*, edited by Leonard Michaels and Christopher Ricks, 562–78. Berkeley: University of California Press, 1980.

Sloterdijk, Peter. *Rage and Time: A Psychopolitical Investigation*. Translated by Mario Wenning. New York: Columbia University Press, 2012.

Smith, Ted A. *Weird John Brown: Divine Violence and the Limits of Ethics*. Stanford, CA: Stanford University Press, 2015.

Smith, William. *Dionysius Longinus on the Sublime, Translated from the Greek*. London, 1739.

Sofsky, Wolfgang. *The Order of Terror: The Concentration Camp*. Translated by William Templer. Princeton, NJ: Princeton University Press, 1999.

Sorel, Georges. *Reflections on Violence*. Translated by T. E. Hulme and J. Roth. London: Collier-Macmillan, 1950.

Spalding, M. J. *The History of the Protestant Reformation in Germany and Switzerland, Fourth Edition*. 2 vols. Baltimore: John Murphy, 1875.

Spevack, Marvin, ed. *The Harvard Concordance to Shakespeare*. Cambridge, MA: Belknap Press of Harvard University Press, 1974.

St. Amand, Pierre. "Hot Terror: *Quatrevingt-treize*." *SubStance* 27, no. 2 (1998): 61–72.

Stampnitzky, Lisa. *Disciplining Terror: How Experts Invented "Terrorism."* Cambridge: Cambridge University Press, 2013.

Stedman Jones, Gareth. *Karl Marx: Greatness and Illusion*. Cambridge, MA: Belknap Press of Harvard University Press, 2016.

Sterling, Claire. *The Terror Network: The Secret War of International Terrorism*. New York: Holt, Rinehart, and Winston, 1981.

Stevenson, Robert Louis, and Fanny van der Grift Stevenson. *The Dynamiter*. New York: International Book Co. n.d.

Stoker, Bram. *Dracula*. Edited by Nina Auerbach and David J. Skal. New York: W. W. Norton and Co., 1997.

———. *The Jewel of Seven Stars*. Edited by Kate Hebblethwaite. London: Penguin, 2008.

Stossel, Scott. *My Age of Anxiety: Fear, Hope, Dread and the Search for Peace of Mind*. New York: Random House, 2013.

Strauss, Jonathan. *Subjects of Terror: Nerval, Hegel, and the Modern Self*. Stanford, CA: Stanford University Press, 1998.

Suárez, Thomas. *State of Terror: How Terrorism Created Modern Israel*. Northampton, MA: Olive Branch Press, 2017.

Tackett, Timothy. *The Coming of the Terror in the French Revolution*. Cambridge, MA: Harvard University Press, 2015.

———. "Interpreting the Terror." *French Historical Studies* 24, no. 4 (2001): 569–78.

Tadmor, Naomi. *The Social Universe of the English Bible: Scripture, Society and Culture in Early Modern England*. Cambridge: Cambridge University Press, 2010.

Taylor, Antony. *London's Burning: Pulp Fiction, the Politics of Terrorism, and the Destruction of the Capital in British Popular Culture, 1840–2005*. London: Bloomsbury, 2012.

"The Terrorist System of Novel-Writing." *Monthly Magazine* 4, no. 21 (August 1797). Reprinted in Rictor Norton, ed., *Gothic Readings: The First Wave, 1764–1840*. Leicester: Leicester University Press, 2000.

Thorup, Mikkel. *An Intellectual History of Terror: War, Violence and the State*. London: Routledge, 2010.

Tomkins, Silvan S. *Affect Imagery Consciousness*. Volume 3. *The Negative Affects: Anger and Fear*. New York: Springer, 1991.

———. *Shame and Its Sisters: A Silvan Tomkins Reader*. Edited by Eve Kosofsky Sedgwick and Adam Frank. Durham, NC: Duke University Press, 1995.

Trollope, Anthony. *The Land-Leaguers*. London: Chatto and Windus, 1884. Available at https://archive.org/details/landleaguers00troluoft.

Trotsky, Leon. "Why Marxists Oppose Individual Terrorism." *Der Kampf*, November 1911. https://www.marxists.org/archive/trotsky/1911/11/tia09.htm.

Ullman, Harlan K., and James P. Wade. *Shock and Awe: Achieving Rapid Dominance*. Washington, DC: National Defense University Press, 1996.

van den Heuvel, Gerd. "Terreur, Terroriste, Terrorisme." In *Handbuch politischsozialer Grundbegriffe in Frankreich, 1680–1820*, 3:89–132. Munich: Oldenburg, 1985.

Virgil. *The Aeneid*. Translated by H. Rushton Fairclough. 2 vols. Cambridge, MA: Harvard University Press, 1986.

———. *The Works of Virgil*. Edited by John Dryden. 3 vols. London, 1730.

Wahnich, Sophie. *In Defence of the Terror: Liberty or Death in the French Revolution*. Translated by David Fernbach. London: Verso, 2012.

Walpole, Horace. *The Castle of Otranto and The Mysterious Mother*. Edited by Frederick S. Frank. Peterborough, ON: Broadview Press, 2003.

Walther, Rudolf. "Terror, Terrorismus." In *Geschichtliche Grundbegriffe: Historisches Lexikon zur politisch-sozialen Sprache in Deutschland*, edited by

Otto Bruner, Werner Conze, and Reinhart Koselleck, 6:323–444. Stuttgart: Klett-Cotta, 1990.

Weber, Caroline. *Terror and Its Discontents: Suspect Words in Revolutionary France*. Minneapolis: University of Minnesota Press, 2003.

Wetmore, Monroe Nichols. *Index Verborum Virgilius*. Hildesheim: Georg Olms, 1961.

Whelehan, Niall. *The Dynamiters: Irish Nationalism and Political Violence in the Wider World, 1867–1900*. Cambridge: Cambridge University Press, 2012.

White House. "Remarks by the President at the National Defense University," press release, May 23, 2013. https://obamawhitehouse.archives.gov/the-press -office/2013/05/23/remarks-president-national-defense-university.

Williams, Helen Maria. *Letters Containing a Sketch of the Politics of France, from the Thirty-First of May, 1793, until the Twenty-Eighth of July, 1794*. 2 vols. London, 1795.

Williams, Raymond. *Keywords: A Vocabulary of Culture and Society*. Rev. ed. New York: Oxford University Press, 1983. Updated online edition available at https://keywords.pitt.edu/williams_keywords.html.

Wittreich, Joseph A. *Why Milton Matters: A New Preface to his Writings*. New York: Palgrave Macmillan, 2006.

Wordsworth, William. *The Prelude: 1799, 1805, 1850*. Edited by Jonathan Words-worth, M. H. Abrams, and Stephen Gill. New York: W. W. Norton and Co., 1979.

———. *Sonnet Series and Itinerary Poems, 1820–45*. Edited by Geoffrey Jackson. Ithaca, NY: Cornell University Press, 2004.

Work, Robert O., and Shawn Brimley. *20YY: Preparing for War in the Robotic Age*. Washington, DC: Center for a New American Security, 2015.

Wright, Angela. *Britain, France and the Gothic, 1764–1820: The Import of Terror*. Cambridge: Cambridge University Press, 2013.

Zaborowski, Robert. *La crainte et le courage dans l'Iliade et l'Odyssee*. War-saw: Stakroos, 2002.

Zemka, Sue. *Time and the Moment in Victorian Literature and Society*. Cam-bridge: Cambridge University Press, 2012.

Žižek, Slavoj. *In Defense of Lost Causes, Second Edition*. London: Verso, 2009.

———. *Violence: Six Sideways Reflections*. New York: Picador, 2008.

Zuleika, Joseba, and William A. Douglass. *Terror and Taboo: The Follies, Fa-bles and Faces of Terrorism*. London: Routledge, 1996.

Index

Lightning Source UK Ltd.
Milton Keynes UK
UKHW020710170219

337440UK00005B/12/P